# LEGAL EASE

## ABOUT THE AUTHORS

**Andrea Campbell** is the author of many books including *Forensic Science: Evidence, Clues and Investigation* and *Rights of the Accused*. She holds a degree in criminal justice and teaches workshops online involving forensic science disciplines and other technical subjects. She is a trained forensic artist and sculptor, and a Diplomate and Fellow with the American College of Forensic Examiners, as well as a member of the International Association for Identification. Andrea lives in Arkansas with her husband, Michael, and Ziggy, a Helping Hands capuchin monkey who will one day be a helper/companion to a quadriplegic. Her two sons are in college. She enjoys walking in the woods, and playing Pinochle and dominoes with her family.

**Ralph C. Ohm** is a Municipal Judge for Hot Springs, Arkansas. He holds a Juris Doctor degree from the University of Arkansas, Little Rock, School of Law. Ralph is a member of the American, Arkansas, and Garland County Bar Associations. He is also affiliated with the Arkansas Trial Lawyers Association and Association of Trial Lawyers of America and licensed to practice before the U.S. Supreme Court, Arkansas Supreme Court, 5th, 8th, and 10th Circuit Court of Appeals; Federal District Courts of Arkansas; and all Arkansas State Courts. Ralph and his family live in Lonsdale, Arkansas. He and his wife, Derri, are the proud parents of daughter Ashlyn. Active in the community, Ralph is on the vestry of St. Luke's Episcopal Church, the Board of Directors for the Lonsdale Volunteer Fire Department, and is a member of Arkansas Spa Pacers.

Second Edition

# LEGAL EASE

## A Guide to Criminal Law, Evidence, and Procedure

*By*

**ANDREA CAMPBELL**

*and*

**RALPH C. OHM**

CHARLES C THOMAS • PUBLISHER, LTD.
*Springfield • Illinois • U.S.A.*

*Published and Distributed Throughout the World by*

CHARLES C THOMAS • PUBLISHER, LTD.
2600 South First Street
Springfield, Illinois 62704

© 2007 by CHARLES C THOMAS • PUBLISHER, LTD.

ISBN 0-398-07297-3 (hard)
ISBN 0-398-07298-1 (paper)
ISBN-13# 978-0-398-07730-3 (hard)
ISBN-13# 978-0-398-07731-0 (paper)

Library of Congress Catalog Card Number: 2006048898

*With* THOMAS BOOKS *careful attention is given to all details of manufacturing
and design. It is the Publisher's desire to present books that are satisfactory as to their
physical qualities and artistic possibilities and appropriate for their particular use.*
THOMAS BOOKS *will be true to those laws of quality that assure a good name
and good will.*

*Printed in the United States of America*
*CR-R-3*

**Library of Congress Cataloging-in-Publication Data**

Campbell, Andrea.
    Legal ease : a guide to criminal law, evidence, and procedure /  by Andrea
Campbell and Ralph C. Ohm. -- 2nd ed.
        p.  cm.
    Includes bibiliographical references and index.
    ISBN-13: 978-0-398-07730-3
    ISBN-10: 0-398-07730-4
    ISBN-13: 978-0-398-07731-0 (pbk.)
    ISBN-10: 0-398-07731-2 (pbk.)
    1. Criminal law--United States. 2 Criminal procedure--United States. 3.
Evidence, Criminal--United States. 4. Criminal justice, Administration of--
United States. I. Ohm, Ralph C., 1957-II. Title.

KF9219.C36 2007
345.73--dc22
                                                                        2006048898

*To my husband, Michael, for all his encouragement*
*—A.S.C.*


*For my loving family*
*—R.C.O.*

# DISCLAIMER

This book is designed to provide information in regard to the subject matter covered. It should not be interpreted as legal advice. The authors assume no liability or responsibility to any person or entity with respect to any loss or damage caused or alleged to be caused, directly or indirectly by the information and illustrations in this book.

In regard to state statutes, procedures, and court rulings, it should be noted that different jurisdictions have their own guidelines and prescriptions. When fact checking, readers should examine their own state's dominion.

# PREFACE

The criminal justice system is a huge machine with many working parts. There are a thousand different outcomes all from the same beginnings. Since criminal law—substantive, procedural, and constitutional—are the grease that keeps the justice wheel moving, it behooves its industry workers (the police, prosecutors, defenders, and law students) to know and learn its principles. But where to start?

Because we believe that criminal law is necessary, helping you to understand it and want to use it is our goal. You know, there's a wonderful, naive quote by actor Leslie Nielsen in the science-fiction film *Forbidden Planet.* As he and his compatriot attempt to enter a private dwelling occupied by a demented inventor and his daughter, with the express purpose of finding evidence of malice, he turns to the other somewhat reticent fellow under his command and says, "We're all part monsters in our subconscious, that's why we have laws and religion."

As cheesy as that film looks to us today, Nielsen's script writer was right on the mark—we are, all of us, part monsters in our subconscious. The term to describe this monster character embedded in our psyche is often referred to as "the dark side."

In fact, society in general, having a tendency to deny that such a thing exists often acts in ways that help to suppress that logic and may, in some instances, *encourage* criminal behavior. It's not surprising that when an atrocity occurs in a quiet neighborhood such as in the case with Jeffrey Dahmer (who was convicted of stalking and cannibalizing young male victims) for his neighbors to exclaim, "He was such a nice, quiet boy! Who would have thought?"

Who would have thought indeed. Well, there are people who think about criminal mentality and motive—men and women who bump up against the mentally ill and evil in our society every day. Over time, these seasoned individuals have developed a method of finding, stopping, and helping to punish those individuals who continue to express their "dark sides," often with menacing regularity.

This book provides an expansive and practical guide to the various aspects of law. Our task was to organize and explain the practicality of law through all phases of the criminal justice system. To that end, this book is divided into three parts.

Part One, Criminal Law Explained, explains the evolution of law, defines what criminal conduct is and breaks it down into its elemental parts. After this, an entire chapter is devoted to providing an explanation of the tools to help you look up your own laws, principles, and precedents. And in Part One we begin to see that there are punishments, yes–but also defenses and justification for unintended conduct and the remedies of the court to understand them.

Part Two, Criminal Procedure and Evidence, teaches the steps of constitutional arrest, search, and seizure. It follows with a rather thorough explanation of our constitutional rights, the equitable rules our founding fathers fought so hard for, which is not only a sacred trust, but a true living document. Later we learn more about law enforcement, the prosecutors, and the defenders, and how it is personified by persons who try to practice lawful ideals in the most difficult of circumstances. They are dedicated to balancing the right of society to feel secure against safeguarding an individual's right to privacy and freedom.

Part Three does just what the section heading sets out to do, takes us on "A Walk Through the Criminal Justice System," incorporating the viewpoints of all the players involved, and culminating where everything in law is supposed to lead–into court.

If you are interested in criminal law, you must not be frustrated by the formal, archaic, or unusual words. Of course, there are technical terms and the law perpetuates a written language that tends to be syntactically complex and dense, mostly because of its historical roots. The unusual sentence structure is meant to be precise. The telegraphic speech of the court–"Objection! Hearsay." "Not offered for the truth of the matter, Your Honor." "Overruled."–is really quite efficient, allowing a brief interruption for what otherwise is predictable content. But don't let the jargon of legal pomposity keep you out of what is thought to be an exclusive club! Embrace it. Embrace it because law stories are about people on edge and they need the law, and, more importantly, they may need you to sort it out for them.

The object of this volume is to give groups who are new to the scene (and even those who aren't), an easy-to-read book of reference for all those nuances the law presses onto the system. So whether the reader needs a primer on search and seizure, a blueprint for the rules of order for the court, or the definitions and parameters of a crime, the authors hope the savvy professional will approach this book as the unconditional resource.

ANDREA CAMPBELL

# INTRODUCTION

In the first edition of *Legal Ease* we talked about how laws evolve and change as if they were a living, breathing entity. And that is never so apparent as in this newer, second version, where we bear witness to how a nation's laws reflect its' happenings. If we could apply metaphor here: laws truly are a mirror, holding up to its face, images of societal change. The events of men and women in desperate situations, entwined within the law in sometimes unbelievable ways, show us a continuing story of how a country deals with population growth, lack of resources and opportunities for all, immigrant expansion, open borders and fanatical hate. There are those same people behind the mirror, who, unfortunately, are so dependable in their delinquent and depraved ways, they will always try to take shortcuts to gains or relief by breaking the law, and creating change and transformation in how we should behave.

Laws also paints a picture of how a nation suffers. A huge revolution was precipitated by the events of September 11, 2001, when radical, Islamic terrorists brought the World Trade Center towers down to Ground Zero in New York City, when our Pentagon in Washington, D.C., was attacked, and when a plane went down in Pennsylvania, never reaching its target because of passengers who bravely decided to take law into their own hands to prevent another tragedy—a human missile from hitting its target.

Now, because of these catastrophic measures, where a country experiences terrorism in new and bolder ways, its' lawmakers begin to find methods for prevention—and anti-terror bills morph into the Patriot Act, a federal administration decree that extends government's reach, and supercedes state protections into what were once, the private records and the movements of its citizens. We are experiencing a nation closing in on itself and asking its people to *bear with* the extra searches at airports, to ignore new, more intrusive privacy and wiretap capabilities, to shore up under identification requests, library, and computer monitoring, and to support other, enveloping steps for our safety.

This new tack filters down to the states, granting regional and local law enforcement more protection, more power, and more depth in terms of service in order to fuse our government assistance into a monitoring, cognizant body. How does this manifest itself? Of course, it makes travel more difficult with additional searches and demands on time, and, for example, toll collection monitoring in New Jersey is now the norm; police dogs can do more, being called in to sniff this and that, and in many states, it's a felony to kill or injure a service animal; the hate crimes statutes become more apparent adding extra years to sentencing; fleeing pursuits are more dangerous and, in the commission of a felony in Mississippi, can add many months onto a felon's prison time; schools are more wary and now able to do drug-testing under new authority; and whistle-blowing is encouraged, both in terms of business fraud, and to counterterroristic threatening and plots.

This shift has also snaked its way into new state laws as well: 9-1-1 calls may be used at trials, DNA collections for felons are everyday protocol, death sentences are available for teens who commit heinous crimes, and gang affiliations are noted on records, and, in Florida, citizens can use deadly force against muggers, carjackers and other attackers, and the idea for personal protection is spreading.

With the advent of new forms of information collection on its citizens, comes more and more computer crime such as identity theft, human trafficking, and statutes for child safeguards against pornography, kidnapping, sexual solicitation, and pedophilia.

A nation protecting itself is alarming, intriguing, and constantly creating new laws, new wrinkles, and new human stories. We hope you are as excited about this fresh, updated look at law as we have been.

# ACKNOWLEDGMENTS

We would like to express our appreciation to the people and associations mentioned here: Paul Bosson and the Prosecuting Attorney's office of Hot Springs; Tom O'Neal, Director of Pupil Personnel; Sgt. Bill Livingston, Lt. Willie McCoy, and the Hot Spring's Sheriff's Department, including Corporal Corky Rowlett and Deputy Judy Daniell; the Hot Springs Municipal Court; the Hot Springs Bail Bond Company; Cummins Prison Administrators; Omar Almobarak; Marsha King and the Law Library; John Ott and the *Law Enforcement Bulletin*; Chief of Police Gary Ashcraft, Corporal Michael Buck, Corporal Steve Cooley, and the Hot Springs Police Department; the Public Relations Department of the FBI including Rex Tomb and Ernie Porter; and Steven Mross with *The Sentinel-Record*, the best police beat reporter around. For their support and vote of confidence we'd also like to thank Kim Kruglick for his reading and commenting on certain sections of the book, Daryl Clemens, Martin White, Jr., Penny Warner, and Carmel Thomaston. And a tip of the hat to Publisher Mike Thomas, who saw the benefit of this work and helped us to make it a reality.

# CONTENTS

# AUTHOR'S NOTE

No man is above the law and no man
is below it; nor do we ask any man's
permission when we require him to obey it.
　　　　　　　　　　　　　—Theodore Roosevelt

As you read through this book, you will notice that the same sub-ject may be addressed in several different chapters. For exam-ple, the term *mens rea* will appear in the first chapter and it may also appear when we talk about prosecutor charging, and, again, when we speak of intent. This unique form of cross-referencing demon-strates the word in all its different contexts.

You will also note that separate, shaded boxes may appear offset from the text, and marked with words such as "Caution," "Other Notes," or "FYI." The *Caution* is to alert you to certain kinds of information that may prove helpful to you in your particular career, or, which are stumbling blocks to be aware of in regard to common-ly practiced procedure. *Other Notes* are other similar areas of impor-tance, and *FYI* notes are just interesting tidbits about the subject itself. None of these should be interpreted as concrete rules, because each police unit or lawyer's office has their own standards and modes of operation. They are simply areas of concern that have pre-sented themselves to management in the past, and they may be ben-eficial to you in the future.

# LEGAL EASE

# PART ONE

## Criminal Law Explained

# Chapter 1

# THE EVOLUTION OF LAW

The life of law has not been logic;
it has been experience.
–Oliver Wendell Holmes Jr.,
*The Common Law*

Every generation in the history of America has been concerned with crime. The Wild West was characterized by vigilantism where posses of angry young men took justice into their own hands. The Civil War period was rife with riots, looting, and mob violence. During the Roaring Twenties, bootlegging was a common occurrence and gangsters gunned each other down on city streets. The Great Depression told tales of banks that were "knocked over" by infamous characters such as Bonnie and Clyde, while dazed citizens followed their cross-country escapades in their daily newspaper.

In fact, crime sprees and criminal dilemmas are the stuff of legends. And the laws that sprung up around them are not static. Laws, sanctions, and the norms that society live by are dynamic, because criminal law grows and changes as if it carries the breath of the people who fought the system. Historically, criminals have been banished, beheaded, impaled, burned, flogged, mutilated, and chained to everything from trees to grinding wheels to the oars on great ships. Lawbreakers have also been enslaved, exiled, and imprisoned.

The criminal procedures used today are fruit borne from the seeds of long-accepted practices of conviction, trial, and error. The beginnings of law and the horrible struggles of war, torture, and inequalities in history paint a glorious if brutal picture. As professionals you will find the foundations of law not only helpful to know and understand, but the historical perspectives may inspire you to read about another time. Many criminal procedures you use today have the past as their underpinnings.

## HAIL CIVILIZATION

When a culture becomes complex enough to support a various number of people and ideas, the unity and close proximity of its inhabitants forms a civilization. That community mindset helps to preserve its past, sponsors innovation, and transmits its inherent style and values. Civilization first emerged some five to six thousand years ago. First, small agricultural villages in the Mesopotamia river valley near the Tigris and Euphrates rivers evolved. Shortly thereafter, in Egypt, around the Nile, communities sprung up. These social organizations had more complex rules for conduct than those that guided cave dwellers or the earliest farmers. In fact, the very word civilization is borrowed from the old French but taken from Latin meaning *civilis*, relating to private rights, state law, and public right, but with an important distinction—it was for city dwellers only.

A civilization evolves only with the aid of a firm foundation, and establishing authority requires a balance between those doing the governing and those being governed. This practical peace calls for certain sophisticated divisions of command and labor. Specific duties, power, and ability pass down through particular families. Who you were born to pretty much determined your lot in life.

Firm authority also requires acceptance. Mesopotamia, and later Egypt, had powerful kings and a priestly caste. Seeking social order, the people gave control to the man or woman who seemed to have some special power, wealth, or cunning. In cruder communities, power was given over to the biggest or strongest of men; and in some cases, to men with red hair. Law or formally accepted codes of conduct were set down and distinctly regarded from the simple customs of a village.

## In less sophisticated communities, power was given over to the biggest or strongest of men; . . .

As a consequence, detailed, historical law codes tell us how societies controlled relations among their people. The best known is the Laws of Hammurabi, sometimes referred to as the Code of Hammurabi. These judgments were issued by an eighteenth-century B.C. Babylonian king who probably adapted them from older Sumerian and Akkadian law. An able administrator, Hammurabi's laws were engraved on a pillar of stone and related to all aspects of life in Babylonia. Four thousand lines of writing expressed what was expected from the people: the sanctity of their oath to God and the necessity of all legal matters and written evidence.

### HAMMURABI'S LAW CODE*

*Here are some examples of the "judgments" laid down by Hammurabi in his famous law code.*

When Marduk [the patron god of Babylon] sent me to rule the people and to bring help to the country, I established law and justice in the language of the land and promoted the welfare of the people. At the time I decreed:

1. If a man accuses another man of murder but cannot prove it, the accuser shall be put to death.
2. If a man bears false witness in a case, or cannot prove his testimony, if that cause involves life or death, he shall be put to death.

---

**FYI**—The cuneiform stone column, which records a long series of the legal judgments published under the name of Hammurabi can be found at the Louvre Museum in Paris, France. The best source of the code was a black diorite stela-upright slab-found at Susa, Iran, in 1901.

---

Translated by Robert F. Harper, 1904, *language modified.*

22. If a man commits robbery and is captured, he shall be put to death.
23. If the robber is not captured, the man who has been robbed shall, in the presence of the god, make a list of what he has lost, and the city and the governor of the province where the robbery was committed shall compensate him for his loss.
142. If a woman hates her husband and says, "You may not possess me," the city council shall inquire into her case; and if she has been careful and without reproach and her husband has been going about and belittling her, she is not to blame. She may take her dowry and return to her father's house.
195. If a son strikes his father, they shall cut off his hand.
196. If a man destroys the eye of another man, they shall destroy his eye.
197. If he breaks another man's bone, they shall break his bone.
200. If a man knocks out a tooth of a man of his own rank, they shall knock out his tooth.

*Lex talionis*, the law of retaliation—or a principle of correspondence between punishment and crime such as, "an eye for an eye and a tooth for a tooth"—is said to be derived from these early beginnings and is a doctrine many cultures still cling to today. In fact, a modern version of talion law is in effect in the Islamic Republic of Iran. Equivalent reprisal takes form in their ideology but is also practiced in the law—with penalties being proportionate to the severity of the offense, such as, "letting the punishment fit the crime." Today, a person found guilty of theft in Iran could be punished by severing his hands.

One important thing to note: talion law in its implementation does not call for retaliatory justice by taking the perpetrator's eye for one lost by the victim, rather, it limits the victim's legitimate claim to *no more* than an eye for a lost eye—not a tooth, an ear, an arm as well.

## EARLY TRIALS

Early due process and primitive versions of the trial—a sophisticated treatment of how controversies were settled in ancient western civilization—are illustrated through what we know about Biblical Israel (c. 1020-922 B.C.) and a system they had called "trial court at the gate."

Since there was a mix of clans in these communities, certain folkways, patterns of behavior and beliefs common to a particular group of people, and mores (pronounced MORe-rays), essential binding customs, were taught to one another. Any violations of these beliefs were dealt with by the trial court, at the gate. Trial convened in the morning near the gates to the community, in front of the elders, and before the townspeople who left to work in the fields for the day. It attracted an audience and was meant to be public. One of the rights of the accused, the basis for a public trial, began here.

The accuser, who acted as the prosecution essentially, was the party on the right hand of the justice, with the judge seated in the center. The accused was assisted by a defender who would stand. Death sentences for serious crimes were common and when the offense warranted "stoning," the accuser got to throw the first stone.

There were penalties for false testimony. It usually meant the liar received the same sentence as the accused. Also, as part of the process, no testimony was allowed that was based either on second-hand information or supposition, bringing to mind today's rule of evidence against hearsay. In addition, two witnesses were needed to convict and this served as the basis for today's theory of corroboration. Plus, if there were a lack of evidence, the accused would take an exculpatory oath; he would call upon God (known as "Yahweh") to punish or curse him should he lie.

The people of that time believed that law was an expression of God's commands and that any violation was a transgression against God. For example, Israeli law commanded that the one who had killed should also be killed. If the blood spirit given to them by God was taken in murder, the law was allowed to take again what rightfully belonged to Yahweh. If no killer was found, a blood sacrifice from an animal was granted to restore balance.

## THE AGE OF REFINEMENT

Two other great western civilizations helped to shape the law's early beginnings, the Greeks and the Romans. Solon, a popular poet and statesman, was well known for his compassionate work which made him a towering figure in Greek history. As chief magistrate of Athens, Solon drafted a code which essentially prohibited slavery for indebtedness, divided classes based on income and property, and granted citizenship to even the lowest peon, thereby allowing men a chance to improve their status economically regardless of ancestry.

Solon's court of appeal, the Heliaea, consisted of a jury drawn from a lot of 6,000 members of the Athenian tribe. With his enactment for more equal citizen participation and responsibility, he pointed the state toward eventual democracy. Three other important contributions from the Heliaea system were 1) guilt or innocence was determined by secret ballot; 2) the trial was finished in one day; and 3) the courts relied on the people's contribution and civil action–in other words, it sanctioned the first citizen's arrest.

Some other concepts survived the Athenian law process, that of filing a complaint, holding preliminary hearings (the notion that the magistrate could dismiss motions or hold them over) and the taking of oath (they also allowed "oath helpers," people within the defendant's family who were sworn in as well). Interestingly, if the defendant had more oath helpers than the accuser, the charges were dismissed.

Also, the Athenians prided themselves on being great orators and perfected the art of the closing argument, summation speeches directed toward the jurists. Other original measures were that monetary fines were imposed as a deterrent to lying, such as, 1,000 drachmas were collected from those who pressed false charges. Court penalties included capital punishment, a common remedy, which primarily consisted of drinking hemlock or being thrown into an open pit and stoned. Noncapital punishments included banishment, public degradation, or the flogging of slaves.

> ## . . . drinking hemlock or being thrown into an open pit and stoned.

## LONG LIVE ROME

A refined system of law and procedure was one of the chief cultural contributions of the Roman civilization. Laws were issued by assemblies made up of citizens who were in the army or who were landholders, and they dealt largely with public issues such as land distribution and military commands overseas. On the other hand, the laws that affected relations between citizens were largely the work of individual magistrates who had a limited term of service, one-year elected, and they needed the consent of their colleagues to govern.

Normally, cases came before a judge–again, a private citizen, who relied on the advice of other citizens reputed to know the law called jurists. They operated under the adversarial trial process and the police force was often called in as an investigating element.

Romans distinguished their own citizens from the rest of the other members of the Empire. Natives were subject to civil law–laying the basis for modern civil law–or law applying only to citizens; others were allowed to maintain their own customs, *ius gentium*, or the law of other nations. These two laws then, logically, were assigned to two kinds of magistrates: the "urban praetor" and the "traveling praetor," their jurisdictions being self-explanatory.

Eventually as the powers of authority within the Empire grew, the law of custom replaced the law of other nations. Public pressure for codes of law spawned ten bronze and wooden tablets, later to become a dozen strikings called the Twelve Tablets. These were fastened to the speaker's stand at the Roman Forum. *Leges*, which were enactments by Roman assembly, is our *legislation* today. These rules of customary conduct morphed into an issuance called *edicts*–public orders or decrees. Later, around 130 A.D., officials codified the edicts and leges into one body of law called *Edictum Perpetuum*, or force of law.

During the height of the Roman Empire, the Emperor Justinian created a written summary of laws called the "Justinian Code." These collected laws had developed for 1,000 years; and with 170 constitutions it became the Corpus Juris Civilus, or, the Body of Civil Law. This served as the basis for canon law–law of the Catholic Church. Later, in large part due to the church, the canon and common law tied together again to form the French Napoleonic Code, which today serves as the influence of a development of law exercised through the Louisiana Purchase, called the Louisiana Civil Code.

## Putting It in Perspective

Although these ancient stories about law and law rendering give an ordered look to their respective societies, a reader of history must look further for the truth. A well-rounded lawyer and law professional would do well to note that Greece was plagued by the lack of law from its early beginnings. Their greatest story, the "Peloponnesian War" was a civil conflict involving Greeks killing Greeks. When they did defend their lands (such as with another famous battle, the "Trojan War"), their enemies were known as barbarians. In other words, the growth of the Greek empire spawned injustice and was one of the key factors in the advancement of the judicial system.

The Roman Empire hit its height with *Pax Romana*, the Roman Peace, celebrating two centuries of solid prosperity. But, it, too, was founded on the backs of slaves, and justice for the captive and disenfranchised was nonexistent.

---

**FYI**—The dichotomy between a land celebrating the height of Roman civil engineering-1 million inhabitants in the greatest city in western civilization, Rome, in the midst of great prosperity-was not as great a time to live through for the slaves and the conquered barbarians, who did all the work. The laws were laws of oppression if you were not a citizen of Rome.

## SOURCES OF AMERICAN CRIMINAL LAW

American criminal law, and the subsequent rights of the accused as we know it today are a blend of two traditions. First, the common law, was developed in Saxon England and was grounded in customs and precedents. The second, civil law, was derived from Roman antecedents and represents laws adapted from the earliest efforts used to control human behavior. These laws survived by means of written and established codes that defined offenses and prescribed penalties for those crimes.

English common law, a tossed salad made up of tribal rules, Roman law, and the customs of invaders and other travelers from France, Scandinavia, and what would become Germany, influenced our methodology as well. In 1066, William the Conqueror, the Norman ruler and a major historical figure, imposed his own public mandates on the existing system in order to consolidate his power and authority. Under the royal justices appointed by William, existing state law became *common law*–named so because it was based on the traditional practices of the realm and was common to all England. And even though common law had its roots in custom and tradition, it evolved through time and used the process of consistent, judicial decision-making.

For this reason, common law is "judge-made law." Think of it as a reproduction of a fine antique, one that has been adapted, changed, polished and buffed to a shine. The whole museum storehouse of common law then, is an actual collection of decisions handed down from generation to generation.

It is important to note that the Norman Conquest had an impact on written legal language as well. In his book, *Legal Language*, Peter M. Tiersma says, "Before the Conquest, both English and Latin were used to write legal documents. After the Normans arrived, the use of English rapidly declined. The Normans were accustomed to writing in Latin."

## Kings and Law

Henry I, King Williams's son, made his own contributions to criminal justice and issued *Leges Henrici*. One prime example and an idea that has matured, was that he established that crimes such as robbery and counterfeiting were "against the King's peace." Thus, these offenses became crimes against the State. This set a precedent for crimes punishable by the state's resources instead of by a person, or crimes of misdemeanor. Later still, King Henry II, developed and extended the King's court system and created a jury system called the Inquisition, where a jury panel determined the miscreant's guilt.

Following was King John, a serious abuser of power. He increased taxes and governed according to his whims. This upset the barons (landowners) and church leaders, and they drew up a list of rights for the people. In 1215, King John was forced to sign the Magna Carta. In it, were such ideas as separation of church and state, additional rights given to the rising middle class; and it now required the King to seek advice from his barons before enacting any laws.

And finally for England, King James, a tyrant king in the late 1600s, was forced to abdicate and this movement helped to produce the English Bill of Rights. As part of these rights there would be no order for suspending laws without the aid of Parliament, no standing army during peace, free elections for members of Parliament, and the people's freedom of speech could not be impeached.

Therefore, when the "new world" was being settled by English colonists in the seventeenth and eighteenth centuries, they had a basis for law and, after throwing off the shackles of English rule with the War of Independence, their rights of freedom and a new, American common law system was left to progress. One man in particular, Sir William Blackstone, helped the new American judges by publishing *Commentaries on the Laws of England* which illustrated the principles of the common law in an encyclopedic treatment. Blackstone had been a jurist and professor at Oxford and his effort aided in demystifying English law. The barristers of England however, were a little put off by Blackstone's seminal effort because they took pride in offering their services to "discover the law" ("hire and decipher" difficult jargon) but his American counterparts found in Blackstone's *Commentaries* something of a "legal bible."

## FIVE SOURCES OF LAW

The sources of American law are the United States Constitution, acts of Congress, state constitutions, state statutes and territorial legislature acts, and the common law. The law of the Constitution is greater than an act of Congress and, when in conflict, can void it out. If a valid act made by Congress clashes with a state constitutional provision, the latter is rendered useless. If a provision of a state constitution goes against the statute or law of the same state, the state law is voided. If a law of a state or one of its territorial legislatures conflicts with a common law provision, the latter is rendered ineffective.

## TYPES OF LAW

A professional should be familiar with the different types of law and what each mean. Lawyers will obviously need to know the various terminology. Law enforcement personnel will find the knowledge of law classifications an asset for their profession as well. Described below are the types of law under the umbrella of the American criminal law system.

Substantive criminal law is the more formal term for criminal law. The key elements of substantive criminal law are:
- the acts
- mental states, and
- accompanying circumstances or consequences that make up the necessary features of crimes.

In other words, it defines the kinds of behavior (act or omissions), the wrongs against the state, and assigns punishments for such conduct. Any references in this book to criminal law are actually references to substantive criminal law.

## DEFINING WORDS FOR LAW

### Procedural Law

Procedural law or "criminal procedure" is how substantive criminal law should be carried out. These are the steps on how to proceed in order to enforce criminal law. It defines arrest, probable cause, rights, and search methods, all elements of the law enforcement plan. Based on fundamental fairness and due process, procedural law tells us how evidence should be collected and what rights are guaranteed to the accused.

### Statutory Laws

Statutory laws are those laws that are made by state legislatures and Congress. This type of law is most important, because all American jurisdictions have extensive statutes dealing with crimes and criminal law. These laws are put together into codes for sorting purposes and are classified under separate headings. The criminal laws of any state are found under the state penal code. So, to find out how Arkansas defines the crimes of kidnapping, false imprisonment, and vehicular piracy you would look in the Arkansas Penal Code, as provided in the Arkansas Statutes 5-11-101, 5-11-102, 5-11-103, 5-11-104 and 5-11-105. State codes are subject to revision at annual legislative sessions.

## Administrative Law

Administrative laws are rulings by government agencies at the federal, state, or local levels. For example, an executive branch may set up and give authority to a board of health in order to establish regulations for specific policy areas (in this instance, health standards). Although most of the content of administrative law is not targeted directly at criminal behavior, certain violations are dealt with in criminal courts.

## Constitutional Law

Constitutional law is the law of the United States Constitution and the constitutions of the individual states. These, by nature, are supreme over other kinds of law and the disputes are most likely handled in state supreme courts, and, sometimes, in its final destination (if it gets that far), the Supreme Court. In the event of a conflict, the federal Constitution law is dominant over state law. The only crime defined in the U.S. Constitution is treason.

## Precedents

This type of law is influenced by the principle of stare decisis–"let the decision stand." Judges use this rule to follow what went before in judicial interpretations. This means that judges today accept the decisions made by judges in the past. These principles, or precedents, help to promote stability and certainty when making legal decisions, although prior decisions are sometimes overturned by the higher authority in a court of appeals, reversing or modifying existing case law.

## Case Law

Case law can be created by judges in their rulings on statutory laws. This is also when they take into account previous rulings and set down in writing an opinion if their own. Supreme Court cases can be read on the Internet and there are entire volumes devoted to their rulings.

## Torte

A torte is a civil remedy for injury to persons and property. The injured party must sue for remedy or reparations. Examples of these would be libel, slander, trespass, and damage from negligence.

## SEVEN BASIC LAW PRINCIPLES REQUIRED FOR A CRIME

We all have ideas about what we think is inappropriate behavior, but what is a crime in the eyes of the law? Are there basic requirements of a criminal act, a laundry list of wrongs? In simple terms, yes.

For a particular behavior to be considered criminal, there are basic elements that must be met. These factors must all be present and are what the legislatures and courts use to prepare and interpret substantive criminal law. Basically, a crime is defined as: "an intentional act or omission in violation of a criminal law, committed without defense or

FYI—This is an interesting concept: there can be no crime unless a law exists that has been violated. Examples of this would be the rather recent laws against carjacking, or offenses that are now being defined as "hate crimes."

justification and sanctioned by the state as a felony or misdemeanor." These are the essential ingredients in every crime:

1. Legality
2. Actus reus
3. Mens rea
4. Concurrence of *actus reus* and *mens rea*
5. Harm
6. Causation
7. Punishment

In defining legality there is an ancient Latin saying Nullum crimen sine lege which means "no crime without a law." You may also hear it as *Nullen crimen, nulla poena, sine lege*, or, "there is no crime, there is no punishment, without law."

Actus reus is simply another way of saying "guilty act." Bad thoughts alone do not constitute a crime. Just because you may wish someone dead, unless you take action to bring about that result, it may be sad, but it's not a crime. It is important though, to distinguish thought from speech, because there are laws that govern that. Also, an agreement to commit a crime is one of the elements required for a criminal conspiracy which we'll talk about later.

*Mens rea* means "guilty mind." This is also referred to as criminal intent. Proving intent is a hurdle all prosecutors train for. It calls for an assessment of the psychology, motives, and intent of the defendant. The concept of *mens rea* is based on the notion that people have the capacity to control their behavior and can choose between alterna-

tive courses of conduct. If a school bus driver drives through an intersection without stopping and causes an accident, he or she will not be charged with a crime if the brakes failed and if the driver did everything possible to prevent the accident.

Concurrence of *actus reus* and *mens rea* means that the act and the mental state, or intent, work together in time for a crime to be committed. For example, the act and mental state are not concurrent if they are separated by a considerable gap in time. A lack of significant time between mental state and the act is a strong argument against the mental state causing the act.

Harm means that only conduct that is in some way harmful can be considered criminal. The essence of the idea of harm is based on due process. For instance, a criminal law is unconstitutional if it can show no relationship to the matter of injury against its citizens. Harm does not have to be physical however. In cases of libel, perjury, and treason no physical harm is inflicted.

Just recently, legislatures have expanded harm to include hate crimes and criminal discrimination. A hate crime is an act of violence or property damage committed because of the victim's race, gender, or sexual preference.

Causation relates to crime in the same way that a defendant's conduct produces a given result. Only crimes like perjury, lying under oath, or forgery (signing a false name) are defined so that the crime consists of both the act itself and the intent to cause the harmful result, without regard to whether the result actually occurs. The harm that occurs must be similar enough to the intended result that the defendant can still be held responsible.

In some instances, cause is difficult to assess. For example, if A shoots a bullet into B and he dies, we can see through ballistics evidence and the wound that the action and the intent was to cause B's death. On the other hand, if A shoots B and leaves him on the freeway and B gets hit by C, who doesn't see him, will A be convicted of B's murder? Only if it can be determined that A's conduct was a substantial factor in bring about B's death or that what happened was a foreseeable consequence of A's behavior.

Punishment means that under the American legal system, citizens must not only be warned about what conduct is forbidden, but they must also be made aware of the consequences of their actions. For this reason, the law stipulates sanctions for every crime.

### REVIEW QUESTIONS AND ANSWERS

Chapter 1 is all about the foundation of criminal law, that is to say, how societies sprung up and policed themselves through history. Here are some of the answers and concepts to the questions at the end of Chapter 1: "The Evolution of Law."

## Key Words to Define

- **Civilization**–when a culture becomes complex enough to support a various number of peoples and ideas. The close proximity and unity of its inhabitants helps to form a civilization.
- **Common law**–Existing state law based on traditional practices common to all England, during the reign of William the Conqueror.

- **Edicts**–Public order or decree
- **Hammurabi**–The 18th B.C. Babylonian king, best known for the Laws of Hammurabi.
- **Justinian Code**–The emperor Justinian of the early Roman Empire created a written summary of laws called the Justinian Code; laws developed over 1,000 years, which became the *Corpus Juris Civilus* or Body of Civil Law.
- **Legality**–No crime without a law; an ancient Latin saying that there can be no crime without a law or, *nullen crimen, nulla poena, sine lege.*
- **Mores**–Accepted codes of conduct within a community.
- **Precedents**–Judges use this law based on what was practiced by other judges, meaning, "Let the decision stand."
- **Substantive criminal law**–The more formal term for criminal law

## Questions for Review and Discussion

1. *Question:* What does "lex talionis" mean? *Answer:* The law of retaliation, an "eye for an eye" remedy or the punishment should fit the crime.

2. *Question:* How were the early trials of Biblical Israel conducted? *Answer:* Trial at the gate was conducted early in the morning before inhabitants left for work; there was an accuser, a judge, and a defender; testimony was given, the use of corroboration was common, penalties for false information, and sentencing performed by a panel or a judge; if death sentencing by stoning, accuser got to throw the first stone.

3. *Question:* What two great western civilizations helped to shape law? *Answer:* Rome and Greece.

4. *Question:* Since the Athenians considered themselves great orators, they perfected the art of _____ or summation

speeches directed at the jurors? *Answer:* The closing arguments.

5. *Question:* Did the Romans allow non-native justice? *Answer:* Natives were subject to civil law, other nations had their own customs *uis gentium* or, law of other nations.

6. *Question:* What is common law? *Answer:* Existing state laws under William the Conqueror based on traditional practices and common to all England.

7. *Question:* Who was William Blackstone? *Answer:* A jurist and professor at Oxford who published *Commentaries on the Laws of England.*

8. *Question:* What are the five sources of law? *Answer:* U.S. Constitution, acts of Congress, state constitutions, state statutes, territorial legislative acts, common law.

9. *Question:* Who uses procedural law the most? *Answer:* Police, because it defines arrest, probable cause, rights and searches—how law is to be carried out.

10. *Question:* Define both "actus reus" and "mens rea." How do they work together? *Answer: Actus reus* means guilty act, *mens rea* means guilty mind. The act and the mental state or the intent, are what come together to make up a crime.

11. *Question:* Explain, "hate crimes." *Answer:* A hate crime is an act of violence or property damage committed because of the victim's race, gender or sexual preference. Since ageism is a modern-day phenomenon, it could also be considered.

## *Essay Assignment: In Your Own Words*

HOW DO THE SEVEN PRINCIPLES OF LAW WORK TOGETHER TO FORM A CRIME? You should be writing about the seven essential ingredients needed for every crime such as: Legality, Actus reus, Mens rea, Concurrence of actus reus and mens rea, Harm, Causation and Punishment. If summary paragraphs demonstrate that you know what each of these factors mean and how they come together to form a criminal act that satisfies the assignment.

# Chapter 2

# CRIMES DEFINED

Crime, like virtue,
has its degrees.
    –Racine, *Phédre*

## INCHOATE OFFENSES

Would you believe there is an extensive body of law that permits punishment for an incomplete or failed crime? Yes, the offenses of attempt, solicitation, and conspiracy are all *inchoate*, or anticipatory crimes. They include any uncompleted activity where the end result would have been, without fail, a crime. So these crimes are a "preparation," if you will. Inchoate offenses were originally created by the courts to give police the power to apprehend dangerous persons who have not yet done the deed, and, thereby, prevent them from completing their criminal objectives.

## INCHOATE CRIMES

Traditionally, inchoate crimes have always been considered misdemeanors, but over the years they have been merged into felonies as society has put more power in the hands of law enforcement and prosecutors to deal with recalcitrant problems such as organized crime, white collar crime, and drug crime.

## ATTEMPT

Of the inchoate crimes, attempt is the most frequent charge. In order to be charged with an attempt, certain conditions must be met:
1. The intent to commit an offense, AND,
2. A substantial step (also called an "overt act"), OR,
3. Conduct that would have been a crime.
The state penal code usually gets specific in defining the attempt to commit murder, but a typical statute reads like this one from Florida: "Whoever attempts to commit an offense prohibited by law and in such attempt does any act toward the commission of an offense, but fails in the perpetration or is intercepted or prevented in execution of the same, commits the offense of criminal attempt."[1]

---

1. West's Fla. Stat. Ann. § 777.04.

## SOLICITATION

Solicitation and attempt are different in that solicitation is complete when the request or inducement to do the act is made. In order words, solicitation is:

1. The intent to promote or facilitate a crime, AND
2. Someone who commands, urges, or requests another to engage in specific conduct that would make up an offense or attempt.

The *Gardner* case[2] illustrates exactly when the crime of solicitation is performed. Roger Gardner, an alleged contract killer, hired a man named Tim McDonald to kill Alvin Blum for $10,000. Gardner met with McDonald, giving him some expense money, a gun, and ammunition. During their conversation at this meeting, Gardner said he would first kill a man named Hollander, and if that did not create the desired result, then McDonald should go on to kill Blum. Gardner's attempt failed when he was arrested and charged with solicitation to murder. It turned out that McDonald worked for police as an informant, and his information led to Gardner's arrest.

### Gardner said he would first kill a man named Hollander, . . .

On appeal, Gardner argued that he did not commit the crime of solicitation because he did not actually direct McDonald to proceed with the murder of Blum, or pay him all the money promised. The Maryland Court of Appeals saw it differently and affirmed Gardner's conviction, saying that "the crime of solicitation was committed when he asked McDonald to commit the murder . . . neither the final direction to pro-

ceed nor fulfillment of conditions precedent [paying of the money] was required." The Court observed that the "gist of the offense is incitement."

One important distinction of solicitation is this: It does not require direct solicitation of another, but may be done through an intermediary. A Connecticut court also found solicitation to be far more dangerous to society than the attempt to commit the same crime. Their reasoning? In *State v. Schleifer*[3] the court said that behind it is an evil purpose, "coupled with the pressure of a stronger intellect upon the weak and criminally inclined."

## CONSPIRACY

On the other hand, the necessary elements of conspiracy are this:

1. An agreement, or what we might call, the meeting of the evil minds, AND
2. The purpose or the intent to commit a crime, AND
3. An overt act.

Now the next logical question is: What constitutes an overt act? An overt act is any act, not necessarily a substantial act but anything that indicates the crime is alive and well. It could be something as trivial, but as visible, as writing a laundry list of supplies needed in order to rob a bank. Also, "mere knowledge" of a crime, or thinking bad thoughts is not enough of a reason to be guilty of a conspiracy.

In the court's mind conspiracy is a distinct offense; it cannot be melded into other target offenses such as arson, kidnapping, homicide, etc. Overall, judges have expressed their feelings about conspiracy like this: That conspiracy deserves its own attention–is itself a crime–because a group association

---

2. *Gardner v. State*, 408 A. 2d 1317, 1322 (Md. 1979).
3. *State v. Scheifer*, 121 A. 805, 809 (Conn. 1923).

**FYI**—Two to Tango:
Okay, now that you have this principle about conspiracy being a distinct offense, here is the exception to the rule. (Rule number one: there is always an exception to a rule of law—we have to expect it and accept it.) So there is an exception where conspiracy does not merge into the target crime. Wharton's Rule, named after a famous commentator on criminal law, says that two people cannot conspire to commit a crime such as adultery, incest, or bigamy, because these offenses can only exist between two participants, meaning: it does not endanger the public generally. (We think this has its limitations also.)

makes it possible to attain more complex crimes than can be perpetrated by one criminal mind; and that crimes unrelated to the original purpose are more likely to happen than for what the group first got together to do. And this is borne out by the fact that the range of conspiracies cuts across all socioeconomic classes in society, an element that means upscale characters may get caught up in someone else's plan.

### . . . conspiracy deserves its own attention–is itself a crime– . . .

There are some important stipulations about conspiracy:

1. All acts of one conspirator are chargeable to all others.
2. All statements by one conspirator are admissible to all conspirators.
3. In a conspiracy, the agreement does not have to be expressed, it can be implied.
4. It takes two or more. In the eyes of the

law, an accomplice's pre-crime assistance makes a conspirator just as guilty as the person who carries out the actual crime. Plus, a person can be convicted and punished for both the conspiracy and the crime IF the crime is actually committed.

### . . . one of four women put to death in California.

### ACCOMPLICE

What are some of the things an accomplice does–someone who helps the principal to commit the crime? For our purposes here, let's assume that Kevin Klever breaks into a jewelry store and steals diamonds. If Naïve Ned is Kevin's accomplice, he may have assisted Kevin by distracting or drugging the night watchman, cutting the wires to the security system, or helping Kevin review the floorplan and layout of the store. Even if

**FYI**—The 1958 film *I Want to Live!* was the story of Barbara Graham, who was convicted five years earlier of collaborating with three others of robbing and murdering a widow. Graham's main function was to help her associates gain access into the widow's home. Graham netted the maximum sentence and was put to death, even though she may not have shared in the actual killing. Two last-minute stays of execution were lifted, making her one of four women put to death in California. Susan Hayward won a Best Actress Academy Award for her portrayal of Barbara Graham.

**Other Notes**—An interesting note to those of you who come up against a husband and wife criminal team. In the past, common law regarded a husband and wife as one person for most purposes, so the couple could not be guilty for conspiring with one another. But with time and experience, the trend in recent years has been to recognize the separate identities of the spouses. Hello, modern thinking.

Naïve Ned were not actually on the scene, such as if he rented a U-Drive-It and left it parked within walking distance of the jewelry store, or if he agreed to baby-sit Kevin's infant son, Kevin II, while Kevin Klever robbed the store, he is subject to the same charges as Kevin when caught.

And although someone can be guilty of three inchoate crimes, he or she cannot be convicted of all of them, just one. But the prosecutor will file as many charges as possible to improve his chances of conviction; sometimes called "overcharging" by defense attorneys. This type of practice also serves as a bargaining chip when it comes to plea negotiation in that the prosecution can offer to dispense with one or more of the lightest charges for the right information.

Now I know you're thinking about certain terms you may have heard used on television or films such as, "accessory after the fact" or, that someone has "aided and abetted," or even the terminology where someone has "hindered the apprehension" of the perpetrator. Who are these people, what are these charges, and why are they different from conspirators?

The difference is basically the factor of time, and one might even refer to them as "hidden crimes." Listen to some of the criminal definitions: A person commits an offense if, with purpose to hinder the apprehension, prosecution, conviction, or punishment of another for an offense he or she:

1. harbors or conceals the person,
2. provides aid, such as weapons, money or transportation,
3. prevents or obstructs anyone from performing an act which might aid in the discovery of said person by force or threats,
4. conceals, alters, or destroys evidence,
5. warns persons of impending discovery, and
6. volunteers false information to police.

Do you see the distinction? The help to the perpetrator comes after the criminal act but still affects the crime or the criminal in some elemental way. And a crime is not actually finished until the criminal has reached a place of temporary safety. Perhaps, because by the time an accessory after the fact becomes involved a crime has already occurred, in most states accessories after the fact face far less punishment than accomplices or their principals.

Okay, so you are one to one with an offender who has gotten caught up in some bad business and begs for advice. Is there

**FYI**—Although defendants may be convicted of separate charges for the same act, they usually cannot be punished separately for each charge. When a complaint is filed, it may say, for example, that the accused, who stole five computers is charged with five counts of burglary plus breaking and entering.

some way to help him or her "get out of trouble?" Is there a defense? It is a practice more commonly used than you would think. It is called renunciation.

## RENUNCIATION

Renunciation is, at the very least, a way to let the transgressor negotiate a better deal with the prosecutor. Renunciation is an active arrangement whereby the one who strayed will terminate complicity in the commission of a crime, AND, deprive the complicity of its effectiveness, OR, will give timely warning to cops, OR, will make a substantial effort to prevent a crime. Maybe the offender will put his or her own life at stake or make a compelling, redeeming, or distinguishing gesture–this provides for the universal fact that we all make mistakes and early deterrence is indeed possible.

## LIABILITY TYPES

Before we leave accessory activities, there is another area of aiding a perpetrator called "supplier's liability." Anytime you hear about strict liability crimes, these are crimes in which intent is not an element. For example: Act + Intent = Criminal Liability. Whereas, Forbidden Act = Strict Liability

Crime. Offenses that involve no mental element but consist of only forbidden acts or omissions are classified as strict liability crimes. Since the Latin term, *mala in se* means "wrongs in themselves," *mala prohibita* refers to "prohibited evils" or offenses deemed wrong by the state. This latter type of statute says that if someone does or doesn't do something which brings about a certain result, he or she is still guilty of a crime. Examples of this would be liquor, narcotics, and food laws; regulatory laws; and traffic regulations. These cases usually involve mostly youthful offenders or matters of public health or welfare.

With supplier's liability, the supplier or "seller" presents goods to the perpetrator, and the supplier has no liability for the "mere knowledge" of the buyer's criminal purpose for the goods unless:
1. The seller acquires a stake, for example, receives a benefit, such as selling goods at inflated prices;
2. No legitimate use for the goods or services exist, for example, the supplier has a directory of prostitutes; or
3. The volume of business conducted is grossly disproportionate to legitimate demand, for example, when a doctor sells Prozac in mass quantities; and
4. the crime that goods are being used for is a felony.

**Caution**—In court, you will often hear about "accomplice testimony" such as, having an accomplice "roll over" on another conspirator. The truth is, judges have historically been distrustful of an accomplice who points the finger or shifts the blame to someone else. Because of this inclination, most states have a safeguard rule that a defendant cannot be convicted merely upon the testimony of an accomplice. If the prosecution presents a witness who qualifies as an accomplice, the prosecutor will have to "corroborate" that witness's testimony with independent evidence linking the defendant to a crime. Use this little known fact to your advantage by ensuring that there is some type of physical evidence that can be linked to the perpetrator. Occasionally, the court may adjourn proceedings when the judge refuses to hear accomplice testimony, and the prosecutor must then change his or her tactics in order to search for further truth. Knowing this going in is the best way to anticipate problems.

## INTENT

We've skirted around the issue of "intent." Does it matter what state of mind the criminal was in at the time of the crime? Frankly, yes. State of mind is a major player, the ace in the hole so to speak, the card used to complete the loaded hand held by the prosecutor and it is called "intent." Since intent is such a crucial factor to proving someone's liability for a crime, here are the four basic terms pertaining to intent–the mental state of mind–and what they mean, in simple terms.

- Purposeful–the conscious objective is to engage in a conduct.
- Knowing–the person is aware of his or her conduct *and* he or she is practically certain that the conduct will cause the result.
- Reckless–conscious "disregarding" of a substantial and unjustified risk *and* the disregard is a gross deviation from the standard of care that a reasonable person would observe.
- Negligence–she or he would be aware of a substantial and unjustifiable risk *and* the risk must be of a nature that the failure to perceive it involves a gross deviation from the standard of care that a reasonable person would observe.

Let's take a hypothetical case to explain this. Suppose that the defender, Colt Packer, fired a gun that hit Charter Arms in the shoulder. There could be a minimum of four different scenarios to explain the shooting and proof of intent. First, Packer could have fired the gun and hit Arms accidentally. Second, Packer may have fired the gun deliberately but did not realize that Arms was in the vicinity. Third, Packer may very well have intended to shoot Arms, wounding him after a dispute but not necessarily killing him. And fourth, Packer may be guilty of attempted murder in that he was trying to prevent Arms from taking another breath. Four very different versions with virtually the same result–hitting Charter Arms with ammunition from a loaded gun.

### . . . Packer may have fired the gun deliberately but did not know that Charter Arms was in the vicinity.

Now just to complicate things a little further, there is also a legal term called "doctrine of transferred intent." This concept says that when a person intends to commit one criminal act but accomplishes another, the law implies that the necessary criminal intent for the second wrongful act is still present. In other words, if the accused intended to hurt one person, and wound up injuring someone else, the intent is still sufficient to make him or her responsible for the second, unintended victim. In the classic illustration, A aims a gun at B intending to kill B. A misses and instead kills C. A's mental state directed against B is said to be transferred to C, the unintended victim. The only intent left now is for the courts to decide what to do with him.

## FUNDAMENTAL COURT SYSTEM

In Chapter 1 we talked about the evolution of law and its historical underpinnings. Before we go much further, you need to get a picture of how the fundamental court system looks on our U.S. criminal justice family tree. For example, the United States Constitution is at the head of the family; it sets forth the general powers and limits of government and specifies the rights of its individual citizens. The U.S. Supreme Court upholds the Constitution and adjudicates questionable trials concerning issues involving constitutional law specifically. In later chapters we'll draw simplified court systems and detail their responsibilities so you will understand it at-a-glance.

On the first tier or branch of this tree is the *federal government.* Our federal government is responsible for defining and punishing federal crimes–crimes against the nation. Next to this, are the *state constitutions.* This is a separate entity which sets forth the powers and limits of the fifty state governments, each which may be distinct from the others.

Just below the federal government are the three great powers, the legislative, executive, and judicial branches. The *legislative branch* is administered by our United States Congress who enacts laws setting forth the various federal crimes and punishments. The *executive branch* of the federal government is responsible for enforcing federal laws, prosecuting cases, and supervising punishments. The *judicial branch* is made up of the federal courts which help to interpret the laws by deciding particular cases.

These three branches: legislative, executive, and judicial have what's called the principle of separation of powers. That means, each branch of government must rely on the other for approval, so that no one power can make decisions without the other. Just to illustrate this tit-for-tat concept: the legislative branch makes laws, the executive branch enforces those laws, and the judicial branch interprets those laws. Now, if the Congress writes a law, the Supreme Court can declare congressional laws unconstitutional. The Congress can also rewrite legislation to circumvent the Court's decisions; and the Senate also confirms the judges and determines the number of judges appointed.

The President of the United States can nominate federal judges, can refuse to enforce the Court's decisions, and can grant pardons. The Congress can override a presidential veto of its legislation, it can remove and impeach a president, and the Senate confirms the presidential appointments. It also controls the power of the purse and provides funds for the president's programs. And, finally, the Supreme Court can declare presidential actions unconstitutional. That is separation of powers!

On the other side of the second tier of authority are the *state constitutions.* Each state has its own constitution that sets forth the powers and limits of their own government. They receive input from their state legislatures, which makes state laws (often called state statutes), and sets forth their own criminal prohibitions and penalties. There is another section under state constitutions called *state and local government.* This body oversees law enforcement, prosecutorial functions, and corrections agencies within that state. And finally, the third branch is the *state court system* which interprets the state laws by deciding particular cases. Each of these entities needs the cooperation of the other in order to operate efficiently.

## COURT TYPES

### Criminal? Civil?
### What's the Difference?

Court cases are fundamentally two types: *criminal* and *civil*. A criminal case means that the government seeks to punish an individual for an act that has been deemed a crime by either Congress or a state legislature. Consequently, in a criminal case, the prosecutor (who is an elected official) undertakes and controls the case, not the victim. He or she will file criminal charges against the offender and does not need the permission of the victim. The prosecutor must prove the defendant's guilt "beyond a reasonable doubt." As a result, the defendant is almost always guaranteed a trial by a jury of his or her peers. The accused also has the option of having a government-appointed attorney. Trials are commonly open to the public.

A civil case has different bones. It has to do with a dispute between individuals or organizations and most often concerns either duties or rights that each legally owe the other. The state has a less direct interest (other than peace) and the attorneys are generally representatives of private firms, so the parties in civil cases pay for their own lawyers. Most civil laws are broken because of a breach of contract, which means that one or both of the parties involved, violated the terms set forth. The injured party is the one who initiates the case.

People held liable in civil cases may have to pay damages, give up property, or suffer some other type of remedy. In a civil case, the plaintiff (the one bringing forth the case), only need prove the facts with a preponderance of evidence that the defendant is liable for damages. Only some types of civil cases involve a jury trial. Usually, an offer of settlement will negate the need for court.

A *tort*, on the other hand, is a wrongful act that does not violate any enforceable agreement, but still violates a legal right on behalf of the injured party. Examples of a tort would be wrongful death or personal injury cases because of either intentional or negligent reasons, including wrongful destruction of goods or property, trespass, and defamation of character–which is, libel, slander, or degradation of one's name or standing.

### Misdemeanors, Felonies, and Infractions

Like people, criminal laws come in an array of sizes and shapes and fit different circumstances. Crimes are separated by their seriousness and, as a consequence, their punishments. Felonies are the most serious crimes and generally speaking, they are punishable by more than a year in prison and fines greater than $1,000. Examples of felonies are murder, rape, robbery, and kidnapping.

Misdemeanors are less serious crimes and typically can be punished by less than one

---

**FYI**—A person can be subjected to both criminal and civil cases—prosecuted by the state for criminal actions and civilly sued for monetary damages. In 1995, in the most publicized case in history, O.J. Simpson was prosecuted for the murder of both Nicole Brown Simpson and Ron Goldman and found not guilty. That did not end his trials however. In an entirely separate case, Simpson was also sued in a civil court for "wrongful death" by the victims' families. At the end of the civil case in 1997, Simpson was found responsible for the victims' deaths and ordered to pay millions of dollars in damages.

> **FYI—Wobbler statutes.** Some crimes may be classified by prosecutors and judges as either a felony or misdemeanor according to criminal statute. Such crimes are often referred to as "wobblers." For instance, some wobbler statutes may allow an assault to be charged as a felony or misdemeanor largely depending on the prosecutor's own discretion. His or her decision will be based on the severity of the injury to the victim, or the nature of the defendant's intent and past criminal record. Likewise, a judge may decide, after hearing the evidence, to reduce a felony assault to a misdemeanor depending on the circumstances presented.

year in jail and fines of no more than $1,000. Examples of common misdemeanors are drunk driving, shoplifting, prostitution, and possession of an unregistered firearm. A unique element of misdemeanors though, first time caught involves less incarceration time, aggravation and a fine, but the second and third go-around with the same crime can net someone felony charges.

Infractions are those violations that are classified as less serious than misdemeanors, which commonly involve traffic laws, and would typically be remedied by a monetary fine. Defendants charged with infractions are not usually eligible for a jury trial. Included in this group may also be municipal laws or offenses called "ordinances." These are rules or laws set up by a particular city or county. A city ordinance may prohibit smoking in government buildings and with some of the old, so-called "blue laws"—archaic ordinances—rules such as no spitting on the sidewalk may be infractions. Violators of municipal laws are typically issued fines to pay.

## Suit and Tie Crime

Another relatively new area of crime in the scope of all law historically, white-collar crime presents special problems for criminologists because it is difficult to define, the conduct involved is often elusive, and no readily quantifiable data exist to tell how often it is done. What in the past may have endured as unethical business, is now redefined as conduct that is criminal. Plus, other offensive behavior such as computer crime, does not fit the mold of developed common law and has only become formalized as a forbidden statute in recent years.

This slippery genus of lawbreaking is usually committed in the course of an occupation or profession and, as such, is thought of as pinstripe crime because of the connection with the red "power" tie and striped suit, and is committed by persons in the upper socioeconomic strata of society primarily. White-collar crimes as a consequence, often fall into federal jurisdiction. These may include violation of statutes such as bid rigging, price fixing, money laundering, insider trading, and tax fraud. Interestingly, white-collar crimes are frequently defined to include prostitution, gambling, obscenity, and offenses relative to the importing, manufacture, and distribution of illegal drugs. It's these same types of crimes that come under the banner of "organized crime" but only when they are committed by groups of people who also attempt to gain political influence through graft and corruption, while balancing their activity with threats and acts of violence.

If a white-collar crime is prosecuted federally, the violation can be tied to statutes enacted by Congress. These laws will be found in Article 1, Section 9 of the U.S. Constitution, which grants the government power over postal, bankruptcy, and taxing matters, and also transfers its authority with regard to domestic and foreign commerce.

Sometimes, a "small fry" gets nicked for white-collar offenses because they have committed fraud or swindled a target. They operate by using telephone or mail solicitations in order to bilk money out of people by sell-

ing "opportunities to buy" unregistered securities, help their marks to obtain undeserved diplomas, participate in phony contests, or just generally perpetrate scams, such as would be done with a real estate scheme or fraudulent land sales. And the variety of offenses will continue to grow and evolve in interpretation as electronics takes over more and more of our lives.

When talking about the law, we often bump up against some common public

**FYI—Murky waters.** In June 1998, in *U.S. v. Singleton,*[4] the U.S. appeals court ruled that it was illegal under federal law for the government to "purchase" accomplice testimony with a promise of leniency. This decision, made by the 10th U.S. Circuit Court of Appeals, rocked the Justice Department. At issue was the moral and legal underpinning of immunity deals that would, essentially, make criminals of the federal prosecutors who offer them. If this ruling was upheld, it would have had implications for thousands of cases, most recently the convictions of McVeigh, Nichols, and Fortier who were tried in connection with bombing the federal building in Oklahoma City, which resulted in the deaths of 168 people.

Timothy McVeigh was charged with first degree murder and sentenced to death. A separate jury convicted Terry Nichols of conspiracy for helping to plan the bombing and collecting supplies and he was sentenced to life in prison. Michael Fortier, another accomplice, received 12 years in prison after pleading guilty to failure to warn authorities of a bomb plot and transporting stolen weapons. But, in part, Fortier's lighter sentence was due to his providing crucial testimony that helped convict McVeigh and Nichols.

The ruling was put on hold until the full, Denver-based appeals court could decide. In its majority opinion, a 12-member panel said that "Statutes of general purport do not apply to the United States unless Congress makes the application clear and indisputable." That if Congress had intended to overturn the accepted practice, "it would have to do so in clear, unmistakable and unarguable language." The reversal pleased Justice Department officials, noting that offering leniency in exchange for truthful testimony was "a longstanding, important aspect of the legal system."

The case that brought up this dispute centered on the Kansas conviction of Sonya Singleton, on charges of cocaine trafficking and money laundering. Three judges said the chief prosecution witness illegally received leniency in exchange for his testimony, violating federal law against bribing witnesses. These same judges did not change their minds with the final vote 9-to-3.

4. *U.S. v. Singleton*, 144 F.3d 1343 (10th Circuit 1998).

beliefs–some key assumptions we make about the criminal justice system that become conventional wisdom. For instance, don't we assume that legal counsel is always competent? Or that guilt will always be determined by the facts? That trials are fair and unbiased? Guess again.

---

**Caution**—The expression "falling through the cracks" is tailor-made for the criminal justice system. For offenders without funds or connections, the odds of getting off are heavily weighed against them. Because the state has such powerful resources, and because the system is overloaded and underfunded, the courts and the public defender's office must do their part to see that due process is indeed a fundamental right for every person accused.

---

## Patriot Act

The Patriot Act[5] began as the United and Strengthening America Act, formed in response to the September 11, 2001 terrorist attacks against our country, and it dramatically expanded the authority of federal government to track and disrupt terrorists, here and overseas.

Some of the laws rewritten under the Patriot Act are immigration law, and banking and money laundering laws. It also adjusted the Foreign Intelligence Surveillance Act (FISA) and created the new crime category of "domestic terrorism."[6]

This U.S. criminal code provision, 18 U.S.C. §2331, reads like this: *domestic terrorism* defines activities that (1) involve acts dangerous to human life that are a violation of the criminal laws of the U.S. or of any state, that (2) appear to be intended (a) to intimidate or coerce a civilian population, (b) to influence the policy of a government by intimidation or coercion, or (c) to affect the conduct of a government by mass destruction, assassination, or kidnapping, and (3) occur primarily within the territorial jurisdiction of the U.S.

## Ten Titles to Fight Terrorism and More

The full Patriot Act has ten titles and each contains several sections, but the following is a slight sketch of the ways it taps into our lives in respect to criminal law and procedure: Along with enhanced security, special funds are set aside for counterterrorist actions including more money for the FBI's Technical Support Center–so they can install and use state-of-the-art tracking technology to monitor Internet traffic in order to detect terrorist cells and head-off terrorist plots. President Bush claims it will be easier for Internet service providers to release customer records voluntarily to the government when emergencies are linked to an immediate risk, and that it will also help victims of hacking crimes get assistance from law enforcement to monitor trespassers on their computer.

Other surveillance measures allow various government agencies the ability to collect business, telephone, bank, and credit records. Bush said it eliminates double standards, by allowing agents to pursue terrorists with the same tools they use against other

---

5. http://www.whitehouse.gov/infocus/patriotact/
6. section 802

criminals. For targeted investigations, intelligence agencies and law enforcement would be able to intercept communications via *pen register*–an electronic device that records all numbers dialed from a particular telephone line–or *trap and trace* devices–an electronic device used to record and trace all message signals from a telecommunication system.

Sections of the Patriot Act also permit the FBI to ask federal judges on the secret FISA court for: "roving" wiretap warrants, and the ability to force businesses to turn over records involved in terrorism or intelligence probes, and businesses many not tell anyone about such orders. *Roving* wiretaps often span more than one district in multiple jurisdictions, making it easier for Act-authorized agents to monitor terrorists who seek to thwart surveillance by rapidly changing locations. There are also "sneak and peek" court-approved warrants so investigators can search premises and take evidence without notifying the occupant for 30 days. In addition, Act II lets the FBI, CIA, and other law enforcement and intelligence agencies share information about terrorist investigations and increases recordkeeping and reporting requirements. The final portion of this title deals with currency smuggling and counterfeiting, including quadrupling the maximum penalty for counterfeiting foreign currency.

Another potent provision is found in Title III and deals primarily with strengthening banking rules specifically against money laundering, especially on the international stage. It outlaws United States laundering of any proceeds from foreign crimes of violence or political corruption, cybercrime or terrorist organizations. Businesses such as check-cashing outfits and other financial institutions must report cash transactions involving more than $10,000 to the IRS, and to file SARs–Suspicious Activity Reports as well.

Title IV–Protecting the border–amends large parts of the Immigration and Nationality Act, giving increased law enforcement and investigative power to the United States Attorney General and to the Immigration and Naturalization Service. Some provisions are designed to prevent alien terrorists from entering the United States, particularly from Canada, and to enable the Attorney General or his deputy to detain and deport alien terrorists or those engaged in activities meant to endanger national security.

Following that are articles that remove obstacles to investigation by offering rewards for information, disclosure of educational records, coordination with law enforcement, and other information-gathering entities such as electronic surveillance or physical search guidelines. Of particular importance are those persons who use the Internet to make plans for bombs, to manufacture or utilize atomic weapons or the production of nuclear material or energy–and people who use terrorist financing through "hawalas" (informal money transfer networks) rather than traditional financial institutions.

## DNA Database and Collection

Section 3 of the Act mandates collecting DNA from Federal prisoners who were convicted of murder, sexual abuse, child sexual abuse, involvement in sex trafficking and slavery, kidnapping, robbery or burglary, or for any military offense against the Uniform Code of Military Justice.

Under the President's initiative, the Attorney General is instructed to improve the use of DNA in the criminal justice system–especially in federal, state, and local forensic laboratories–by granting funds, training and assistance to eliminate backlogs, strengthen crime lab capacity, and to stimulate research and development. State law enforcement can tap into the FBI's Combined DNA Index System–CODIS–to exchange and compare DNA profiles electronically, thereby linking crimes to each other and to convicted offenders. An interesting statistic,[7] as of July 2006 the profile composition of the National DNA Index System (NDIS) is as follows: Total number of profiles: 3,557,154, total forensic profiles: 144,582, total convicted offender profiles: 3,412,572.

Title VII of the Patriot Act increases information sharing with an emphasis on critical infrastructure protection. So, not only would it allow law enforcement to counter terrorism in our own country, but makes it easier to enter into grants or contracts that cross jurisdiction boundaries.

Vehicles of mass transportation are handled, and clearer standards and tough penalties are assessed for land-and water-based systems as well as commercial aviation. The U.S. railroads already had a number of regulations but even vehicles and ferries are mentioned. Since biological agents and toxins can hurt or kill large numbers of commuters, such as in 1995, when the Aum Shinrikyo cult, released sarin nerve gas in a Japanese subway, chemicals are also factored in for stiff punishments.

Conspiracy provisions were added to criminal statutes that cover arson or destruction of property within the special maritime and territorial jurisdiction of the United States, killings in Federal facilities, the destruction of communications lines, stations, or systems, material support to terrorists, torture, the sabotage of nuclear facilities or fuel, interfering with flight crews; carrying weapons or explosives onto an aircraft, and the destruction of interstate gas or hazardous liquid pipeline facility.

## Meth in the Patriot Act

Surprising to some citizens who read the Patriot Act for the first time, the Reauthorization of 2006[8] includes the Combat Methamphetamine Epidemic Act. This bill introduces a comprehensive anti-methamphetamine package restricting the sale of products containing ingredients needed to cook the drug, and providing new tools to police and prosecutors to combat dealers. For example, the bill places limits on large-scale purchases of over-the-counter drugs that are used to manufacture methamphetamines, and requires stores to keep these ingredients behind the counter or in locked display cases. It increases penalties for smuggling and selling methamphetamines. An additional $99 million a year for the next five years is available to train state and local law enforcement to investigate and lock up meth offenders and the bill expands available funding for personnel and equipment for enforcement, prosecution and environmental cleanup.

## Americans Have Opinions

According to a recent Gallup poll,[9] when citizens were asked about the topic of civil liberties, 38 percent of those polled said the Bush administration has gone too far in restricting civil liberties, while 40 percent said the government's approach has been "about right," and 19 percent said the government had not gone far enough. Surveys

7. http://www.fbi.gov/hq/lab/codis/clickmap/htm
8. http://www.whitehousedrugpolicy.gov/NEWS/press06/030906.html
9. http://www.cnn.com/2006/POLITICS/01/10/poll.wiretaps/index.html?section=cnn_topstories

conducted between the 2002 poll and the most recent numbers of a 2006 poll show the percentage of people who think the administration has gone too far has gradually increased.

In response to critics such as the American Civil Liberties Union (ACLU), and to reply to the many criticisms of the Patriot Act, the U.S. Government setup the web site http://www.lifeandliberty.gov.

## REVIEW QUESTIONS AND ANSWERS

Chapter 2 illustrates the elements of a criminal act–how they are structured and what ingredients are needed to form a crime, beginning with the attempt to construct a crime through to liability, misdemeanors and felonies. The foundations of government structure in regards to crime and laws are also begun here; allowing students to see what makes a crime, where crime comes from and the basics of the types of degrees of crime.

## *Key Words to Define*

- **Conspiracy**–an agreement between two of more people to commit an act of crime, plus intent, *and* an overt action, these three things combined
- **Inchoate**–Anticipatory crimes
- **Intent**–a state of mind with purpose to commit
- **Legislative branch**–U.S. Congress enacts laws for federal crimes and punishments
- **Misdemeanor**–less serious crimes punishable by less than one year in jail and no more than $1,000 in fines
- **Negligence**–a person is aware of a risk and has an avoidance of care that a reasonable person would assume

- **Overt act**–a substantial step toward a crime
- **Renunciation**–a perpetrators substantial effort to prevent a crime, usually done for lenience in prosecution

## *Questions for Review and Discussion*

1. *Question:* What are the three elements that make up an attempt? *Answer:* Intent, a substantial step (or overt act) and conduct that would have been a crime

2. *Question:* What makes "solicitation" and "attempt" different? *Answer:* Solicitation is complete when the request to do the act is made.

3. *Question:* What is Wharton's Rule? *Answer:* Two people cannot conspire to commit a crime such as adultery, incest, or bigamy because these offenses are between two people and does not endanger the public generally.

4. *Question:* Name some things an accomplice might do? *Answer:* Distract a security guard, review a floor plan or blueprint for a crime, and rent a get-away vehicle.

5. *Question:* What makes a crime such as "aiding and abetting" different from an inchoate crime? *Answer:* The element of time–help that comes after the criminal act but is still elemental to the crime.

6. *Question:* Strict liability is different from criminal liability, how? *Answer:* These are offenses of harm but have no "intent" or mental element; example, selling liquor to a minor. It's done for profit but without thinking of the consequence.

7. *Question:* Could the example of strict liability in question 6 be called "supplier's liability"? *Answer:* Yes. The seller receives money from the underage purchaser and the goods contribute to drunkenness.

8. *Question:* Does each state have its own constitution? *Answer:* Yes. What does this document do? A state constitution sets forth the powers and limits of state government.

9. *Question:* Name the three branches of our federal government. *Answer:* Executive, legislative and judicial.

10. *Question:* What are the two types of court cases? *Answer:* Criminal and civil.

11. *Question:* How are civil and criminal cases different? *Answer:* In a criminal case the government seeks to adjudicate; civil trials however, are wrongdoings or a dispute between individuals or organizations and those concerns are rights or duties that each legally owe each other.

12. *Question:* People held liable in a civil case have what sort of remedy hurled at them? *Answer:* They may pay damages, lose property, pay fines or are required to perform a service.

13. *Question:* Name a tort or wrongful act. *Answer:* Wrongful death, destruction of property, slander, etc.

14. *Question:* Are infractions more or less serious than misdemeanors? *Answer:* Less serious, such as traffic violations.

15. *Question:* A "suit and tie" crime is also called? *Answer:* a white-collar crime.

## *Essay Assignment*

EXPLAIN THE REMEDY FOR "ACCOMPLICE TESTIMONY" AND WHY IT'S NEEDED. Accomplices who "roll over" on their co-conspirators for leniency or a reduced sentence are not valued as dependable with judges and others. Most states have a safeguard rule against accomplices who shift the blame to another conspirator with accomplice testimony: it is called *corroboration*. Corroboration occurs when another witness can back up the truth or testimony of the accomplice.

# Chapter 3

# CRIMES AGAINST THE PERSON

The soul of a murderer is blind.
–Albert Camus, *The Plague*

These are what people say they fear the most: violent crimes and bodily harm. "Crimes against the person" have a profound psychological aftermath. They affect people as a personal violation and these feelings fuse themselves onto the victim's thoughts forever (if they live to regret it). This is an important concept for law enforcement and lawyers to grasp because it is difficult to imagine and it affects every action the victim takes. This chapter will seek to define personal crimes and provide insight for the professional.

Though often used interchangeably, homicide and murder are not necessarily the same thing. A *homicide* is any killing of a human being by another. There are some homicides that are justifiably legal, such as the killing of a suspect by police or a killing in self-defense. Whereas, *murder* on the other hand, is an unlawful killing with malice aforethought. In other words, in order to charge someone with murder, it must be proven that there was premeditation.

Premeditation doesn't mean that the killer acted out because of spite or hate as most people believe, it means that the killer intended to kill a person–a different distinction. In most states, malice aforethought is not limited to intentional killings but it also exists if: A killer intentionally inflicts very serious bodily harm which causes a death; OR, If a killer's behavior demonstrates "extreme reckless disregard for the value of human life" and results in a victim's death. For example, the perpetrator could have been involved both in a dangerous act *and* demonstrated wanton disregard for other human life on the scene at the time.

It is important that a professional look up his or her particular state's law when becoming involved in loss of life. Some part of the definition, and even the words used to describe a law or a crime, may be unique. For example, here is a simplified outline of an Arkansas statute for homicide that has several distinguishing features from other states' laws:

## HOMICIDE

**Capital murder**: A person commits or attempts to commit capital murder if he engages in (one of the seven below), and in the course of or the furtherance of that felony, *he causes the death of another under* circumstances manifesting *extreme indifference to the value of a human life*:

**A. Limited Felony Murder:**
1. Rape
2. Kidnapping
3. Arson
4. Vehicular piracy
5. Robbery
6. Burglary
7. First-degree escape

**B. Kills a *Public Servant*:**
1. A police officer
2. A judge
3. A firefighter
4. A jailer
5. A prison official, when they are acting in the line of duty or performing their jobs.

**C. A Double Death:** with purpose to kill one, kills two

**D. Public Official:** with purpose of killing an elected official, he kills anybody, any time, e.g., a sheriff

**E. Life Sentence:** under a life sentence, he *purposely* kills another

**F. Contract Killing:** the hitter; pursuant to an agreement, he kills someone in return for anything of value

**G. Contract Killing:** hirer; a contract killing (agreement) in which he "hires" someone to kill another.

## CLASS Y FELONY

*Important notes in Arkansas law:*

- Conduct must be the proximate cause of death; this means that the victim's death must have been the natural and probable result of the defendant's unlawful conduct.
- Death does not have to be foreseeable (or intended).
- Death used to be defined as the end of heart and lung function; now, death is cessation or termination of brain activity.
- In Arkansas, there are five classifications of homicide, and a Capital Murder receives the death penalty. The other classifications are Murder in the first degree, Murder in the second degree, Manslaughter, and Negligent Homicide.

Homicide and the degree of culpability—in other words, blame—are also somewhat different in each state. Most states classify murder as either first degree or second degree. And the law regards some killers as more dangerous and morally blameworthy than others. Murder in the first degree is willful, deliberate, and premeditated. Now the period of time required for premeditation does not have to be a long duration. Just long enough to consider the gravity of the situation; it could be as brief as going into the next room to get the Glock.

We've also seen, as in the Arkansas statute above, murder in the first degree includes

---

**Caution**—Say a small Korean market has been assailed by a gang intent on robbing the vendor. One of the transgressors wants to take the money and run but, in the process of the heist, he frightens the merchant and his gun accidentally discharges, killing the owner. The felony murder rule makes this offender strictly liable because he kills the citizen in the process of committing a crime. Sound familiar? A writer used this concept and Nakita, of *La Femme Nakita* was born. Realistically though, the murderer will not get to work in covert operations.

any murder in the course of committing a felony. And it only follows that murder in the first degree usually carries a more severe punishment than second-degree murder charges too. Currently, in a majority of states, the ultimate penalty is death. In some other states, instead of capital punishment, sentencing is life in prison without the possibility of parole. Second-degree murder convictions are usually served by a term of years in prison rather than a life sentence, and are almost always eligible for parole.

## Currently, in a majority of states, the ultimate penalty is death.

An important note that we've found in the first degree murder statute in Arkansas is that in the case of a death involving a fetus, the prosecution has to prove that the fetus was viable, and, as of this writing, we believe that constitutes twenty weeks. Check out this anomaly in your own state's laws and you may have an interesting case to build on. If you're dealing with a repeat offender, perhaps he or she "got away with murder" because of this little-known pregnancy rule. That's sure to inflame a lot of your other, more determined witnesses who set out to seek justice for those who are seldom represented–infants and children.

## PREMEDITATION OR SPECULATION?

*State v. Bingham*[1] is a case that illustrates the dilemma between deciding whether it is a sound policy to separate out premeditated killings in order to impose more severe penalties than for other murders.

Leslie Cook, a retarded adult living at the Laurisden Home in Port Angeles, was raped and strangled on February 15, 1982. Bingham was the last person with whom she was seen. The two of them got off the Port Los Angeles–Sequim bus together at Sequim about 6 P.M. The pair visited a grocery store and two residences. The last of these was Enid Pratt's where Bingham asked for a ride back to Port Angeles. When he was refused, he said they would hitchhike. They took the infrequently traveled Old Olympic Highway. Three days later, Cook's body was discovered in a field approximately one quarter mile from the Pratt residence.

At trial, the state's expert testified that, in order to cause death by strangulation, Cook's assailant would have had to maintain substantial and continuous pressure on her windpipe for three to five minutes. The state contended that this alone was enough to raise an inference that the murder was premeditated. The trial judge agreed. Therefore, it allowed the issue of premeditation to go to the jury. The jury convicted Bingham of aggravated first-degree murder, rape being the aggravating circumstance.

On appeal, Bingham's attorney conceded that a finding of guilty of murder was justified, but he challenged the finding of premeditation, and contended that the evidence was insufficient to support it.

In an opinion given by Chief Judge Worswick, the Supreme Court agreed. There was no evidence presented that proved Bingham had known Cook before February 15 or that he had a motive to kill her. By chance, they took the same bus. Judge Worswick said that while it could be inferred Bingham raped her, a reasonable jury could not infer from this beyond a reasonable doubt that he also planned to kill her. There was really no evidence to support premeditation. The case was reversed and remanded for judgment and sentencing for second degree murder.

---

1. *State v. Bingham*, 40 Wn. App. 553, 699 P.2d 262 (Wash. 1985).

## MORE MURDER

The definition of murder in the second degree includes: the conscious objective to cause the death of someone, and causes the death of another, *or*, to knowingly cause death under circumstances of extreme indifference to the value of a human life, *or*, with purpose to cause a serious physical injury to someone, cause a death, any death. It's a killing in which malice aforethought is present, but the premeditation factor is not. This could mean a death resulted from a barroom fight, it could also include parents who abuse children with fatal results.

### CLASS B FELONY

## Depraved Mind

You will also hear the words "depraved mind or heart" in connection with second-degree murder. An apt example of this would be a case where the state of New York charged a fifteen-and-a-half-year-old boy with murder in the second degree for reckless conduct that created a grave indifference to human life. In *People v. Roe*[2] the evidence at trial revealed that the defendant had loaded a mix of live and dummy shells into a 12-gauge shotgun, pumped a shell into the firing chamber, not knowing whether it was potentially dangerous or not. Then he callously raised the gun to his shoulder, and pointed it directly at the victim, stating they would play a game of "Polish roulette" and asked, "Who is first?" The defendant then proceeded to discharge a live round into the chest of a thirteen-year-old boy, which resulted in his death.

On appeal, the boy's defender argued that it must be shown that his defendant's reckless conduct was imminently dangerous

and presented a grave risk of death, whereas, in manslaughter, a much lesser charge, the conduct need only present the lesser "substantial risk" of death.

The New York Court of Appeals held that they felt the evidence presented was such that the defendant had an intense interest in weapons, possessed a detailed knowledge of weapons, and they therefore reasoned that with this type of information available to him, the macabre game of chance was legally sufficient to support second-degree murder.

## MANSLAUGHTER AND ITS PARTNER, PROVOCATION

Provocation frequently is an ingredient in manslaughter trials. There are two classes of manslaughter under common law: voluntary and involuntary.

Voluntary manslaughter, also known as manslaughter in the first degree, arises when a person is suddenly provoked and kills in "the heat of passion" or extreme emotional disturbance. The words hate, rage, or jealousy come to mind. Human weakness helps to define voluntary manslaughter in that the circumstances are likely to provoke any reasonable person into action. The killer may act intentionally, but the emotional context prevents them from being able to control their behavior, reducing their moral blameworthiness. It is a Class C felony under Arkansas law.

A common scenario is the husband who returns home unexpectedly to find his wife in bed with another man. One other vital characteristic in this state's law is that "mere words" are not sufficient enough to provoke a person to kill. However, informational words—those words that are highly inflam-

---

2. *People v. Roe*, 542 N.E. 2d 610 (NY 1989).

matory–such as "your husband is sleeping around" and not simply calling someone an "idiot," which would be insulting but not necessarily informational, make the difference between provoking extreme emotion and not. Intricacies? The law is full of them and, as a professional, you can use these subtle characteristics to your advantage when it comes to the prosecutor charging your key players if the offender demonstrates a hot temper. These are the details that make for properly balanced legal cases.

The key difference between voluntary and involuntary manslaughter is that a person's reckless disregard is of a substantial risk and results in death, but it involves mainly a carelessness and not a definite intent. Involuntary manslaughter has also been called "criminally negligent homicide" and is sometimes referred to as manslaughter in the second degree.

In order for the prosecution to assign voluntary manslaughter to the charges, he or she may have to unearth a defendant's specific intent. On the other hand, in a criminal charge involving involuntary manslaughter, the defendant's intent only need be general, in terms of not being partial to the victim, and inferred from the defendant's act and

surrounding circumstances. Two examples of this would be waving a loaded gun around that results in someone's death or throwing bricks off an overpass onto oncoming traffic, which also results in an accidental death.

## Vehicular Homicide

Road rage and the bloodshed on American highways have spawned many states to enact vehicular homicide as a specific felony, rather than the charge of manslaughter for causing a traffic death. An excerpt from the Florida statutes reads like this: "Vehicular homicide" is the killing of a human being by the operation of a motor vehicle by another in a reckless manner likely to cause death of, or great bodily harm to, another."[3]

By using this unique language, the state in effect has enabled the prosecutor to secure a conviction where the state is otherwise unable to meet the level of proof for establishing manslaughter. For a professional, when an offender operates a motor vehicle in such a negligent manner that it causes a death, legal eagles had best consult their individual state statutes for the charges.

---

**Other Notes**—Why, why, why? Research tells us that some typical motives for homicide may include: revenge, sadism, personal gain, mental deficiency, self-defense, sex, mercy, fear, love, feuding, contract killings, ambition, rivalry, protecting someone or something, motive in order to cover up another crime, jealousy, to frame another, blackmail, debt, and probably the least viable and the hardest to demonstrate, thrill killing. For investigators, these powerful key words should conjure up a potential motive for your case. Meaning, if you construct your fact-finding with one or more of these motives in mind, and continually allow the suspected intent to poke itself into your thesis—the why, why, why did it happen?—you will have a better idea about what drove your offender into action. Investigative brainstorming should always provide plenty of importance to motive.

---

3. West's Fla. Stat. Ann. § 782.071.

## Real Life versus Fiction

When it comes to homicide, fiction is more optimistic than reality. Unlike the characters in your favorite crime novel, in the United States today, you will not find a homicide detective who has solved every case. And while the numbers of murders committed has dropped, statistics[4] from 1992-2000, tell us the homicide rate declined and recent levels have fallen to numbers last seen in the late 1960s, but the percentage of homicides cleared by arrest has also been declining. In 2004, 63 percent of all homicides were cleared compared to 79 percent in 1976. Cases are getting harder to crack!

Experts provide several reasons for this disparity. More murders today are committed by strangers rather than by spouses or friends. James Fox, a criminologist at Northeastern University says, "Now we have taken the home out of homicide. There is a greater distance between victims and offenders, and the greater the distance, the more difficult it is to solve the crime."

Other, more apparent, frustrating factors continue to complicate cases and leave more and more investigators baffled. Robert Ressler, a retired FBI agent, says that murderers today have become more sophisticated, and that killers know more about crime-solving techniques. Also, a lot of the victims of homicide lie on the fringe of society. Coupled together with this "invisible people" problem, is the fact that the homeless, runaway, and prostitute victims have lifestyles that make it harder to track their killers. And finally, witnesses today seem more likely to refuse to talk, especially when the offenders are connected to gangs or deal in drugs. Fox has said that the good old days of 80 percent clearance rates will probably never return.

## Methodology

Homicides can be accomplished by several methods, including shooting, strangulation, knifing, poisoning, electrical shock, gassing, vehicular, hanging, beating, suffocation, and burning.

## Hospital Homicide

Technological advances in medicine have given physicians the option of using sophisticated life-support systems to prolong life for indefinite periods of time. Along with this is a burden, whose ramifications involve moral, ethical, and religious concerns. A landmark case, In *re Quinlan*,[5] involving Karen Ann Quinlan, who lay in a comatose state with no reasonable medical probability of regaining a sentient life, tells the tale of parents who requested her removal from life-support systems and were granted their petition. The court said that withdrawal of such life-support systems, under the circumstances, would not constitute a criminal homicide.

**FYI**—According to the Bureau of Justice Statistics *Sourcebook*, law enforcement agencies clear or solve offenses when at least one person is arrested, charged, and turned over to the court for prosecution. For example, in 1994, the number of violent crimes—murder, nonnegligent manslaughter, forcible rape, robbery, and aggravated assault—cleared by arrest were 45.3 percent.

4. http://www.ojp.usdoj.gov/bjs/homicide/cleared.htm
5. In *re Quinlan*, 355 A.2d 647 (NJ 1976).

But there are other issues and varying judicial opinions as to when, under what circumstances, and by whom, cessation may be ordered for minors and incompetents. And haven't we read stories in the news about people who work in hospitals who have taken it upon themselves to relieve certain patients of their life? This, too, is a powerful controversy. Just be aware that there is no statutory or judicial consensus on the viability of, or the procedures to, execute termination of a life. And, there is a vast difference between a nurse or doctor who goes haywire with power and discretion versus the procedures that have been granted in good faith, based on competent medical advice and the consent of an equally competent patient and family.

## THREATS AND PHYSICAL HARM

The assaultive offenses, assault and battery, are commonly used as a pair, but are really separate offenses at common law. Under most states' laws, a simple assault would include a threat to strike someone with the fist, or a missed punch. Assault also carries two different manners of distribution: an assault is an "attempt" to commit battery, or the intentional creation, other than by mere words alone, of a reasonable fear in the mind of the victim of immediate bodily harm. As an example, in a majority of American jurisdictions, the pointing of a gun at another would be an assault since it places another in reasonable apprehension of receiving a battery.

A battery, on the other hand, requires some physical contact with the victim. Simple battery would include hitting or pushing someone, but it could even encompass offensive touching against someone's will, intentionally tripping someone, or when a parent or teacher is using excessive force in disciplining a child. Simple assaults and batteries generally remain misdemeanors unless they are perpetrated against public officers like police or firefighters and then they are frequently classified as felonies.

When these offenses are labeled "aggravated," they cease to be called simple, and take on new meaning. For example, as aptly explained by authors Scheb and Scheb in their textbook, *Criminal Law & Procedure* (1999), "A frequently litigated issue in prosecutions for aggravated assault and aggravated battery is whether the instrument used by the defendant is a dangerous weapon capable of producing death or great bodily harm. An air pistol, a hammer, a club, or an ice pick—and under some circumstances, even a person's fist—have been found to qualify. Courts generally reason that the test is not whether great bodily harm resulted, but whether the instrument used was capable of producing such harm" (p. 103).

The definitions often require that although a completed battery can be committed recklessly, an assault of either type requires that the defendant have acted purposely or with knowledge. This next Supreme Court case presents several of these interesting points.

In *Harrod v. State*,[6] the appeals' court needed to decide whether a person could be convicted of assaulting another who has suffered no harm and was never aware of the alleged assault. The appellant, John G. Harrod, was charged with and convicted of two counts of assault. Here are notes from his first court case. You decide:

A confrontation between John Harrod, his wife Cheryl, and her friend Calvin

---

6. *Harrod v. State*, 65 Md. App. 128, 499 A.2d 959 (Md. 1985).

Crigger occurred on September 15, 1983. Cheryl testified that Calvin Crigger came over to visit when she thought her husband had gone to work; and that, "all of a sudden [John Harrod] came out of the bedroom with a hammer in his hand, swinging it around, coming after me and my friend." Calvin ran out of the house and down the steps. Then Cheryl testified that her husband then threw the hammer over the top of their son Christopher's port-a-crib in the living room, and it went into the wall. After that, he reentered the bedroom and returned with a hunting knife with a five-inch blade, and told Cheryl he was going to kill her and that if she took his son away from him, he was going to kill Christopher, wherein, John Harrod then put the knife into the banister near Cheryl's arm. He then followed Cheryl out to Calvin's car and "went after Calvin, going around and around the car."

John Harrod told his side of the story next, saying that he had missed his ride to work that day and returned back home around 10:00 A.M. and went to sleep in a back room when he heard Calvin's deep voice. He confessed to picking up the hammer, walking into the room and suggesting Calvin leave. Cheryl protested saying he didn't have to go, and John Harrod said, "Buddy, if you want your head busted in, stand here; if you want to be healthy and leave, go." Harrod claims that Calvin just stood there, so he swung the hammer. Calvin moved his head back and the hammer stuck in the wall over the crib, which was near the door.

## "Buddy, if you want your head busted in, stand here . . ."

The court in rendering its verdict, decided that beyond a reasonable doubt and to a moral certainty Mr. Harrod did go after Cheryl and Calvin, swinging a hammer and missing, wielding a knife and missing, and that he was guilty of two counts of carrying a deadly weapon–the knife and the hammer–and also two counts of assault, one against Cheryl and one against the minor child.

What do you think?

On appeal, the Supreme Court judges dismissed the charge of assault against Christopher saying that there was no evidence in the record that Christopher was in fact aware of the occurrences in his home on the morning in question. Therefore, there was insignificant evidence to find Mr. Harrod guilty of putting that victim in fear-type assault. And because the trial was erroneous in finding the appellant guilty of an assault on Christopher, they reversed that conviction.

**Other Notes**—As of April 2001, the House voted on a bill to make it a federal crime to harm a fetus during an assault on its mother, urging action on behalf of "unborn victims." Voted on in previous years, this bill now has the support of the White House. "This legislation affirms our commitment to a culture of life, which welcomes and protects children," said President Bush in a prepared statement for the press in Houston. The bill would only apply to crimes in federal jurisdiction, but about half the states have similar laws. The Supreme Court in 1989 upheld Missouri's version, one of the broadest, which describes an "unborn child" at any stage of prenatal development as a person.

## Whistle Blowing

Whistle blowing has been on the horizon of many crimes–corporate in the last ten years mainly–in Texas, someone who witnesses the commission of a felony[7] that could cause serious bodily injury or death and does not immediately report the crime to the police can be prosecuted for a Class A misdemeanor, which is punishable by a fine not to exceed $4,000, up to a year in jail, or both.

## Mayhem

Mayhem is an old-fashioned word, but it is still on the books in California. Their statute states: Every person who unlawfully and maliciously deprives a human being of a member of his body, or disables, disfigures, or renders it useless, or cuts or disables the tongue, or puts out an eye, or slits the nose, ear, or lip, is guilty of mayhem.[8]

Originally, the mayhem definition meant to willfully and maliciously injure another in order to render them unable to fight. In some states that was changed to include injuries that disfigure a person. The prosecutor, in other instances, has to prove the offender's intent to maim or disfigure the victim. These types of offenses are typically associated with revenge and, an aggravated case, would be to permanently disable the victim, something we often associate with organized crime. Again, we suggest that a professional consult his or her specific state's law because mayhem may be rolled into other statutory crimes and is often referred to as aggravated battery or attempted murder.

## Stalking

Times do change and, at the end of the '80s decade, police noticed an increase in complaints from persons who were continually being followed, harassed, or threatened. In order to name the language that seeks to describe this type of behavior, they came up with the term *stalking*, and noted that the complaints came primarily from women who were targeted by men.

By 1993, several states met the challenges presented by this new nuisance and further defined stalking, turning it into a crime. The general stipulation is that a person who willfully, maliciously and repeatedly follows or harasses, or makes a credible threat against another is guilty of stalking. The words "credible threat," which showed up in many state law books, have been struck from most of the definitions since being questioned under litigation. Certain other challenges have been made, such as with the Illinois Supreme Court fairly recently, over whether the law held up against a person's right to

---

**Other Notes**—Investigators interested in following this type of behavior for their clients should also watch for complaints being filed by women (and men) who are victim(s) nowadays, to relentless e-mail messages. This ceaseless terror (although it may have started as a simple amorous advance) may lead to enactment of new laws, both through federal and state channels.

---

7. Texas HB 325
8. West's Ann. Cal. Penal Code § 203.

freedom of speech. The Illinois law still stands, but another attempt at dismantling the statute came from Georgia, who had to decide whether attempted stalking was really a criminal offense at all, and not merely an assault misdemeanor. But the Georgia Supreme Court, in *State v. Rooks*,[9] confirmed that stalking is an offense because such conduct: constitutes an attempt to follow, place under surveillance, or contact another person.

## RAPE AND STATUTORY RAPE

Rape laws have gone through many versions and incarnations from the times since the common-law scheme as first defined in the early English common law period. Questions about force, consent, gender terminology, and what constitutes the physical act, have all been disputed as the decades pass and charges are challenged. Statutory rape, the purpose of which was to protect young women from all acts of sexual intercourse, has also been subject to definition refining when it comes to age limits, gender discrimination, and whether or not carnal knowledge is sexual intercourse, including other, sexual encounters involving minors.

One of the most significant legal reforms concerning rape came about during the late 1970s and 1980s in respect to rape shield laws. This enactment precludes presenting evidence in court of a victim's prior sexual activity with anyone other than the defendant. Some state's laws require that certain evidence be first submitted *in camera*–in chambers–for a determination as to whether the evidence of the defendant's prior relationship with the victim is relevant to the victim's consent.

Today Michigan has a modern, comprehensive law for first-degree criminal sexual offense. The criminal sexual conduct is defined by various degrees: it tells whether it involves sexual penetration or sexual contact and spells it out. Some of its provisions are: sexual penetration is sexual intercourse, cunnilingus, fellatio, anal intercourse, or any other intrusion, however slight, of any part of a person's body or of any object into the genital or anal openings of another person's body, but emission of seed is not required. In addition, the statute is a gender-neutral offense, which has become a basic reform. It also makes provisions for those people who commit sexual batteries against the helpless; those who take advantage of their family position or supervisory authority; or an offense that occurs between a doctor and his or her patient. For an example of this statute, see Mich. Comp. Laws Ann. § 750.520.[10]

If, as an investigator, you have a rape scenario as your primary focus, in order to provide a complete and thorough analysis, you should also seek to find your state's explanation of spousal rape, and whether it carries lesser penalties than the traditional rape statutes. The entire issue was once held together by a universally-accepted dictum called Hale's Rule. Lord Hale, a seventeenth

---

**Caution**—As in all criminal cases, the prosecution bears the burden of *corpus delicti*, proving that the crime has been committed. One common problem in sexual battery prosecutions is the lack of independent eyewitness testimony. It may all boil down to the victim's word against the defendant's word, and here is an

---

9. *State v. Rooks*, 468 S.E. 2d 354 (Ga. 1996).
10. Mich. Comp. Laws Ann. § 750.520.

area an investigator must be clear on because this is such as emotional issue.

Police and prosecutors, while being sympathetic, almost always rely on hard evidence—the preservation of semen, pubic hairs, and evidence of bruises in the form of photographs—in order to pull a sexual assault case together. The credibility of a witness is hardly ever more important than in a rape case. Consequently, the use of a rape counselor, nurse, or someone well versed in this type of abuse is a godsend.

century English jurist wrote that a husband could not be guilty of the rape of his wife because: she was chattel belonging to her husband; a husband and wife are "one" and as such, he cannot rape himself; and finally, that marriage means the wife irrevocably consents to intercourse with her husband on a continuing basis. Unbelievably for those independent women of today, it wasn't until the 1980s that Hale's Rule began its erosion, but investigators should still check the specifics of their state.

## MODERN CONCEPTS: ABUSE

Spurred on by social agencies, certain laws have sprung up to define the problem associated with abuse to members of society who either cannot take care of themselves, or for those who require protection because of age, disability, or lack of resources. These abusive offenses sometimes show up in state statutes as strict liability crimes–criminal penalties that do not require intent. *Child abuse* falls under this category and is often referred to as "endangering the welfare of a child." Normally these offenses would be prosecuted under the category of assault and battery or, "aggravated" categories of each, but with the rise of neglect and abuse, certain states have child abuse laws covering a broader range of abusive behavior.

Instances of *spousal abuse*, which would likely fall under the umbrella of the criminal assaults laws, are now being set aside by some states for individual treatment and definition. Because these new statutes sometimes make provisions for an issuance of court injunctions–for example, a temporary restraining order–for those spouses who are subject to domestic violence, verify your state's laws for certain.

*Abuse of the elderly* can take many forms and will most likely result in physical abuse, neglect, abandonment, isolation, fiduciary abuse or any other treatment resulting in harm, pain, mental suffering, deprivation of

**Caution**—Why would offenses such as child abuse, spousal abuse, or even abuse of the elderly make a difference to your investigation if you are looking for evidence of a major crime? Because generally, people who are committing crimes have many other problems, family life among them. Therefore, in order to document their disposition correctly, you need to show some dimension to their behavior. Typically, a perpetrator doesn't just go down to a bank and blow people away because he needs to; rather, a person who is under great stressors such as problems with unemployment, marital discord, demands from parents, that, when coupled together with character flaws such as laziness, belligerence toward authority, and perhaps a drug problem, all go into the big stew that makes for a pretty dangerous, unbalanced, and unsettled character. Caution in dealing with these types of people is mandatory.

food, or services, or continued mental suffering. Regulatory agencies, social workers, etc., are usually the ones who detect abuse of the elderly the most, but, often, procedures will require handling by a civil court. Abuse of the elderly is generally reported to law enforcement and prosecution as a matter of process, and has been known to incorporate the citing of one or more of the traditional statutes of assault and battery. Today, some progressive state legislatures have passed bills that call for enhanced penalties for those who commit violence against elderly persons.

## Leaving Is Not An Option

There are a couple of key differences between *false imprisonment* and *kidnapping*. Not all states have laws against false imprisonment. False imprisonment is usually classified as a misdemeanor, but, in Texas, if the restrained victim is exposed to a substantial risk of bodily harm, guess what? It jumps into the felony pool. Also, to illustrate the difference between these two offenses, false imprisonment is a restraining offense against a victim, whereas, kidnapping is an unlawful taking and forcible carrying away–often referred to as *asportation*–of a person without their consent and it is classified as a serious felony, universally forbidden by both state and federal jurisdictions.

There are several ways to paint a picture of false imprisonment and it is often employed in movies with seemingly no mention or notice. For example, if a police officer takes a person into custody without either probable cause or a warrant, that could be an unlawful arrest, or false imprisonment. What about a storekeeper who detains a customer suspected of shoplifting, but has no reasonable basis for the suspicion? Or how about the employer who holds an employee, using supervisory authority, in order to suppress the employee's departure in order to obtain information? False imprisonment is not a commonly charged offense so you probably won't see it, but know that it has elements of kidnapping and usually the victim tends to want to take the person to civil court for damages rather than press criminal charges. This is not a scenario the professional wants to be a part of, while they should note it in others.

Kidnapping is not only a felony but can also have its degrees. And it can jump into federal jurisdiction, say, for example, if a minor is taken out of one state and transported into another. To begin, it could be labeled kidnapping in the first degree if the intent involves the extorting of money or property for the return of the victim, and if the offender restrains a person for a certain number of hours (under a New York penal code it is twelve hours)[11] with the intent to inflict physical injury, or abuse her or him sexually, *or*, while in the process of committing another felony, *or* if the perpetrator terrorizes someone, *or*, if the kidnapper inter-

---

11. McKinney's N.Y. Penal Code § 135.25.

> **FYI**—An interesting note, the Federal Kidnapping Act is commonly called the Lindbergh Law, as a result of the case where the Lindbergh's infant son was taken from the home of Charles A. Lindbergh, the man who became famous for making the first nonstop solo flight across the Atlantic Ocean, dubbing him the "Lone Eagle." Bruno Richard Hauptmann, a man of German descent, was convicted of the crime, which made for a spectacular hunt, a multitude of newspaper headlines, and a well-documented trial, the result of which was the execution of Hauptmann in 1936.

feres with the performance of a governmental or political function, *and* if the person taken dies during the abduction, *or*, before she or he is able to return to safety.

## Torture

There is little written about torture in criminal law books. David S. Mullally in his book *Order in the Court* (2000), defines it as ". . . the intentional infliction of great bodily injury on another" (pp. 65–66). As an illustration to defining torture, he refers to a character named Frank who uses a blowtorch and pliers to burn and peel the skin off Jack's face. With the final comment, "Frank is guilty of torture." No argument there!

Since torture is an aberration often associated with serial murder, it might behoove you to check with your individual state's law for further information as to the statute's elements and punishment, and then alert your commander for further disposition.

## The Hostage Situation

Another more recent statute makes hostage taking a federal offense and to elucidate its description, it requires that: it is a crime to knowingly receive, possess, or dispose of any money or property that has been delivered as ransom for a victim of a kidnapping; *or*, it is unlawful for a bank robber to avoid apprehension by forcing someone to accompany him or her. And one sure thing about violating federal statutes, the manpower and resources available can be quite overwhelming for the culprit. When the government is in pursuit of an offender it is a sure thing the case will present larger-than-life drama requiring an alert police command and SWAT team if necessary.

For domestic interference, much has been written about parents who abduct their own children as a result of a divorce or custody program and, in this scenario, one parent seizes the child from its custodial parent and travels to another state. As a consequence, most states have made child snatching a felony, and one of the stipulations is the ability to extradite violators to the state in which the offense took place. There are additional provisions in some states' laws and an act called the Uniform Child Custody Jurisdiction Act (UCCJA) is enforced in all fifty states. The UCCJA helps to continue jurisdiction for custody in the home or resident state of the child, which means cooperation between different states and judges is now mostly assured.

## REVIEW QUESTIONS AND ANSWERS

Chapter 3 begins to address the definitions for crimes against the person and cites some examples and cases to think about.

## Key Words to Define

- **Battery**–physical hurting, hitting, etc.
- **Blame**–degree of culpability.
- **Capital punishment**–penalty of death.
- **Depraved mind**–a grave indifference to human life.
- **Homicide**–Any killing of a human being by another.
- **Malice aforethought**–intentional killing or afflicting bodily harm which causes death or extreme reckless disregard that results in death.
- **Premeditation**–intent to kill.
- **Stalking**–a person willfully, maliciously and repeatedly follows or harasses; a credible threat.
- **Uniform Child Custody Jurisdiction Act**–a state of cooperation for child custody operations between states and judges.

## Questions for Review and Discussion

1. *Question:* Name two "justifiable" homicides. *Answer:* The killing of a suspect by police or killing in self-defense.

2. *Question:* How long is the period of time for premeditation? *Answer:* Long enough to consider the gravity of a situation; ex. used: going into the next room to get a Glock, then using it.

3. *Question:* What is the key difference between voluntary and involuntary manslaughter? *Answer:* A reckless disregard that involves substantial risk, results in death, involves carelessness but is not provoked as in *voluntary* manslaughter.

4. *Question:* What is the difference between "assault" and "battery"? *Answer:* Assault is an attempt to threat to commit battery, actual physical contact.

5. *Question:* What makes a crime "aggravated"? *Answer:* Defendant acted purposely and uses a weapon capable of death or great harm (optimum word is "purposely").

6. *Question:* Can mayhem involve disfigurement? *Answer:* Yes, when intent can be proven.

7. *Question:* What does "in camera" mean? *Answer:* In chambers.

8. *Question:* What was Hale's Rule? *Answer:* That a husband cannot rape his wife; she was chattel.

9. *Question:* Name a few ways how the abuse of elderly can take shape. *Answer:* Physical abuse, neglect, abandonment, fiduciary harm, mental suffering, and deprivation are the worst.

10. *Question:* What takes false imprisonment into "kidnapping" in Texas? *Answer:* The restrained victim is exposed to substantial risk of bodily harm; terror.

## Essay Exploration

EXPLAIN WHY HOSTAGE-TAKING IS A FEDERAL OFFENSE: The perpetrator knowingly receives, possesses, or disposes of money or property that has been delivered as ransom for a victim or kidnapping. Often related to bank robbery or some other offense on federal property.

# Chapter 4

# COPS AND ROBBERS AND MORE

The loser is always suspicious.
–Publilius Syrus, *Moral Sayings*

## REPORTS GALORE

The justice system is buried in paper. A variety of federal government agencies collect crime-related data and ultimately publish the information in order to respond to issues and to help develop law enforcement plans. For example, the Department of Justice, the Federal Bureau of Investigation, the National Institute of Justice, the Office of Juvenile Justice and Delinquency Prevention, the Bureau of Justice Statistics, and the Bureau of Prisons each collect data and participate in the distribution of important information about the study of crime.

The FBI also publishes an annual report "Crime in the U.S."–in this, they have divided offenses into categories called *Index Crimes.* These eight Index Crimes are included because of their seriousness, frequency of occurrence, and the likelihood of their being reported to and by police.

Its subsidiary program, Uniform Crime Reporting (UCR), is a useful tool. The primary goal with UCR is to generate reliable criminal statistics for use in law enforcement, and, of interest, these are the reports that the average citizen is exposed to through the media, by listening to the radio, viewing television, or reading the daily newspaper. Few laypersons realize that the news reports refer to only eight categories: murder and non-negligent manslaughter, aggravated assault, forcible rape, robbery, burglary, larceny-theft, motor vehicle theft, and arson. UCR is also used by criminal justice practitioners, scholars, and citizens-in-the-know.

Why is this important to professionals? Because these reports can provide facts, statistics, actual cases, and analyses, and it's all available for the asking. One can read reports at government sites on the Internet or receive hard copies free, or for a nominal fee, through the mail. By utilizing these services–you can even get e-mail about updates–you will have your finger on the pulse of new legislation and the most current justice department and law enforcement thinking. In the Appendices is a listing for a variety of web sites that provide a motherlode of information.

A redesigned UCR program called the National Incident-Based Reporting System, or NIBRS, was developed to expand the reporting, maximize integrity, and prevent false clearing of the books–a version of improving police clearance rates–and to modernize crime information records. By knowing that these documents exist, it will add verisimilitude when police have to file reports, and it will give the professional lawyer or criminal justice employee inside information into the methodology and current rational of the various government branches.

## VARIATIONS ON STEALING

Some of the more common crimes are also called crimes against property, crimes against habitation, and acquisition offenses. Huh? Do you know the differences between robbery, theft, burglary, and larceny? Basically, the distinctions include whether they threaten the owner's enjoyment of property but pose no immediate risk of safety; whether they involve other interests, or in the case of robbery, if they use physical force. We'll talk about the different and varied divisions of these crimes so you'll understand more about cops and robbers.

### It Wasn't Phony Money

Brian Donovan and Robert Grant were pretty proud of themselves. While in a bar one night, the pair were overheard talking about a "helluv an idea" they had of using a phony deposit box. The Massachusetts jury did not have quite the same take on the affair when they convicted the two of larceny. Evidence introduced at trial showed that they had constructed a phony night-deposit box and attached it to the wall of a building. Looking just like a real depository, the box

was constructed of heavy-gauge steel. Seven depositors lost an estimated $37,000 by putting deposits into the phony box. Although the actual box was never discovered, their bar conversation was used against them in court. Another witness said that Grant had admitted to her that he had robbed a bank using a fake bank box.

On appeal, the Massachusetts Supreme Court[1] rejected the defendant's contentions that certain evidence had been improperly admitted into evidence and that the evidence produced at trial was legally sufficient to prove the crime of larceny.

Larceny is one of the more clearly defined crimes in common law, although the old-fashioned terminology first used to describe it will sometimes confuse. For example, the phrase "caption" was employed instead of the word *taking*; the term "asportation" meant *carrying away*; and the personal property involved had to be "corporeal" which meant it had to have a physical presence. In order to simplify it here, let's use these steps: Larceny consists of (1) taking, (2) carrying away, (3) personal property, (4) of another, and (5) with the intent to permanently deprive the owner of the property. Some examples of larceny are shoplifting; theft of objects, parts, or accessories from motor vehicles; purse-snatching; and bicycle theft.

Now real estate, land, and fixtures cannot be part of the list because the property must consist of tangible items which can be carried away. Larceny is more easily remembered if you think of it as a crime against possession. Some modern laws have used the term *theft*, which allows for the distinction that items are taken "while on the premise lawfully."

---

1. *Commonwealth v. Donovan*, 478 N.E.2d 727 (Mass. 1985).

## Grand Theft

Now we may come upon the question, what is the difference between grand theft and petty theft? In this sense, grand theft is the equivalent of first-degree theft and subject to more serious consequences. For example, the property taken is worth more than a minimum amount. It usually involves property valued at $200 to $400 or more depending on the state. The theft of cars—sometimes called grand theft auto—and some type of stealing animals are often classified as grand theft regardless of their actual market value.

Motor vehicle theft has become big business, perpetrated by car theft rings. Thieves pop a door lock to obtain the ignition key code number, and with a portable key maker, they make a duplicate key and drive away with the vehicle in about seven minutes or less. Nissan Pathfinders and Toyota Forerunners are the cars of choice because they're easy to steal.

## Thieves pop a door lock to obtain the ignition key code number, . . .

Where stolen cars once went through a transformation with painting and disguising of ownership, today they are merely transported—taken across state lines and delivered to unsuspecting or unscrupulous car dealers or shipped out of the country. The United States is fast becoming a supplier of stolen vehicles to Third World countries.

## Petty Theft

Petty theft (*petit theft*) sometimes includes property that is taken directly from a person but by means other than force or fear, and with property having a value under $300. A pickpocket crime would be a good example of this offense. And, for those who know a character with sticky fingers: petty theft, a misdemeanor, can graduate to grand theft and a felony charge if there are prior convictions. In order to make the charge more serious, the prosecutor would have to name the prior conviction on the complaint or information.

Another favorite question among law students is: When someone finds "lost" property is it still a theft for them to keep it? When someone takes control of property without taking a reasonable measure to restore it—yes, it is a crime. For example, if Charles sees a $100 bill fall out of Marie's wallet and she is unaware she has dropped the money, and then Charles skates over to claim it, Charles has committed theft. Since Charles knows the money belongs to Marie and he had a reasonable opportunity to return it to her, he commits a crime by not attempting to return the money. That is called "constructive" taking.

Now if Charles was skating by and discovers a $100 bill blowing down the street with no one in sight, it's his lucky day, and he would not be guilty of theft if he kept it. Although it might start the beginning of a different kind of problem if his wind-blown

**Other Notes**—An interesting and popular question from law students is: If property is stolen from a thief who has stolen it previously, is it still illegal? Sorry, but, yes. Although we sometimes want to take the side of those who steal from stealers (the movie *Sneakers* comes to mind), theft is illegal even if the person from whom property is stolen had no right to the property in the first place.

bill turned out to be counterfeit, and led to other trouble . . .

## ACQUISITION CRIMES

Larceny is known as one of the acquisition crimes. Two others are *embezzlement,* and *false pretenses*–also known as fraud. Embezzlement has these elements: (1) Fraud, (2) in conversion, (3) of the property, (4) of another, (5) by one who is already in lawful possession thereof, (6) with the intent to defraud the victim. The main acquisition element and what makes this offense so successful for abusers is the conversion stipulation. As a consequence, this undertaking is commonly perpetrated by accountants, lawyers, store managers, and the treasurers of organizations. Conversion could be diverting the money or property intended for the employer into the representative's personal hidden reserve or working account.

## . . . what makes this offense so successful for abusers is the conversion stipulation.

False pretense is acquiring someone else's property through the use of fraud, a slight distinction from the other acquisition offenses. If someone (1) obtains a title, (2) to property, (3) by means of material false representation, (4) with the intent to defraud the victim that is false pretense. There is a double *mens rea* to the crime of false pretense. The defendant must know that he or she is lying, and must also intend to defraud the victim. This usually means that the property was acquired by means of lies, trickery, deceit, or some type of scam played out by the defendant.

Conditionally, the element of misrepresentation must involve a concern of a past or present fact, and not something happening in the future. This key lynchpin of time points up the fact that the victim was scammed so completely that he or she is not giving up temporary possession to his or her goods, but will give up all of the money or goods to the thief due specifically to the scam. In other words, a thief tricks the victim into *voluntarily* handing over money or property, usually through a cruel and devastating hoax. False pretense then, is a prime situation for perpetuating revenge, and a continuing criminal device for a character who has been burned.

## Home Repair Fraud

Most people want to believe that other human beings are good, like themselves. That belief is fuel for scammers, the desperate, and the sociopaths. According to a government survey taken between May 2003 and May 2004, more than one in ten Americans were the victim of fraud.[2] The Federal Trade Commission's first survey of consumer fraud found that nearly 25 million adults in the U.S., or 11.2 percent of the adult population, were victims of fraud, and that certain racial and ethnic minorities more often fell prey to fraudulent schemes.

Unfortunately, when people need help and support the most, such as with the case of victims of the 2005 hurricane season under the wrath of Rita and Katrina, thieves descend on storm victims and put them at greater risk. Legal authorities say they've seen scams like price gouging, home repair fraud, vehicle license forgery and even identity theft related to the hurricanes.[3]

2. "FTC: 1 in 10 fall for fraud", Katie Benner, *CNN/Money*, August 5, 2004 staff writer
3. "Scammers Target Katrina, Rita Survivors . . ." Eric Noe, November 8, 2005, *ABC News.*

**Other Notes**—"Any felony" will often do for the crime of burglary. Even if you picture the typical burglar donning a mask, waving a flashlight, and carrying a sack for the booty—entry into a building with the specific intent to commit any type of felony, whether that includes molesting a child, or burning the building down, is sufficient for burglary, and you'd better believe a smart prosecutor will throw everything into the charges. Also, degrees of burglary exist; for example, the danger of physical harm is greatest when a burglar enters an inhabited building, so, in many states, this constitutes a first-degree burglary.

Complaints about home repair fraud run the gamut from people pretending to be licensed contractors; laborers doing substandard or incomplete work projects; gouging or raising prices to unrealistic levels, and simply taking a deposit and not returning.

Mississippi, another hard-hit state besides Louisiana, has a law on their books called Offenses Affecting Trade, Business and Professions:[4] Home repair fraud, that essentially includes all forms of home repair from construction, installation, replacement or improvement of every outdoor and indoor structure, such as driveways and swimming pools to central heating and plumbing fixtures and everything adjacent and in-between.

To paraphrase, the basics read: A person commits the offense of home repair fraud when he knowingly enters into an agreement or contract, written or oral, with a person for home repair and misrepresents a material fact relating to the terms of the contract or the existing condition of any portion of the property involved, or creates another's impression which is false or promises performance, which he does not intend to perform or knows will not be performed.

Any form of deception, false pretense or false promises; or if he conceals either his real name, the name of his business or uses coercion to force the victim's consent to work; or damages the property, is a criminal offense.

Violation and a first conviction is a misdemeanor when the amount of the fraud is less than Five Thousand Dollars ($5,000.00) and shall be punished by a fine not to exceed One Thousand Dollars ($1,000.00) or imprisonment in the county jail not to exceed six months, or both. A second or subsequent conviction becomes a felony punishable by imprisonment in the custody of the Department of Corrections not to exceed two years when the amount of the fraud is more than One Thousand Dollars ($1,000.00) but less than Five Thousand Dollars ($5,000.00).

There are many other details in regards to the type of work, the degree of misrepresentation and the amount of escalating damages and sentencing to go with–but one *very important aspect* to this law is that the court orders the defendant to make restitution to the victim, either within a specified period of time or in specified installments, and if the defendant refuses to obey the repayment penalty, he will most likely not receive either probation or suspension of his sentence.

In Texas they also have a statute[5] that requires home repair or delivery companies to check the criminal histories of their employees who enter private residences as part of the service or an installation they provide. Not a bad idea.

---

4. Mississippi Title 97-23-103, Ch. 499, § 10; Laws, 2006, Ch. 348, § 1
5. Texas HB 705.

# Burglary

Burglary is also referred to as a *habitation offense* by certain criminal justice researchers. A burglary occurs when a culprit 1) breaks into, 2) and enters, 3) the dwelling, 4) of another, without consent, 5) with the intent to commit a felony or steal property. The original common law burglary was set up to protect buildings under the cover of night. Today, many states have enacted the statutes proscribing breaking and entering, thereby making the law extend beyond dwelling houses and eliminating the requirement of night. In addition, some law codes specify not only buildings of any type, such as shops, barns, and outhouses at risk, but the offense even extends to portable structures such as cars, boats, and mobile homes. Be aware that the courts have a tendency to liberally construe what breaking and entering mean. For instance, there is no force required to satisfy the breaking initiative. Even going into a building through an open window qualifies.

And entering can be defined as a hand, foot, or even a finger reaching within the dwelling; just the slightest touch and toe is both enough for a sufficient breaking and entering element. The prosecution does have to prove that a defendant meant to commit a felony or theft inside a building at the very moment the defendant entered it.

# Fake Gun a Threat?

*Jones v. Commonwealth*[6] is a case with the question of whether the evidence is sufficient enough to support the conviction of robbery. On March 17, 1989, Deputy John Stanton of the Williamsburg Sheriff's Department was transporting Jerry Earl Jones from the Richmond Penitentiary to Williamsburg. The defendant was in leg chains and a waist chain with handcuffs attached to each side. Stanton was driving an unmarked vehicle with Jones in the back and no divider between them.

---

**Caution**—a quick way to distinguish between
**Robbery**—Theft with threat of "physical force or fear"
**Burglary**—Unlawful attendance or entry
**Theft**—Items taken while on premise lawfully
**Larceny**—Taking; the carrying away of personal property of another, intent is to permanently deprive owner

---

**FYI**—This temporal relationship to the force of taking is an area for professionals to ponder, and many interesting cases have come up regarding both when the force was applied, and how much force is required to qualify for robbery. Also, robbery is a "specific intent" crime. The government has to prove that a thief intended to permanently deprive a victim of stolen property. Usually, a prosecutor relies on circumstantial evidence to prove intent, and implores the judge and jury

---

6. *Jones v. Commonwealth*, 13 Va. App. 566, 414 S.E. 2d 193 (Va. 1992).

to use their common sense to infer a thief's intent from the circumstances. Of course, if police have uncovered the actual goods, well, the intent is well met.

In addition, degrees of robbery exist, for example, *aggravated* robbery or *first-degree* robbery, makes for another, more serious class of crime and punishment. Remember, when researching it is important to check the state's law where the crime was committed. For example, under Colorado law, robbery of the elderly or handicapped is afforded the same punishment as the offense of aggravated robbery.[7]

En route, the defendant suddenly yelled, "Sheriff, don't make me blow your damn brains out." Stanton, startled and scared, jerked to see what was going on. He observed an object of metal that appeared to be the barrel of a pistol. Travelling 65 miles per hour, Stanton lost control briefly until he managed to direct the car to a grassy median.

Stanton immediately began to look and feel for his gun, which was missing from his holster, and the car went out of control.

Figure 1. Evidence comes in many forms as demonstrated in this evidence room at the Hot Springs Police Department, Hot Springs, Arkansas.

---

7. West's Colo. Rev. Stat. Ann. § 18-4-304.

Unarmed, Stanton did not get the car back on the road as ordered, and, in an effort to "wreck" the car and "bail out," he steered toward the guardrail and jumped into the grass. Jones, however, gained control of the car and sped away.

Later, the car was found without a radio antennae and several hubcaps removed. A "fake gun" was found on the rear seat. Jones was arrested shortly thereafter, and indicted on March 20, 1989.

The evidence was challenged on appeal—the fake gun—but the conviction was affirmed. Judge Bray, who gave the opinion, said, ". . . Stanton was fearful and surrendered the vehicle to defendant. Defendant then escaped with both the automobile and Stanton's pistol, apparently taken by defendant while Stanton was in extremity. These circumstances amply support a robbery conviction."

## ROBBERY DEFINED

Robbery is the taking, or the attempt to take, anything of value from the care, custody or control of a person by force, threat of violence, actual violence, or by putting the victim in fear. Because of its personal and violent nature, robbery is another crime against person, and, as such, is feared greatly by the public.

A couple of distinctive notes help to define the offense of robbery: mainly, the force used, does not have to be major. A threat of violence is enough, even though the classification between a robbery and larceny is marginal. Also, in some state courts, the force applied or implied does not have to occur simultaneously with the taking. A typical example of robbery is the hold-up of a convenience store using a gun, but it could also be a purse-snatching if the person is still attached to it or if it results in a confrontation.

## Bank Hi-Jinks

In 1997, Floyd J. Carter donned a ski mask and entered the Collective Federal Savings Bank unarmed. Carter confronted an exiting customer and pushed her back inside. She screamed, startling others in the bank. Undeterred, Carter ran inside and leaped over a counter and through one of the teller windows. A teller rushed into the manager's office. Meanwhile, Carter opened several teller drawers and emptied the money into a bag. After removing almost $16,000, he jumped back over the counter and fled.

After his apprehension, Carter was charged with federal bank robbery, 18 USC Section 2113(a), which punishes "[w]hoever, by force and violence, or by intimidation, takes . . . any . . . thing of value [from a] bank." Carter pleaded not guilty, claiming that he had not taken the bank's money by force, violence, or intimidation as required of robbery. Carter moved that the District Court instruct the jury that they consider whether he committed federal bank *larceny*, a lesser offense in the broader crime of robbery, in which case, Carter could be guilty of larceny without being guilty of robbery. The larceny law punishes "[w]hoever takes and carries away, with intent to steal or purloin, any . . . thing of value exceeding $1,000 [from a] . . . bank," with a maximum penalty of 10 years in prison, as opposed to robbery's 20-year maximum.

In a 5-4 opinion delivered by Justice Clarence Thomas, the Court[1] held that fed-

---

8. *Carter v. United States* (99-5716) 530 U.S. 255 (2000) 185 F.3d 863.

eral bank larceny is not a "lesser included offense" of federal bank robbery.

## Carjacking–A New Breed of Crime

The force of taking cannot be better demonstrated than in the forcible taking of another's vehicle, referred to under a fairly new statutory offense called *carjacking.* In February 1993, the first trial under the new federal law–the Anti-Car Theft Act of 1992– was upheld in Orlando, Florida, when three young males were accused of carjacking. They had stolen two vehicles and committed execution-style slaying of two young men, and injured a third. The prosecution built its case on the fact that they were guilty of (1) stealing a car involved in interstate commerce, (2) doing it by force, and (3) using a firearm. The defense lawyers, on the other hand, held the posture that although the defendants may have been guilty of some offenses under state law, they were not guilty of violating the new federal law on armed carjacking involving violence. To the aid of the state's case, and as a detriment to the others, a fourth defendant pleaded guilty and testified against the other three. Six hours of deliberation produced a jury verdict which found the three defendants guilty of conspir-

acy, two counts of armed carjacking involving death, and two counts of using a firearm during a felony. In April 1993, the three defendants were sentenced to life terms, plus twenty-five years. The fourth perp? Well, we don't know his sentence, but he is probably looking over his back a lot.

# TECHNOLOGY CRIME

## Theft or Identity

With modern technology and its accompanying changes to the way we live come new risks and new crimes. As more about our lives become reduced to data: such as writing checks for purchases, ordering movie tickets on the Internet, renting a car, using a cell phone, applying for a credit card, submitting medical information to a doctor or even mailing in tax returns, an electronic paper trail is being created. These documents reveal bits of personal information, like bank and credit card account numbers, income, Social Security number (SSN); or name, address, and phone numbers–a goldmine of information for an identity thief. Once a data pickpocket has that information, it can be used without someone's knowledge

**FYI**—This brings to mind an historical idea called "hue and cry." Alfred the Great (840-899 A.D.) established a strong system—while waiting for the Danish invasion—called "mutual pledge." It was developed in order to organize local citizenry into an association for tithing and protection. Alfred instituted the program *hue and cry*, which meant that any person who discovered a crime, was to give out a hue and cry in order to rally people to catch the offender "red-handed"—with blood on their hands. When the criminal was brought to the tithe chief, the people enforced murder by death, and usually theft was subject to civil restitution, bondage, or servitude. This, then, was the historical basis for the civil code remedy of restitution.

to commit fraud or theft. Identity theft,[9] or the appropriating another person's identity, is a serious crime. In 2004,[10] 3.6 million households, representing three percent of the households in the United States, discovered that at least one member of the household had been the victim of identity theft during the previous six months. People whose identities have been stolen lose money through bogus credit card transactions; can unwittingly help someone get a passport, academic credentials, or any number of identifying characteristics we spend a lifetime securing. Time and money spent cleaning up the mess thieves have made of a person's good name and credit record is taxing financially and emotionally. Victims may lose out on job opportunities, or loans for education, housing, or cars. They may even get arrested for crimes they didn't commit.

Mail gets stolen, wallets and purses are taken, and people get ripped off by scammers and online "phishing." Thieves can divert anyone's mail with a change of address, get financial reports, and run up credit card charges until maxed out. The elderly are especially susceptible and often fall for phony telephone scams. Identity theft hunters can even get information from old, discarded computers.

Over 37 states have made laws specifically relating to identity theft as a crime. In some states, people found guilty of theft under the Theft of Identity Statute will automatically be guilty of a felony, no matter the amount stolen. There is considerable variation among states: some providing provisions that make "trafficking" in identities illegal; others have included certain aggravating factors making for enhanced crimes and punishments; and another feature is that police must make reports. What follows is Arizona's statute:[11]

Taking identity of another person or entity; classification:

A. A person commits taking the identity of another person or entity if the person knowingly takes, purchases, manufactures, records, possesses or uses any personal identifying information or entity identifying information of another person or entity, including a real or fictitious person or entity, without the consent of that other person or entity, with the intent to obtain or use the other person's or entity's identity for any unlawful purpose or to cause loss to a person or entity whether or not the person or entity actually suffers any economic loss as a result of the offense.

B. On the request of a person or entity, a peace officer in any jurisdiction in which an element of the offense is committed, a result of the offense occurs or the person or entity whose identity is taken resides or is located shall take a report. The peace officer may provide a copy of the report to any other law enforcement agency that is located in a jurisdiction in which a violation of this section occurred.

The statute even goes on to increase the penalties if there are multiple violations. Taking the identity of another person or entity is a class 4 felony in Arizona.

---

9. identification fraud (18 U.S.C. § 1028), credit card fraud (18 U.S.C. § 1029), computer fraud (18 U.S.C. § 1030), mail fraud (18 U.S.C. § 1341), wire fraud (18 U.S.C. § 1343), or financial institution fraud (18 U.S.C. § 1344)
10. *Identity Theft, 2004* Bureau of Justice Statistics, April 2006, NCJ212213
11. Arizona Rev. Stat. § 13-2008-2009 (2005)

## Laser Pointer

Late in 2004, David Banach of Parsippany, New Jersey, was identified and arrested after pointing a high power, green laser pointer into the cockpit of an airplane. In response to such incidents, the US[12] Terrorist laws recently made it a Federal offense to point a laser at an aircraft: "Whoever knowingly aims the beam of a laser pointer at an aircraft in the special aircraft jurisdiction of the United States, or at the flight path of such an aircraft, shall be fined under this title or imprisoned not more than 5 years, or both."

Powerful handheld green lasers have become popular and irresponsible use of green lasers can be disastrous. Experts say that a direct shot to the eye from a laser over 15 mW–a radiation of electromagnetic wavelength longer than that of visible light, but shorter than that of radio wave–can permanently damage the eye, within a fraction of a second. Several states have code for this as well, such as this with Mississippi.[13]

Laser Pointer at Police, Fire, or Emergency with intent to harm; Misdemeanor, up to $1000 fine, no imprisonment.

We think penalties will increase if a death ensues from what seems like a harmless prank.

## Extortion

Similar to the crime of robbery, extortion is made up of four elements: (1) obtaining (2) property (3) by threats (4) with the intent to obtain the property by fear and coercion. It is often called *blackmail*, which is actually a federal statute (the blackmail statute) and reads something like this: "Whoever, under a threat of informing, or as a consideration for not informing, against any violation of any law of the United States, demands, or receives any money or other valuable thing, shall be fined. . . ." Later on, in section 876, "it is a crime to demand ransom or to threaten someone through the mails, using the Postal Service."[14]

The threats used by extortionists are often intimidation to either accuse a person of a crime, expose a secret affair affecting another, and, when that doesn't work, a threat to use injury to the person or a member of his family. Once a common theme of motivation running through episodes of "Murder, She Wrote," blackmailing often involved important characters who were seeking to hide some type of past indiscretion, infraction, or family secret, and there are a lot of variations on this theme. A professional investigator can only imagine the real-life possibilities.

## Getting the Goods

Receiving stolen property is a convenient way for a naïve citizen to get into trouble. What makes it a crime is that a person receives property of another knowing that it has been stolen, or believing that it probably has been stolen, with the purpose to deprive the owner thereof. So, if an individual recognizes that serial numbers or store names have been obliterated from merchandise, he or she has a good indication that the goods are "hot." Receivers, thinking that they are far removed from the crime and it's worth the risk, are often indignant when evidence or testimony points back to them.

## Arson, Investigation Required

*Arson* consists of any willful or malicious burning or attempt to burn, a dwelling,

12. Chapter 2 of title 18, United States Code, Sec. 39. Aiming a laser pointer at an aircraft
13. Mississippi Code: Title 97 Crimes: Chapter 35 Crimes Against Public Peace and Safety § 97-35-49.
14. 18 U.S.C.A. § 876.

house, public building, motor vehicle, aircraft, or property of another. As originally stated in common law, though, setting fire to one's own home was not considered arson. Modern statutes today, however, have extended the offense to include the intentional burning of buildings, structures, and vehicles of all types, and frequently this includes a person's own property.

But there are areas to exploit here, and many differences of law opinion. For example, a Michigan court held in *People v. Williams*[15] that to establish the *corpus delicti* of arson of a dwelling house, the state must show not only a burned house, but also that it resulted from an intentional criminal act. The presumption here was that a burned building showed presence of fire, but it could have been accidentally caused.

In Kennedy v. State,[16] a Georgia court upheld the conviction on appeal of Henry Xavier Kennedy, saying a fire in a building belonging to the defendant was incendiary in origin. The case at issue was this: One early morning, at approximately 3:42 A.M., Kennedy's log cabin was reported burning and was eventually destroyed. Investigators found a hot plate with its switch in the "on" position, in the most heavily burned area of the cabin. Investigators also testified that kerosene had been poured around the area of the hot plate, and that is what had accelerated the fire.

Kennedy might have gotten away with it had he not renewed a $40,000 insurance policy a mere five days before the fire. In addition, evidence presented showed that Kennedy's building business had been slow and even though he had his own evidence of an alibi from midnight until about 4 A.M., investigators testified that an incendiary device could have been set before midnight.

## CRIMES AGAINST PROPERTY

Malicious mischief, forgery, and bad checks are unlike the acquisition offenses in that with these crimes the owner is still in possession of a version of the property upon completion of the crime. However, unique to this particular transgression, his or her property is now damaged or impaired in some way.

*Malicious mischief* is sometimes referred to as vandalism and it occurs when a person: 1) maliciously, 2) inflicts injury 3) on the property 4) of another. With malicious mischief the real legal issue is how much damage needs to be done to qualify. The courts have generally agreed that if the damage prevents the property from being used as it is most often, or, if the damage significantly diminishes its value, then the injury to the property is sufficient.

In *State v. Tonnisen*,[17] the defendant appealed his conviction for malicious mischief. The state produced evidence that the defendant allowed for a tank trailer truck to dump its load of caustic soda all over the road during a strike and employee walk-out. In testifying in his own defense, Tonnisen said that he had not put his hand "anywheres in the vicinity of between the truck and the trailer."

Unfortunately for him, a police officer on duty, along with other observant persons, watched the defendant go over to the truck, stick his hand between the vehicles and pull it back full of grease.

## Forgery

Because of the importance of written and printed documents, both federal and state statutes generally classify forgery as a felony. Almost every type of public or private legal

---

15. *People v. Williams,* 318 N.W.2d 671 (Mich. App. 1982).
16. *Kennedy v. State,* 323 S.E.2d 169 (Ga. App. 1984).
17. State v. Tonnisen, 92 N.J. Super. 452, 224 A2d. 21 (N.J. 1966).

instrument in most all the American jurisdictions is covered by the crime of forgery. It's that important. Also, it is not necessary to show that anyone was actually defrauded by the forgery for the crime to be complete. That said, here are the elements of forgery: (1) The fraudulent (2) making (3) of a false writing 4) that has apparent legal significance (5) knowing the writing is false (6) with the intent to deceive.

The Arizona Criminal Code uses the same principles stated above but goes even a step further. It reads:

A. A person commits forgery if, with intent to defraud, such person:

1. Falsely makes, completes or alters a written instrument; OR

2. Knowingly possesses a forged instrument; OR

3. Offers or presents, whether accepted or not, a forged instrument or one which contains false information.[18]

Arizona then, has expanded the offense by including the offering or passing of such a document (which is also referred to as "uttering a forged instrument").

Common examples of forgery and uttering a forged instrument are signing another's name to an application for a driver's license, or to transfer a certificate of stock; writing a check on another's bank account without authority; or altering grades or credits on a college transcript; printing bogus tickets to a concert or sporting event; altering the amount of a check or note; or changing a legal description on a deed of property. Since computers are being used extensively for forms and applications more commonly today, new statutes proscribing both forgery and uttering a forged instrument need to be updated.

Now, with this area so broadly banned, one would think that presenting a worthless check on a bank account would be a forgery. And, indeed, as commercial banking grew in terms of numbers of customers and transactions, this presented a problem in trying to prove that the accused fraudulently obtained goods–or, the flip side of the forgery question was: did they simply miscalculate their checking account balances? In order to cope with this uncertainty, state legislatures created what is commonly called "bad check statutes" or worthless check statutes. Texas law sums it up nicely in their state law by saying: (a) A person commits an offense if he issues or passes a check or similar sight order for the payment of money knowing that the issuer does not have sufficient funds in or on deposit with the bank. . . .[19]

## Easy Credit

In the past, a person who used a stolen credit card, or otherwise obtained a card through fraud, was subject to the laws of larceny and theft. But due to credit cards' widespread use, many states have enacted laws actually proscribing credit card fraud. Pennsylvania probably has the most in-depth statute and, summarized, it requires that: a person commits an offense if he or she: (1) uses a credit card for obtaining property or service knowing (2) the card is stolen, forged, or fictitious, (3) belongs to another, (4) has been revoked or cancelled, (5) Unauthorized use, (6) makes, knowingly sells, aid and abets, (7) publishes code or numbering to avoid payment for property or services.

---

18. Ariz. Rev. Stat. § 13-2002.
19. Vernon's Tex. Penal Code Ann., § 32.41 (a).

## OFFENSES AGAINST PUBLIC MORALITY

Criminal justice scholars are always interested in crimes against morality for many reasons. Originally, common law did not address these issues because they were the domain of the church known as *ecclesiastical crimes*, and were normally tried and punished by the Church of England. Consequently, in the early part of American history, the Puritans, a religious group, made a concerted effort to ensure that all the offenses against morality were criminalized by state statutes in keeping with their beliefs. For the most part they were successful, although, today, many of those laws have been revised or removed because there are constitutional limitations to be considered on each. For example, when talking about the practicality of instituting moral codes, many people believe the aphorism "you can't legislate morality." A prime example of this is illustrated in a landmark case, *Griswold v. Connecticut.*[20] The U.S. Supreme Court struck down a state law that made it a crime for all persons, even married couples, to use birth control devices. Who would have thought that a law like that could ever be instituted, especially since the case law is dated 1965?

> ... many people believe the aphorism "you can't legislate morality."

Debate will always continue over morality crime and public opinion about the law changes, but, even so, every state has at least one, if not all, of the following five crimes against morality: fornication, adultery, illicit cohabitation, bigamy, and incest. But because of changing societal attitudes, forni-

cation, adultery, and seduction–the unfulfilled promise of marriage–are rarely, if ever, prosecuted.

And what does an angry spurned lover do with crimes against morality? Well, if a civilian wants to particularly add angst to another's life, he or she can accuse the other of incest or bigamy. Between the cost of proving it isn't so, and the insult and injury to character, that additional poke in the eye could add up to a lot of revenge and an additional nuisance. So for those professionals who need to know-it-all, incest is a crime which prohibits intermarriage or sexual relations between certain persons of kinship, which is also referred to as "blood relations" such as, parents and children, brothers and sisters, etc. And while bigamy still occurs, however occasionally, it is defined as a marriage between two persons when one is legally married to another.

A rarely prosecuted offense, sodomy, which was described originally as a "crime against nature," in general: includes oral or anal sex between humans and sexual intercourse between human and animals (sometimes called "bestiality"). While less than half the states retain this offense, you may hear of it when it is incident to a charge of rape and sexual battery. Note: When sodomy is nonconsensual, it is considered a crime against a person, not as an offense against morality.

## Prostitution, Pimping, and Pandering

Sometimes called the "oldest profession," prostitution is about a person who engages in sexual activity for hire. Today, prostitution is illegal in all states except Nevada, where it exists by local option in some counties, although it is strictly regulated by law.[21] In

---

20. Griswold v. Connecticut, 381 U.S. 479, 85 S.Ct. 1678, 14 L.Ed.2d 510 (1965).
21. Nevada Rev. Stat. §§ 201.380, 201.430, 201.440.

the past, statutes have been directed at females but increasingly, enforcement has come to include males as well. And, originally, the definitive language was aimed almost exclusively at the prostitute, but now there is conviction for the customers, and also those who live off the earnings of a person practicing prostitution. In addition, there exists a loophole here: if the statutes are not all inclusive with respect to both pimps, partners, and clients–they might be vulnerable to constitutional attack as a denial of equal protection of the law.

Normally listed as a misdemeanor, in Texas it is a serious felony for a person to cause another by force, threat, or fraud to commit prostitution. The federal government has gotten into the problem too with the Mann Act,[22] which prohibits interstate transportation of individuals for prostitution or for compelling them to engage in immoral practice. The Supreme Court has ruled that the act applies to transporting persons for immoral purposes whether or not commercial vice is involved.

## Private Parts

Indecent exposure is a misdemeanor offense for persons showing their private parts in a public place. Frequently referred to as "lewd and lascivious conduct," the laws generally stipulate that exposure must be done willfully and in an offensive manner, and not by mere accident. Some statutes, such as the one in Florida, have defined that in order for an act to be offensive exposure, it has to "incorporate sensory awareness as well as physical proximity" so that a man[23] who was convicted of masturbating in the

presence of his thirteen-month-old child had his charges reversed by the state's supreme court. In the court's view, the child did not have sensory awareness.

The sunny state of Florida must have its problems making its civilians keep their clothes on because there is a statute that prohibits public nudity on beaches and other recreational areas. Arrests under this provision are not common, however, and certain sectors are set aside where topless or nude sunbathing is permitted.

## Just What Is Obscene?

In the highly-expressive 1970s, a high school boy extended his middle finger toward a highway trooper from the back of a school bus. In *State v. Anonymous*[24] the court got to consider whether it was an offense to make an obscene gesture in a public place with "intent to cause inconvenience, annoyance or alarm or recklessly creating a risk thereof." The court found the rambunctious student not guilty, stating, that to be obscene, an expression "must be in a significant way erotic."

## Children in a New World

Dietrich Bonhoeffer,[25] born 1906, died in 1945, was a German Lutheran pastor, theologian and participant in the German resistance movement against Nazism. He once said, "The test of the morality of a society is what it does for its children."

The protections for children in the law ever increase, in spite of what that says about the nature of today's world. The Wetterling Act of 1994[26] is a United States law that

22. The Mann Act, 18 U.S.C.A. § 2421 et seq.
23. *State v. Werner*, 609 So2d. 585 (Fla. 1992).
24. *State v. Anonymous*, 377 A.2d 1342 (Conn. Super. 1977).
25. http://www.dbonhoeffer.org/
26. U.S. Code Title 42, Chapter 136, Subchapter VI § 14071

requires registration of sexually violent offenders of children. The Federal version of "Megan's Law"[27] (1996) amended the Wetterling Act to require a certain degree of community notification rather than leaving it to the discretion of local law enforcement agencies. The Pam Lyncher Sexual Offender Tracking and Identification Act which came later, requires the creation of a national computer database to track sex offenders and calls for the FBI to handle registration in states that lack "minimally sufficient programs." All states have this federal rule, and penalty to register is determined by each state.

Opponents to registration say that notification is intended to help law-abiding citizens feel safer. They explain that, many, if not most, sex offenders pose little risk to neighbors and strangers. Challengers to the register feel that by lumping large numbers of sex offenders into one group, widespread notification will exaggerate the apparent danger and actually make people feel more vulnerable rather than safe.

Not too much accurate research on the subject exists, but we do know that the majority of child victims[28] are molested by relatives and family friends.

In addition to congressional action that legislates state tracking of sex offenders, the U.S. Government recently began tracking sex offenders internationally. Operation Predator is a new initiative developed by the Department of Homeland Securitys Bureau of Immigration and Customs Enforcement (ICE) to protect young people from "child pornographers, alien smugglers, human traffickers, and other predatory criminals" worldwide.

# Child Porn

Hand in glove with sexual abuse and assaults on children go child pornography. The Arkansas[29] laws are strict in this regard and read as follows:

Engaging children in sexually explicit conduct for use in visual or print medium.

(a) Any person who employs, uses, persuades, induces, entices, or coerces any child to engage in or who has a child assist any other person to engage in any sexually explicit conduct for the purpose of producing any visual or print medium depicting the sexually explicit conduct is guilty of a: (1) Class B felony for the first offense; and (2) Class A felony for a subsequent offense. The second part of this law, section (b) sadly applies to any parent, legal guardian, or person having custody or control of a child.

# Internet Stalking of a Child

Here in Arkansas, unfortunately, we have learned about Internet stalking all too well. Kacie Rene Woody, 13, met a La Mesa, California, man on the Internet who killed her after traveling to Conway, Arkansas, to lure her out of her home.[30] Her body, along with the body of David Fuller, was found in a van at a storage garage in Arkansas, both suffering from gunshot wounds. Police suspect that the girl had been sexually assaulted.

Authorities said that Fuller had struck up an Internet relationship with Kacie and might have tricked her into believing he was a teenager by using fictitious photographs. Police spent most of December 4 searching for Kacie and went to a nearby storage facil-

27. http://www.registeredoffenderslist.org/megans-law.htm
28. http://jeffersonsheriff.org/characteristics.html
29. Arkansas criminal code: 5-27-303
30. "FBI scours ex-home of La Mesan who killed girl, self" *Union Tribune Publishing* http://www.signonsandiego.com/news/metro/20021207-9999_2m7chat.html

ity after receiving a tip. Upon arriving at the storage garage, they heard a gunshot. Police believe the shot was Fuller–committing suicide. The Arkansas Internet stalking law[31] provides that a person commits the offense of Internet stalking of a child if the person being twenty-one (21) years of age or older knowingly uses a computer online service, internet service, or local Internet bulletin board service to: (1) Seduce, solicit, lure, or entice a child fifteen (15) years of age or younger in an effort to arrange a meeting with the child for the purpose of engaging in: (A) Sexual intercourse; (B) Sexually explicit conduct; or (C) Deviate sexual activity.[32] Internet stalking of a child is a: Class C felony if the person attempts to arrange a meeting with a child fifteen (15) years of age or younger, even if a meeting with the child never takes place; or Class C felony if the person attempts to arrange a meeting with an individual that the person believes to be

fifteen (15) years of age or younger, even if a meeting with the individual never takes place; or Class A felony if an actual meeting with the child takes place, even if the person fails to engage the child in any sexual activity.

## History Check for Predators

A Texas law[33] allows an administrator of a non-profit youth program to check the criminal history of a volunteer or applicant for a program that provides athletic, civic or cultural activities to children under the age of 17. High incidence of teachers[34] having sexual activity with students has prompted criminal history checks for any employees in direct relationship or regular contact with minors.

---

**Caution**—Obscenity is a great vehicle to use to irritate a police officer, prosecutor, or offender. It is one of those needling statutes that is hard to define. Literally dozens of cases have dealt with obscenity issues and, more distinctly, how to define what the Supreme Court has called, "utterly without redeeming social importance"[35]—so as not to deny its people with the right to free speech. There are cases involving nude dancing in clubs, obscene mail in the post, lewd movies and plays, and child pornography. By the way, child pornography, like obscenity, is unprotected by the First Amendment to the Constitution.[36] And, be aware that legislation for pornography on the Internet is in the looming.

By the late 1800s, Congress had made it an offense to mail any obscene, lewd, or lascivious paper or writing,[37] and decreed that the word *obscene* should be treated the same as it had by common law, which was considered a public nuisance and was punishable as a misdemeanor.

---

31. Arkansas code 5-27-306. Internet stalking of a child.
32. § 5-14-101
33. SB 443
34. Texas15 USC 1681 b
35. *Roth v. United States*, 354 U.S. 476. 77 S.Ct. 1304, 1 L.Ed.2d 1498 (1957).
36. *New York v. Ferber*, 458 U.S. 747, 102 S.Ct. 3348, 73 L.Ed.2d 1113 (1982).
37. *Knowles v. United States*, 170 F. 409 (8th Cir. 1909).

## "One Man's Vulgarity . . .

. . . is another's lyric." Profanity is another offense that is hard to uphold. In *Cohen v. California, supra*[38] the Supreme Court invalidated the "offensive conduct" conviction of a man who entered a courthouse wearing a jacket emblazoned with the slogan "Fuck the Draft." Justice Harlan agreed that the four-letter word being litigated was indeed tasteless, but nonetheless, it was his right to say it. In order for something to be profane, right now (although watch current news releases because it is subject to change) the defendant's language either must be deemed "fighting words" or a breach of the peace.

## Gambling–A Roll of the Dice Against Public Morality

Gambling crept in under the wire of offenses against public morality, and sits next to sexual offenses. This may seem an incongruity since common law did not regard gambling as an offense. Today federal laws and a variety of state statutes and local ordinances make all or certain forms of gambling illegal. Laws regulating gambling come under the police power of the state. And a trip to the U.S. Supreme Court has determined that there is no constitutional right to gamble. Common forms of gambling are craps, bingo, poker, bookmaking, and slot machines. Betting on sports events, horses, and card games is included as well. Since there are so many types of gambling, they are separated by the legal versus the illegal. Buying a lottery ticket in many states is not only legal, it is an important source of revenue for the state, with resources going toward education and other improvements. In the same vein, a common form of illegal gambling is running numbers. In order to play, a bet is placed on a number in the hopes that it will match a preselected number for a win.

So, what it gambling? It must consist of these elements: (1) a consideration, (2) a prize, and (3) a chance. This seems to fit under a lot of categories including raffles, promotional schemes, local carnivals and fairs, and a variety of games played for prizes. It is hard to tell the difference between games of chance and games of skill. In order to define the difference for your needs, each individual state statute will spell out the distinction. And, often, the only way to be absolutely sure, is with court distinction.

Some statutes prohibiting gambling exclude athletics or other contests in which participants must pit their physical or mental skills against one another for a prize. In some states nonprofit organizations benefit from particular forms of gambling that are otherwise forbidden. The paradox continues because there are states that will allow dog tracks for betting while an individual may be prosecuted for making a wager on the Kentucky Derby in his or her own home. Certain pinball operators have had their trade defined for them by an Ohio appellate court, which decided that the outcome of the operation was largely determined by the skill of the user and was therefore, not a game of chance.

## BREACHES OF THE PEACE: OFFENSES AGAINST PUBLIC ORDER AND SAFETY

### Illegal Weapons

According to a report by The Center on Crime Communities & Culture, 35 states require no registration or licensing for guns. A whopping 43 states require no permit or

---

38. *Cohen v. California*, supra, 403 U.S. at 25, 91 S.Ct. at 1788, 29 L.Ed.2d at 294.

registration in order to purchase assault weapons. And, 18 states have no minimum age to possess rifles or shotguns. With statistics like that, you can be assured that illegal weapons are big business and will provide big business and havoc for your law enforcement bureaus. Keep listening to the media, however, as the gun debate rages on.

## Concealed Weapons

Some states have statutes making it unlawful to carry a concealed weapon. To further define *concealed*, it means one carried on or about a person in such a manner as to hide it from sight. That makes sense. And story has it that a defendant was properly convicted of carrying a concealed weapon in her purse when the metal detector went off at the courthouse. But, sometimes, it is not as clear as all that. Once a Georgia appellate court decided that even though the handle of a gun could be seen peeking out of a defendant's pants, the weapon was concealed.[39] And, many concealed-weapon laws make it unlawful to carry a concealed weapon in a vehicle. Check into this further for added assurance.

The term "brandishing a weapon" is an ancient relic of a law meaning that someone draws or exhibits a weapon in an angry or threatening manner. Consult your individual state's ruling as you may have another "nuisance" offense with which to use in your charges.

## Disturbing the Peace

The common law recognized the right of the people to assemble peaceably for lawful purposes. In spite of that, preserving public order was given a high priority. And

Figure 2. A small sampling of illegal guns collected every year in a medium-sized community (population 38,000).

although the state and local government bore most of the burden for maintaining peace, the federal government has a significant role as well.

Unlawful assembly and riot is aimed at group behavior, while laws proscribing dis-

---

39. *Marshall v. State*, 200 S.E. 2d 902 (Ga. App. 1973).

orderly conduct are more for both group and individual conduct. To illustrate the distinction, the Indiana Code defines *unlawful assembly* as "an assembly of five or more persons whose common object is to commit an unlawful act, or a lawful act by unlawful means."[40] To further define the riotous conduct, the statute goes on to say it is "conduct that results in, or is likely to result in, serious bodily injury to a person or substantial damage to property." The conduct itself is held as a misdemeanor, unless it is committed while armed with a deadly weapon, and then it becomes a felony. The Federal Anti-Riot Act of 1968 was spurred on by the high incidence of controversy over the Vietnam War, racial unrest, and other social ills experienced in the turbulent 1960s.

Disorderly conduct rides the rails with unlawful assembly but it is applied to a person who recklessly, knowingly, or intentionally (1) engages in fighting or tumultuous conduct, (2) makes unreasonable noise and continues to do so after being asked to stop, (3) disrupts a lawful assembly of persons. . . .

The Supreme Court has ruled on the utterance of fighting words in several cases and feels it is beyond the protection of the First Amendment. In *Chaplinsky v. New Hampshire, supra*[41] the Court said that fighting words are those that (1) inflict injury, (2) tend to create a breach of the peace, and (3) are not an essential part of the exposition of ideas. In other words, when profanity is aimed at a police officer, some courts view that type of behavior by a different standard—they feel the officer should know how to handle the situation and, consequently, hesitate to convict. Regardless of the circumstances, the prosecution must establish that these words intended to incite violence. For law enforcement, these offenses tend to mix

it up when opposing groups get together to hash things out.

## I Hate "Hate Crimes"

As to the growing incidence with hate crimes—which is bigotry expressed toward minorities using symbols, objects, or characterizations that cause alarm, anger, or resentment on the basis of race, color, religion, or gender—some jurisdictions have enacted measures prohibiting hate crimes and have fixed them as misdemeanors. These offenses will continue to change and adapt and must always be weighed against the First Amendment right to free speech.

## Vagrancy and Loitering

Those elite in feudal England sure knew how to control a serf. That's where this business with vagrancy and loitering came from. Apparently, the higher-ups did not want their laborers to search for improved working conditions, and, in the same breath, they did not want the idlers to become public charges. So in order to regulate the economics of the populace, the common law developed a misdemeanor called *vagrancy*. The offense normally required three parts: (1) being without a visible means of support, (2) being unemployed, and (3) being able to work but refusing to do so.

"Get off my bench! . . . oh, excuse me," but, Americans weren't much better and used the vagrancy laws as broad discretion for taking people into custody in order to control the undesirables, or, to "shake them down." Since the indigents who were rousted were the most unlikely candidates to realize the unconstitutionality of the laws—how

40. West's Ann. Ind. Code § 35-45-1-1.
41. Champlinsky v. New Hampshire, 315 U.S. 568. 571, 62 S.Ct. 766, 769, 86 L.Ed. 1031, 1035 (1942).

**Example of an Arkansas Statute**

**Incite to Riot:**

5-71-203. Inciting riot.

(a)  A person commits the offense of inciting riot if he knowingly:

(1)  By speech or conduct urges others to participate in a riot under circumstances that produce a clear and present danger that they will participate in a riot; or

(2)  Gives commands, instructions, or signals to others in furtherance of a riot.

(b)  Inciting riot is a Class D felony if injury to persons or damage to property results therefrom.
Otherwise it is a Class A misdemeanor.

History. Acts 1975, No. 280, § 2904; A.S.A. 1947, § 41-2904.

5-71-201. Riot.

(a)  A person commits the offense of riot if, with two (2) or more other persons, he knowingly engages in tumultuous or violent conduct that creates a substantial risk of:

(1)  Causing public alarm;

(2)  Disrupting the performance of a governmental function; or

(3)  Damaging or injuring property or persons.

(b)  Riot is a Class A misdemeanor.

History. Acts 1975, No. 280, § 2902; A.S.A. 1947, § 41-2902.

5-51-206. Advocating personal injury, destruction of property, or overthrow of government—Use of symbols.

(a)  It shall be unlawful for any person or persons to wear, use, exhibit, display, or have in possession any symbol, token, device, or flag, the meaning, object, purpose, or intent of which is to encourage, aid, assist, or abet, with such intent, or incite with such intent to, or which is calculated to encourage, aid, assist, abet, or incite any person in:

(1) The infliction of personal injury upon any other person; or

(2) The taking of human life; or

(3) The destruction of either public or private property without due process of law; or

(4) The destruction or overthrow of, or that which tends to destroy or overthrow, the present form of government of either the State of Arkansas or the United States of America.

(b) Any person violating this section shall be deemed guilty of a misdemeanor and, upon conviction, shall be punished by fine of not less than ten dollars ($10.00) and not more than one thousand dollars ($1,000) and may be imprisoned in the county jail not exceeding six (6) months, or both, at the discretion of the court.

History. Acts 1919, No. 512, § 2; C. & M. Dig., § 2319; Pope's Dig., § 2945; A.S.A. 1947, § 41-3954.

do you proscribe laws for doing nothing?– over the years, there have been terrible injustices aimed toward loafers, alcoholics, derelicts, and tramps. By 1960, the constitutionality of the vagrancy laws was frequently being challenged on the grounds that the laws were vague, that they violated due process of law requirements, and exceeded the police power of the states. The courts generally upheld the right of the legislature of the states to define its own terms, however, until much later, when the long-awaited blow of vagrancy laws finally showed signs of vagueness to the judges, and were struck down. In one Jacksonville, Florida,[42] case, it collapsed under vagueness and, for the fact that it served as a vehicle for "arbitrary and erratic arrests and convictions." Incidentally, you don't have to look too hard to see police still using loitering ordinances today; it's a convenient subterfuge in which to remove suspected drug dealers from the streets.

## TRAFFIC VIOLATIONS

In the past, traffic offenses such as failure to yield, and failure to observe traffic signs and signals were treated as misdemeanors; and people committing them were arrested and required to post bond to avoid confinement pending adjudication. Since the 1960s these offenses have turned the corner to become civil infractions, rather than misdemeanors. As a result, offenders are now given tickets or citations instead of being subject to arrest. And given the modern-day mobility of travel, states updated their thinking and adopted "model" laws which make traffic offenses fairly uniform across boundaries. When a driver is stopped for a viola-

---

42. 405 U.S. at 162, 92 S. Ct. at 843, 31 L.Ed.2d at 115.

tion, however, police may observe his or her conduct, and direct a search based on reasonable suspicion, which may further move the police officer's instinct to probable cause and, finally, to an arrest based on the evidence found.

## Mobile: Alcohol and Drug Offenses

There are many different names for driving under the influence (DUI). Some are driving while intoxicated (DWI), driving under the influence of liquor (DUIL), operating a motor vehicle intoxicated (OMVI), operating while intoxicated (OWI), operating under the influence (OUI), and the latest, driving with an unlawful blood-alcohol level (DUBAL). All states have attempted to enact laws to keep American roadways free of drunk driver carnage. According to the California Vehicle Code, it is unlawful: 1) For any person who is under the influence of an alcohol beverage or any drug, or under the combined influence of an alcoholic beverage and any drug, to drive a vehicle. 2) It is unlawful for any person who has 0.08 percent or more, by weight, of alcohol in his or her blood to drive a vehicle.[43]

One defendant tried to get around this statute by claiming that the prosecution failed to prove he was "driving the vehicle." In *State v. Harrison*,[44] evidence supported the fact that Harrison was found asleep behind the steering wheel of his car parked on the roadway with the key in the ignition, motor running, and the transmission in drive. The court didn't see it his way and concluded that this evidence established that he was in actual physical control of the vehicle and, therefore, it was sufficient to prove that the defendant was driving the automobile.

## . . . the prosecution failed to prove he was "driving the vehicle."

Standard sentencing for DUI generally falls along the line of probation, plus fine, plus treatment program, and some time in jail. We'll take another look, from a different point of view, about driving while under the influence and drug use offenses in later chapters–unfortunately, it's that common–and if you are a police officer, well, you may see it every day.

## REVIEW QUESTIONS AND ANSWERS

Chapter 4 again explains the statutes, this time the laws we are defining deal with taking, altering and destroying property.

### *Key Words to Define*

What are some of the "key words" in Chapter 4 and what do they mean? Can you explain these terms?

- **Burglary**–Breaks into and enters the dwelling of another without consent to steal property or commit a felony.
- **Carjacking**–Forcible taking of a car using a firearm.
- **Concealed** (as in "concealed weapon")–Carried on or about a person in such a manner as to hide it from sight.

---

43. West's Cal. Ann. Vehicle Code § 23152 (a) (b).
44. *State v. Harrison*, 846 P.2d 1082 (N.M. App. 1992).

- **Ecclesiastical crimes**–Morality offenses adjudicated by the Church of England (historical doctrine).
- **Larceny**–The taking, carrying away the personal property of another with the intent to deprive the owner.
- **Lewd and lascivious conduct**–Exposing private body parts.
- **Malicious mischief**–Maliciously inflicts injury or damage on the property of another.

## Questions for Review and Discussion

1. *Question:* What are Index Crimes? *Answer:* FBI annual report offenses are divided into eight categories based on their seriousness, frequency and likelihood of being reported.

2. *Question:* What are some of the ways you can you get government reports? *Answer:* At government Web sites, hard copy orders by postal mails, e-mail updates and by telephone orders.

3. *Question:* What is a quick way to distinguish between:

**Burglary**–unlawful attendance and entry
**Larceny**–carrying away personal property of another; ex. pickpocket
**Robbery**–theft with the threat of physical force or fear
**Theft**–items taken while on the premises lawfully

4. *Question:* What is the key factor between grand theft and petty theft? *Answer:* The property is worth more with grand theft and the seriousness of the offense.

5. *Question:* What makes malicious mischief different from theft? *Answer:* While on the premise lawfully the owner is still in possession of property but it is damaged or impaired.

6. *Question:* Name some common examples of forgery and altering a forged instrument. *Answer:* Fake driver's license signature, (same with certificates of stock); checks written on another's account, altering grades or credit hours on college transcripts, bogus tickets for events, altering a deed, etc.

7. *Question:* Why is forgery different from a "bad check" statute? *Answer:* A person commits an offense of a bad check if he knowingly issues and passes a check for payment when the issuing body has insufficient funds.

8. *Question:* Why do so many people believe you can't legislate morality? *Answer:* There will always be debates on what is moral.

9. *Question:* Is buying a lottery ticket gambling? Yes. Why? *Answer:* Because it is consistent with: a consideration, a prize and a chance.

10. *Question:* Unlawful assembly and riot is aimed at a _____ behavior. *Answer:* Group (usually five or more people).

## Essay Exploration

Explain how a driving citation can result in an arrest. When a driver is stopped for a violation police may observe their behavior and conduct, then ask for a search based on reasonable suspicion, which may culminate in probable cause and arrest based on evidence found, or suspected.

# Chapter 5

# BEHIND ENEMY LINES

The rich rob the poor
and the poor rob one another.
–Sojourner Truth Saying

The best reward for authoring a book like this is the satisfaction of knowing that we have laid a trail for you through the maze of the legal process, so that you can come and go at will, confident of finding your way with the exit just beyond. The most lasting quality we could hope for is that we have assisted you in tackling research. Since only you can know what it is you're looking for, by giving you the skills with which to investigate, we will be giving you the key to a fascinating and challenging world.

## RESEARCH AIDS

In that interest then, this chapter covers the nature and the basics of legal research. To begin, the correct mindset of a researcher should be like that of the adventurer; know that in order to seek out the unknown, you most likely will find a few blind alleys or dead-end situations. Two of the best qualities a professional and pilgrim can possess are to have patience and be persistent. So it is with the law and law research.

There are billions of words written on legal facts and opinions. Seeking and finding information requires a plan, something similar to building a cabinet or sewing a dress. To illustrate–we will use the cabinet analogy–you must choose from French, English, Country, etc., categories of design. Next, you will find one or two good woodworking books that will provide you with an overview of the techniques common to that style; for example, does it have dentil molding, Queen Anne legs, mortise and tendon joints? From there, you get more specific and decide on a set of plans, learning any unfamiliar terms, and making a list of the tools and parts required. Finally, you assemble the components and machinery required and follow the instructions in the plan. After heavy doses of labor, if all goes well, you will have something to put your law books into at the end.

## LEGAL EXPERTS

The first and easiest way to research some

legal aspect is to ask another person who is most likely to know the answer. Your local prosecutor is an elected official and, as such, may answer your question or at the very least, lead you to a source. Law librarians are most knowledgeable and can be helpful in pointing out further resources and how to use them. (They are also held captive in the correct venue, a most encouraging component; make friends of them.) Courtroom clerks can answer some procedural details such as providing jury instructions, voir dire stipulations, and court rules, just be aware they are also likely overwhelmed by the sheer numbers of people who pass through the system or are subject to rude and desperate people, so act humble and polite and don't be offended when they tell you they cannot offer legal advice. A criminal lawyer can certainly help (at cost) but again, their tight calendars mean you will not be a priority and, again, research tips are the most you can hope for. And, finally, the Internet is a compelling and exciting medium with which to explore. The possibilities are endless and we will talk about both the tips, trends, and traps of using the World Wide Web.

## LAW HELPMATES IN PRINT

Let's move on then to books. Reliable law dictionaries can help to explain specific words and unfamiliar terms or just to help you get ideas. Some good resources are:

- *Law Dictionary for Non-Lawyers* by Daniel Oran (West Publishing Co.)
- *Dictionary of Legal Terms: A Simplified Guide to the Language of Law* by Stephen Gifis (Barrons); and,
- *Dictionary of American Legal Usage* by David Melinkoff (West Publishing Co.)
- *Burton's Legal Thesaurus* by William C. Burton (Macmillan)
- *Black's Law Dictionary* (6th ed.)

## Books of Knowledge

Legal encyclopedias–alphabetically arranged–may provide more basic background information. There are two main, national law encyclopedias called *American Jurisprudence* 2d edition and *Corpus Juris Secundum*. These tomes will hold broad-based discussions on the laws in all fifty states. In addition, many of the largest states have their own encyclopedias as well.

Try also the website: http://www.nolo.com which has a comprehensive legal encyclopedia.

## A Model to Follow

Form books may aid you, especially if you

---

**FYI—Homicide**
Professionals, there is a terrific book entitled *Homicide A Bibliography* by Bal K. Jerath and Rajinder Jerath (CRC Press). The publisher explains *Homicide* as: "This volume represents an exhaustive search of the world's literature regarding homicide. More than 7,000 entries have been compiled from references selected from major indexes in libraries from outstanding universities, government agencies, the Library of Congress, and other sources." If you are in need of a case that parallels your situation, consult this directory—it may very well be the gateway to your answer.

need to see the types of documents that most lawyers copy, instead of inventing their own legal papers. Inside, you will find collections of sample legal documents, mostly, fill-in-the-blank forms for a specific procedural task. Commonly, form books will provide an overview of the procedure required to go along with the form chosen, and additional notes on how to make the document specific by using the most common modifications. Want to see a complaint, a subpoena, a change-your-name document? Look here. One suggestion—start with a form book that is specific to your state, if there is one. For example, forms in the *American Jurisprudence Legal Forms* are primarily national in scope.

Practice manuals, like the old *Cliff Notes* we used to use to summarize a book, give lawyers hands-on information logically organized, covering a specialized area of practice. Don't know how to defend a drunk driving case? Find the practice manual called *Defense of Drunk Driving* written by Richard Erwin and Marilyn Minzer. It is referred to as the "bible" and contains everything an attorney would need to know about handling this specific offense. Practice manuals are available on a variety of topics such as family law, search and seizure issues, and a number of other subjects. *Prosecution and Defense of Criminal Conspiracy Cases* by Matthew Bender is a further one of interest. Another Bancroft-Whitney book meriting attention is *Bender's Forms of Discovery.*

The proof of facts book, *American Jurisprudence Proof of Facts* (Bancroft-Whitney/Lawyers Coop) gives detailed discussions of the burden of proof issues in practically every kind of civil and criminal case. The subject index will point you to an excellent general summary of circumstances that may be related to your case.

Law reviews and journals will give you articles about recent legislation, important or landmark cases, and certain legal philosophy as published by various law schools, commercial publishers, and professional legal societies or bar associations. The topics are authored by professors of law, law students, and well-known practicing attorneys. You will usually find them in paperback pamphlets and libraries will often bind them into hardcover editions at the end of a year. The Internet articles can be found in the Findlaw index at: http://www.findlaw.com where you will locate the law school heading and click on the law journals link. From there you can search for articles by keyword.

Treatises and monographs are different resources for the law student or professional/researcher who has a fairly good background because these vehicles tend to provide a much deeper expertise than what is offered in other reference materials. The difference between a treatise and a monograph is one of length. A treatise is rather formal and covers an entire area of law, whereas a monograph either zeroes in on a small portion of a general legal field, and is a discourse on a single subject—hence the suffix "mono"—or it introduces a new concept or way of thinking. Sometimes the author of a monograph will present much second- and third-level theoretical evidence, so these articles call for both patience and rereading.

## SCHOOL PRIMERS

Textbooks, most of them published by West Publishing, offer an excellent, basic understanding of criminal law and its accompanying procedures. These can be found in campus bookstores, ordered through commercial outlets, or found on the Internet. The best feature about textbooks are the summaries at the end of chapters, the lists of definitions, and queries designed to make the student think more in-depth. In addition to school books, there is a new self-help book trend in the market for those who wish to either educate themselves with the intent of avoiding the high costs of a lawyer or who use these materials as an adjunct to their continuing edification. Nolo Press has a variety of self-help books and a favorite of ours (and the one I most frequently recommend) is entitled *The Criminal Law Handbook: Know Your Rights, Survive the System* by attorneys Paul Bergman and Sara J. Berman-Barrett. It is a highly readable, step-by-step guide to anyone interested in the machinations involved within the criminal justice system. Nolo Press also has a fine web site with a legal encyclopedia, explaining many issues in common English. You can find them on the Internet at: http://www.nolo.com.

## Research for the Die-Hard

One of the very best sources for legal research is the book *Legal Research: How to Find & Understand the Law* by attorneys Stephen Elias and Susan Levinkind. They have taken painstaking effort to offer the reader gradual and continuous methods for finding material both in hard copy, along with examples of Internet methodology, which are similar to small tutorials that walk you through the process by showing what appears on each page or web site screen view.

## Questions and Plotting Ideas

After you are familiar with certain terms, try to formulate questions in order to help categorize your legal issue. Start with these:

### • *Does the situation encompass a federal or state crime?*

Discussions and the specifics of state law and federal law are commonly found in different books, and for good reasons. Our founding

fathers were concerned about government's overwhelming power and potential abuse, so they created the constitutional guidelines. Consequently, most legal research customarily involves state rather than federal law. Congress' power–and the results of their power, federal law–is held to a few specific areas under constitutional direction, so most of the lawmaking decisions are left to state governments. Federal law, as a result, generally affects a broad range of social welfare, health, and environmental questions. There is overlap though, say, with environmental law as an example, because the government helps to regulate and fund these laws for states too. For crimes under this type of situation, such as kidnapping, you may have to look at both state and federal law background.

Some criminal actions also involve multiple offenses. For example, robbing a bank can involve conspiracy, robbery, and possession of a deadly weapon, etc., violations against both the state and the federally protected banking administration. Typically, a prosecutor will charge for every possible crime, some easier to prove than others, and the defendant can be prosecuted for violating both sets of laws. Although this may smack of double jeopardy, it is not. The jurisdictions are not the same in spite of the fact that rulings may be similar, and usually only one prosecutor will pursue the case, so as not to tie up valuable resources from both offices.

### • *Does it involve criminal law or civil law?*

Criminal law is any type of behavior–a crime–punishable by incarceration and/or a fine. The party bringing charges is usually the prosecutor who represents the state, who has the "burden of guilt" as well. The defendant may receive a government-paid attorney and have the right to a trial.

In contrast, for a civil case, the injured party is the one who sues, usually over rights and duties of individuals and organizations named in the dispute, the result of which may be money damages or the loss of property. The lawyers in a civil case are usually private attorneys who charge a fee for services and, in a civil case, the plaintiff must provide a "preponderance of the evidence" in order to collect damages.

### • *Does it pertain to the substance of the law or legal procedure?*

To reiterate the difference between substantive criminal law and criminal procedure, substantive criminal law concerns the definition and punishment of crimes, written and published in order to meet the edict, "no crime without a law." Criminal procedure, on the other hand, is interested in how people accused of crimes are treated by the criminal justice system.

| SUBSTANTIVE CRIMINAL LAW | CRIMINAL PROCEDURE |
| --- | --- |
| Assault | Arraignment |
| Breaking and entering | Arrest |
| Burglary | Confessions |
| Conspiracy | Cross-examination |
| Disorderly conduct | Extradition |
| Drug and narcotic offenses | Grand jury |
| Driving under the influence | Indictments |
| Juvenile offenses | Jury selection; jury verdicts |
| Kidnapping | Miranda warning |
| Larceny | Plea bargaining |
| Lewd and lascivious behavior | Preliminary hearings |
| Malicious mischief | Probation; probation reports |
| Murder | Right to counsel |
| Rape | Search and seizure |
| Robbery | Sentencing |
| Shoplifting | Speedy trial |
| Smuggling | Suppression of evidence |
| Tax evasion | Trials |
| Trespass | Witnesses |
| Weapons offenses | |

### • *What legal category does it fit?*

It will also help your research if you find a subject area for your idea; for example, most law books contain indexes organized by content such as Motor Vehicles, Traffic Rules, etc. Under each of these major headings, you will see an alphabetized list of still smaller subjects or narrower areas, such as:
• Evaluation facility referral,
• Evidence,
• Fines and penalties, and, listed underneath again, terms such as,
• Alcohol and drug substance abuse courses, with a section number and pages;
• Personal injury accident, section and pages;
• Sentencing options, and a different section number, etc. (You see it is narrowing, narrowing until you find the legal description of what you want to zero in on.)

## Down to the Meat of It

We now have backgrounding tools for the idea we wish to explore. We have defined the terms, reduced the jargon to understandable English, and used any number of general resource materials listed above; we have spent some time thinking about questions that have logical answers, and now we need to get down to the meat of the issue. If you want to write about criminal law and constitutional matters, the first best idea would be to consult a primary source. Say you want to write about a manhunt and a difficult arrest. First ask yourself: What does the amendment say about search and seizure? Remember, all criminal law and procedure comes out of the Bill of Rights. Read the Fourth Amendment.

Next, we need to find statute material, and then the applications of that material, or, "cases in point." Okay, let's back up to finding statutes or law codes. Federal offenses are defined in statutes enacted by the United States Congress, and state offenses are defined in statutes enacted by state legislatures. Federal statutes are published annually in the *United States Statutes at Large.* The states have their own volumes called session laws, and these include all the new laws enacted in a given session in any state legislature. Later on, these will be merged into the existing laws which will then be arranged systematically by subject and put into an index.

## OUR SOURCES OF LAW

The U.S. Constitution has amendments and its interpretations are referred to as *constitutional law.*

State constitutions and the cases that result from it are *state constitutional law.*

Congress passes law called "statutes," which decree federal statutory law; and the federal courts decide on federal cases and write opinions that make up a body of *federal case law.*

Federal courts also decide cases and write opinions about state statutes but only when the parties before the court are from different states.

Federal administrative agencies are created by Congress and staffed by the executive branch, such as the Federal Aviation Administration or the Federal Communications Commission, etc., and they issue regulations that constitute the *federal administrative law.*

State legislatures pass statutes, which constitute *state statutory law.* Also, state courts rule on court cases and write opinions, which constitute *state case law.*

State administrative agencies (created by state legislature and staffed by the governor's appointees) write regulations which help to make up *state administrative law.*

Sovereign Indian tribes have their own courts and their own law stipulations, and it empowers their government in what is called *tribal law.*

Local city and county governments pass *ordinances* that become police codes, building codes, health codes, etc., for small communities and local cities.

## Finding Federal Statutes

One popular source has compiled all the federal laws–which started out as "bills" presented to Congress–in a series of books called the *United States Code Annotated,* also known as the U.S.C.A. and published by West Publishing. The laws typically have labels and numbers describing which house of Congress they originally came from such as, Senate Bill (S.5), for a bill introduced in the Senate; or a House of Representatives Bill 116 (H.R. 116).

The U.S.C.A. incorporates fifty separate titles that correspond to the text of the Official Code of the Laws of the United States. Title 18, for instance, is entitled "Crimes and Criminal Procedure." The fact that the codes are annotated means that they contain other information pertaining to each statute such as one-sentence summaries, historical notes, cross-references to other relevant statutes, etc.

Here is an example on how to read a citation (or cite) which is a reference to any primary law source under the United States

Code Annotated. The one illustrated below is the Civil Rights Act of 1964.

18 U.S.C.A. § 3109a–h
18 is the Title Number
U.S.C..A. stands for "United States Annotated Code"
§ means "Session"
3109a–h is the Section Number/Subsection

## Finding Code on the Internet

There are two sites that contain the U.S. Code on the Internet; each is given in a distinct way:

- The U.S. House of Representatives Internet Law Library has a current version of Code at: http://www.rose.net/remote/22.htm
- Cornell Law School at: http://www4.law.cornell.edu/uscode

## STATE STATUTES

State statutes can be organized in a couple of different ways, either annotated–containing notes and references–or not, using just the text of the statute. Legal students most often prefer the annotated versions which convey not only the actual language of the statute, but give listings for significant court cases. State statutes also can be organized into books according to subject matter, by codes, such as the Penal Code for criminal statutes, specifically; or by title number, chapter; and, finally, in books that are numbered sequentially. Books that contain collections of statutes usually include an index in the last volume with directions to the whereabouts of particular statutes according to their subject matter. The word "code" in most instances is synonymous for "law." Below is an example of a statute in an Arkansas code book for burglary.

If you are not finding your topic in the index, say, it involves *arrest*, try looking under a couple of different headings such as: "Search and Seizure," or "Fourth Amendment."

## BURGLARY, ARSON

Here is an example of The Model Penal Code (Official Draft, 1985):

### 221.0 Definitions

In this Article, unless a different meaning plainly is required:

(1) "Occupied structure" means any structure, vehicle or place adapted for overnight accommodation of persons, or for carrying on business therein, whether or not a person is actually present.

(2) "Night" means the period between thirty minutes past sunset and thirty minutes before sunrise.

### 221.1 Burglary

(1) *Burglary Defined.* A person is guilty of burglary if he enters a building or occupied structure, or separately secured or occupied portion thereof, with purpose to commit a crime therein, unless the premises are at the time open to the public or the actor is licensed or privileged to enter. It is an affirmative defense to prosecution for burglary that the building or structure was abandoned.

(2) Grading. Burglary is a felony of the second degree if it is perpetrated in the dwelling of another at night, or if, in the course of committing the offense, the actor:

(a) purposely, knowingly or recklessly inflicts or attempts to inflict bodily injury on anyone; or

(b) is armed with explosives or a deadly weapon.

Otherwise, burglary is a felony of the third degree. An act shall be deemed "in the course of committing" an offense if it occurs in an attempt to commit the offense or in flight after the attempt or commission.

(3) *Multiple Convictions.* A person may not be convicted both for burglary and for the offense which it was his purpose to commit after the burglarious entry or for an attempt to commit that offense, unless the additional offense constitutes a felony of the first or second degree.

## HOW STATE STATUTES LOOK

A state statute may look like the example below:
**West's Annotated California Codes, Vol. 51A, § 1524**

A typical state statutory citation may break down like this:
**Example: 46 Vt. Stat. Ann. § 1247**
- **46** would be the Title/volume number
- **Vt. Stat. Ann.** stands for "Vermont Statutes Annotated"
- **§** stands for session
- **1247** is the section number

To find state statutes on the Internet, go to:
- Findlaw: http://www.findlaw.com/11state gov/
- The U.S. House of Representatives Internet Law Library and use the search engine feature: http://rose.net/remote/22htm
- Cornell University: http://www.law.cornell.edu/states/index.html

## Citations Are Not Easy Reading

Case citations have usually five or six items:
- the case name which are the names of the plaintiff and the defendant
- the volume number of the reporter where the case is published
- the name of the reporter
- the page number of the volume

- the year the case was decided
- for federal appeals cases or federal district cases a designation of the circuit; or for state cases the judicial district where the state is located.

**Example: State v. Rooks, 468 S.E.2d, 354 (Ga. 1996)**
- **State v. Rooks**, are the names in the case, the State versus an individual named Rooks,
- **468** is the Volume number
- **S.E.2d** designates the reporter; S.E. means Southeastern (First and Second series)
- **354** is a page number
- **(Ga. 1996)** is the state; and year; Georgia, in 1996

## Rhyme or Reason?

One of the reasons for this type of system is that the work has undergone many drafts by many editors, most of whom use legalese on a daily basis. Another reason is that for every law there is an exception or many exceptions. Legal research experts suggest that you read the material several times. Be aware of the differences between **And** and **OR**. The "And" designation usually means that these two factors must be employed together. The "OR" stipulation on the other hand, means that the conditions must be met by one condition OR the other.

Make an attempt to look up every word that is unfamiliar, or that could be construed to mean different variations on a similar theme. If a Latin term such as *Prima facie* arises in any of your reading, and you find out that it means "lawfully sufficient," before moving further, see how that definition applies to the rest of the text; does it make more sense if it means, the "minimum of facts in order to proceed"?

Check to see if the other statutes mentioned along with yours relate to the one you are reading. Remember there is a concept among justice scholars called "strict interpretation." Basically, this means that laws must be interpreted *literally*–verbatim–and the prosecution (the more knowledgeable source of the law than the defendant) must show that the offense of the accused meets all the elements listed for each crime in order for it to stick. And bear in mind that all statutes must be interpreted by judges and lawyers and interpretations about statutes are almost always subject to varying ideology. By reading the history of a decision, and working up to present day, it can help you to see how the law has evolved through use. Plan on spending some time to backtrack at least one decade, if you can.

If someone will argue a case based on a state statute, make sure that you have the latest version. Laws are often updated and revised. In collections of annotated versions, updates are posted in what is called the *pocket parts*. A pocket part is an add-on version that fits into the hardcover volume and is usually stored in a pocket. Any changes such as additions will be underlined; and deletions will be indicated by an asterisk. If the particular law is still pending, probably the best source for the latest developments will be with your local representative. Call that office and request a copy of the bill (even if you do not have the number of the bill, knowing what the bill is about and who sponsors it, should be enough for identification). In addition, your local law librarian might have an amended copy of the latest version called a *slip law*.

## INTERPRETING STATUTES

When the law is applied and the defendant and lawyer find reasons not to accept the decision, they make an appeal to a high-

er court. The appeals court is not in the position to decide guilt or innocence, their primary concern is to read the transcript of the trial and make a decision about the lawfulness of the decision. Does it violate the defendant's constitutional rights? Is the law too vague to enforce as written? Is there room for more than one interpretation? These judge-rendered decisions are kept and published as case notes. Case reading is fun and interesting in that it tells the actual facts of the case as it came down. Case notes accompany the statutes in annotated codes and also in books that publish cases and materials. A couple of good books housing Supreme Court cases–cases involving constitutional law–and their decisions are:

• *Basic Criminal Law: Cases and Materials*, 3rd ed., by George E. Dix and M. Michael Sharlot (West's Criminal Justice Series)
• *Basic Criminal Procedure: Cases, Comments and Questions*, 8th ed., by Yale Kamisar, Wayne R. LaFave and Jerold H. Israel (American Casebook Series, West Publishing Co.)

In addition, there are a series of books called *Shepard's Citations for Statutes*. These dark red, hardcover volumes provide a complete listing of each time a particular statute or constitutional provision has been referred to and perhaps interpreted by a federal or state court. Legal researchers have a nickname for finding how their statute has been reported and it is called "Shepardizing" a case. In order to use Shepard's, you will need to know the exact number (citation) of the statute and it is helpful to know the year it was passed.

For instructions on how to shepardize federal and state statutes we suggest *Legal Research: How to Find & Understand the Law* by Elias and Levinkind, Nolo Press, pages 9/10 and 9/11.

## THE REPORTER SYSTEM

There are volumes that contain appellate court decisions specifically. These are called reporters. The National Reporter System includes decisions from the United States Supreme Court, lower federal courts, and the state appellate courts. The National Reporter System contains the text of each reported decision plus a brief summary of the decision called a syllabus and a section for topics called headnotes. These headnotes briefly describe the principles involved and are indexed by a series of key numbers. For example, decisions about first-degree murder are classified under the heading "homicide" and there is a key number for each aspect of the crime. Therefore, homicide with intent to kill in the first-degree might be classified as "Homicide 9-Intent and design to effect death."

There are also a series of regional reporters which are decisions of the highest state courts (but not always the supreme courts) and the decisions of the intermediate state courts called appellate courts, are found in seven regional reporters.

## INFORMATIVE INTERNET SITES

We would be remiss by not mentioning a particular web site run by friend and defense attorney, Kim Kruglick. Kim's pages are not only thorough in respect to the law and criminal law sources, but there is a nice section on forensic web sites. You can find the site at: http://www.kruglaw.com

For much lighter research, check out these other Internet resources:
• http://www.courttv.com
• http://www.ljx.com
And for a glimpse into the legal organizations there is the American Bar Association at: http://www.abanet.org and the National District Attorney's Association at: http://www.ndaa-apri.org

## MINDFULNESS

There is a concept called *synchronicity* that comes from Carl Jung, a Swiss psychiatrist who was famous for expounding his views on introversion and extroversion. Jung gave a name to the phenomenon and described it like this: that once someone becomes *mindful* of a subject, the amount of repeat awareness of that subject increases considerably with each new encounter. Now that you have the basics of law research, we hope that you will develop a synchronicity of your own and find law everywhere: in the newspaper, on television, in the films you watch, etc. Your knowledge and mindfulness will make those instances of application–of your writing and reading about the subject–that much more interesting.

Good hunting!

## REVIEW QUESTIONS AND ANSWERS

### *Key Words to Define*

• **Annotated**–Containing notes and references
• **Civil law**–Injured party sues using paid, private lawyers; preponderance of evidence is the criteria for cause and settlement
• **Criminal procedure**–How people who are accused of crimes are treated and processed by the criminal justice system
• **Findlaw**–An Internet Web site with articles, catalogs to state's laws and other information; www.findlaw.com
• **Ordinances**–Local city and county governments pass ordinances that become

building codes, health codes, etc.; for the well-being of the community

- **Pocket parts**–Updates or add-ons to versions of annotations, histories, etc.; usually in the front or back of books, journals.
- **Practice manual**–Hands-on information logically organized
- **Prima facie**–Lawfully sufficient, minimum of facts needed in order to proceed
- **Proof of facts**–Detailed discussions on burden of proof issues
- **Statutes**–Also referred to as "codes," are laws
- **Treatise**–Formal documents covering an entire area of law
- **U.S.C.A.**–United States Code Annotated

## *Questions for Review and Discussion*

1. *Question:* Name three sources for the beginner to research some legal aspect of the law. *Answer:* Local prosecutor, law librarian, courtroom clerk, attorney, guides, books, law university library

2. *Question:* What are form books? *Answer:* They contain the types of documents most lawyers use; procedural, fill-in-the-blank sheets.

3. *Question:* Can a crime involve multiple offenses? *Answer:* Yes. Robbing a bank can involve conspiracy, robbery, possession of a weapon, even hostage taking, etc., violations against both the state and federal laws.

4. *Question:* In this example: 18 U.S.C.A. § 3109 a-h what does the symbol § mean? *Answer:* Session. 18 is what? The title number in U.S. Code.

5. *Question:* What is an "appeal" supposed to accomplish? *Answer:* The appeals court does not decide guilt or innocence, but is to make a decision about the lawfulness of the process, verdict or sentencing.

## *Essay Exploration*

Explain why laws are written in legalese. Laws developed from different cultures, that is to say, Roman, Greek, Anglo Saxon, etc., and have deep historical underpinnings. Many laws are based on precedents or opinions from judges as the centuries have passed. Consequently, old English interpretations use arcane language, and are meant to be read by other law professionals. Also, laws are subject to updating, amendments and rendered historical opinions and thus, undergo many drafts. In addition, many of the terms are Latin and require deciphering or knowledge not normally taught today.

# Chapter 6

# DEFENSES, JUSTIFICATION, AND EXCUSE

Laws are like spiders' webs: If some poor
creature come up against them, it is caught;
but a big one can break through and get away.
–Solon, *Lives of Eminent Philosophers*

Ever hear of the "Twinkie defense," the "abuse excuse," or the "insanity plea"? American criminal jurisprudence admits that even though someone may have perpetrated the crime he or she is charged with, this does not necessarily mean the defendant is guilty of crime. What one may call "loopholes" are defenses which, if believed to be true by the jury, must as a matter of law negate the criminal responsibility of the accused. Remember, to begin, the prosecution must prove all elements of a crime, for example, that he or she did the act, that the act and the intent happened in concert, that there were no attendant circumstances such as self-defense that would cancel out criminal liability, and that the outcome was caused by a criminal act.

This chapter introduces a number of defenses. No *imagined* defense will work because the experts know them, but that does not stop the creativity of defense lawyers from creating new ones every year. If they can find expert witnesses to back up their claims (such as what may be presented by forensic psychologists and psychiatrists)

their testimony may change the landscape of the case. And, both common law, as well as state's law, allow the accused to come forward and present credible evidence that such a defense is factually possible.

## Allege It, Prove It

In general, a defendant may likely plead "Not guilty, Sir" to the charges. In addition, he or she may offer up a defense–sometimes called a *negative defense*–and the defendant (since now the tables have turned), has the burden of raising some evidence to back it up. That process is called the "burden of production of evidence." Later, when the defense evidence is presented, the prosecution needs to counter the negative defense in order to overcome it. As an example, say our defendant is charged with manslaughter because he killed a person who forced entry into his home. On the night in question, the defendant asserts he was asleep, and claims to have used deadly force to *defend his home.* If any evidence proves that he did, in fact,

act in self-defense–say, the offender had weapons that showed usage–the prosecution must prove the defendant did not act reasonably. (We see an acquittal here, don't you?) In some jurisdictions though, it gets harder to prove, as the defendant is labored with the burden of proving defense by the greater weight of the evidence, usually referred to as a *preponderance of the evidence.*

Remember, the most common and powerful defense argument is a principle called the *presumption of innocence.* Anytime defendants takes their own defense upon themselves, they also will be taking on many other burdens, leaving themselves and their witnesses open to cross-examination. For the defendant who chooses to remain silent and presents no witnesses, the prosecution has the burden of *proof beyond a reasonable doubt*–and the defendant can later claim the prosecution's case is too weak for the burden, even if everything the prosecution witnesses said was accurate. In addition, the defense attorney can poke holes in the guilty argument by cross-examining the prosecution's witnesses–and holes make for reasonable doubt.

Another very important point and a boon to the defense in both theory and practice: if the defense presents no argument, the prosecution is not allowed to comment on the fact that the defendant chooses not to testify or has failed to put on an affirmative case. The risk here, though, is that jurors have a tendency to disregard this rule. The juror's assumption–or first impression perhaps–is that the defendant won't stand up for him or

herself because he has something to hide.

## . . . holes make for reasonable doubt

### DID IT, DEFEND IT

A defense that must be specifically pled is called an *affirmative,* or *"true" defense.* To be lawfully defined, the only true defense arguments are those where the defendant admittedly committed a crime, but seeks to avoid punishment based on a legal excuse or justification. Some examples of this kind of defense are: duress, self-defense, entrapment, etc.

To get a clearer picture of *affirmative defenses,* they can be ordered into five different categories:
1. Those asserting lack of capacity: infancy, insanity, intoxication, and automatism
2. Those alleging justification or excuse: duress, consent, necessity, mistake of law, mistake of fact
3. Those justifying a use of force: self-defense, defense of habitation, defense of property, defense of others, and using force to resist an arrest
4. Those depending on constitutional or statutory rights: immunity, double jeopardy, or statutes of limitation
5. Those attacking government conduct: entrapment or selective prosecution

Of course, it is up to the prosecution to produce evidence *beyond a reasonable doubt* that negates the affirmative defense.

---

**FYI**—Affirmative defense makes possible the "twist" every plot cries out for. It is up to the prosecutor to anticipate every possible scenario that the defense could present based on the time of death, hard evidence, alibi, or whatever. By allowing the accused the chance to defend him- or herself, the defense strategy becomes very iffy, very edgy. Prosecution should be prepared to "quick study" some alternative explanations, which may call for many, late-night brainstorming sessions.

Let's look at the affirmative defenses individually for a better understanding of how they work, starting with the lack of capacity defenses.

## Infancy: He's So Young

At common law, a child under seven is assumed unconditionally unable to form criminal intent. This is the basis of the defense of infancy. For this reason, most of these cases are "adjudicated in juvenile court." But the same charge for a child between seven and fourteen is debatable, and some jurisdictions permit the child to be tried as an adult, especially if the crime is particularly heinous. However, the prosecution must be able to introduce evidence that shows the delinquent child knew what he or she was doing. How is this done? Well, if the child tried to conceal the crime, bribe a witness, or accuse others of the deed, he or she is showing that hand.

Laws are still evolving as the age of murderers drops and modern statutes differ in their treatment–some have raised the age while some have modified it–but all agree that it is the child's age *at the time of commission* of the crime and not the age at trial that determines the waiver from a juvenile court to adult venues.

## I Thought I Was Napoleon

In a twist of affairs, all offenders are presumed sane unless pronounced by agreement as insane (although we may not agree with their general assessment). Contrary to popular belief, the insanity defense is not a frequently used ploy, and the accused are not really getting away with anything when it actually works out in their favor. Confinement to a mental facility is not syn-

onymous with either a "rest home" or a "spa." Any preconceived notions of a mental hospital as housing quaint, eccentric, or dingy people is wholly incorrect. The will of a mentally ill patient is no less than our own, it's just directed in a different fashion.

## M'Naghten Rule

The original rule for insanity is based on a historical English case and aptly named the *M'Naghten rule*. A man named Daniel M'Naghten suffered under the delusion that he was being persecuted by government officials. In his mind, the best way to be rid of this situation was to kill Sir Robert Peel, the founder of the British Police System and the man for whom the term "Bobbies" is crafted. To end his torture, M'Naghten positioned himself outside Peel's domicile and, instead of shooting him, shot and killed his secretary, Edward Drummond. At trial, M'Naghten's barristers argued their client insane at the time of the shooting and the jury agreed. Queen Victoria was outraged by the outcome and insisted a yardstick for the insanity defense be set. The House of Lords responded with this:

> . . . it must be clearly proved that, at the time of committing the act, the party accused as labouring under such a defect of reason, from disease of the mind, as not to know the nature and quality of the act he was doing; or, if he did know it, that he did not know what he was doing was wrong.[1]

As new theories involving mental capacity developed among those who practiced psychology and psychiatry, the rule seemed a bad fit. Since it was based solely on intellect, it ignored that powerful notion of irresistible impulse, an emotional concept built on self-control. In other words, this new notion allowed that there were people who,

---

1. M'Naghten's Case, 8 Eng. Rep. 718 (1843).

while knowing an act was wrong, still succumbed to an uncontrollable desire or the duress of a mental disease and did the act anyway, and therefore should be excused from criminal liability.

Since this formula did not fit all forms of perpetrators either, the *Durham test* came to fruition which said: the accused is not criminally responsible if that person's unlawful act was the "product of mental disease or defect."[2] Now this was a definition a psychiatrist could live with, but the electorate could not, and it was eventually discarded.

In 1962, the *ALI standard*, named for the American Law Institute, proposed this version:

> *A person is not responsible for criminal conduct if at the time of such conduct, as a result of mental disease or defect, a person lacks substantial capacity either to appreciate the wrongfulness of his conduct or to conform his conduct to the requirements of law.*

The idea of combining both cognitive and volitional capacities as a test for sanity was adopted by the federal courts and was used as a test for the Hinckley case, where a man named John Hinckley was found not guilty by reason of insanity for his attack on former president Reagan.

Congress wasn't happy with this rendition and soon passed the Insanity Defense Reform Act of 1984 for the federal government. It reads like this:

> *It is an affirmative defense to a prosecution under any Federal statute that, at the time of the commission of the acts constituting the offense, the defendant, as a result of a severe mental disease or defect, was unable to appreciate the nature and quality or the wrongfulness of his act. Mental disease or defect does not otherwise constitute a defense.*[3]

An interesting facet of the revised act, now provided a clause that stated the "defen-

dant has the burden of proving the defense of insanity by clear and convincing evidence." This requirement puts the evidence in the middle as far as strictness, as much as standards can be defined. It is higher than the "preponderance of evidence" as required by civil evidence, but still lower than the evidence "beyond a reasonable doubt" variety.

## INSANITY DEFENSE TODAY

Seventeen-year-old Eric Michael Clark took the keys to his brother's truck, and while his brother slept, drove around a nearby neighborhood for 40 minutes disturbing residents with loud music. Flagstaff Police Officer Jeffrey Moritz responded to the call and pulled Clark over. Clark was acting psychotic and suffering from chronic, paranoid schizophrenia, thinking the policeman was an alien. He proceeded to shoot Moritz several times, severing a major artery and killing him. For a year and a half prior to the shooting, Clark had suffered from mood swings, as well as episodes where he screamed, alternating with whispered gibberish. He spent time in a psychiatric hospital and was released against medical advice.

At trial Clark wanted to use this evidence not only to prove that he was insane (a claim on which he bore the burden of proof) but also to show that he could not form the criminal intent that the government required him to prove beyond a reasonable doubt. The trial judge, however, ruled that Arizona law confined the use to expert evidence for his insanity claim; and that he could not use that argument to show he could not form the necessary criminal intent. The court ruled he had not sufficiently proved his insanity defense, and Clark was convicted and sen-

---

2. Durham test: 214 F.2d 862, 876 (D.C. Cir. 1954).
3. 18 U.S.C.A. § 17 (a).

tenced to 25 years to life in prison. In the higher Arizona state court, there was no dispute of these facts.

The U.S. Supreme Court heard argument on Clark's case to determine whether a defendant has a Fourteenth Amendment due process right, separate from his insanity plea, to present expert evidence about his mental state in order to counter the prosecution's evidence of criminal intent?

In a 5-to-4 decision, the Supreme Court held that Arizona could constitutionally limit the use of expert evidence about a defendant's mental state to his insanity defense. A defendant is presumed sane until he proves otherwise, and Justice Souter argued that allowing a defendant to use evidence of insanity to show that he could not form the necessary criminal intent would enable him to get around that presumption.

## Mothers Who Murder

In Houston, Andrea Yates, a suburban housewife, admitted to drowning her five children–ages 7 years to six months–to save them from Satan. Despite a long and documented history of schizophrenia and postpartum depression, in 2002, Yates was found sane and guilty in the first trial. A different jury just recently found Yates not guilty by reason of insanity. The verdict, reached after 13 hours of deliberation over three days– means Yates will be committed to a state mental facility in Texas until she is deemed to be no longer a threat.

Russell Yates, her former husband, said the prosecution failed to understand "that Andrea was ordinarily a loving mother who fell to this disease and did an unthinkable act." He claimed, "We took her to a psychiatrist and the psychiatrist failed us," he said.

Notwithstanding Harris County Assistant District Attorney Joe Owmby told reporters he was disappointed by the verdict. "Yates was not insane when she killed her children," he said. "She knew it was a sin, knew it was legally wrong and knew society would disapprove of her actions." Still, he said, he would not recommend that the district attorney bring further charges related to the drownings. "The charges we filed were intended to conclude this case one way or another." Owmby said the heavy media coverage, including a series of editorial opinions in the local paper, "must have had an effect, in a general way, on the jury." He said he was not accusing the jurors of not following instructions, "but they're human beings, and they have been living with this for the past five years."

In 30 days a hearing will be held to determine whether Yates represents a danger to herself or others and whether she will comply with a treatment plan. Every year thereafter, a hearing before a judge or a jury will be held to decide whether she should be released into the community.

The past five years have witnessed several murder defendants who killed their children believing they were acting on orders from a higher authority. In McKinney, Texas, Dena Schlosser was tried for a second time and found not guilty by reason of insanity (after a first jury deadlocked) in the killing of her 10-month-old daughter, Maggie, on orders from God. In Lamar, Colorado, Rebekah Amaya was tried after telling police she killed her two kids upon orders from a spider. She was found insane. In Tyler, Texas, Deanna Laney was found insane after she crushed the skulls of her three children; she believed she was given instructions, like Abraham, from God.

San Francisco has the trial of Lashaun Harris, who is charged with the murder of her three children. She is accused of throwing them over Pier 7 into the San Francisco Bay. Two of the bodies were never recovered. Harris has pleaded not guilty. She was diagnosed as a paranoid schizophrenic with delusional thought disorder, her attorney Caffese said, and was hospitalized once because she said God was telling her to jump out a window.

Debbie Mesloh, a spokeswoman for San Francisco District Attorney Kamala Harris, said it was up to the defense to present prosecutors with a psychiatric evaluation proving that Lashuan Harris' actions were not "willful, deliberate and premeditated," the standard for first-degree murder. "Until we are presented evidence on her mental state that she could not control herself or something else was driving her, the evidence remains the same," Mesloh said. Harris will most likely face a hearing to determine if she is mentally competent to stand trial, and psychiatrists will eventually attempt to determine whether she was insane at the time of the killings.

California is one of about 20 states that uses the strictest legal standard for assessing a plea of not guilty by reason of insanity. Under the rule, criminal defendants must show not only evidence of mental illness, but that they were incapable of determining right from wrong.

State courts remain divided on this issue and there is a lack of consistency with definitions. Currently, four states–Idaho, Kansas, Montana and Utah–have abolished the defense of insanity altogether. Many states, such as Arizona, allow insanity to be used as defense only when defendants could not understand that their conduct was wrong.

If you are moving in the direction of using mental culpability in a case, you will probably come up against the term *diminished capacity.* This is a partial defense related to insanity. What it boils down to, if used, is it can reduce the criminal responsibility of defendants whose acts are the result of mental illness falling short of insanity. In the 1980s, diminished capacity played a pivotal role in an important California trial when a jury accepted a diminished capacity defense and convicted Dan White of manslaughter for killing San Francisco Mayor George Moscone and Harvey Milk, an openly gay county supervisor. White brought to the fore the so-called "Twinkie defense." His claim was that eating food high in sugar had rendered him temporarily unable to control his actions. The public was so incensed after the verdict, that the California legislature outlawed the diminished capacity defense;[4] many other states have done likewise.

## I Had One Too Many and . . .

The voluntary ingestion of drugs or alcohol does not provide a defense to a criminal charge, but it can serve as a partial defense, that is, if a defendant's intoxication produced mental impairment, enough to be unable to form premeditated intent, then he or she might be convicted of a lesser crime.

**Other Notes**—The insanity defense does not sit well with many people who suggest that a victim who is killed by an insane person is just as dead as someone who is killed by a sane person. Also, many citizens are doubtful of the competence of the psychiatrists and judges who pronounce mental disease and are more uncomfortable still with its connection—or disconnection—between a mental disease and the commission of a crime. Is this an area that is exploited because of its controversy?

4. Penal Code (Calif.) Sec/ 28-b.

But, like insanity, this defense will need to be validated by either medical or psychiatric testimony or both.

A rather interesting case about this concept is found in *Montana v. Egelhoff*[5] In July 1992, Egelhoff was camping in the Yaak region of northwestern Montana in order to pick mushrooms. Egelhoff made friends with two others, Roberta Pavola and John Christenson, who were doing likewise. On Sunday, July 12, the three sold the mushrooms they had collected and spent the rest of the day and evening drinking, in bars and at a private party in Troy, Montana. Some time after 9:00 P.M. they left the party and got into Christenson's 1974 Ford Galaxy station wagon. Egelhoff was seen buying beer at 9:20 P.M. at the IGA grocery store, and the drinking binge continued, because Egelhoff recalled, "sitting on a hill or a bank and passing a bottle of Black Velvet back and forth" with Christenson.

Officers from the Lincoln County, Montana, sheriff's department were called about midnight that night in response to reports about a possible drunk driver. They discovered Christenson's station wagon stuck in a ditch along U.S. Highway 2. In the front seat were Pavola and Christenson, each dead from a single gunshot to the head. In the rear of the car lay Egelhoff, alive and yelling obscenities. His blood alcohol content measured .36 percent over one hour later. Near the brake pedal on the floor of the car, was Egelhoff's .38-caliber handgun, with four loaded rounds and two empty casings; Egelhoff had gunshot residue on his hands.

The defendant was charged with two counts of deliberate homicide, a crime defined by Montana law as "purposely" or "knowingly" causing the death of another human being. The defendant's defense tactic

at trial was that an unidentified fourth person must have committed the murders because he claimed his own intoxication had rendered him physically incapable of committing the murders, or even recalling the events of the night of July 12. Although he was able to present this scenario, the jury was instructed to ignore the defendant's intoxicated condition in determining the existence of a mental state, an element of the offense. The jury decided Egelhoff was guilty and sentenced him to 84 years imprisonment.

Apparently, the Supreme Court of Montana reversed his sentence on appeal when they agreed that respondent "had a due process right to present and have considered by the jury all relevant evidence to rebut the State's evidence on all elements of the offense charged. . . ." In their opinion, the Montana justices believed it was an issue whether the respondent acted knowingly and purposely.

The cornerstone of the case review when it reached the Supreme Court was the due process clause guaranteeing a defendant the right to present all relevant evidence. Egelhoff's attorney claimed that the instruction to the jury, stating that "a person who is in an intoxicated condition is criminally responsible for his conduct" and is not a defense is unconstitutional because it has the effect of negating the requirement that the State prove a mental state when proving deliberate homicide. She also argued that it shifts the burden of proof on the element of mental state from the prosecution to the defendant. And, in opinion, the Supreme Court judges did not disagree with that essential, categorical rule. But, they said, "The accused *does not* have an unfettered right to offer [evidence] this is incompetent,

---

5. Montana v. Egelhoff, (518 U.S. 375.Ct. 1996).

privileged, or otherwise inadmissible under standard rules of evidence . . . that a defendant's voluntary intoxication provided neither an 'excuse' nor a 'justification' for his crimes. . . ." The gist of the matter at hand though, was that the jury had instructions that affected the defendant's due process. The case is reversed and remanded for a new trial.

With involuntary intoxication, the scenario is much different: perhaps as a result of the offender consuming drugs, alcohol, or a prescription medicine through no fault of his own and, then, finding he cannot control his behavior, he may be allowed to go free. Of course, the judge and jury must agree and the weight of the evidence is on the defendant's shoulders.

Since the rules under intoxication can vary widely between states–and change

Figure 3. Deputy Daniell readies the Breathalyzer for a test at the Garland County Sheriff's Department and Jail, Hot Springs, AR.

quickly besides–be sure to check your current individual state statutes before using this as a defense.

## I Did It in a Dream

Under the umbrella of the insanity defense, automatism is a stretch for most people to accept, and for that reason, it is used infrequently. It requires the jury to believe that an unlawful act is committed because of an involuntary condition like somnambulism, that is, sleepwalking. A defendant in Butler, Pennsylvania, contended in November 1994, that his condition, a sleep apnea disorder, depleted his oxygen supply so much it caused him to shoot his wife. The jury saw otherwise and convicted him of murder.

In one Wyoming case, the court gave a good reason for separating automatism from the insanity plea and its consequences. The outcome, they said, is that generally, no follow-up such as institutionalization is needed with sleepwalking, and that is where the road should part from whose who are legally insane. Perhaps they had not met the man from Butler, Pennsylvania.

## I Did It Because He Made Me

*Duress* is another one of those borderline, better check-your-local-statutes defenses. Also referred to as *coercion* or *compulsion*, it is recognized today, although used most frequently by defendants who have committed robberies and thefts, or by prisoners who have escaped from custody. Intertwined with duress is also a notion called "the common-law presumption" which means that if a wife committed a felony other than murder or treason in her husband's presence, she did so because of his coercion. That rendering has been abolished in most jurisdictions, but, because all things about the law are dynam-

---

**FYI**—While we are on the subject of involuntary intoxication, here is a summary of a House of Representatives Bill H.R.2130[6] about the "Date Rape Drug" that recently became law:

Sponsor: *Rep Upton, Fred* (introduced 6/10/1999)

Related Bills: *H.R.3457, S.1561*

Latest Major Action: 2/18/2000 Became Public Law No: 106-172.

Title: An act to amend the Controlled Substances Act to direct the emergency scheduling of gamma hydroxybutyric acid, to provide for a national awareness campaign, and for other purposes. Amends the Controlled Substances Act (CSA) and the Controlled Substances Import and Export Act to provide additional penalties relating to GHB. Adds gamma butyrolactone (GBL) as an additional list I chemical.

2/18/2000:

Became Public Law No: 106-172.

---

ic, other new affirmative defenses are emerging, some of which have taken root in certain states, for example, the battered woman's defense. In 1992, a California appellate court agreed to a new development in the law of duress: battered woman syndrome. The battered woman syndrome was allowed as a defense in support of a woman who committed robbery offenses under the fear that the man she lived with would kill her if she didn't comply.

In another case, *People v. Merhige*,[7] a cab driver used the duress defense rather effectively when he claimed a gun was held to his head while he was ordered to transport his passengers to a bank, despite knowing they would commit a robbery. The Michigan Supreme Court believed the cabby when he told them he feared for his life had he not cooperated, and they reversed his conviction.

## I Did It Because I Could

Generally, we are a forgiving lot. Despite our nature, historically the courts have said

that a victim may not excuse a criminal act and, therefore, consent is not an excuse or a defense. There are exceptions though, such as with larceny, consent is a defense because lack of consent is an element of the offense. And it may also be true in rape situations, but only where competent adults freely consent to sexual relations. We also give consent to physicians before going under the knife, and to sports teams' owners when we agree to accept "contact" in contact sports.

## I Did It But Didn't Like It

Different from duress, where the crime has as its source the actions of others, the defense of *necessity* is defined as the choice between the lesser of two evils. To explain, a man with a suspended driver's license, no telephone, and the absence of a neighbor, drove to a telephone booth in order to call a relative to get someone to take his pregnant wife to the hospital. As timing would have it, he was stopped for a broken tail light, and then arrested for driving without a license. The Supreme Court of South Carolina[8] ruled

---

6. H.R. 2130, became Public Law No. 106-172.

7. *People v. Merhige*, 180 N.W. 419 (Mich. 1920).

8. *State v. Cole*, 403 S.E.2d 117 (S.C. 1991).

---

**Caution**—Because of its vagueness, duress will crop up again and again. Kansas has allowed a person to plead duress as a defense to crimes—other than murder—where the threat is against one's spouse, parent, child, brother, or sister.[9]

---

in a 3-2 decision that, under the circumstances, the defendant could use the defense of necessity. (We're sure his wife appreciates that.)

Likewise, Florida gave the necessity defense to a couple who had contracted AIDS and claimed they used the possession and cultivation of marijuana to help them get through their disease.

On another front, in *Commonwealth v. Berrigan*, the antinuclear activists were sanctioned, even though their plea of necessity got them all the way to the appellate court. The necessity defense did not serve their cause though, after the Pennsylvania Supreme Court heard of their escapade with entering a Pennsylvania factory, damaging nuclear bomb components, and pouring blood on the premises. In fact, other activist activities have not done well and the Alaska Supreme Court re-outlined the three steps required for their citizens who want to claim necessity defense: (1) The act charged must have been done to prevent a significant evil; (2) There must have been no adequate alternative; and, (3) The harm caused must not have been disproportionate to the harm avoided.[10]

## I Did It But I Didn't Know It Was Wrong

The Model Penal Code generally lumps the mistake or ignorance of "fact" and "law" in a single provision, but for our purposes of illustration, and because the judicial discussions have a tendency to treat them as separate distinctions when they make rulings, we will take them individually.

You may, in your studies, come across the principle "ignorance of the law is no excuse." The demands of society are such that just because a person claims not to know he or she had committed a criminal act, it does not excuse the crime. But, again, there are exceptions called the *mistake of law*. A defendant's honest, but mistaken view of the law is sometimes considered a defense. One example is where such a mistake negates the specific-intent element of a crime. For example, a person who trusts in the validity of his divorce, and who mistakenly takes that situation on faith as being legal–a "done deed"– may not be guilty of bigamy when he marries again.

Certain state's codes also have *exceptions to the general rule* that a person's ignorance of the law does not excuse unlawful conduct. The Illinois Criminal Code sets forth four examples where a person's "reasonable belief" that certain conduct does not constitute a criminal offense can be used as a defense. The term *reasonable* is the optimum word here, but, simplified, these are when: The offense is defined by an administrative regulation which is not known to the offender (such as fishing without a license pending legislation); OR, If he relies on a law that is later determined to be invalid; OR, If he sets forth into an activity which is later overruled by an appellate court; OR, If he acts in the

---

9. Kan. Stat. Ann § 21-3209.
10. *Cleveland v. Municipality of Anchorage*, 631 P.2d 1073, 1078 (Alaska 1981).

belief that an official interpretation of a statute or regulation made by a public officer or agency and one who is legally authorized to interpret such things, is law.

## I Did It But I Mistakenly Thought It Was Alright

An often talked about *mistake of fact* is a case that occurred in Mississippi in the fall. A group of hunters were charged with the murder of two fellow hunters during the deer hunting season. A deer camp had a Halloween party and two of the hunters invited were extremely intoxicated. Thinking it would be good fun, they donned a costume where one put a deer head in front of them and the other put a blanket over their backs and left for the party. Within five minutes they got shot and received 23 bullet wounds. All of the men who discharged weapons were charged with murder. The defense alleged their clients mistakenly thought they were shooting at a deer. The jury agreed this was a "reasonable" mistake of fact, clearing them of the criminal responsibility for homicide.

## I Did It in Self-Defense

Using the defense of self-defense sometimes breaks down to provocation and begs the question, "Who started it?" Although, here, too, there is wiggle room; because a person who claims self-defense can strike someone before they are hit if, in fact, a reasonable person could come to the conclusion that physical harm was in the offing and the defendant therefore, used force to "prevent" an attack. Meaning, people do not have to wait until they are actually struck to act in self-defense. And some of the charges that can be vacated vary from battery and assault, to assault with a deadly weapon, manslaughter, and even first- or second-

degree murder. This defense, then, is the linchpin of many cases where the "woman is in jeopardy."

Since self-defense is such an important feature in the denouement of many confrontation cases–we will look at the specific elements of self-defense. The first requirement is that the defendant must believe that force was necessary for his or her own protection. This belief must also be qualified as a reasonable belief, such that a reasonable person in the same or similar situation would have formed the same strategy; and, in some cases, even if the belief is wrong, the defense may still hold. For example, one recently famous case brought forth in 1993 cites the behavior of defendant Rodney Peairs. Peairs, age 31, a meat market manager, was charged with the manslaughter of an exchange student from Japan, Yoshi Hattori. In October 1992, Hattori, dressed as a character from *Saturday Night Fever*, and along with his American host brother, got lost while looking for a Halloween party. When Hattori and his "brother" sought their bearings and knocked on the wrong door, they were met by a panicked man who shouted "Freeze!" Hattori's English was sketchy at best, and he apparently did not understand, moved forward, and was shot once in the chest. The Japanese press descended on the town of Baton Rouge, Louisiana, in order to cover the court case's every turn. In trial, Peairs claimed the boys had made a commotion that had scared his wife. As a consequence, he claimed he grabbed his .44-caliber Magnum with the intent of defending his family. Peairs later apologized for the shooting saying he didn't have time to think. A Louisiana jury wound up acquitting Peairs and, within the parameters of the law, ruled his fear reasonable and his self-defense lawful.

One other requirement as established by some states are the elements of retreat and deadly force. Most courts reject a common-law doctrine which requires a person to retreat to the greatest extent possible before meeting force with force. While the Oklahoma law on this principle is clear: "There is no duty to retreat if one is threatened with bodily harm"[11]–the Tennessee Supreme Court has said that a person who can safely retreat must do so before using deadly force.[12] And, again, the exception here is that most courts that follow the retreat rule also have taken on the standard that a person does not have to retreat in his or her own home.

This question of the amount of force to be used must be addressed too, as there are different schools of thought. How much force is reasonable depends on the circumstances of each situation, particularly the amount of force a supposed victim is using against the defendant. There are two tests that usually support the issue. The first, a traditional standard, is the *subjective standard of reasonableness*. This requires that the jury place itself "in the defendant's own shoes."

Another frame of mind embraces the *objective test*, whereupon the jury is expected to place itself in the shoes of a hypothetical "reasonable and prudent person." In general though, the whole concept has been tweaked somewhat, and what is generally known now as "climbing into the shoes of the victim," has made the subjective argument the more popular standard as a result of a majority of cases where women have had to use deadly force against the assaultive or homicidal offenses of men, in order to protect their own lives.

Following the battered woman syndrome of self-defense, there is a rationale called the battered child syndrome, which is the defense of a child accused of assaulting or

killing a parent. In 1993, when California charged Erik and Lyle Menendez, ages 18 and 21 respectively, with the brutal murder of their parents, many prosecutors felt their claim amounted to an "abuse excuse" and that it was undermining the law of self-defense. Should the brothers have been allowed this "imperfect self-defense," the punishment would have been reduced to manslaughter. Despite the highly publicized perceptions held by the state, the first two trials ended with the jurors locked into mistrial because they could not agreed on a verdict. However, in March 1996, the Menendez brothers were convicted and sentenced to life in prison without the possibility of parole.

## I Did It Because I Was Defending My Home

Sometimes this will be called the *defense of habitation*. The historical view on the security of a person's dwelling is demonstrated best by Sir Edward Coke, who said in his *Commentaries*: "A man's home is his castle–for where shall a man be safe if it not be in his house?" In fact, in *The Third Part of the Institutes of the Laws of England* (1628) it says, "et domus sua cuique est tutissimum refugium" meaning, "and each man's home is his safest refuge." In a more recent case adjudicated by the Illinois Supreme Court, *People v. Eatman*, the Eatman court was of the opinion that "he may use all of the force apparently necessary to repel any invasion of his home."[13] This principle is referred to as the castle doctrine. Since then, the use of deadly force to protect one's home has undergone some revision in that, the deadly part is justifiable only in such situations where the occupant reasonably believes that

---

11. *Neal v. State*, 597 P.2d 334, 337 (Okl. Crim. App. 1979).
12. *State v. Kennamore*, 604 S.W.2d 856, 860 (Tenn. 1980).
13. *People v. Eatman*, 91 N.E. 2d at 390 (Ill. 1950).

---

FYI—Using self-defense expands the scope of admissible evidence, evidence that might not normally be there in the absence of the defense. For instance, witnesses testifying on what would be termed "rumors" is ordinarily not allowed. But a self-defense claim can lead to any information that might point to the defendant believing his use of force was necessary. So, if the victim were rumored to have been violent, for example, the defendant can verbalize that belief as part of his or her testimony.

---

death or bodily injury will be imminent to himself or to the other occupants of the house, or if he believes the assailant intends to commit a felony.

## I Did It Because I Was Defending My Property

Society places a pretty high premium on the preservation of human life, more than on the protection of property. For that reason, the right to use force to defend one's property will not allow the same exceptions as if you were protecting your home. The use of deadly force in this instance must be measured against the amount of force encountered. So, for our purposes here, using only nondeadly force to protect real property, personal property, and possessions, is acceptable against an unlawful interference. Now even this usage carries a stipulation: A prior request to desist from interfering with the property must be issued. Of course, for the layperson, if someone is breaking into his or her car and the warning to stop is either dangerous, useless, or not viable, common sense says "Let it go." It's just a thing and you are you. More respect is afforded the person who chooses to not overreact.

## Deadly Self-Defense

Florida was the first state to allow citizens to use deadly self-defense against muggers, carjackers and other attackers. South Dakota came on board next with a similar law and ten other states are have passed a version of the law. Previously, self-defense meant that the person victimized felt their life was in danger of serious harm or death, and that the level of response needed to match the threat, not exceed it; also attached was the premise that the person about to take defensive steps had a *duty to retreat* whenever possible, and to warn the perpetrator if it would seem to do any good. Many of the laws specify that people can use deadly force if they believe they are in danger in any place they have a legal right to be, such as a church, a bar, a parking lot, and so forth. In other words, deadly force was reserved as a last resort.

Supporters of deadly self-defense have named the new defense measures "stand your ground" laws, but critics say it is a "shoot first" policy. Oklahoma state Representative Kevin Calvey, who introduced the bill at the request of his local National Rifle Association chapter, said, "It's going to give crooks second thoughts about carjackings and things like that. They're going to get a face full of lead," Calvey said. The House agreed 83–4, the Senate 39–5.

Police Chief Nathanial H. Sawyer Jr. of New Hampton, New Hampshire, said the legislation addressed a problem that does not exist. In 26 years in law enforcement, he claims he has never seen anyone wrongfully charged with a crime for self-defense. "I think it increases the chance for violence,"

> **Caution**—In the opinion of many community and minority groups, police killing of civilians is extreme and unjust. The trend is to limit the use of deadly force to situations involving self-defense, defense of others, and apprehending only those engaged in felony conduct or potentially violent crimes. In certain states, the statute and departmental policy allow officers discretion that goes beyond the mandate of self-defense. Know your jurisdiction policies! Financial liability may result, as well as sanctions against the officer.

Sawyer said. Others feel it could give defense attorneys a potential avenue to seek acquittal for crimes, that criminals will benefit much more than any innocent victim. Critics also say that the NRA is overstating its success. Only six of those states expanded self-defense into public places, said Zach Ragbourn, a spokesman at the Brady Campaign to Prevent Gun Violence. There is already a presumption in law that a person does not have to retreat in his home or car, he said.

Just recently in Arizona, the state appellate court delayed the start of jury deliberations in the trial of a retired schoolteacher charged with second-degree murder for shooting a man on a hiking trail in May, 2004. The court is deciding whether this new law applies to his claim of self-defense.

## I Did It To Defend Another

The defense of defending another follows the same dictum as protecting oneself and many a court has noted that "What one may do for himself, he may do for another."[14] So, basically, irrespective of relationship, there could always be someone out there who may be available to protect a third person. Just remember: it must be a reasonable amount of force, and then, if it turns deadly, he or she must be in his or her own home in order to truly justify a killing, and it must be nec-

essary, not retaliatory.

## I Did It Because I Didn't Want To Be Arrested

When common law was knee-high to a grasshopper, a person had a right to use any force necessary, short of killing, towards resisting an unlawful arrest. This concept was largely the result of unfair English practices such as arrest without bail, arraignments assured "when hell freezes over," and terrible conditions in jail. In some states it is still allowed. Over time though, certain courts have become aware that resistance often begets violence and, the outrage has a tendency to escalate relative to the amount of resisting performed. This is an obscure concept so check your individual state statute for the ruling.

Now the right of a private person to use force to effect an arrest is given less credence than that of a police officer, who can do it on reasonable grounds. A "citizen's arrest" and the use of force must be held together by the fact that the offender was committing a felony. And, still, the courts say a private individual acts at his or her own peril when using deadly force. In other words, the action has to be the result of a good, tough, felonious situation in order to rank as a justifiable defense in a court of law.

---

14. *State v. Grier*, 609 S.W. 2d 201, 203 (Mo. App. 1980).

We can take this one step further to when a police officer requires the assistance of a private individual to effect an arrest. Under these circumstances, the civilian has the same privileges as does the officer. This is reasonable because it is against the law to resist helping an officer make an arrest when asked. And the suspect's innocence (oops, made a mistake!) will not negate the defense. Model Penal Code is somewhat trickier with who-gets-what-power, in that a private person effecting an arrest and using deadly force, must believe they are assisting a police officer.[15]

## I'm Not Telling If I Did It or Not

Two years after signing the Constitution, James Madison—who would later become president—came forth with twelve more constitutional amendments. Congress approved ten of them and these became the Bill of Rights. The significance of the Bill of Rights is that it restricts governments, rather than individuals and private groups. The Fifth Amendment has to do with constitutional immunity, the concept that a person cannot be compelled to say anything that might be self-incriminating. The states also abide by this ruling as a result of the Fourteenth Amendment (which incorporates federal laws for the states) but even some states have written similar protections in their own constitutions. This self-incrimination clause means that a person does not have to say anything in a court of law which may put him into trouble such as might be unlawful in another proceeding whether it is a civil, criminal, in a formal or informal proceeding, now or in the future. And the federal version of this guarantee applies only to natural persons (read this as a "native born" person) and not corporations.

So when a witness invokes the Fifth Amendment—"I refuse to answer on the grounds that it may incriminate me"—the court needs some course of action in order to compel that person to speak. This is achieved by extending immunity, which is a grant of amnesty, or we could say "exemption," from prosecution through the use of compelled testimony. This process is called giving a witness *use immunity* and is sometimes referred to as *derivative immunity* as well. Use immunity though, only bars the use of the witness's testimony against him or her in a subsequent prosecution. Federal grand juries are authorized to grant use immunity.[16]

Another type of immunity in some states is called *transactional immunity*. This is a broader protection than use immunity in that it protects a witness from prosecution for any activity mentioned in the witness's testimony.

Then there is *contractual immunity*. The intent with this umbrella is to prompt a suspect to testify against someone else, thereby enabling the prosecution to win a conviction not otherwise available because of constitutional protection against self-incrimination. This type of immunity is rarely given if other available evidence will result in a conviction. Only the United States Attorney, with approval of the Attorney General or certain authorized assistants, is authorized to grant immunity in federal courts. At the state level, such authoritative power is generally approved by the chief prosecuting officer, that is, the district or state's attorney.

Under international law, there are those who enjoy *diplomatic immunity* as part and

---

15. Model Penal Code, Section 3.07 (2)(b)(ii).
16. 18 U.S.C.A. § 6002.

> **FYI**—The interesting part of immunity is that it allows our government a way to get around the Fifth Amendment. But there is a price to pay, because by granting immunity, the compelled witness can confess to the TWA bombing and there is nothing that can be done about it. So, what if the truth is actually worse than the deal?

parcel of their political status. A person who serves as part of a diplomatic mission, as well as members of the diplomatic staff and household, is immune from arrest and prosecution. The expectation, of course, is that American diplomats and their dependents and staff members will enjoy like immunity in foreign nations. This type of immunity is most often found in areas around an embassy or areas of formal foreign function.

## You Can't Try Me Twice For The Same Offense

The double jeopardy clause is one of the great conundrums of legal principles. Basically, it means that if the accused has gone through a trial, been convicted or acquitted, he or she cannot be retried by the same jurisdiction for the same crime. The subject of double jeopardy is very complex and we will deal with it extensively in Chapter 8–Rights of the Accused.

## You Won't Know If I Did It or Not Because Time Ran Out

All crimes, except murder, have a statute of limitations. By law, that means there is a time limit on the prosecution of a crime. There is no historical basis for this time limit, but nevertheless, both federal government and almost all the states have laws that define certain time limits. There are two reasons for this time limit enactment: (1) It is believed a

person should not have to live under the onus of prosecution for a long period of time; (2) proof is usually absent after a prolonged duration, or at the least, not credible anymore. Of course, there is no time limit on murder or other equally serious offenses.

According to the parameters of most statutes, the period for prosecution begins when a crime is committed, rather than when it is discovered. And the ending of the period is triggered by different actions such as, when an arrest warrant is issued, an indictment is returned, or an information is filed. A period can also be interrupted, an effect called *tolling*, and that begins when a perpetrator is a fugitive or is concealed from authorities.

Generally, for federal statutes there is a five-year limitation for prosecution on non-capital crimes. The states have varying times, although, for a basic representation, Ohio seems to have a rudimentary provision that says: a felony other than aggravated murder or murder is six years; a misdemeanor other than a minor misdemeanor is two years; and a minor misdemeanor holds for six months.[17]

Some jurisdictions do not agree on whether a statute of limitations in a criminal action is an *affirmative defense*. For it to be an affirmative defense, it must be pled as such; if not, it is considered waived. (Any action either ignored or unused is relinquished.) Other states will differ though, in that the minute the prosecution files an indictment

---

17. Page's Ohio Rev. Code Ann. § 2901.13 (A).

beyond the designated period allowed by the statute of limitations, the prosecution is barred from proceeding. Can we say timing is everything?

## I Did It Because The Cops Talked Me Into It

Entrapment is a double-edged sword for the accused. Truth is, if the government induces someone into committing a crime, they cannot punish that person for doing it. However, if the defendant is a doer and wants to plead entrapment as a defense, he or she is left open for more trouble, because now the prosecution gets to introduce evidence that shows the defendant was "predisposed" to commit the crime anyway. Get it?

I know you do, and your offenders will have a hard time proving they did not want to do the deed. Defendants who claim they were entrapped into committing illegal acts normally have the burden of convincing a judge or jury—by a preponderance of the evidence—that they were induced to do the crime and not just predisposed to doing it. This defense is most often heard of in connection with prostitution or narcotics sting operations.

There are two tests (or schools of thought) that magistrates use to determine the focus of the criminal intent. The first is called the *subjective test of entrapment*. This presupposes that the defendant did the crime but what is in question, is whether the criminal intent originated because of predisposition to do it, or whether the defendant was induced into action by the police. This means that in order to sustain this as a defense, the defendant would need to show the methods of persuasion police actually used to make a law-abiding person commit a crime.

The *objective test of entrapment* means the court would simply determine whether police methods were so improper that they likely induced or ensnared the person into committing a crime, and that position would be decided by a judge, not a jury.

Using entrapment is a rather hackneyed approach to certain defenses, and making the government a conspirator is nothing new—government officials are often held out as conspiring or manipulative.

## I'm Being Picked On, Man

*Selective prosecution,* also referred to as *discriminatory enforcement of statute* is a concept involving directed police or prosecution unfairness. Although many defendants claim they were unjustly charged with crimes because they are black, Catholic, or because the ". . . police don't like me." This is not a constitutional violation and rather imperceptible or abstract in nature. Because of these characteristics, it is difficult to prove that one was singled out for prejudice. In order to prevail with this defense, the defendant must show that other like persons have also been persecuted and that the wielding of power is aimed at people who are different either by race, religion, gender, or because their free speech has offended those in command.

In May 1996, a decision based on this notion was decided in the Supreme Court, *United States v. Armstrong.*[18] The defendant, Christopher Lee Armstrong, was indicted for crack cocaine and other federal charges. Armstrong filed a pretrial motion for discovery or dismissal, claiming that he and his friends were selected for prosecution because they are black. The Court held that the defendants failed to produce any credible evidence that similarly situated defen-

---

18. *United States v. Armstrong,* 517 U.S. 456, 116 S.Ct. 1480, 134 L.Ed.2d 687 (1996).

dants of other races could have been prosecuted, but were not.

The prosecution showed that their decision to prosecute was because, "there was over 100 grams of cocaine base involved, twice the threshold necessary for a ten year mandatory minimum sentence; there were multiple sales involving multiple defendants, thereby indicating a fairly substantial crack cocaine ring; . . . there were multiple federal firearms violations . . . including audio and videotapes of defendants . . . and several of the defendants had criminal histories including narcotics and firearms violations."

The Court agreed that a defendant did have a right to examine documents material to his defense, but it did not give him the right to work product in his own case. Also, the defendant would have had to eventually identify individuals who were not black, who could have been prosecuted for the same offense but were not. And finally, a newspaper article, which the defendant claimed supported his case, was thrown out because it was based on hearsay and other reported personal conclusions based on anecdotal evidence. So, although they had managed to get as far as the Supreme Court, the case was reversed and remanded; in other words, it didn't work.

## NONTRADITIONAL DEFENSES

The battered woman syndrome served as an acquittal for many women before it was sanctioned as a viable form of self-defense. When a new defense leads to an acquittal, the appellate courts do not have a chance to intervene nor do they have the opportunity to evaluate the decision because an acquittal is the end of the process. In the list below are some of the nontraditional defenses that have been tried unsuccessfully.

## Religious Beliefs and Practices

Some of the issues here have been about laws prohibiting religious rites that are dangerous; parents' rights to raise their children according to religious beliefs; failure to supply medical care to children; and certain marriage statutes.

## Victim's Negligence

Because the victim was negligent does not negate a crime and several defenses also contend wrongdoing on behalf of the victim; also a victim's forgiveness does not relieve someone of criminal wrongdoing.

## Compulsive Gambling

Gambling is out of the realm of defense unless it involves insanity, and pathological behavior does not allow someone to rob a bank.

## Post-Traumatic Stress Syndrome (PTSS)

Stresses involved with combat, or other symptoms such as blackouts, blocked memory, or outbursts commonly called "shell shock" can be introduced to help explain the defendant's state of mind, or difficulties adjusting to civilian life, and although they will not excuse a criminal act, they may help to lighten punishment.

## Premenstrual Syndrome (PMS)

Although the changes a woman undergoes during the days close to the onset of menstruation do cause physiological changes including depression, hormone imbalance, and irritability, they are not a defense to criminal conduct. In Great Britain though,

PMS has been used as a basis to lighten punishment.

## Television Intoxication

Establishing insanity on the basis of psychiatric testimony with regard to a cycle called "involuntary subliminal television intoxication" is a difficult claim. The evidence must still meet the requirement of the M'Naghten rule.

## Pornographic Intoxication

There have been cases, along with academic debate over the effect of pornography on the psyche. So far it has not passed muster, an appellate court held that acting under "pornographic intoxication" does not mitigate the defendant's death sentence for rape and murder.

## "Junk Food" or "Sugar Defense"

While the jury may have been affected in the case of Dan White–a former city supervisor, who shot and killed the mayor of San Francisco and his aide–this has not set a precedence for using the gorging of junk foods as a defense.

## Other Defense Claims

There have been cases argued on behalf of a defendant's propensity for violence because of black rage, multiple personalities, the urban survival syndrome, and a chromosome XYY abnormality. Since breaking-edge medical research has indicated that a person's behavior is influenced greatly by his or her genes, will this assertion be the next possible plea for excuse? Another possible justification is a recent behavior called "wilding." This urban slang terminology has come about as the result of a pack of young men who ran amuck through Central Park stripping and groping at least four women. The attacks came at the end of a steamy weekend in New York in which six people were killed and fifty-nine others stabbed or shot. Will this phenomena be the latest in justification?

## REVIEW QUESTIONS AND ANSWERS

### *Key Words to Define*

- **Affirmative defense**–Five categories of how a defendant can present an excuse or justification.
- **ALI standard**–Name for the American Law Institution; defendant not responsible if at the time, as a result of mental disease, he lacks substantial capacity to appreciate wrongfulness; combines both cognitive and volitional capabilities.
- **Battered woman syndrome**–Commits crime for fear of being killed by spouse.
- **Burden of production of evidence**–Defendant has the burden of raising "proof" evidence; usually associated with insanity defense.
- **Duress**–Coercion, compulsion on victim
- **Durham test**–Not criminally responsible if the unlawful act was the product of mental disease.
- **Mistake of law**–A defendant's honest, but mistaken view of the law can be a defense.
- **Objective test**–Jury places itself in the shoes of a hypothetical "reasonable and prudent" person.
- **Preponderance of the evidence**–Burden of proving evidence by the greater weight of the evidence.

- **Presumption of innocence**–Defendant comes in clean, prosecution must prove guilt.
- **Proof beyond a reasonable doubt**– Prosecution's burden.
- **Statute of limitations**–A time limit on the prosecution of a crime.
- **Use immunity**–Bars witness from testifying against himself.

## Questions for Review and Discussion

1. *Question:* What is the most common and powerful defense argument? *Answer:* Presumption of innocence.

2. *Question:* Name two categories of affirmative defenses. *Answer:* Lack of capacity, Justification or excuse, Use of force, Constitution or legal right, Government conduct.

3. *Question:* Daniel M'Naghten killed who? *Answer:* Sir Robert Peel, founder of the British Police System, Bobbies named for him.

4. *Question:* Do all states have an insanity defense option? *Answer:* No.

5. *Question:* Explain mistake of law. *Answer:* A defendant's honest but mistaken view of the law. Ex.: if someone thinks they are legally divorced and remarry-he or she are not bigamists.

6. *Question:* Defending your home is also called: defense of _____. *Answer:* Habituation.

7. *Question:* What level of law accepts diplomatic immunity? *Answer:* International law, for example, diplomats in foreign lands.

8. *Question:* What is tolling? *Answer:* Statute time for a crime begins when the act is committed but tolling occurs when the fugitive is concealed from authorities; meaning a period of interruption.

9. *Question:* Why is it wise for the defendant to not speak on his own behalf? *Answer:* He cannot be questioned by the prosecution as a witness and the jury cannot use the fact of his not speaking (or defending himself) against him.

10. *Question:* Name two nontraditional defenses. *Answer:* Religious beliefs, compulsive gambling, Post-traumatic Stress Syndrome, Premenstrual Syndrome (PMS), TV intoxication, pornographic intoxication, junk food or sugar high.

## Essay Exploration

In your own words explain entrapment. As long as the student understands it is the government inducing a crime, the punishment is nullified. They should also mention defendant's burden of proof as a "preponderance of evidence."

## Extra Credit

Split the class into two teams. One team must choose the defendant's defense strategy, and the other side must counter their arguments. More advanced students are encouraged to use actual case histories for examination and reflection. They can use Findlaw for search engine specifics, or any other case illustration vehicle.

# PART TWO

# Criminal Procedure and Evidence

# Chapter 7

# ARREST, SEARCH, AND SEIZURE

A bill of rights is what the people are entitled
to against every government on earth.
–Thomas Jefferson, *letter to James Madison*

Some information came to light that a man named Rochin was believed to be selling narcotics. Based on this tip, three deputy sheriffs forced open the door of his room. They found him, partially dressed, sitting on the side of the bed, next to where his wife was lying.

"On a 'night stand' beside the bed the deputies spied two capsules. No sooner had the question, 'Whose stuff is this?' come out and Rochin seized the capsules and put them in his mouth." A scuffle ensued in the course of which the three officers "jumped upon him" and unsuccessfully attempted to extract the capsules from his mouth.

Rochin was then handcuffed and taken to a hospital. Under instructions from one of the officers, a doctor forced an emetic solution through a tube into Rochin's stomach against his will. This procedure is also called "stomach pumping" and the result induces vomiting. The maneuver worked on Rochin in the desired manner and in the vomited matter were found two capsules. The cap-sules contained morphine. Rochin was convicted of possessing morphine and sentenced to sixty days imprisonment. The chief evidence against him was the two capsules.

## . . . a doctor forced an emetic solution through a tube into Rochin's stomach . . .

When officers broke into Rochin's residence, they violated Rochin's right to privacy and his right to feel secure in his home. Police cannot direct a pumping of a person's stomach without violating his personal right of privacy. There are limits placed upon the conduct of police officers and prosecutors. In this particular case, the police were skipping required steps and violating procedure.

The issues presented in Rochin's case[1] are all about "due process," the constitutional guarantee of fairness in the administration of justice. These protections, and certain other rights, are granted under the Bill of Rights and are widely debated every day of our

---

1. *Rochin v. California*, 342 U.S. 165, 72 S.Ct. 205, 96 L.Ed. 183 (1952).

lives and in many situations such as that illustrated above with Mr. Rochin. The police who raided Mr. Rochin's home believed they were doing what was needed in order to catch this criminal. Amendments Four, Five, Six, and Eight in the Bill of Rights, and within the document of our Constitution, are directly aimed at rights individuals are supposed to receive when subject to a criminal investigation, trial, and sentence. The importance of the Bill of Rights is that it restricts governments, rather than individuals and private groups.

By the way, what was the outcome for Mr. Rochin? The Supreme Court, under the opinion of Judge Frankfurter, concluded that the police conduct against Mr. Rochin violated the Fourteenth Amendment due process. He said:

> *This is conduct that shocks the conscience. Illegally breaking into the privacy of the petitioner, the struggle to open his mouth and remove what was there, the forcible extraction of his stomach's contents–this course of proceeding by agents of government to obtain evidence is bound to offend even hardened sensibilities. They are methods too close to the rack and the screw to permit of constitutional differentiation.*

Justice Douglas wrote a separate, concurring opinion on this case, comparing elements of it to the Fifth Amendment rule of self-incrimination. He maintains that the privilege against self-incrimination applies to the states as well as the federal government and because of this privilege "words taken from [an accused's] lips, capsules taken from his stomach, blood taken from his veins are all inadmissible provided they are taken from him without consent. [This] is an unequivocal, definite and workable rule of evidence for state and federal courts."

Only the most confounding cases and fascinating real-life stories reach the Supreme Court. These are the kinds of cases where

reasonable men in all good conscience can choose to disagree. And appellate cases usually form the basis for an interesting conundrum.

## TROUBLING DICHOTOMY

It's true that we live in times of violent crime–although the incidence of violent crimes like homicide, rape, robbery, and assault have gone down in general–more than 80 percent of Americans will experience some sort of violent crime in their own lifetime. According to national polls taken in the last decade, the number one concern of Americans is the element of crime.

It's a given that we want to feel safe from crime and, as a consequence, we give great authority to police in order to handle difficult situations. If you asked most Americans if they would relinquish their Bill of Rights, you would receive a resounding "NO!" But what about our right to be left alone? What can be searched, and seized and when? This tug-of-war, between the desire for security versus the respect for rights, is an ongoing question because rights change, and rights change laws. And there are always political forces that seem to stress either favoring law and order or increasing individual rights. There are a lot of shades of gray between what we want and how it's gotten.

The Constitution sets forth the basic guidelines for the ever-changing balance between what rights the accused are guaranteed with the rights of society to feel protected. Almost half of the amendments in the Bill of Rights deal with personal rights and civil liberties. Similarly, one of the main principles of the justice system is that: It is better for a thousand guilty men to go free than one innocent man to be punished. Today, some law enforcement, government officials, and citizen action groups think that

FYI—Do not sell history short. People who are in the criminal justice system every day—lawyers, judges, and most law enforcement personnel—know the history of the law they have vowed to uphold. Criminal justice, and more specifically, those amendments pertaining to rights, are extremely fascinating because only the most puzzling cases and personal enigmas reach the Supreme Court level for adjudication.

rights have shifted dangerously to favor suspects. Our law system is based on the ideal of the presumption of innocence beyond reasonable doubt. But today, certain of these rights are in question and the pendulum seems to be swinging again.

Mary Broderick, who is with the National Legal Aid and Defense Association, says that most people believe that the justice system favors the criminal too much. "In fact," she says, "the rights of the accused are a symptom of a society myth–that most persons arrested for a crime are convicted." Broderick says that law enforcement officials and judges often send the message that conviction is more important than justice is. Society, in general, supports the idea that the same procedures ought to be followed for everyone, whether they are citizens of our country or not, anyone who is accused of a crime. And in connection with the Fourth Amendment, it protects all people within the United States: that includes adults, children, citizens, aliens both legal and illegal, persons on parole or probation, and corporations.

But we don't usually think twice about procedural rights and we almost never realize how important they are until the accusing finger is pointed at us. The dichotomy between a citizen's desire for security and society's longstanding desire to extend rights clash often, because inevitably those rights will enable some people who are guilty to escape punishment.

## HISTORICAL EMPHASIS

The Bill of Rights, as originally written, was about injustice concerning national government only–until the Fourteenth Amendment . . ." nor shall any State deprive any person of life, liberty, or property without due process of law; nor deny to any person within its jurisdiction the equal protection of the laws." Up until then, the individual states were not required to abide by those implied rights.

Each amendment was written to address an existing violation of the citizens' rights by the British Empire: to prevent abuses by the governing authorities. The Fifth Amendment, due process of law, is a direct descendant of the Magna Carta, which predates the Constitution by some 500 years.

The main rights of the accused are spelled out in the Fourth, Fifth, Sixth, and Eighth Amendments. In the Fourth Amendment, suspects are guaranteed rights against unreasonable search and seizure. This sprung up as a result of the abuse of "general warrants by the British Crown." The general warrants statute meant the British government could search anywhere, any time, and for any reason "as long as the King lives."

The Fifth Amendment works in sync with the Fourth in protecting a suspect's rights. It guarantees that the accused won't be made to confess, stipulates the right against self-incrimination, and set standards for the right to remain silent. This was an enormous gain

*Legal Ease*

from what was in operation previously!

In the Sixth Amendment, the right to be represented by counsel and the right to a trial by your own peers is paramount. It helped to guarantee that the poor would not be underrepresented and thereby made a victim of the courts.

The Eighth Amendment is all about the right against excessive bail and cruel and unusual punishment with respect to detainment and sentencing.

Lives have been lost over these constitutional rights, and lives have been given over to these constitutional rights. The judiciary and interested citizens will debate the rights of the accused for as long as they exist. Because of these passions you are entering a most engaging debate–where laws can affect a man or woman's life so completely, even to the point of death. We hope you will never have to bear witness to these rights or be on the receiving end.

## AMENDMENT IV

### Searches and Seizures

The right of the people to be secure in their persons, houses, papers, and effects, against unreasonable searches and seizures, shall not be violated, and no Warrants shall issue, but upon probable cause, supported by Oath or affirmation, and particularly describing the place to be searched, and the persons or things to be seized.

### Explanation

The word "warrant" in this context means *justification* and refers to a document issued by a judge or magistrate which must indicate the name, address, and possible offenses committed by that person. In addition, anyone requesting the warrant, such as a police officer, must be able to convince the judge or magistrate that an offense most likely has been committed by this person (this is the basis for "probable cause").

### *The Fourth Amendment's Basic Principles Are:*

- Constitutional arrest
- No unreasonable search and seizure
- No warrant will be granted without probable cause
- The warrant must describe the place to be searched and items to be seized, specifically

## CONSTITUTIONAL ARREST

It is the Fourth Amendment that provides the principles for a constitutional arrest. Placing a person under arrest establishes a seizure of the body, obviously because authorities are actually taking away the person's freedom to leave. Defense attorneys will admit there is a big difference as to how suspects are treated, what their rights are, and what is required of them depending on whether they are under "arrest" or not. Michael Saeger, author of the book *Defend Yourself Against Criminal Charges* (1997) says the easiest way for a person to know if he or she is being detained is to inquire: "Am I under arrest?" He suggests that, as much as a suspect would like to believe that he or she is not under arrest, until it is actually known there is no way to determine if he or she can come and go and no way to decide if he or she must abide by the instructions given.

### Probable Cause

Police will have specific details they must adhere to in order to meet their objective with a constitutional arrest. An arrest, with or without a warrant, needs to meet the requirement of probable cause. Probable cause, in layman's terms, means that the facts and circumstances the officer believes to be true at the time of arrest, must be based on reasonably trustworthy information. The area of probable cause is fuzzy, because the probable cause rationale must be more than a "suspicion"–but does not have to show proof beyond a reasonable doubt. Some of the criteria for probable cause include:

- suspicious conduct
- a repetitious pattern of conduct, such as "casing" the place
- demonstrated unfamiliarity with the surroundings
- if subject is carrying tools or having difficulty with a vehicle, etc.
- a remarkable activity at an inappropriate time of day
- activity in a high crime area
- a known criminal record or profile
- reaction to police officers
- failing an encounter or giving demonstrably false responses
- noncooperation with a request
- nervousness during an encounter
- collective knowledge
- information from an informant
- failure to have I.D. or identify oneself

## Reasonable Suspicion

The courts have struggled with the meaning of reasonable suspicion and there are many cases to back up this effort. The nature of reasonable suspicion is certainly related to probable cause and the analysis between the two has some similarities. Mainly, common sense is used to evaluate the factors of the case. The expertise of the law enforcement officer is given preference. The circumstances are taken in their totality, so they cannot be so quickly explained away. And the reasonableness of mistakes of fact are taken into consideration meaning, certainty is not required for either standard.

The difference between reasonable suspicion and probable cause is that reasonable suspicion as a standard is less demanding. Some courts define reasonable suspicion as a fair probability of criminal activity, or, in another way, it can be called *possible cause*.

## The Affidavit

The next step in the process is to secure a warrant. A warrant for arrest is valid only if it is based on a complaint or a document called an *affidavit* that sets forth certain facts showing both the commission of an offense and the accuser's responsibility attached to it. The information, or the "basis of knowledge," used to secure the warrant need not be trial-ready though, meaning, information can be obtained from an established confidential informant; it can come from a victim of a crime related to the search; it can be based on a statement from a witness to the crime; or information can come from another police officer. In other words, it can be hearsay that seems reliable!

## Confidential Informant

When police officers do not have personal knowledge of the facts, they rely on information from other parties. *Hearsay evidence* is an out-of-court statement offered for the truth of the matter asserted. Since probable cause may be based on hearsay, confidential or anonymous informant sources other than other police officers–often referred to as *snitches* in the vernacular–are an effective investigative tool. This provides a unique problem: An affidavit based on an informant's tip must meet a two-prong test, sometimes called the *Aguilar-Spinelli test.*

1. The affidavit must also establish the reliability of the informant by showing one of the following:

- "Prior use" and reliability of the informant, meaning the informant must have a

### GARLAND COUNTY CIRCUIT/CHANCERY COURT

<u>STATE OF ARKANSAS</u>                               <u>AFFIDAVIT</u>
     <u>VS</u>                                          <u>FOR</u>

_____       <u>SEARCH</u>
_____       <u>WARRANT</u>

**BEFORE** the Honorable _____, Judge of the Garland County _____ Court comes now the affiant, _____ _____ of the Garland County Sheriffs Office who deposes and says that he has reason to believe that on the person/property of _____ _____ located/described as _____ _____ now being concealed certain property, _____
_____
_____
_____

and that the facts tending to support this brief are as follows: The affiant _____
_____
_____
_____
_____
_____
_____

The affiant respectfully requests that Search Warrant be granted for the property and person listed and that permission be granted to execute it _____
_____

     **Affiant:  Investigator** _____
     **Garland County Sheriffs Office**

Sworn to and subscribed before me on this _____ day of _____ 199___.

_____
       Judge

Structure 1.

good track record with the police, having given reliable information on numerous occasions.

- A declaration against interest, meaning, the informant describes activity against his own penal interest. For example, if he is willing to say "I bought dope from her," which shows he is criminally liable too.
- Clear and precise details in the tip, indicating personal observation and knowledge of the location of the evidence.
- The informant has a membership in a reliable group such as the clergy, a civic group, students, etc.).

2. The affidavit must set forth sufficient underlying circumstances in order to permit a neutral and detached magistrate to understand how the informant reached the conclusion. This is known as the *basis of knowledge* and details items such as, who, what, where, when, and why.

## The Magistrate

The judge who issues the warrant must be neutral and detached from the law enforcement officers and the situation presented. The judge cannot enforce the search warrant; and likewise, cannot receive compensation when warrants are issued. The first thing that should pop into your mind: Is the judge neutral and detached?

Obtaining that warrant follows certain constitutional standards, too; a judge will only sign it if the probable cause is spelled out in writing. At least that's the way it should operate. Realistically, the potential for a problem always exists. A drawing of the warrant picture would look like this:

## BASIS OF KNOWLEDGE

The first thing that has to be included in an affidavit: who, what, when, where and why.

## AFFIDAVIT

An affidavit based on an informant's tip must set forth sufficient underlying circumstances in order to permit further investigation.

## JUDGE

"Probable cause" is required for a signature from a neutral and detached magistrate, who has to understand how the informant reached his or her conclusion.

## WARRANT

Describing the place to be searched; describing the things to be seized; oath or affirmation that the statements in the request are true.

## EVIDENCE

## TRIAL COURT

## SENTENCING

## JAIL/PRISON

## SEARCH WARRANT: DESCRIBING CHARACTERISTICS IN A SEARCH WARRANT

### Place

Even if there is probable cause to search a certain location, the warrant must describe the location with reasonable particularity, that is, it should have a street address, an apartment number, and for rural settings, a rural mailbox designation or requisite landmark.

## Things To Be Seized

In theft cases, warrants may contain detailed descriptions or specific brand names of property and goods. For documents evidence, records pertaining to fraud including tax forms and accounting books would suffice. And it has always been the case that instruments of crime, such as a gun used in a robbery, the fruits of a crime such as money or illegal narcotics where possession is prohibited by law may be picked up as well.

## Warrant Loopholes

Some jurisdictions allow magistrates to issue search warrants over the phone. The police officer will sign the magistrate's name to the duplicate original warrant and the magistrate signs the other duplicate original in his or her possession. On return of the officer's duplicate, the judge will sign it too, and file both with the court clerk. This is only applied to emergency situations where time is a critical factor.

## Executing a Warrant

First of all, the power to execute a warrant doesn't rest with just anyone. In most states, the person must have a "peace officer" stamp of approval or some similar classification. We can call them the "ppp"–publicly paid police. They could be with the local police, the deputy sheriff, or a member of another investigative agency, and they will usually wear special uniforms and will always have law enforcement identification.

## Timeliness of a Search Warrant

Time is an important factor for a warrant! The best reason for executing a timely warrant is that probable cause may disappear. If the information that is the basis for probable cause is stale, the warrant will not issue. For example, during ongoing criminal activity, say, a drug lab operation, a lapse of ten to thirty days is acceptable, if the police believe that evidence will still be in a particular place. Information older than that will be dismissed. A warrant is allowable if the probable cause is anticipatory, such as waiting for a shipment of stolen goods. And a search warrant can be issued for a future date as long as probable cause exists.

Ten days is about the most a jurisdiction allows for the execution of a search warrant. After a statutory time limit (or the time limit set by the judge) has passed, the warrant is dead; and evidence seized on a dead warrant can be suppressed in court. (See Structures 3–7.)

## Nighttime Searches

The time of day a search warrant can be executed is also a consideration. Slightly less than half the states restrict execution of searches to daylight hours absent special circumstances. Most jurisdictions go with 6 A.M. to 10 P.M. as daylight and anything after that needs a showing of qualifying factors.

Executing a search warrant in the absence of the occupant has been done, and the lower courts generally agree it passes, but judges also make it relevant to consider whether or not police made an attempt to locate the occupants. And, covert and surreptitious entries are constitutionally defective. The court holds that "the mere thought of strangers walking through and examining the center of our privacy interest, our home,

GARLAND COUNTY CIRCUIT/CHANCERY COURT

STATE OF ARKANSAS                                        SEARCH
        VS                                              WARRANT

TO ANY SHERIFF, CONSTABLE, OR POLICE OFFICER IN THE STATE OF ARKANSAS.
AFFIDAVIT HAVING BEEN MADE BEFORE ME BY _____
_____ THAT HE HAS REASON TO BELIEVE THAT ON THE PROPERTY
OF _____
_____ DESCRIBED AS _____
_____
_____ WHICH IS LOCATED _____
_____
_____ THERE IS NOW BEING CONCEALED
CERTAIN PROPERTY NAMELY _____
_____ WHICH ARE IN VIOLATION OF _____
_____
_____

I AM SATISFIED THAT THERE IS PROBABLE CAUSE TO BELIEVE THAT THE
PROPERTY SO DESCRIBED IS BEING CONCEALED ON THE PREMISES ABOVE AND
THAT THE FOREGOING GROUNDS FOR APPLICATION FOR ISSUANCE OF THE SEARCH
WARRANT EXIST.

YOU ARE HEREBY COMMANDED TO SEARCH FORTHWITH THE PLACE NAMED FOR THE
PROPERTY SPECIFIED, SERVING THIS WARRANT AND MAKING THE SEARCH DURING
THE   DAYTIME   NIGHT   AND IF THE PROPERTY BE FOUND THERE TO SEIZE
IT, LEAVING A COPY OF THIS WARRANT AND A RECEIPT FOR THE PROPERTY
TAKEN, AND PREPARE A WRITTEN INVENTORY OF THE PROPERTY SEIZED AND
RETURN THIS WARRANT AND BEING THE PROPERTY AS REQUIRED BY LAW.

THIS SEARCH WARRANT SHALL BE RETURNED TO THE _____ COURT
OF HOT SPRINGS, GARLAND COUNTY ON OR BEFORE THE HOUR OF _____
(AM) (PM)  ON THE DAY OF _____, 19 _____.

DATED THIS DAY OF _____, 19 _____.


                              _____
                                            Judge

Structure 2.

arouses our passion for freedom as does nothing else."

## Home Search Warrant

We all have an expectation of privacy within our own home, the most protected area, and the courts respect that. There is also an expectation of privacy for papers inside our briefcases, inside our homes. For this reason, a warrant is required for home searches and must meet certain criteria, specificity of interest being the main objective for a search. A search warrant can be used to search premises belonging to a person not suspected of a crime as long as there is "probable cause to believe that evidence of someone's guilt will be found." (The key is always "probable cause.")

## Knock and Announce Rule

The police must knock and announce their authority and purpose in order to search a house except in cases of true emergencies. They also have latitude if the situation would endanger the lives of the officers. Under federal law[2] an officer is required to knock and announce on arrival at the place to be searched. The purpose of this requirement is to reduce the potential for violence and protect the right to privacy of the occupants.

For entry, officers should wait a reasonable amount of time (which can be mere seconds) anticipating a response. There is also the rationale that, if after giving notice, they are refused admittance or must extricate themselves from danger, they may break into premises to execute a search warrant. The notice requirement is also excused if the officers believe the occupants already know they are there, or they hear the sound of "running feet," meaning that stating their authority and the purpose of the visit is a useless gesture.

## No-Knock Evidence

Police obtained a warrant authorizing a search for drugs and firearms at the home of Booker Hudson but failed to follow the Fourth Amendment "knock and announce" rule, which requires police officers to wait 20–30 seconds after knocking and announcing their presence before they enter the home. They discovered large quantities of drugs and cocaine rocks in Hudson's pocket. A loaded gun was found lodged between the cushion and the chair in which he was sitting.

The common-law principle that law enforcement officers must announce their presence and provide residents an opportunity to open the door is an ancient one. The trial judge ruled that the evidence found in the home could therefore not be used. The question presented to the Supreme Court[3] was: does the general rule excluding evidence obtained in violation of the Fourth Amendment apply to the "knock-and-announce" rule? *No.* In a 5–4 decision, the Court ruled that evidence seized at a home can be used at trial even if police failed to knock and announce their presence. The rule requiring improperly seized evidence to be suppressed does not apply in such instances when police have a valid search warrant.

The opinion by Justice Scalia reaffirmed the validity of both the knock-and-announce rule and the "exclusionary rule" for evidence

---

2. 18 U.S.C.A. § 3109.
3. *Hudson v. Michigan* (No. 04-1360) Argued January 9, 2006––Reargued May 18, 2006––Decided June 15, 2006.

```
                              RETURN


I RECEIVED THE ATTACHED SEARCH WARRANT _____,
   19_____, AND HAVE EXECUTED IT AS FOLLOWS;


   ON _____, 19_____, AT _____ O'CLOCK, _____M, I
SEARCHED THE _PERSON PREMISES_ DESCRIBED IN THE WARRANT AND I LEFT
A
COPY OF THE WARRANT WITH _____
_____
(NAME OF PERSON SEARCHED OR OWNER OR AT THE PLACE OF SEARCH)

TOGETHER WITH A RECEIPT FOR THE ITEMS SEIZED.

THE FOLLOWING IS AN INVENTORY OF PROPERTY TAKEN PURSUANT TO THE
WARRANT:
_____
_____
_____
_____
_____
_____
_____
_____
_____
_____
_____
_____


THIS INVENTORY WAS MADE IN THE PRESENCE OF _____
_____ AND _____
_____.


I SEAR THAT THIS INVENTORY IS A TRUE AND DETAILED ACCOUNT OF ALL THE
PROPERTY TAKEN BY ME ON THE WARRANT.


                          _____
                                          OFFICER

SUBSCRIBED AND SWORN TO AND RETURNED BEFORE ME THIS _____ DAY
OF _____, 19_____.


                          _____
                                          JUDGE
```

Structure 3.

obtained by police in most cases of Fourth Amendment violation. However, the majority held that the exclusionary rule could not be invoked for evidence obtained after a knock-and-announce violation, because the interests violated by the abrupt entry of the police "have nothing to do with the seizure of the evidence." Justice Scalia wrote that the knock-and-announce rule was meant to prevent violence, property-damage, and impositions on privacy, not to prevent police from conducting a search for which they have a valid warrant. The Court also found that the social costs of the exclusionary rule as applied to the knock-and-announce rule outweighed any possible "deterrence benefits," and that alternative measures such as civil suits and internal police discipline could adequately deter violations.

And, an entry by ruse does not constitute a "breaking" requiring prior notice. In other words, if police officers sense danger by having to use the knock and announce stipulation, they may choose instead to pretend to be making a delivery or even to be narcotics customers if the situation involves substance abuse and sales.

There is also something called a *no-knock warrant* if there is probable cause to believe there is evidence to be destroyed or the situation could be harmful to police. The court will issue a warrant waiving the "knock" requirement.

The actual execution of the warrant means the police are supposed to present or serve a copy of the warrant on the homeowner, seize the items listed and, on return, present it to the issuing magistrate.

## My House, Your House

A divided Supreme Court[4] ruled that police may not enter a home to conduct a search if one resident gives permission but the other says no. The 5–3 decision in a Georgia drug case involved a feuding couple. Police saw what appeared to be a straw coated with cocaine in the bedroom of Scott Fitz Randolph and it cannot be used in a prosecution of him. Apparently, Randolph's wife, Janet, called police during a domestic dispute in their home in Americus, Georgia. She told the officer her husband used drugs and led him to the straw, even though Scott Randolph had refused the officer's request for a search.

Chief Justice Souter referred to a social custom and property law that gives spouses and co-tenants equal claim on who enters a person's property. He said that no guest would enter at one occupant's invitation if another told the guest to stay out, and, that police, absent a search warrant, should not enter either. This decision reverses a pattern among U.S. lower courts that had favored police if one resident allowed a search over the objections of another.

Chief Justice John Roberts dissented from majority and argued that people who share a home have a reduced expectation of privacy and assume the risk that another resident might agree to a search by police. He said the ruling would endanger spouses who are abused and want police to come to a home, but does not make it clear to police that a threat exists. Nonetheless, Thomas Goldstein, who represented Randolph, praised the decision as an affirmation of the Fourth Amendment's privacy protection.

---

4. *Georgia v. Randolph,* U.S. 04-1067 (2006) 278 Ga. 614, 604 S.E. 2d 835

## SCOPE AND INTENSITY OF A SEARCH WARRANT

### Premises Described

In setting the legal boundaries of a search and defining the premises of an address, you may come upon a term called *curtilage.* Curtilage is an old-fashioned French word meaning "the area attached to a house and forming one enclosure with it," so we are not only talking about searching the house, but the grounds associated with it. Courts have usually stipulated this includes backyards, courtyards, and associated buildings on farms and ranches, including one's car or vehicles. But, the reverse is not true. If a search warrant grants authority to search a vehicle, that will not include entry into any private buildings within the scope of that document.

### Personal Effects

A valid search warrant does not have to include specific descriptions of rooms, cabinets, or furniture. In general, a warrant authorizing the search of a premises, justifies a search of the occupant's personal effects, especially if they represent plausible places for safekeeping the objects specified in the warrant. For example, if a warrant specifies stolen jewelry, it is not out of the realm of possibility that the item may found be in a coat pocket or pinned to clothing.

### Search the Person, Plus . . .

A warrant can justify the search of a person either exclusively or jointly with the search of a particular location. And when searching an individual, this also includes property carried by the suspect, such as a purse or any recognizable personal effect. Now as to whether other persons not listed on the warrant, such as visiting friends or someone else on the scene may be searched, this is not acceptable without probable cause, or unless the officer can pinpoint with reasonable suspicion that the onlooker is also engaged in criminal activity. If the police have "probable cause" to arrest a person discovered on the premises to be searched, they may search that person incident to the arrest.

### Fruits of the Deed

When executing a warrant the police generally may seize contraband or any fruits or instrumentality of a crime that they discover, whether specified in the warrant or not. A search continued beyond the limitations of the warrant may contain evidence that is excluded, and any further intrusion must cease.

### Limits of Search In Re: Length and Damage

A warrant to search for evidence founded on probable cause implicitly carries with it the limited authority to detain occupants of the premises while a proper search is conducted. The court has a permit for police officers to receive assistance from private citizens if it will allow for a more quick and efficient search. For example, telephone company employees may help to locate certain electronic devices used in surreptitious wire communications. Officers may remain on the premises as long as is reasonably necessary to complete the search up to and including hours. If damage is reasonably necessary to the search, such as digging a hole where fresh dirt is laid or opening a wall newly patched in order to find evidence within the scope of the warrant, it is justified. However, officers must refrain from tearing up a place and using the warrant as an excuse for destruction. For any wanton destruction, officers may be liable for civil damages.

## SEIZURE OF THE PERSON

There are literally thousands of variations on the search-seizure issue that wind up in appellate court and which serve to recreate, or carve out the process. In this next case, the issue of how to approach and touch a person suspected of a potential crime is defined.

## Stop and Frisk

A Cleveland plainclothes detective, Officer McFadden, observed several men who were standing on a street corner in the downtown area about 2:30 in the afternoon. He became suspicious of their behavior. One of the suspects walked up Huron Road, peered into a store, walked on and then started back, looked into the store again, and then conferred with his companion. The other suspect followed the same procedure and went through this process some twelve times, as if they were "casing" the store prior to a robbery. They also talked with a third man, and then followed him up the street about ten minutes after his departure. McFadden thought the men might be armed; he followed too, and confronted the men as they were talking. He identified himself and asked for the suspects' names. The men responded by mumbling something and the officer spun around a man named Terry and patted his breast pocket. He felt a pistol, which he then removed. A "frisk" of Terry's companion revealed another weapon, but the third man was unarmed and he was not searched any further.

Terry was charged with possessing a concealed weapon, and he moved to have the weapon suppressed as evidence. The motion was denied by a trial judge, the Ohio court of appeals confirmed it, and the state supreme court dismissed Terry's appeal.

This case eventually wound up in front of the Supreme Court of the United States and the result is known as a landmark decision. The Supreme Court ruled in *Terry v. Ohio*[5] (1968), that in circumstances where dangerous situations are unfolding on city streets, the police need to have an escalating set of flexible responses, graduating in response to the amount of information they possess. The judges agreed that a distinction should be made between a "stop" and an "arrest," and between a "frisk" and a "search." Police should be allowed to "stop" a person and detain him or her briefly for questioning on suspicion of connection to a criminal activity. Then, if the police officer is again suspicious the person may be armed, a protective frisk for weapons only should be conducted if it is reasonable to believe that the person is presently dangerous. The scope of the frisk is generally limited to a pat-down of the outer clothing for a concealed weapon. If the stop and frisk leads to probable cause that the suspect may have committed a crime, the police officer should be empowered further to make a formal arrest that allows for a full search. The judges felt that these further definitive rules to procedure were justified, because it amounted to a "minor inconvenience and petty indignity" imposed on a citizen in the interest of effective law enforcement.

---

5. *Terry v. Ohio*, 392 U.S. 1, 88 S.Ct. 1868, 20 L.Ed.2d 899 (1968).

Information from the Arkansas Law Enforcement Training Academy has a chart that spells out the difference:

|  | The "STOP" | ARREST |
|---|---|---|
| Justification | Reasonable suspicion | Probable cause |
| Search | Possibly a "pat-down" | Complete body search |
| Record | Minimal | Fingerprints, photographs, and booking |
| Intent of Officer | To resolve ambiguous situation | To make a formal charge |

## An Encounter

The courts felt there needed to be a distinction made between an encounter and a stop. If an officer cannot form reasonable suspicion for illegal activity, a citizen cannot be stopped because a stop would be a seizure that requires justification. But an encounter is a way to engage a citizen and is irrelevant under the Fourth Amendment. Would a person ever feel free to leave if approached by an officer to answer questions? Since the court wanted to develop a system so that officers could conduct a preliminary inquiry without the stigma of a stop, they devised the *Mendenhall Test.*

## Mendenhall Test

These factors help to delineate whether the officer has employed tactics satisfactory enough to constitute a stop:

Physical obstruction of movement–if officers block a suspect's forward movement, that is a good indication it is a stop.

Show of force–Drawn guns or any other form of menacing behavior is a convincing indication a stop has occurred.

Keeping identification or travel documents–An officer can approach a person and politely request identification or an airline ticket in an encounter. The person is free to reject that request. If the person honors that request, the officer is not permitted, absent of reasonable suspicion, to retain the ID or ticket in order to prolong the inquiry.

Coercive orders or threatening tones–Any threat of detention or accusation of criminal activity signals a stop.

Brevity–Even polite questioning must be brief; anything in length poses reasonable suspicion.

Polite requests to consent to search or moving the questioning–Like brevity, if a request to search luggage in an airport goes beyond cursory, the consensual encounter takes on coercive factors. Likewise, if an officer politely questions a citizen and then asks for a longer conversation that is fine, but the minute the conversation is moved to an investigative office, that is considered a stop.

The right to terminate an encounter or refuse consent–An officer is not obligated to tell a citizen that he or she has a right to refuse either conversation or consent to search or both.

Coercive surroundings–Close encounters on a bus, or questioning in a cramped space is not coercive per se; it's when the questioning occurs in an area not visible to the public, that may be a stop.

---

**Situations where police will question someone.**

• Is a citizen legally obligated to answer a policeman's questions?

Basically, no. It is not a crime, and a civilian cannot be arrested for failure to respond. Why? Because the Fifth Amendment guarantees a "right to silence." (That doesn't mean that police will not try to intimidate someone either—they will!)

• If a person starts to answer, can he or she stop the questioning and walk away?

Yes. Unless a police officer has "probable cause" to make an arrest, or a "reasonable suspicion" that a person's conduct is criminal, he or she may leave. Now if the officer has information that gives a legal basis to conduct a "stop and frisk," he or she can detain anyone. The best thing to do is ask: "Am I under arrest?"

• If pulled over by an officer for a traffic offense, can someone be arrested if he or she does not supply identification?

Yes, traffic infractions are generally given "citations"—tickets that specify a court appearance or fine. But if the citizen approached cannot supply personal information in connection with a traffic stop he or she can be detained or arrested. "Be prepared to cooperate and identify yourself" are the optimum passwords for civilians en route.

• If stopped for drunk driving, must a person answer questions?

No. But the officer has the right to put the offender through a sobriety field test and an arrest may ensue if he or she fails the test.

• Does a person get Miranda rights before questions?

No. A Miranda warning advises people of their right to not answer questions and is only required if someone is in custody and the police want to later use the statements in court.

• Can a citizen be harmed by answering?

It's possible. Sometimes people who have done nothing are still subject to being accused, plus, they may unwittingly disclose information implicating themselves.

• If a person gives false information about a friend, is he or she in trouble?

Yes. When an individual lies to police, he or she may be charged with "accessory after the fact"—as an accomplice if he or she is more closely involved, and, in the case of knowing about a felony beforehand, he or she could be charged with conspiracy.

• Can civilians talk their way out of a crime?

It's not suggested. Self-incrimination is protected under the Fifth Amendment.

---

## Who Are You?

A Nevada rancher, who refused to identify himself to a sheriff's deputy in May 2000, pushed a dozen "stop-and-identify" state statutes into accepted procedure for police. The case taken up by the Supreme Court[6] said that a police officer could now force a person to identify himself. A sheriff's deputy in Humboldt County, Nevada, questioned

---

6. *Hiibel v. Sixth Judicial District Court of Nevada, Humboldt County*, 542 U.S. 177 (2004)

Larry Hiibel, subject of the dispute, after the department alerted officers to a call that a man was assaulting a woman in a red-and-silver truck. Hiibel was found standing outside a truck parked by the side of the road that matched that description. A young woman was in the truck.

When the deputy tried to get Hiible to identify himself, he refused, put both hands behind his back, and told the officer to arrest him and take him to jail. Hiibel, a small ranch owner, said he believed he had done nothing wrong and, thus, there was no reason to reveal who he was to police, or that of his daughter, in the truck.

"Asking questions is an essential part of police investigations," Justice Anthony Kennedy wrote for the court. "In the ordinary course, a police officer is free to ask a person for identification without implicating the Fourth Amendment," He also said that giving one's name is unlikely to be incriminating under the Fifth Amendment as well. By a 5–4 vote, the Supreme Court justices ruled that as long as an officer reasonably suspects wrongdoing is underway, the state law under which the rancher was charged does not violate his Fourth Amendment right to be free of unreasonable searches and seizures.

## WARRANTLESS REQUIREMENTS

Perhaps you remember an instance on a television show or movie where an arrest was made without a warrant. Yes, that happens, but it is fraught with danger for both the arrestee and the arresting officer. Sometimes states' investigators, and even the FBI, will bring along a local, uniformed officer to facilitate arrest. One reason for this is

the peace officer has to have enough power to restrain the suspect. As citizens and justice professionals we need to know and understand that law enforcement will have the willingness to use a billy club, a chemical or electric device, a gun, or some other instrument as aid. But a police officer is also restrained in using too much force, which opens up a whole host of risky consequences. But, for now, you recognize the pattern of requirement involved in getting an affidavit and a warrant and you see police have certain, defined limitations.

## FELONY ARREST

Under common law, an arrest made without a warrant must meet certain circumstances. If the publicly paid police have reasonable grounds to believe that a felony has been committed, and if they have a particular person in mind, a felony arrest is possible. Also, if a misdemeanor is committed in the presence of law enforcement personnel, there is another reason for valid arrest. And still, there are more situations for warrantless arrests, and one of them is if the police are arresting a person in a public place.

In this case involving a public situation, *United States v. Watson*[7] (1976), a reliable informant named Khoury told a postal inspector that he had supplied a man named Watson with a stolen credit card, and had agreed to turn over additional cards at their next meeting which was scheduled for a few days later a restaurant location. As decided ahead of time, Khoury signaled the inspector when Watson had the cards, at which point the postal inspector arrested Watson without a warrant as he was authorized to do under postal regulations.

---

7. *U.S. v. Watson*, 423 U.S. 411, 96 S.Ct. 820, 46 L.Ed.2d 598 (1976).

The court of appeals held the arrest unconstitutional because the inspector had failed to secure a warrant, even though he admitted having time to do so. This error in judgment had bearing on the court's additional ruling that Watson's consent to a search of his car was not voluntary.

Eventually, the Supreme Court reversed the earlier decision made with Watson on the grounds that each case should be considered under historical guidelines–if the felony were committed in his presence, or if there were reasonable grounds to arrest–that to permit felony arrests only with a warrant or in exigent circumstances could severely hamper effective law enforcement's capabilities.

Four years later, in *Adams v. Williams*[8] (1972) the Court said: "The Fourth Amendment does not require a policeman who lacks the precise level of information necessary for probable cause to arrest to simply shrug his shoulders and allow a crime to occur or a criminal to escape. On the contrary, *Terry v. Ohio*, recognizes that it may be the essence of good police work to adopt an intermediate response. . . . A brief stop of a suspicious individual, in order to determine his identity or to maintain the status quo momentarily, while obtaining more information, may be the most reasonable in light of the facts known to the officer at the time." Indeed, stopping citizens in the course of an investigation is a practice that can be traced back to thirteenth century England.

One other important right to note about arrest protocol is that if someone is arrested without a warrant, he or she must receive a probable cause hearing within forty-eight hours. Otherwise detainment would have no limitations, and could feasibly produce dire consequences for the both the people accused, their business, and family. For with-

out this safeguarding of rights, the enormous power and resources of the state dwarf what the individual accused of a crime can bring to bear. To compensate for this and to ensure a degree of fairness, the playing field has to be tilted somewhat in favor of the accused.

## Traffic Arrest News

A Texas woman named Gail Atwater faced a new Supreme Court ruling with trepidation. Divided on the issue, the court ruled 5-4 that police can arrest and handcuff people for minor traffic offenses. The authority, they say, proceeds naturally from the right to pull someone over. Ms. Atwater is white, and was stopped by police officer Bart Turek. In front of her small children, Atwater was handcuffed, and then briefly jailed for failing to wear a seat belt. Atwater claims she and her passengers were unfastened only briefly, to aid them in looking for a distraught 4-year-old's lost toy. A police officer saw it differently, claiming she endangered her children and ordered her to jail.

"The question is whether the Fourth Amendment forbids a warrantless arrest for a minor criminal offense, such as a misdemeanor seat belt violation punishable by only a fine. We hold that it does not," Justice David H. Souter wrote for the court majority. Justice Sandra Day O'Connor took the minority view and said that the ruling "cloaks the pointless indignity that Gail Atwater suffered with the mantle of reasonableness."

The issue for the court was not whether Officer Bart Turek had the right to stop Atwater in the 1997 incident in Lago Vista, Texas–he did. Turek claims that when he saw 4-year-old Mackinley's face pressed against the windshield of Atwater's pickup truck, he knew he was seeing a clear viola-

---

8. *Adams v. Williams*, 407 U.S. 143, 92 S.Ct. 1921, 32 L.Ed.2d 612 (1972).

tion. Apparently a prized toy flew onto the roadside, and Atwater allowed her children to unbuckle their seat belts, just as she had, so all could crane their necks while she slowly retraced their path.

Truek saw a problem with their method of locating the toy, they were all in danger despite the fact there was no other traffic on the road. Soon after, Atwater's children were picked up by a friend, while she was taken to the police station. Police took her mug shot, and she was placed in a cell alone, until she posted $310 in bail. She later pleaded no contest and paid the $50 fine. Atwater and her husband decided to file a suit against the city, claiming the arrest violated her constitutional rights. The case never went to trial and *Atwater v. Lago Vista*, 99-1408, stands as a valid arrest.

## Held for Questioning

If circumstances are insufficient to arrest an individual on a criminal charge, there is no power (without consent or special statute) to lock a person in jail for questioning or for investigation, except that a judge or magistrate may be authorized to consign a material witness in a criminal case who refuses to make an effort to appear and testify in court after having been directed to do so.

While our system of justice makes allowances for self-incrimination, there is no immunity which entitles a mere witness to refuse to give information relative to the guilt of someone else, unless there is some special protection in the particular case, as for example where the two are husband and wife. Historically, witnesses were always subject to punishment for failure to give officers—outside the courtroom—any first-hand felony information.

## SEARCH INCIDENT TO ARREST

There is another commonly invoked exception the police use during seizure that eliminates the need for a search warrant requirement and it involves searches incident to arrest. Here, the search occurs at the same time and in the same place the police arrest a suspect. If the arrest is lawful, that is, based on probable cause, the courts have said it is not unreasonable for the police to search a suspect.

In *Robinson v. United States*[9] (1986), the Court held that the police may automatically search any person subjected to a custodial arrest, regardless of the nature or severity of the crime. There is no requirement that they actually must fear for their safety or even believe that they will find evidence of a crime. This concept fostered ideas loosely referred to as the "bright-line rules": the search is based on a need to avoid the endless fine distinctions required of police about making on-the-spot determinations. The theory is that each individual case has unique facts in frequently occurring situations and that knowledge must be considered, relative to the minor intrusions to a person's privacy and the safety of the officer. It also means that a suspect's personal effects are transportable—can be carried off to the jail—including his or her automobile if they are in or near it, and it may include a search of the area of arrest, even as much as covering an entire home or area of business.

But what if you're not under arrest, what about your reasonable expectations of privacy then? What are the circumstances for police entering a person's home? Who bears the burden of proof of demonstrating emergency circumstances? And what exactly is an emergency?

Last things first.

---

9. *Robinson v. United States*, 506 A.2d 572, 575 (D.C. App. 1986).

## Emergency Searches

An emergency situation, or exigent circumstance, provides an exception to the warrant requirement, meaning, a police officer can enter a person's home to make an arrest without a warrant. Some emergency circumstances exist in these hypothetical situations: For example, a police officer checks on an injured motorist and discovers illegal drugs; maybe an officer rushes into a house where the owner has alerted someone to flush drugs down the toilet; or officers can intervene if a child is screaming in danger. But officers operating under this exception must still meet the probable cause demand. Some emergency situations are:

- hot pursuit of a fleeing criminal
- vanishing evidence
- children in trouble
- property involving fire
- risks to police or public safety

## Hot Pursuit

If police officers are chasing down a suspect, it is unrealistic to expect them to get an arrest warrant. Some type of harm may occur and to allow the suspect to get away would render the warrant meaningless anyway. The "hot pursuit" exception is based on the fact that the suspect knows he or she is being pursued and will either try to escape or destroy evidence.

## Vanishing Evidence

Vanishing evidence is a frequently invoked justification for a warrantless search and seizure and is also called evanescent evidence. The best example for vanishing evidence can be found in *United States v. Riley.*[10] Police officers had a suspected drug house

under surveillance. They observed someone leaving the house with a white bag and followed. This person, Terry Moore, drove to a hotel and made an exchange. Police arrested Moore and found a bag containing cocaine. Moore then informed the officers that a large sum of money, a gun, and another person were at the house. While detailing this evidence, police noticed Moore had a cellular phone. They immediately dispatched nine officers to the house for a bust sans warrant. The entry was justified on the grounds that the evidence could have been quickly and easily destroyed. Evidence which is likely to disappear before a warrant can be obtained could also mean a blood sample containing alcohol or any product that could convey an urgent need.

The government bears the burden of proof of demonstrating exigent circumstances and police officers must have an arrest warrant in order to enter a person's home or arrest him or her absent emergency circumstances or consent. However, the scope of the search they use may be limited by the scope of the consent. In fact, there are situations and various rules about expectations of privacy and consent that are worth knowing.

## CONSENT TO SEARCH

No warrant is necessary when a consent to search is voluntarily offered, but the consent must come from a competent individual who either owns or possesses authority over the premises to be searched or items inspected. Knowledge of the right to withhold consent is not necessary to establish a voluntary, intelligent consent. The scope of the search may be limited by the scope of the consent. Likewise, the consent may be revoked or

---

10. *United States v. Riley*, 968 F.2d 422 (5th Cir. 1992).

withdrawn at any time and the search must cease. So, if a homeowner gets nervous about the search, he or she may refuse at any time.

The person consenting to a property search must have standing, and a person has standing if: he or she owns or possesses the place searched, or if the place searched was his or her home, whether or not he or she owned the land. So, for example, an employer cannot give consent to search an employee's desk, and some state courts do not allow parents to give consent to search a child's diary or a locked storage box in the child's personal room. High school searches? Yes, the principal is allowed to offer up consent for school lockers, usually in connection with published school rules or when in a violation of law. But in college, usually students must provide consent to search over their own dorm rooms and locked possessions.

## Unusual In-Home Arrest Situations

**Doorway arrests**–The courts have waffled on whether when a defendant answers a door, he or she is arrested in the home or in public. Some courts have said that if the officer remains outside the doorway and informs the defendant he or she is under arrest, the arrest is public–or incident to arrest–and no warrant is needed. However, if the arrest is made after entry, then there is a *Payton violation* and the

information discovered thereafter is illegally obtained. Best to check your individual state's rulings.

**Common hallways**–Anyone standing in a common hallway is fair game for a public arrest.

**Hotels and motels**–As long as the person has rightful possession of the room, a warrant is needed. The minute the rental period has expired, however, the turf designation is nada.

**Homeless persons**–Originally the courts claimed that a homeless person's claim of violation of warrantless arrest was nonexistent. Increasingly, however, the courts have been sympathetic to the privacy interests of homeless persons and have begun to hold flexible ideas as to what constitutes a home, even if it is within a public area.

## Consent Doctrine

The following is a story of third-party consent to searches, *Illinois v. Rodriguez*[11] (1990). Someone suspected of committing a crime may not want to allow police entry to his or her home for various reasons, and will demand a warrant for search; but what if the consent was given by someone other than the accused?

On July 26, 1985, police were summoned to the residence of Dorothy Jackson on South Wolcott in Chicago. Gail Fischer, Ms. Jackson's daughter, met them. She showed

---

**FYI**—Homeowners arrested outside the house are wise to not ask to go back in to get clothes or feed the dog. Police officers are allowed to make a "protective sweep" of the area following an arrest. This means they can make a "cursory visual inspection" of places where an accomplice might be hiding. If a sweep is lawful, any contraband or evidence of a crime in plain view is okay to take.

---

11. *Illinois v. Rodriguez*, 497 U.S. 177, 110 S.Ct. 2793, 111 L.Ed.2d 148 (1990).

signs of a severe beating. Fischer told the officers she had been assaulted by Edward Rodriguez earlier that day in an apartment on South California. "Rodriguez is asleep," she told the officers, and then consented to go there with police to unlock the door with her key so they could arrest him. The police noted that Fischer referred to the place as "our" apartment and admitted she had clothes and furniture there. It was unclear whether she lived there currently, or that she had lived there in the past.

Police drove to South California accompanied by Fischer. They did not obtain an arrest warrant for Rodriguez or seek a search warrant for the apartment. Once they arrived, Fischer unlocked the door and gave permission for the police to enter.

## PLAIN VIEW

In the living room, they observed in plain view drug paraphernalia and containers filled with white powder they assumed was cocaine just lying about. In the bedroom Rodriguez was asleep; some of the same containers of powder were nearby in open attaché cases. Officers arrested him and seized the drugs and related goods. He was charged with possession of a controlled substance with intent to deliver. Rodriguez's lawyer moved to suppress all evidence seized, claiming that Fischer had vacated the apartment several weeks earlier and had no authority to consent to entry.

The Cook County Circuit Court granted the motion. They believed that, at the time, Fischer did not have common authority over the apartment. She was an "infrequent visitor" and, based on later findings, discovered her name was not on the lease, she did not contribute to the rent, was not allowed to invite others in, and did not have access when the respondent was away. The Circuit Court also rejected the State's contention that even if Fischer did not have common authority over the premises, there was no Fourth Amendment violation if the police reasonably believed at the time that Fischer did have standing. (Adapted from Basic Criminal Procedure: American Casebook Series, West Publishing; *Illinois v. Rodriguez*, pp. 353–360.)

What do you think? The outcome is below.

The Supreme Court *reversed the judgment* of the Illinois Appellate Court and remanded it back for further proceedings. Their opinion was based on the theory that "Because many situations which confront officers in the course of executing their duties are more or less ambiguous, room must be allowed for some mistakes on their part. But the mistakes must be those of *reasonable men*, acting on facts leading sensibly to their conclusions of probability." They said further, that the Constitution is no more violated when officers enter without a warrant because they reasonably (though erroneously) believe that the person who has consented to their entry is a resident of the premises, than it is violated when they enter without a warrant because they reasonably (though erroneously) believe they are in pursuit of a violent felon who is about to escape.

## More About Plain View

If an officer has the legitimate right to be in a particular location, any evidence seen is up for grabs. Evidence of a crime must be inadvertently (or accidentally) discovered. The evidence must be in "plain view." Police can also use drug-sniffing dogs to ferret out evidence in "public areas." An overheard conversation also is subject to use as evidence and sometimes officers can use flashlights to find evidence. Binoculars or sound amplifiers have also been used, within reason.

A warrantless search is considered constitutional if the prosecution can show, by a preponderance of evidence,[12] that it was made in accordance with an exception, such as plain view, with consent, or under exigent circumstances.

A person does not have a reasonable expectation of privacy in objects held out to the public such as:

- the sound of a person's voice,
- paint on the outside of a car, and,
- account records held by a bank.

These are obviously things put out into the universe without restraint. And although these terms may sound ridiculous because of their narrow definition, there is a legal phrase, *Nullum crimen sine lege*, which states, "No crime without a law." Meaning, in order for a law to be violated, it must exist. It follows then, that citizens cannot expect privacy in the things they freely offer out to the public because the law delineates what exactly is meant by private.

## AUTOMOBILE SEARCH

What about someone traveling in a car? Are police allowed to search a person's car willy nilly? Why? And under what circumstances? This is an interesting consideration where the situation itself changes according to different circumstances, but on grounds quite different from the general consent notion and those other issues having to do with home privacy concerns.

## Traffic Stop

A police officer who stops a car for a traffic infraction can ask the driver and any passengers to exit the car as a safety precaution. A cursory check for weapons can be made if the officer reasonably suspects one of them may be engaged in criminal activity. However, stopping a car to issue a traffic citation does not allow a full-scale search of either the car or its occupants. Police still must have probable cause to believe that the car contains evidence of a crime in order to conduct a search. And because it is rare that the danger of a car or something in the trunk of a car could be used as a weapon against police, the rationale of police safety alone does not justify a reason to search the trunk. Still, the statistics bear out that most car searches pass constitutional muster; but for a different reason. Why? Automobiles are mobile. There has to be an exigency created by mobility. It must be likely that the vehicle will be unavailable by the time a warrant can be obtained. Police know and understand that if they don't look in the trunk now, there is a good chance that whatever was in the trunk will be gone by the time they secure a warrant.

## Man's Best Friend

It all goes back to 1998, when an Illinois State Trooper stopped Roy Caballes for going 71 mph in a 65 mph zone. The trooper issued a warning ticket, while another trooper walked his drug-sniffing dog around the car. The dog alerted at the trunk and a search uncovered marijuana. Caballes was sentenced to twelve years in prison and fined $256,136. for approximately $250,000 worth of marijuana.

The Supreme Court[13] took up the issue that pits individual liberties versus a popular police tactic, and ruled 6-2 that police can

---

12. Preponderance of evidence: evidence is more likely than not.
13. *Illinois v. Caballes*, (03-923) 543 U.S. 405 (205) 207 Ill. 2d 504, 802 N. E. 2d 202

Figure 4. This officer can check for warrants on his computer as he patrols.

use drug-sniffing dogs during routine traffic stops, even when officers have no reason to suspect the vehicle is carrying narcotics. This reverses an Illinois Supreme Court ruling that said the use of a dog wrongly converts a routine traffic stop into a drug investigation.

Attorneys for Caballes and the American Civil Liberties Union claimed that permitting dogs to sniff a motorist's vehicle without "reasonable suspicion" that the motorist may have committed crimes, gives police too much power to invade citizens' privacy.

It is interesting to note that while almost all municipalities have ordinances against interfering with police dogs (and sometimes horses) such as this one from New Hampshire: Maiming or Causing the Death of or Willful Interference With Police Dogs or Horses. -

I. Whoever willfully tortures, beats, kicks, strikes, mutilates, injures, disables, or otherwise mistreats, or whoever willfully causes the death of a dog or horse owned or employed by or on behalf of a law enforcement agency . . . ;

many new state's laws have made it a felony, for example, as with this Mississippi law: to kill or injure a police dog, punishable by $5,000.00 fine and/or five (5) years Mississippi Department of Corrections.

## WING SPAN

And there are distinct stipulations about where police officers can look. They cannot tear out the seats or open up the glove compartment; they can only search a person's "wing span" worth of reach–far enough for a suspect to be able to stash something under the seat. And as usually always associated with a vehicle, individuals should also assume a lesser expectation of privacy in their car because law enforcement may have enough probable cause to impound the car–the search of a vehicle under this exception does not have to occur at the time of the stop. They can have it towed to the police department and search it on their own good time. There they may make a warrantless seizure of property found during a routine inventory of an impounded vehicle because police have searched cars by declaring it is an inventory. But because it's not an emergency, the search should be made under a warrant based on probable cause, just as if it were a nonemergency search of someone's home.

## A DIFFERENT KIND OF SEARCH

### Mail Search

After a jury trial, a small-town Nebraska school bus driver was found guilty in 1987 of violating a provision of the Child Protection Act of 1984, by committing the crime of receiving child pornography through the mail. Years later, in *Jacobson v. United States*[14] (1992), a ruling came down from the Supreme Court reversing the decision that 61-year-old Keith Jacobson, a round-faced, gray-haired farmer who had lawfully ordered a nudist magazine was guilty.

Previously, the 56-year-old veteran-turned-farmer, who supported his elderly father in Nebraska, ordered two magazines and a brochure from a California adult bookstore. The magazines he ordered, *Bare Boys I* and *Bare Boys II*, contained photographs of nude preteen and teenaged boys. The contents of the magazines surprised Jacobson, who later testified that he had expected to receive photographs of "young men 18 years or older." But since the young men depicted in the magazines were not engaged in sexual activity, Jacobson's receipt of the magazines was legal under both federal and Nebraska law. Within three months though, the law with respect to child pornography changed. Congress passed the Act making it illegal to receive sexually explicit pictures of children through the mail. Jacobson was then the target of twenty-six months of mailings from government sting operators. Postal inspection teams masqueraded as organizations dedicated to sexual freedom.

Finally, after considerable government planning, Jacobson yielded to the temptations of a postal sting called Project Looking Glass and ordered a magazine entitled, *Boys Who Love Boys*. Entrapment is the inducement, and in this case, the active encouragement by law enforcement officials of an individual to commit a crime, not contemplated by him or her, undertaken for the sole purpose of instituting a criminal prosecution against that person. Justice Byron R. White wrote the decision for the majority court overturning Jacobson's conviction by saying, "When the government's quest for convictions lead to the apprehension of an otherwise law-abiding citizen who, if left to his own devices, likely would never run afoul of the law, the courts should intervene."

---

14. *Jacobson v. U.S.*, 503 U.S. 540, 112 S.Ct. 1535, 118 L.Ed.2d 174 (1992).

Jacobson's arrest drove him into seclusion for months and cost him his job of driving children to and from school. He wound up serving a two-year probation and completed some 250 hours of community service. Afterwards, Jacobson said, "I feel happy, grateful and humble. It's a victory for all Americans. It means you have a right to be let alone if you're minding your own business and not involved in some kind of criminal enterprise."

Justice Sandra Day O'Connor protested the Jacobson decision and produced a dissenting opinion. Her concern was that the court had introduced "a new requirement" that she believed could hamper later drug, bribery, and pornography stings. Government agents often mimic criminal behavior to induce criminals to show their true colors. O'Connor felt that this decision might put a damper on any helpful government sting operations in the future, simply by producing the fear of officials in creating a predisposition in its suspects.

As a practical matter, undercover police work often creates opportunities for crime and the methodology has become increasingly commonplace. In law enforcement's effort to control drug trafficking, for example, inducement is a significant component in their procedure, demonstrated by the fact that it is the subject matter of many Supreme Court cases. "Sting" operations are also employed in investigations involving burglars and corrupt public officials. In the case of burglaries, for example, criminals are often identified as a result of their selling stolen goods to police-operated fencing fronts. And concerning the latter, corrupt public officials are the subject of elaborate purported bribery attempts and the results have been documented in some famous cases of abuse of the public trust. An example of this would be an operation called Abscam, where, in February 1980, an FBI agent posed as an Arab sheik and offered bribes to certain congressmen in exchange for political favors.

In *State v. Sainz*[15] (1972), the New Mexico Court of Appeals adopted this formulation of the entrapment defense:

> When the state's participation in the criminal enterprise reaches the point where it can be said that except for the conduct of the state a crime would probably not have been committed or because the conduct is such that it is likely to induce those to commit a crime who would normally avoid crime, or, if the conduct is such that if allowed to continue would shake the public's confidence in the fair and honorable administration of justice, this then becomes entrapment as a matter of law.

The strain between keeping and preserving a person's rights and wanting to preserve security through enforcement have many shades of gray where nothing is ever clearly black or white. But when cases such as these involving surveillance and entrapment come before the courts, it is getting harder to tell who is the criminal and who are the police.

## Wiretapping: Another Form of Search and Seizure

Electronic eavesdropping, also called wiretapping, is considered to be a search under the Fourth Amendment. In order to get a valid warrant authorizing a wiretap, you must have the following:

1. A showing of probable cause to believe that a specific crime has been or is being committed.;
2. The defendant whose conversations are being overheard must be named.;

---

15. *State v. Sainz*, 84 N.M. 259, 261, 501 P.2d 1247, 1249 (App. 1972).

3. The warrant must describe the nature of the conversation which can be over-heard.;
4. The wiretap must be limited to a short period of time.;
5. Officers must make provisions to terminate the wiretap when the desired information has been obtained.;
6. A return must be made to the court showing what conversations have been intercepted.

The surveillance is usually for a thirty-day period of time.[16]

## Exceptions to the Warrant Requirement on Seizing Conversations

The Fourth Amendment protects only "legitimate" interests; in other words, if the person has undertaken an illegal activity, there is no legitimate privacy interest. However, since it is not possible to know in advance of the search that their activity is illegal, certain interests must be presumed and protected before the intrusion takes place.

**The "unreliable ear"**–A speaker assumes the risk that the person to whom he is talking is unreliable. If the person turns out to be an informer, the speaker has no basis under the Fourth Amendment to object to the recording of the conversation as a warrantless search. You assume the risk that whomever you tell things may tattle.

**The "uninvited ear"**–A speaker has no Fourth Amendment claim if he or she makes no attempt to keep the conversation private, for example, if calls are made on a public telephone.

## Airport Searches

As you approach the concourse, a sign is posted that warns "all bags are subject to search." This announcement places passengers on notice that ordinary Fourth Amendment protections do not apply. Because of increased concerns over airplane hijacking and terrorism, increased security at airports, such as walking through the metal detector, the x-raying of baggage, or the inspection of carry-on items will be the norm. These are valid administrative guidelines as established by the Federal Aviation Administration and there is little question these searches are reasonable.

\* \* \*

If the government becomes a lawbreaker, it breeds contempt for the law."
*–Justice of the Supreme Court*

## Ms. Mapp, Landmark Case

Remember earlier I mentioned a case involving Ms. Mapp? It was all about how we are guaranteed a citizen's right against unreasonable search and seizure. Well, the courts frequently determine the degree of unreasonableness. The landmark case for this decision is based on *Mapp v. Ohio*[17] set down in 1961.

On May 20, 1957, someone set off a bomb that demolished the front porch and wall of Don King's house. Three days after the bombing, three Cleveland men drove to a two-family home run by Dollree Mapp. Acting on a phone tip, the three plain-clothesmen went to Mapp's thinking that a suspect connected to the bombing, Virgil Ogiltree, would be there; his car was parked

---

16. 18 U.S.C.A. § 2518 (5).
17. *Mapp v. Ohio*, 367 U.S. 643, 81 S.Ct. 1684, 6 L.Ed.2d 1081 (1961).

outside. Because Ogiltree never came out, officers became inpatient and knocked on the door to make inquiries. Ms. Mapp answered but denied them entrance, stating that she would not allow them to search without a warrant, nor would she open the door without first calling her lawyer. The men kept the house under surveillance, yet radioed another officer to obtain a warrant.

Later, a half-dozen uniformed men came back, and claimed they had a warrant. Mapp again refused to open the door. They entered the residence by breaking out a pane of glass, unlatching the door, and charging up to Mapp's second-floor apartment. She met them on the landing. "Where's the warrant?" she demanded. Delau, one of the officers, held up a piece of paper. Mapp grabbed the paper and stuffed it under her turtleneck. The officers proceeded to cuff her and snatched back the paper from inside her shirt. While searching the residence, officers confiscated some obscene materials—pencil sketches of nude models and four books— and artifacts for betting equipment. Dollree Mapp was arrested and charged with possession of gambling equipment and obscene materials. The latter offense was listed as a felony under a newly amended state statute on antipornography. By the time Mapp was brought to trial in September 1958, the "search warrant" she had tried so hard to keep, had disappeared. (Twenty years later the arresting officer, Sgt. Delau, would admit that contradictory to his trial testimony his lieutenant had only obtained an affidavit, a document spelling out the reasons for wanting a warrant.)

Mapp was found guilty on the obscenity charge and sentenced to one to seven years in the Ohio State Reformatory for Women. She appealed and the Supreme Court of Ohio upheld the conviction. Eventually, in 1961, the U.S. Supreme Court consented to hear her appeal on the issue that the Fourth Amendment guarantee of the right of people to be secure in their houses, papers, and effects, and against unreasonable searches and seizures and warrants, was in question. In this instance, the police conducted an illegal search and seizure. They not only violated Ms. Mapp's privacy but the search warrant was issued for a bombing suspect, and not for the things they collected. This was really one of the first early applications of the exclusionary rule—a policy forbidding the use of illegally obtained evidence.

But the story does not end here, and the pendulum keeps moving. A bill was passed in 1984 to modify the *Mapp v. Ohio* ruling. Now it limits the exclusion of evidence under certain circumstances, such as: if the excluded evidence was gotten through a reasonable, "good-faith" belief on the part of police yet still conforms with the Fourth Amendment. Of course, each state gets to craft its own definitions of what constitutes an "illegal" search and seizure. And, later again, the Supreme Court had another chance to modify an exception to the exclusionary rule. In the same year, 1984, they decided on an "inevitable discovery" exception. This means that any evidence discovered in violation of a defendant's rights can be used in a trial if the prosecution can establish that the evidence would have been found in the course of a lawful search.

The rules involving search and seizure are constantly being tested, although, contrary to popular belief, the number of criminals freed by the exclusionary rule has been small—less than 1 percent of federal cases have not been pressed due to inadmissible evidence.

## EXCLUSIONARY RULE EXCEPTIONS

Exclusionary rule exceptions: (Enforced with a "Suppression of Evidence Hearing"–

the judge needs to suppress the evidence.)
- Does not apply to live witnesses (they can still be compelled to testify)
- Does not apply to grand juries (they do not determine guilt or innocence–just probable cause)
- Does not apply to civil proceedings
- Does not apply when cops act in "good faith"
- Does not apply to evidence obtained by a private individual (unless he or she is working on behalf of the cops)
- Excluded evidence can still be used for impeachment (proving a lie)

## Citizen's Arrest

A store security guard can arrest a shoplifter, the owner of a car can arrest a punk trying to break into her car . . . and in "extraordinary cases" a police officer can conscript a private citizen into aiding a capture of suspect. . . .

It's rare for a citizen to make arrests but a private detective often will. It is legal for an ordinary citizen to make an arrest but there are problems. There is limited protection for private citizens who make mistakes during an arrest. Most states will recognize a private arrest if:
- they observe the commission of a crime;
- the person arrested actually committed a felony;
- a felony was done, and the private citizen has probable cause to believe the arrested person did it.

If a private citizen arrests an innocent person–they are civilly liable. The charge most likely would be false imprisonment.

Now if a private citizen uses deadly force, courts are rather hostile toward that type of service. Then too, if mistakes are made here,

a citizen may be sued both civilly and criminally.

## THE FOURTH AMENDMENT AND THE INTERNET

Since 9/11, the Electronic Communications Privacy Act has morphed and things have changed but here are the basics in regards to computers and the government obtaining stored information:

- To determine whether an individual has a reasonable expectation of privacy in information stored in a computer,[18] it helps to treat the computer like a closed container such as a briefcase or file cabinet. The Fourth Amendment generally prohibits law enforcement from accessing and viewing information stored in a computer without a warrant if it would be prohibited from opening a closed container and examining its contents in the same situation.
- Individuals may lose Fourth Amendment protection in their computer files if they lose control of the files.
- The permitted scope of consent searches depends on the facts of each case and agents need written consent that states explicitly that the extent of consent includes consent to search computers and other electronic storage devices.
- Most spousal consent searches are valid.
- Parents can consent to searches of their children's rooms when the children are under 18 years old. If the children are 18 or older, the parents may or may not be able to consent, depending on the facts.
- The plain view doctrine does not autho-

---

18. Title III of the Omnibus Crime Control and Safe Streets Act, 1968, and §§ 2701-12 as "ECPA."

rize agents to open and view the contents of a computer file that they are not otherwise authorized to open and review.

• Government employers and their agents can conduct "reasonable" work-related searches even if those searches violate an employee's reasonable expectation of privacy.

• When a search may result in the incidental seizure of network accounts belonging to innocent third parties, agents should take every step to protect the integrity of the third party accounts to avoid potential ECPA liability.

• Agents should obtain multiple warrants if they have reason to believe that a network search will retrieve data stored in multiple locations.

• When agents have reason to believe that a search may result in a seizure of materials relating to First Amendment activities such as publishing or posting materials on the World Wide Web, they must consider the effect of the Privacy Protection Act[19] (PPA). Every federal computer search that implicates the PPA must be approved by the Justice Department, coordinated through CCIPS.[20]

Currently, the foundation of the cyber-crime prosecution program is the Computer Crime & Intellectual Property Section known as CCIPS. CCIPS was founded in 1991 as the Computer Crime Unit, and became a section in 1996. Keep an eye out for new laws and developments in this area.

In a computer context, the Electronic Communications Privacy Act (ECPA: 18 U.S.C. §§ 2701-11) established a three-tier system by which government can obtain stored information from electronic service providers:

1. In general, the government needs a search warrant to obtain the content of unopened communications such as e-mail;
2. a court order to obtain transactional records; and
3. a subpoena to obtain subscriber information.

Some challenges to apprehension exist, in that cybercriminals cloak their illegal activity by weaving communications through a series of anonymous remailers, thus creating forged e-mail headers with powerful point-and-click tools readily downloadable from hacker web sites, or by using a "free trial" account or two, and then are often able to "wipe clean" the logging records that would be evidence of their activity.

One emerging concern is the growing problem of online harassment or threats amounting to cyberstalking. One California woman was awakened repeatedly through the night by men knocking on her door offering to "rape" her. A rejected suitor had posted personal advertisements on the Internet pretending to be her. The ads contained her home address and telephone number and claimed that she fantasized about being raped.

Currently, the foundation of the cyber-crime prosecution program is the Criminal Division's Computer Crime and Intellectual Property Section known as CCIPS. CCIPS was founded in 1991 as the Computer Crime Unit, and became a section in 1996.

---

19. 42 U.S.C. § 2000aa
20. http://www.cybercrime.gov/ccips.html

# REVIEW QUESTIONS AND ANSWERS

## *Key Words to Define*

- **Affidavit**–Facts showing both the commission of an offense and accuser's responsibilities.
- **Curtilage**–Areas in conjunction with a house.
- **Evanescent evidence**–Vanishing evidence.
- **Exclusionary rule**–A policy forbidding the use of illegally obtained evidence.
- **Fourteenth Amendment**–Nor shall any state deprive any person of life, liberty or property without due process of law; nor deny to any person within its jurisdiction the equal protection of the law.
- **Fourth Amendment**–Guaranteed right against unreasonable search and seizure.
- **Fruits of the deed**–Evidence of wrongdoing not specified in a warrant.
- **Hearsay evidence**–Out of court statements offered for the truth.
- **Knock and announce rule**–Police must knock and announce themselves on arrival at a place to be searched; notice requirement.
- **No-knock warrant**–If probable cause leads police/authorities to believe that evidence is being destroyed or some type of harm can occur to an individual, police can waive the "knock" stipulation.
- **Preponderance of evidence**–Evidence is likely than not to prove something.
- **Probable cause**–Facts and circumstances the officer believes to be true at the time of arrest, cased on reasonable

trustworthy information and experience.
- **Seizure of the body**–Law says, "arrest."
- **"Uninvited ear"**–No Fourth Amendment right or claim if someone makes no attempt to keep his conversations private.
- **Warrant**–Justification; document issued by a judge to indicate possible offenses committed by that person.

## *Questions for Review and Discussion*

1. *Question:* What do almost half of the Amendments in the Bill of Rights deal with? *Answer:* Personal rights and civil liberties.

2. *Question:* Our law system is based on what ideal? *Answer:* The presumption of innocence beyond a reasonable doubt.

3. *Question:* Name four criteria for probable cause. *Answer:* Suspicious conduct, casing a place, a known criminal record, high activity at an inappropriate time, activity in a high crime region, a reaction to police, supplying false responses, non-cooperation with a request, failure to have I.D., nervousness during an encounter, information from an informant, etc.

4. *Question:* The information basis of knowledge used to secure a warrant can be gotten how? *Answer:* Information from an informant, from a victim of a crime related to the search, statement from a witness, another policeman's information, hearsay, suspicious activity, etc.

5. *Question:* What are the first few things to be included in an affidavit as the basis of knowledge? *Answer:* Who, what, when, where and why?

6. *Question:* Who can execute a warrant? *Answer:* Local police, sheriff, deputy, or member of a government investigative agency.

7. *Question:* Is some latitude given over the knock-and-announce rule? *Answer:* Yes. If police believe evidence is being destroyed, or if there is exigent circumstances, e.g., danger to a child or another person.

8. *Question:* Can police pretend to be delivering a package? Flowers? When trying to gain access to a house? *Answer:* Yes.

9. *Question:* Can answering the police harm a person? *Answer:* Yes, if they implicate themselves or act strangely suspicious.

10. *Question:* How soon after arrest without a warrant must someone get his probable cause hearing? *Answer:* Within 48 hours.

11. *Question:* What is a search incident to arrest? *Answer:* The search occurs at the same time and place police arrest a suspect.

12. *Question:* When does a person not have a reasonable expectation of privacy in objects held out to the public? *Answer:* Sound of a person's voice, paint on the outside of a car, account records held by a bank. What else? Garbage on the street.

## *Essay Exploration*

WRITE A SHORT 500-WORD ESSAY: tell about whether or not you feel that today the law limits our privacy and state whether you feel this is good or bad. Try to back up your argument with specifics and not just your opinion.

Students can mention anything from the Patriot Act such as Internet monitoring, ISP reporting, bank monitoring, wiretaps, ID checks, airport searches, car searches, cell phone taps and accounts monitoring, and so forth.

# Chapter 8

# RIGHTS OF THE ACCUSED

The public good is in nothing more essentially
interested than in the protection of every
individual's private rights.
–William Blackstone, *Commentaries*

The law of criminal procedure is a
unique and uncertain balancing act. It is
best described as a set of conflicting rules the
government must follow in order to maintain law and order, while at the same time
protecting the rights of its individual citizens.
This "uncertainty" of procedure is due to the
nature of periods in United States history
where the political emphasis shifts. What the
law says is illegal today may not be the same
as what the law says was illegal yesterday.
And the future is up for revision also.

## AMENDMENT V

## Grand Juries, Self-Incrimination, Double Jeopardy, Due Process, and Eminent Domain

No person shall be held to answer for a capital, or otherwise infamous crime, unless on a
presentment or indictment of a Grand Jury,
except in cases arising in the land or naval
forces, or in the Militia, when in actual service
in time of War or public danger; nor shall any
person be subject for the same offence to be
twice put in jeopardy of life or limb; nor shall
be compelled in any criminal case to be a witness against himself, nor be deprived of life,
liberty, or property, without due process of
law; nor shall private property be taken for
public use, without just compensation.

## Explanation

There are two types of juries. A *grand jury*
looks at physical evidence and listens to the
testimony of witnesses and then decides
whether there is sufficient reason to bring a
case to trial. A *petit jury* hears the case at trial
and makes a decision about it. ". . . [T]o be
twice put in jeopardy" means a person cannot be tried two times for the same crime
and cannot be forced to give evidence or testimony against himself or herself. Plus, no
person's right to life, liberty, or property
may be taken away except by following lawful means, called "the due process of law."
Private property taken for use in public pur-

poses must be paid for by the government.

## Rights of Persons:
## Interrogations and Confessions

At one time or another we've all heard an actor playing a witness tell the judge, "I take the Fifth, Your Honor." What is he asking for? How can someone take the fifth? Among the many provisions in the Fifth Amendment is the right of protection against self-incrimination. In other words: "No person . . . shall be compelled in any criminal case to be a witness against himself." Since an American trial by its nature is supposed to operate under an adversary system, it implies that the state must prove the guilt of the accused, not just assume guilt. "Innocent until proven guilty" are the watchwords of the American system. Self-incrimination has been expanded by interpretation, however, to protect not only a defendant, but also a witness, in all manner of questioning before a court, grand jury or coroner's inquest, and in investigations by legislative body or administrative official.

This concept is most important when it comes to interrogation. Under the protection of the Fifth, basically it means that no person can be abused or tortured in order to give up a confession. In the cases of *Escobedo v. Illinois* and *Miranda v. Arizona*, the Courts added that to secure the validity of confessions, suspects must be notified of their rights against self-incrimination and have a right to counsel. Because of this, certain hurdles must be removed before any self-incriminating statements can be introduced as evidence:

1. the State must demonstrate that the confession was not coerced; defendants' statements should not violate the voluntariness requirement of the due process clause of the Fifth and Fourteenth Amendments;
2. incriminating statements may not be admitted if the accused did not have right to counsel; or,
3. if the statement was made without Miranda warnings; and finally,
4. the state has to be prepared to show the defendant knowingly and intelligently waived his or her rights.

## WHAT IS AN INTERROGATION?

Commonly thought of as questioning at the station house after arrest, interrogation can occur anywhere. The Supreme Court has defined interrogation as "express questioning or its functional equivalent," including "any words or actions on the part of the police that the police should know are reasonably likely to elicit an incriminating response from the suspect."[1]

## Determining the Risk
## of Incrimination

A judge must determine whether the information demanded might incriminate a witness in the future. He or she uses the system that if the testimony provides a link in a chain of evidence that might be used to show that a witness had committed a crime, it is incriminating.[2]

## MIRANDIZING

- **You have a right to remain silent.**
- **Anything you say can and will be used against you in a court of law.**
- **You have the right to talk to a lawyer and have him present with you while**

1. *Rhode Island v. Innis*, 446 U.S. 291, 301, 100 S.Ct. 1682, 1693, 64 L.Ed.2d 297, 308 (1980).
2. *Hoffman v. United States*, 341 U.S. 479, 71 S.Ct. 814, 95 L.Ed. 1118 (1951).

you are being questioned.

- If you can not afford to hire a lawyer one will be appointed to represent you before any questioning, if you wish one.
- You can decide at any time to exercise these rights and not answer any questions or make any statements.

## Waiver

After the warning and in order to secure a waiver, the following questions should be asked and an affirmative reply secured to each question.

## "Do you understand each of these rights I have explained to you?"

## "Having these rights in mind, do you wish to talk to us now?"

## Remember, this only applies if the person being questioned is in *custody*!

We're all familiar with these warnings as read by police and law-based officials. But who was Miranda? What did he do? And why do these words mean so much to law enforcement personnel and, in turn, those accused of a crime? Entire volumes have been written about the specifics of this case. It unfolds here:

Lois Ann Jameson (not her real name) was on her way home from work at the Paramount Theater in downtown Phoenix, Arizona, when things went wrong. She stepped off the bus a few minutes after midnight, heading toward home, when a car suddenly pulled out of a driveway and blocked her path. The driver dragged her into his car, tied her hands and ankles, and warned her not to move. In an outlying desert area she was made to disrobe, was raped, and robbed of four dollars. Later, she was allowed to get dressed and returned to the neighborhood where she had been abducted.

Phoenix Metro Police were called into the case and on March 4, 1963, Detective Carroll Cooley began his investigation. Through their vigilance with watching the habits of Ms. Jameson, evidence soon led law enforcement to the home of Twila Hoffman, who lived in the nearby suburb of Mesa. They discovered that Hoffman lived with a man named Ernest Miranda, who roughly fit the description of Jameson's assailant.

Checking his work record, they found him absent his job at United Produce the night of the crime. Further checking uncovered Miranda had a rather lengthy criminal record.

Cooley and Wilfred Young went to Twila Hoffman's residence and asked Miranda to accompany them downtown to the police station, to discuss a case they were investigating. At police headquarters, Miranda participated in a lineup and was identified by Lois Ann Jameson. Detectives informed Miranda he had been identified and began questioning him in greater detail. Later, the detectives would tell the courts that "neither threats nor promises had been made" toward Miranda who had just admitted that he had raped Jameson and then confessed to a second robbery.

The entire interrogation took a little more than two hours. Officers had used his testimony against him and it had become self-incriminating, and he wound up signing a confession. There was no evidence of police brutality and really nothing out of the ordinary.

Ernest Miranda's charges were for kidnapping and rape and he was tried and sentenced to two concurrent (running simultaneously rather than one after the other) terms, twenty to thirty years on each charge, to be served at the Arizona State Prison. It is hard to believe that less than three years later, Ernest Miranda would be responsible for a landmark Supreme Court decision. And the Miranda warning would create a series of repercussions that would change the standard of police procedure from that time forward. The Fifth Amendment guarantee resolved in the *Miranda v. Arizona*[3] case provides that a suspect has a right to remain silent; and that he or she is entitled to an attorney *before* questioning.

## First Challenge

Later, police officials complained that Miranda rulings placed the rights of criminal suspects over the rights of society. In response, the Courts' new philosophy was that law enforcement would be made more reliable if founded on independently obtained evidence, rather than confessions secured under coercive interrogation and without benefit of counsel, and that this should be the new test for justice. But in 1968, in an attempt to rebalance the rights again, several exceptions to the Miranda ruling transpired. The Omnibus Crime Control and Safe Streets Act provided that in federal cases, a voluntary confession could be used as evidence even if the accused person was not informed of his or her rights. As a result, even in cases not tried in federal courts, confessions have been allowed in evidence under certain circumstances, such as when public safety requires action.

In the 1980s, there was a slight shift toward restricting a person's rights again. In *New York v. Quarles*[4] the question was if a police officer could ask a suspect for his or

her gun before receiving Miranda rights. The court upheld that the procedure for securing the gun was all right, because police were applying a "concern for public safety" in a public place over the rights of the accused. This was a much-needed "first-things-first" issue for protecting police security many said, and extremely important in the minds of law enforcement officers who were facing new and increasing dangers.

## Blanket Assumptions

The theory that criminals are "getting off" because the police didn't read them their rights is incorrect as a blanket assumption. It is more likely that statements or confessions violating Miranda will be inadmissible as evidence in a trial. It doesn't necessarily mean that the charges against a suspect will be dropped, certainly not if the prosecutor and investigators have other evidence they can use against him or her. But still, there are always exceptions. The following is a case that illustrates another result.

Police were investigating a series of purse-snatch robberies in California. One of the victims died as a result of the injuries sustained by her assailant, Roy Allen Stewart. Stewart was caught after he endorsed one of the dividend checks taken in one of the robberies; bank authorities had alerted police of his activity right away. At about 7:15 on the evening on January 31, 1963, police officers went to Stewart's home and arrested him. On arrival, one of the officers asked Stewart if they could search the house and Stewart replied, "Go ahead." The search turned up various items taken from the five robbery victims.

At the time of Stewart's arrest, police also arrested Stewart's wife and three other per-

3. *Miranda v. Arizona*, 384 U.S. 436, 86 S.Ct. 1602, 16 L.Ed.2d 694 (1966).
4. *N.Y. v. Quarles*, 467 U.S. 649, 104 S.Ct. 2626, 81 L.Ed.2d 550 (1984).

sons who were visiting. The four were taken to the jail, along with Stewart, and questioned. Then Stewart was taken to the University Station of the Los Angeles Police Department where he was placed in a cell. During the next five days, police interrogated Stewart on nine different occasions. On one occasion, Stewart was confronted by an accusing witness; during the other sessions he was isolated with his interrogators.

Sometime during the ninth interrogation, Stewart broke down and admitted that he had robbed the deceased but had not meant to hurt her. Police then brought Stewart before a magistrate for the first time. The other four people arrested with Stewart were released for lack of involvement.

Nothing in the record indicated Stewart had been advised of his right to remain silent, or his right to counsel. In follow-up, the interrogating officers were asked to recount their conversations and no one mentioned that Stewart had been advised of his rights.

In court, the jury found Stewart guilty of robbery and first-degree murder and fixed his penalty as death. On appeal though, the Supreme Court of California reversed the decision on the basis that Stewart should have been advised of his right to remain silent and his right to counsel. The court said it could not presume, in the face of a silent record, that the police had done the required advisement. The Supreme Court affirmed the decision clarifying their decision further by saying that, . . . "Nor can a knowing and intelligent waiver of these rights be assumed on a silent record. Furthermore, Stewart's steadfast denial of the alleged offenses through eight of the nine interrogations over a period of five days is subject to no other construction than that he was compelled by persistent interrogation to forgo his Fifth Amendment privilege."

## Miranda, I Thought I Knew You

In *Missouri v. Seibert,*[5] Patrice Seibert was convicted of plotting to set a fire in 1997 that killed a teenager who had been staying at the family's trailer in Rolla, Missouri. Police explained that she arranged to have her home burned to cover up the death of her 12-year-old son, who had cerebral palsy, to avoid allegations of neglect.

The Supreme Court became involved because police used a strategy to extract a confession that was believed to be against her right to remain silent. The court, on a 5–4 vote, said that deliberately questioning a suspect twice, the first time without reading the Miranda warning, was usually improper, but the court left open the possibility that some confessions obtained after double interviews would be acceptable, providing police could prove the interrogation wasn't intended to undermine the Miranda warning.

The case considered was in regards to the treatment of murder suspect, Patrice Seibert, in *Missouri v. Seibert.* The Missouri Supreme Court issued a ruling that they believed that the two-step interrogation process used in her case was improper and that decision was upheld by the nation's highest court.

In a dissent, Justice Sandra Day O'Connor voiced her opinion that it would be tough for lower courts to determine if officers had gone too far.

---

5. *Missouri v. Sibert* (02-1371) 542 U.S. 600 (2004) 93 S. W. 3d 700

---

**Caution**—Date and time are critical on signed documents.

---

## DEFINING TERMS

### Confessions

A confession is a statement either oral or written by a person that tends to prove the commission of a crime and is self-incriminating. If it's not self-incriminating, it's not a confession.

### "Waive the Right"

A person can waive his or her Miranda rights but the prosecutor must prove that the waiver was knowing, voluntary, and intelligent. The proof is generally to have them sign a form.

### When Can Confessions Be Used Against You?

A truly involuntary confession is not admissible for any purpose. The Miranda warning and a valid waiver are prerequisites to the admissibility to any statement made by an accused during custodial interrogation. An interrogation will be considered "custodial" if the individual is not free to leave.

A confession obtained in violation of a defendant's Miranda rights but otherwise voluntary, may be used to impeach the defendant's testimony if he or she takes the stand at trial even though it is not admissible in the prosecutor's case to prove guilt.

The Miranda requirements do not apply to a witness testifying before a grand jury even if the witness is under compulsion of a subpoena.

## Closing in on the Word: Interrogation

Miranda does not apply to spontaneous talk not made in response to interrogation. However, cops must give the warnings before they can follow up. An interrogation is not only limited to questioning but also to actions by law enforcement designed to illicit incriminating statements. The question of psychological coercion is looked at in a case-by-case approach.

## Miranda, Don't Bother

A Miranda-based case involved Samuel Patane in United States v. Patane.[6] At issue here was a decision made by the Colorado Supreme Court in favor of Patane, a man who had told an officer not to bother reading him the Miranda warnings.

In June 2001, Samuel Francis Patane was arrested for harassing his ex-girlfriend, Linda O'Donnell. He was released on bond, subject to a temporary restraining order that prohibited him from contacting O'Donnell. Respondent apparently violated the restraining order by attempting to telephone O'Donnell. On June 6, Officer Tracy Fox of the Colorado Springs Police Department began to investigate the matter. On the same day, a county probation officer informed an agent of the Bureau of Alcohol, Tobacco, and Firearms (ATF), that Patane, a convicted felon, illegally possessed a .40 Glock pistol. The ATF relayed this information to

---

6. *United States v. Patane* (02-1183), 542 U.S. 630 (2004) 304 F.3d 1013

Detective Josh Benner, who worked closely with the ATF. Together, Detective Benner and Officer Fox went to Patane's house to question him about the domestic case, and they told him he had a right to remain silent, which he waived. After inquiring into respondent's attempts to contact O'Donnell, Officer Fox arrested the man for violating the restraining order. He was asked about the firearm, and reluctantly directed them to a gun in his bedroom, and was charged with illegal possession of a firearm.

A grand jury indicted Patane for possession of a firearm by a convicted felon, in violation of 18 United States Code. The District Court granted respondent's motion to suppress the firearm, reasoning that the officers lacked probable cause to arrest respondent for violating the restraining order.

The Denver-based 10th U.S. Circuit Court of Appeals ruled that the gun could not be used as evidence against Patane, because its discovery was the result of a statement made without a Miranda warning. Supreme Court's Justice Thomas and two other justices said a failure to give a suspect Miranda warnings did not make such evidence inadmissible in court. The "Self-Incrimination Clause" in Miranda is not implicated by the admission into evidence the physical fruit of a *voluntary* statement. Accordingly, there is no justification for extending the *Miranda* rule to this context. The *Miranda* rule is not a code of police conduct, and police do not violate the Constitution (or even the *Miranda* rule, for that matter) by mere failures to warn.

## Interrogations and "Right to Counsel"

The accused has the right to terminate the interrogation. If he or she indicates in any manner, at any time prior to or during questioning that he or she wants to remain silent the interrogation must stop.

Likewise, when the accused requests counsel, all questions must stop until he or she either gets a lawyer or initiates further communication.

## New: Wider Leeway in Interrogations

By a 5-4 vote, the Supreme Court just recently ruled against Texas defendant Raymond Levi Cobb, who had been charged with burglary and, months later, confessed to murdering a woman and her toddler during the burglary.

In 1993, the Owings family home was burglarized in Walker County, Texas. Margaret Owings and her 16-month-old daughter were reported missing. A neighbor, Cobb, confessed to the crime and claimed to know nothing of the disappearances.

After being indicted on a burglary charge and released on bond, Cobb confided to his father that he had killed Owings and her daughter. His father contacted the sheriff's office and Cobb was arrested. Apparently, he waived his right to be silent, and told officers about stabbing Owings during the burglary. After the deed, he says he dragged her body to a wooded area and discovered the baby when he went back to get a shovel. Cobb put the baby on the ground near her mother's body and he said while digging the hole, the baby fell into the pit.

The Sixth Amendment affords the right to counsel in criminal prosecutions. That right begins once someone is charged with a crime. At issue in the *Cobb* case, was whether as some lower courts have ruled, rights extend to crimes that are "factually related" to those that have actually been charged.

In response, the Supreme Court said the Sixth Amendment right is linked only to the specific offense being prosecuted at a given time. Chief Justice William Renquist said this: "To exclude evidence simply because other charges were pending at the time would unnecessarily frustrate . . . the investigation of criminal activities." He also noted that suspects still must be told of their right against self-incrimination. Those who dissented on the opinion, along with Alan Raphael, a law professor at Loyola University in Chicago, said basically that the decision limits what many lower courts had believed was the reach of the right to counsel.

The pendulum swings toward justice once again.

## THE DUE PROCESS '60s

The due process revolution of the Supreme Court in the 1960s, epitomized the social tensions of the period. A series of constitutional judgments were made that included such procedural issues as a defendant's right to an attorney, the right to exclude evidence seized illegally by the police, the right to a jury trial, and the protection against coerced confessions.

Not only does *Miranda* speak to the issue of coerced confessions, but it brought to the forefront critical right to counsel issues once again. A basic, fundamental liberty in the American criminal justice system is the right to be represented by counsel. An important notion, because more than 90 percent of all citizens accused of a crime in this country cannot afford to retain counsel. As stated in the Sixth Amendment of the Bill of Rights, in all criminal prosecutions the accused shall enjoy the right to have assistance of counsel for his or her defense.

### *Gideon v. Wainwright*[7] (1963)

Just before dawn on June 3, 1961, a Panama City, Florida, police officer was making his rounds. He noticed that the front door of the Bay Harbor Poolroom was slightly open. Upon investigation, he discovered the rear window of the building had been shattered, and a cigarette machine and a jukebox had apparently been robbed.

A local bystander informed the policeman that he had seen a man in the poolroom earlier, a man named Clarence Gideon. On the basis of this information, Gideon was arrested and charged with breaking and entering with intent to commit a misdemeanor, which is a felony under Florida law.

Gideon had been convicted and served time for a variety of previous offenses including burglary, possession of government property, other burglary attempts, and had escaped from prison, was captured, and served a full term, only to repeat another burglary in a different state. Paul B. Wice says in his book *Gideon v. Wainwright*, "On the surface, Gideon appeared to be a typical repeat-offender, a lawbreaker who started his lawbreaking early in life and continued to have trouble conforming to society's rules. On closer examination, however, Gideon, though handicapped by poor health and a forbidding criminal record, was attempting by the early 1950s to provide for his economically distraught family" (p. 11).

In any event, after the above Florida incident, Judge McCrary listened to the defendant's request for counsel because, Gideon argued, he was destitute and could not afford to pay a lawyer. The judge denied his application. Under Florida law and the current federal constitutional precedent at the time, the court was required to appoint counsel to represent a defendant charged with a capital offense only, a crime which held the potential for the death penalty.

Unable to muster the forces needed for defense, Gideon was sentenced to the maxi-

---

7. *Gideon v. Wainwright*, 372 U.S. 335, 83 S.Ct. 792, 9 L.Ed.2d 799 (1963).

mum penalty, five years imprisonment. Still without counsel, Gideon proceeded to teach himself the law and made appeals on his own behalf. Gideon's handwritten appeal, written in pencil on notebook paper, eventually caught the attention of the Supreme Court. In some instances, Gideon discovered among the inmates that counsel was actually not denied, but there was no consistency about when it was applied.

This time, Gideon did have counsel when his petition was heard during the 1962-63 Supreme Court term. A successful Washington lawyer, Abe Fortas, was appointed for the case. In its decision, the Supreme Court stated that: ". . . reason and reflection require us to recognize that in our adversary system, the accused cannot be assured a fair trial unless counsel is provided for him." The court overturned his conviction. Through his efforts, the *Gideon* decision extended right to counsel to all state indigent defendants–people who could not afford to hire counsel–facing felony trials, and helped to regulate the right to counsel by defining the question of when it should be practiced. This notion helped to bolster the adversarial system which formed the very basis of the U.S. system of justice. It was believed that two advocates battling before an impartial judge and jury would produce facts and that the resulting verdict would be fairly determined.

Over the years, various rulings have come down pertaining to this principle of counsel. The dramatic outcome for today is, if a defendant was entitled to a lawyer by law, the failure to provide him or her with counsel is an automatic reversal of the conviction, even without showing any specific unfairness in the proceeding. At nontrial proceedings though, defendants must show they were actually harmed as a result of their denial to counsel.

**Times when the accused DOES NOT have a right to a government-appointed lawyer:**
- for a discretionary appeal
- blood sampling
- handwriting sample
- photo identification
- pre-charge investigative lineup
- during a parole or probation revocation proceeding
- at a postconviction proceeding where a "writ of habeous corpus" is served–meaning, the person is to be brought forth to court to determine if detention is lawful

**Times when the accused HAS A RIGHT to government-appointed counsel; if indigent and in:**
- custodial police interrogation (in custody, held by publicly paid police, in a question-and-answer session)
- postindictment interrogation: whether custodial or not, charges have been filed, cops cannot interrogate without a lawyer
- preliminary hearings to determine probable cause–before that hearing can be held, must provide a lawyer
- at an arraignment, guilty plea or not
- postcharge lineup; the lawyer cannot stop the lineup, his or her main function is to make sure it's done properly
- at a guilty plea or sentencing
- during all felony trials (either a $1,000 or more fine; or a year in jail)
- misdemeanor trials when imprisonment is actually imposed
- participating in an appeal as a matter of right (see below)

**FYI**—The self-representation or "pro se" defense is seldom used but it will show up in your tenure. The Constitution places a defendant's "free choice" above the need for effective representation, although most lawyers have said, "The defendant who chooses to represent himself has a fool for a client!"

In 1984, the Supreme Court also added on some other factors to self-representation, namely, that a defendant does not have the right to personal instruction from the trial judge, he does not have the right to obstruct the workings of the criminal process, and he may not be represented by another person who is not a member of the bar. Judges sometimes appoint standby counsel, someone who assists defendants who wish to defend themselves.

TRIAL

▼

LOSE

▼

RIGHT TO APPEAL
(have to have a lawyer)

▼

TO COURT OF APPEALS

▼

STATE SUPREME COURT
can accept or reject case
(don't have to have a lawyer
for discretionary appeals)

▼

U.S. SUPREME COURT
(may accept or reject appeal).
Will need representation.

## INDIGENTS

An indigent is a person who does not have enough money or property to hire counsel, but it does not mean they are totally devoid of funds.

- Any doubts of indigency are resolved in favor of the individual.
- Right to counsel includes the right to "effective" counsel.
- An ineffective assistance of counsel claimed by the convicted defendant is the most often raised grounds for appeal. (If

the defendant is successful on appeal, the case is remanded back for a new trial.)

## RIGHTS OF PERSONS IN CRIMINAL PROSECUTIONS

### Privilege and Confidentiality

If the testimony before the court were based on information the accused told his or her attorney in confidence, should the attorney be made to admit the client's statements? And what is the difference between so-called "privileged communication" and "confidential communication"? Or is there a difference?

"Sidebar? Your Honor?"

*Privileged communications* are those protected by law, such as transmissions of information that take place between an attorney and client, or a priest and the penitent. The person on the receiving end of the information cannot be compelled to divulge the contents of the communication unless the person doing the confiding waives his or her legal right to secrecy. Likewise, private talks between husband and wife are also privileged; however, in some states, a person is allowed to testify on behalf of their spouse. Some other areas where privileged state-

**Caution**—A client's statements to his or her lawyer concerning an intention to commit a crime in the future are not confidential. In emergency or life-threatening situations, a lawyer might have to reveal such a statement to the police even before a crime is committed. Likewise, a defendant cannot ask his or her lawyer to hold on to an incriminating tangible object, such as a knife that was used in a stabbing.

ments may occur are: between police informers and police; physicians, therapists and their patients; and newspaper reporters and their secret, anonymous sources.

*Confidentiality* carries a different interpretation. Confidentiality refers to an ethical obligation on the part of a skilled specialist to safeguard information given by a client, or clients, in a professional capacity. Confidential sharing has no legal protection in the court, unless it is also privileged communication as well. For example, a marriage counselor ethically would not divulge any statements made to him or her by clients. But in the courtroom venue, the information the counselor possesses is not considered privileged and he or she will be compelled to tell, or risk a contempt of court citation (a remedy of a fine or imprisonment levied by the judge is available for refusing).

## Eavesdropping

Discussing the case in a restaurant can be dangerous for a defendant who speaks confidentially with his or her lawyer over dinner. Clients may get more than dessert, they may get "just desserts!" A loudmouth defendant

has no reasonable expectation of privacy in a public place; the confession is subject to eavesdroppers.

## AMENDMENT VI

## Criminal Court Procedures

In all criminal prosecutions, the accused shall enjoy the right to a speedy and public trial, by an impartial jury of the State and district wherein the crime shall have been committed, which district shall have been previously ascertained by law, and to be informed of the nature and cause of the accusation; to be confronted with the witnesses against him; to have compulsory process for obtaining witnesses in his favor, and to have the assistance of counsel for his defence.

## Explanation

Any person accused of a crime has a right to a fair and public trial by a jury in the state in which the crime took place. The charges against the person must be spelled out and any accused person has the right to know who his or her accusers are. The accused

**Other Notes**—The defendant who brings his "girl" along to a confidential attorney-client meeting, risks losing the privilege of confidentiality according to protocol. The District Attorney might be able to ask the girlfriend about what was said during the conference.

also has a right to a lawyer to defend him or her, and to question those who testify against the defense. The attorney may also call people to speak in favor of the client at trial.

## SIXTH AMENDMENT: RIGHTS OF PERSONS IN CRIMINAL TRIALS

*For Evelyn Stevens, wife of the deceased and murdered subject of this trial, it had seemed like years since she'd last heard those words from police officers, Lieutenants Haley and McGrew, "Ms. Stevens, it's about your husband, Douglas Stevens." Looking into the mirror this morning at tired swollen eyes and strained nerves, she would swear she'd aged seven years in the waiting.*

## Speedy and Public

The Sixth Amendment to the Constitution guarantees all criminal defendants "the right to a speedy and public trial." And while some defendants get trials that they feel are altogether too speedy, the constitutional guarantee really serves two purposes. First, a speedy trial relieves a defendant of the pervasive consequences involved with being accused. If the accused is subject to incarceration, any length of time in jail will seem oppressive–not to mention the drain of personal finances, loss of business, personal anxiety, public scorn, and the weakening of his or her defense. Second, a speedy trial is to promote society's interest in the prompt disposition of charges. Common, law-abiding citizens are often concerned about proper and timely administration of justice when it occurs in "their own backyard"; they may feel threatened by the unresolved details surrounding the crime, and the potential for

additional harm should the perpetrator be out "on the loose."

One very important note on timing–the right to a speedy trial begins to apply its pressure only after the person has been accused, that is, after he or she has been indicted, received information, or is taken into custody and under arrest. Because of this stipulation, the right is not violated by a delay in filing charges where such delay might violate the person's other rights. Once arrested, however, the accused is entitled to a speedy trial, even if subsequently released and not recalled for a substantial period of time.

The actual amount of time that denotes speedy is the judge's call. The conduct of both the prosecution and the defendant must be weighed by a judge, who also takes in additional factors such as: the length of delay, the reason for the delay, the defendant's declaration or denial of rights, and actual prejudice to the defendant. Length of delay alone does not establish a violation of a speedy trial, because unless the delay has been sufficiently long enough to be prejudicial, there is no need to examine the other relevant factors.

Some states, however, exact specific time limits within which an accused must be brought to trial. Often they will use the federal guidelines which are published under the Speedy Trial Act.[8] Two of the federal time limits are: The government must formally charge a defendant with a crime within thirty days of the defendant's arrest, and the government should bring a case to trial not less than thirty nor more than seventy days after charging a defendant with a crime. Under state statutes (Florida, for example), a nonincarcerated defendant must go to trial within one hundred twenty days, and an

---

8. Speedy Trial Act, 18 U.S.C. § 3161.

incarcerated defendant has a shorter trial date time limit of ninety days. These are not set in concrete and are typically subject to a host of exceptions. Often, both defendants and prosecutors agree to delay proceedings.

The reason for delay is legally significant. If the prosecutor deliberately attempts to delay the trial to his or her advantage, this weighs heavily for the defendant and the speedy trial claim is taken seriously. It can, ultimately, result in dismissal of the case. However, if the delay is sustained through efforts by the accused, then the accused will be deemed to have waived his or her right to a speedy trial.

One final note: The nature and amount of prejudice coming from the delay is considered in light of the consequences the right is designed to protect. For example, if the delay has created a lengthy or oppressive incarceration, has resulted in the loss of evidence, the death of a witness, inaccuracy of witness testimony, or has increased the anxiety of the accused measurably, a showing of prejudice will be strongly considered by the judge when the time comes for making a "speedy trial analysis."

## Right To Be Present at Trial

In all criminal trials the defendant has the right to be present during the proceeding from arraignment to sentence unless the right has been waived or forfeited. The Federal Rules state that presence is required at every stage, including the impaneling of the jury, the return of the verdict, and the imposition of sentence. A defendant who voluntarily fails to show up for trial may be tried "in absentia."

A few instances where continued presence is not required is if the defendant is: voluntarily absent after the trial has commenced; involved in a noncapital case; OR, can be dismissed after being warned about disruptive behavior. Also, if the defendant is an organization and represented by an attorney he may be absent, OR, for a punishment and fine and or imprisonment for not more than one year; OR, if the proceeding is only a conference or a hearing involving a question of law; OR, when it involves a correction of sentence. Generally, though, the courts deem that it is essential to the proper administration of criminal justice that a defendant be present, and that the courts should indulge every reasonable basis against the loss of this constitutional right. Of course, if a defendant must be removed from the courtroom for belligerent behavior, the court makes communication with his or her attorney possible, until such time when he or she agrees to behave and return to the court.

## PUBLIC TRIAL

In addition to the timeliness of trials and presence at trials, the Sixth Amendment also provides that in "all criminal prosecutions the accused shall enjoy the right to . . . public trial. . . ." This right to a trial which is available to the public is grounded in history and the Anglo-American distrust of secret goings-on. The purpose of a public trial is to safeguard against any attempts at employing the courts as instruments of prosecution and to keep citizens apprised of actions against its own. There are, however, certain instances where trials take place as closed proceedings. The judge has the ability to exclude members of the public from the trial, if he or she feels the need arises. One example may be in the case of a rape violation. Another reason to close a trial is if it involves youthful offenders. As recently as 1990, a New York trial case of an investment banker who was mugged was closed to spectators during the victim's testimony, and her name was never printed in the media.

An area of major concern currently exists about whether to bar the media from a trial. The courts have said that even if the government, the defendant, and the judge have all agreed to a closed hearing, that the Fifth, Sixth, and First Amendments could be raised by members of the media. Because of this, rules have been laid down in respect to when the media can and cannot attend a trial. Neither the defendant nor anyone else has a right to require the judge to admit unneeded persons into the courtroom. In addition, if seating capacity is exhausted, exclusion of nonessential persons is totally appropriate.

## Sequestration Rules

Sequestration are rules that attempt to prevent witnesses from being influenced by the testimony of other witnesses. Witnesses who are sequestered must sit outside the courtroom until called to testify. Normally, they cannot discuss their testimony with anyone else who is waiting. Once excused from giving further testimony however, they are free to go. Typically, if a defendant's family or friends are going to testify, sequestration rules prevent them from being physically present in the courtroom for much of the trial.

\* \* \*

*"In the legal matter of the State of Ohio versus Derrick Borehead," the clerk called out, "the charge is one count, murder in the first degree with special circumstances. A plea of not guilty has been entered."*

*Judge Wheedel peered over the top of his spectacles from one table to the other. "Are we ready?"*

*The people at both tables stood up in deference to his Honor. Assistant District Attorney Henry Cassin said, "Ready for the prosecution, your honor."*

*"Ready for the defense," Attorney Jensen declared. His assistant, a young man with thick hair and generous eyebrows was shaking his head in the affirmative, bobbing his head all round like the fake toy terrier in the rear window of a car.*

*"Good," the judge said, "Let's impanel a jury and get underway."*

## SELECTION OF THE JURY

The primary phase of any criminal trial is the selection of a jury. For the accused, now the defendant, it is probably the most important procedure. The right to a trial by jury is a distinctive feature in the system of jurisprudence, dating back more than seven centuries. The English Magna Carta of 1215 contained the stipulation that no freeholder would be deprived of life or property except by judgment of his peers. Article III of the Constitution incorporates this principle with the following statement: "A trial of all crimes except in cases of impeachment shall be by jury." The Sixth Amendment holds that, "in all criminal prosecutions the accused shall enjoy the right to a speedy trial by an impartial jury."

The accused also has a right to dispense with a jury and can request to be tried by a judge alone. These trials are called *bench trials*. In some states, defendants must file a request for a jury trial either when they enter a plea, or at some time before the beginning of a court term in which a jury would be impaneled. Failure to file constitutes a waiver of the right. In all criminal matters in which jail is a potential penalty, though, the accused have an absolute right to a jury trial.

The primary purpose of a jury is to serve as a check against arbitrary or vindictive law enforcement. In *Duncan v. Louisiana*[9] (1968) the U.S. Supreme Court recognized that

9. *Duncan v. Louisiana*, 391 U.S. 145, 88 S.Ct. 1444, 20 L.Ed.2d 491 (1968).

juries advance the means needed for a fact-finding process: they are selected by law and sworn in to determine matters of fact and, sometimes, matters pertaining to sentencing in a criminal action. But, in reality, most often, the judge is both the fact-finder and the person who decides what law to apply to those facts. It is almost unique to the American system that ordinary citizens have the responsibility to decide a criminal defendant's ultimate fate. The judge's power—and the power of precedent or previous law—help in defining the rules of law and the sentencing guidelines, and thus, provide him or her certain amounts of discretionary authority.

It is important for the accused to know what size jury he or she is entitled to. Over the years, jury costs have forced states to limit jury size and in many states a litigant is likely to get a six-person jury if he or she is not charged with a felony. Given the choice, the twelve-person panel would be to the accused's advantage. Since the prosecution needs a unanimous jury to convict, it makes sense that he or she is more likely to find sympathetic individuals within a larger group. But still, there are states which provide for less than unanimous verdicts in criminal cases, but they are non-death penalty cases primarily. Using that scenario, for example, conviction could be based on nine out of twelve jurors voting for guilty, and this would be constitutionally valid for that state.

Each side in a case is given a list of the potential jurors. There are perhaps 120 names on the call-up list, so an initial examination of them is difficult. A much smaller percentage will be represented in court on the day of the trial and, through attrition and nearing the end of the term of service, the numbers will be smaller still. From this pool, fourteen names (twelve jurors and two alternates), will be drawn at random from the attendees. This first batch will undergo a *voir dire* examination by the judge and the attorneys for both sides.

## Voir Dire

*Voir dire*, French for "to speak truly," is the questioning of the jurors by both opposing attorneys. The process is meant to ferret out those who will, in their administration, act fairly, and remain unbiased for any reason. The prosecution and the defense are each allowed a specific number of "preemptory challenges," the ability to remove prospective jurors from their duty with no explanation given. Jurors can also be removed for "cause." This occurs when there is some fact that is disclosed which would make the prospective juror unfit to serve. Some common reasons for removal may be if there is a relationship between one of the jurors and a witness; a juror may be a conscientious objector when it comes to alcohol, religion, or guns which would render a prejudice; or if a potential juror is a member of a specific race or ethnic group of which someone involved is a member. And in cases involving a capital offense, such as murder, jurors are often subjected to complex questions about their attitudes toward the death penalty. A juror who could never vote to put a defendant to death is likely to be excused for cause, as is one who would always vote for death for any defendant convicted of murder.

## The "CSI Effect"

Unlike television infotainment, true criminal evidence collection and methodology can be at its extremes: both boring *and unpredictable* science. Juxtaposed against real life, however, its inherent nature produces stories stranger and more interesting than anything made up.

The "CSI Effect" is a phenomenon[10] we have been documenting for a few years now and it means that many people enjoy and watch the CSI-type television programs—*CSI-Las Vegas, Miami* and *New York, Crossing Jordan, Bones,* and others of that ilk. Because viewers feel they are getting an education in forensic science, they become "armchair detectives." Consequently, when they are called up for jury duty, as the result of this occurrence, they have unrealistic expectations about what forensic science can actually accomplish and many defendants are going free.

Here are some things about police that you may be unaware of:

- Criminalists or evidence collection officers are sometimes police officers but never process the evidence.
- Gunshot does not "pick up" people and most victims don't realize they've been shot right away and are able to return fire.
- Car windshields do not shatter under a bullet firing.
- Hiding behind a car will get you killed.
- Homicides represent less than 10% of all major crimes.

## Voir Dire Changes

Because of the "CSI Effect," many lawyers are now questioning potential jurors about their television viewing habits and asking if what they see on TV, they believe is true. If yes, and they are true fans, some jurors are being disqualified at *voir dire* because of their faith in this mis- and disinformation about the realities of the criminal justice system.

## Truth in the Lab

- Most criminal labs have an average backlog of 15,000 cases.
- Lab results often take *months*—if extremely high profile with political pressure, or, if an especially heinous crime, many weeks are common.
- Drugs cases are the majority of work.
- Forensic scientists are lab technicians who *never* interview suspects, and most never testify in court or even know the outcome of the case.
- Forensic scientists almost never crossover into another discipline but do only one thing, such as fingerprints—day in, day out.

## Grand Jury Basics

Before we leave this information on juries, a few notes about grand juries. A grand jury is made up of a number of private citizens selected either to review or investigate felony cases for terms lasting prescribed periods of time. Traditionally, a grand jury consists of twenty-three persons and requires a majority vote to indict. At this time, two-thirds of American states do not use grand juries.

The grand jury system and due process rights generally are recognized as two of the great "checks"—of the checks and balances principle—charged with protecting private citizens from the dangers of an overzealous prosecutor and a person's due process rights. In the case *United States v. Dionisio,*[11] the Supreme Court proclaimed that the purpose of the grand jury is to stand between government agents and the suspect as an unbiased evaluator of evidence. Thus, in theory, the grand jury should protect suspects from

---

10. http://www.the-CSI-effect.com
11. *U.S. v. Dionisio,* 410 U.S. 1, 93 S.Ct. 764, 35 L.Ed.2d 67 (1973).

indictments based on unsubstantiated information presented to it by the prosecutor.

Over the years, a build-up of constitutional restraints have been placed on traditional, crime investigation agencies. As a consequence, there has been an increase in the popularity for using investigative grand juries. In grand jury proceedings the target of the investigation is not afforded the normal due process rights that a criminal suspect receives at the stationhouse because of its very nature–its coercive behavior. For example, in a federal grand jury proceeding, a witness is only allowed to speak with counsel by stepping outside the courtroom.

* * *

*The young defense attorney's assistant unconsciously pushed his fingers through his thick hair, it was beginning an afternoon curl. He would be the first one to admit he was nervous, and excited; excited at the prospect of actually being able to sit in on the Stevens murder case, and excited at the idea of keeping good notes on the prosecution's ploys. He wanted to write a book one day, and this was the stuff of good fiction. And when the prosecution brought in Ms. Gaines, a surprise witness, he thought that Defense Attorney Jensen would cave, but, wow! The prosecution's move, even though it had been sprung on Jensen–"We were just able to locate Ms. Gaines, your Honor"–did not shake him for a minute. Jensen ended the session with a sigh and the words, "This comes as a complete surprise to us, your Honor. We will need a few days to prepare our cross-examination."*

## Confronting Witnesses

The right to confront witnesses is protected by the Sixth Amendment, an all-purpose amendment for the important aspects of a trial, and this clause is no exception. The confrontation provision serves three purposes. The first has to do with oath, and oath-taking was an integral component in the tri-

als of ancient western civilization. The oath helps to ensure the reliability of the witnesses' testimony. Secondly, confrontation exposes the witness to further examination by means of the defense's cross-examination and, finally, it allows the judge and jury a chance to weigh the demeanor of the witness and helps them to discern credibility.

Since the right to confront witnesses was deemed a fundamental right in federal and state prosecutions, it is applicable to state's law under the Fourteenth Amendment due process clause. This right includes the right of the accused to be physically present during the course of a trial. However, the accused can waive this right also, by voluntarily absenting him- or herself from the proceedings which will continue on in his or her absence.

The right to confront witnesses is essentially the right to cross-examine witnesses. Being able to cross-examine witnesses is an important skill to master and one of the more significant tools for the trial attorney. When witnesses claim to tell the truth as they know it, that truth may be tainted because of their viewpoint or exposure. It is up to the defense attorney to bring the truth back to the middle by careful questioning. There are many reasons the answers to questions will be skewed: the witnesses are trying to shield themselves; they may have a desire to punish the accused; or they may become confused, misinformed or fail to see the importance of what they say, against what they believe. Witnesses may not want to follow through on the adage of the law principle that states, the accused is innocent until proven guilty. So the defense must have some way to sift out beliefs from the facts; they hold the right to impeach the witnesses' own words or to present an alternate theory to the crime.

There is another part to the confrontation process. For what good would it do to have questions of a person if he or she doesn't show up? The omission itself could be damaging. The Sixth Amendment holds another expressly provided provision. It is not spelled out, but there should be some way to make the right to confront witnesses part of a compulsory process. There should be a way for the defendant to assure that there is the means to compel someone to come to court, just as the prosecutor has the power to subpoena witnesses on the state's behalf. The defendant must depend on others for this claim.

## Little Catches

There are other questions inherent in the trial process too. What if the trial judge makes threatening remarks that drive the only defense witness off the stand? Or what if the government decides to deport a witness? The courts have said in *Webb v. Texas* (1972),[12] that this tactic of the threatening judge, in effect, prevents the accused from presenting his or her witnesses and their version of the facts, and is not allowed. Furthermore, exclusion of crucial defense evidence by the trial judge impairs the right of the accused to present a defense, even where the evidence offered is technically inadmissible under appropriate local rules. For example, in *Chambers v. Mississippi*

(1973),[13] the defendant offered evidence that the crime he was accused of was committed by someone else and had an oral confession to prove it. The evidence was excluded on the grounds that it was hearsay under the rules of evidence. The Supreme Court reversed that decision, saying that if the evidence were held back for a substantial assurance of trustworthiness, it would impair the defendant's right to present a defense.

And what happens when the government deports a witness? If the deported witness and his or her testimony were material and favorable to the defendant's constitutional claim for defense, then the compulsory process for right to compel witnesses to testify was violated, and the defense gets another trial.

## Double Jeopardy, the Movie

Since most people have deeply rooted ideas about justice, certain cases and their outcome seem to inflame their sensibilities. These are the ideas that law students debate ad nauseum. The movie *Double Jeopardy* illustrates one of these controversial cases. In the film, a woman and her husband are sailing overnight on a new boat they bought. The woman wakes up to find blood everywhere and her husband is gone. In a panic, she

---

**Other Notes**—Here is an interesting take on evidence elsewhere. The state of Virginia has something called the 21-Day Rule. The Virginia General Assembly has repeatedly protected Rule 1:1 of the Virginia Supreme Court—an archaic statute that prevents incarcerated individuals from having their guilt or sentencing reviewed on the basis of new evidence twenty-one days or more after their initial sentencing. Virginia's 21-Day Rule, which was issued to give the citizens of Virginia "finality," prevents the admission of evidence that at the time of sentencing may have appeared inconsequential or inconclusive due to underdeveloped technology or facts. This is particularly poignant in rape and murder cases for which DNA is now available. Expect more head-butting for those seeking to repeal the 21-Day Rule.

---

12. *Web v. Texas*, 409 U.S. 95 (1972).
13. *Chambers v. Mississippi*, 410 U.S. 284 (1973).

finds a blood-stained knife and picks it up. In a nutshell, she is later tried and convicted for her husband's murder for which she is sentenced. Desperate and afraid, she asks her best friend to take care of her six-year-old son who is now the recipient of his father's $2 million life insurance policy. She spends ten years in prison.

During this time inside, her friend disappears and when the woman finally finds this "so-called" friend and talks to her son on the telephone, the husband, who was supposedly murdered, walks in. While on the phone, the little boy says, "Hi, Daddy!" This alerts his mother to the set-up between her friend and her husband to get the life insurance money and run away together.

## While on the phone, the little boy says, "Hi, Daddy!"

Incensed and incarcerated, another inmate tells her that when she gets out, she can walk right up to her husband, who is already declared legally "dead," and shoot him in the face. She learns how to get paroled and her plan is set in motion. The rational behind this idea is that she has already been tried, convicted, and served her time for his murder. The question is: Would it be double jeopardy to try, convict, and sentence her again?

## Double Jeopardy for Real

Another characteristic of the important Fifth Amendment, is a clause that says, no person shall "be subject for the same offense to be twice put in jeopardy of life or limb." This is our constitutional prohibition against double jeopardy. Basically, it means that if the defendant is found "not guilty" at trial, or is placed in jeopardy for a significant portion of the trial, he or she cannot be tried again for the same offense even if overwhelming

evidence comes in later that proves his or her guilt.

But, as with every other law, there are exceptions here too. The first exception to the rule is when with the defendant's consent the first trial ends in a mistrial. He or she can be tried again for the same offense in the same courtroom. But if a mistrial happens to be declared without his or her consent, it can be moved forward for "the ends of public justice."

## FILING A MOTION

Defendants can only be subjected to another trial if they "file a motion" to move for a new trial. They must typically do so very soon after the jury reaches a verdict. In federal court, new trial motions must be made within seven days and based on newly discovered evidence. An example of this is if a witness for the defendant was out of the country or fled for some reason; or, if new DNA testing became available. A request for a new trial by a defendant is considered a "waiver" of double jeopardy rights and he or she must abide by the new ruling.

A defendant can be tried for the same offense twice if the first case was dismissed, either at trial or during trial, but before conviction. If the trial was already begun, the dismissal must be based on a reason other than the defendant's guilt or innocence.

Another way to get a second trial is in consideration of either a hung jury (they cannot agree), or when the death or illness of judge, juror, or defendant stalls the trial.

## Double Jeopardy Timing

You do know that double jeopardy does not exist as long as the statute of limitations (period of time within which a case can be filed following a crime) has not run out and there is no one charged. There is no statute of limitations on a homicide (although a "solved" case can be "cleared or closed").

Also, defendants are not considered in double jeopardy until the actual trial begins. Jeopardy attaches once a jury is sworn in or when the first witness is sworn in to testify in a nonjury trial.

But, as soon as a judge or jury finds a defendant "not guilty" to all charges, the prosecution cannot appeal, nor can the prosecution ask the judge to set aside the verdict and order a new trial. So, in essence, even if the judge and half the world knows the decision is wrong–hello, O.J. Simpson–a "not guilty" verdict is final.

If a defendant was convicted and appeals his or her case to a higher court, and, the higher court reverses the conviction based on an error made in the first trial and a new trial is sanctioned, (the phrase is: the Court remands or returns the case to the court of original jurisdiction for a new trial), by simply initiating the appeals process the defendant has "waived his claim to double jeopardy" meaning, the second time is law. But there are always exceptions to the rules, and rules for the exceptions, and in the case of appeals there is one additional consideration: the new trial must be for the same offense and not for a greater offense nor a greater degree of offense. For example, a class B felony cannot become a class A felony, namely because each "class" or classification carries with it different extremes of punishment.

## Unsatisfied with the Movie

It is a done deal for Ashley Judd, the star of the movie *Double Jeopardy* and the end is satisfactory with some minor liberties. But a good friend of mine tells me a prosecutor in a federal court would probably try to get Judd on another charge if she really killed

her husband after her prison term; and, remember, there is nothing that says she can't be sued in a civil court, which is another trial procedure with a different basis of proof. It's just that the results of this new civil trial would be remuneration or some other type of restitution.

Of course, if no one knew about the killing or, if they didn't care (such as with a sympathetic detective), or, if they didn't file charges (lack of evidence) for the actual death, she is free.

As you can see, the Fifth and Sixth Amendments are loaded with promises, rules, and guarantees so important to the rights of the accused. Still, in preparation for an investigation and subsequent trial, the defendant may not fully realize the imbalance of power. While the prosecution can freely grant immunity and compel witnesses to testify, the defense has no such power; defendants can only protect themselves against third-degree tactics, hope for reliable evidence in their favor, and rely on the wisdom of the judge and jury to sort things out.

## AMENDMENT VIII

## Bail, Cruel and Unusual Punishment

Excessive bail shall not be required, nor excessive fines imposed, nor cruel and unusual punishments inflicted.

## Explanation

Usually an amount of money is requested by the court to ensure that an accused person will return for his or her court case and final judgment and this is called *bail*. The amount of bail or the fine imposed as punishment for a crime must be reasonable compared with the seriousness of the crime involved. Any punishment deemed too harsh or too severe for a crime is prohibited.

The last important right in respect to criminal prosecution involves the Eighth Amendment and its guarantees against excessive bail, and cruel and unusual punishment. The exercising of this right does not mean that the accused has a constitutional right to bail. The Supreme Court has not declared it to be a due process right. The accused may be denied bail if the prosecution demonstrates clear and convincing evidence that his or her release might cause danger to the public. Some critics have become clearly upset with this decision citing that it automatically negates the presumption of innocence. This is one of the subtle incongruities of the law.

Also, the Supreme Court has never expressly said that the excessive bail clause is enforceable against the states via the Fourteenth Amendment. The matter is left up to the individual states. So although the idea of bail is to insure the appearance of the accused in court, it is up to the states to define what is excessive.

In one case, cruel and unusual punishment was used to help *define* the punishment. The Supreme Court invalidated a provision that prescribed a state death penalty law that allowed capital punishment in cases of rape.[14]

The cruel and unusual punishment clause is a throw-back to the use of excessive physical punishment of prisoners common in early European history.

## Bad Prison Conditions

The Supreme Court has made it tougher

Figure 5. Bail bonds are a 24-hour service.

14. *Coke v. Georgia*, 433 U.S. 584, 97 S.Ct. 2861, 53 L.Ed.2d 982 (1977).

for prisoners to file fictitious lawsuits claiming poor prison conditions. In order to challenge substandard prison conditions as cruel and unusual, their complaints must meet certain standards. A prisoner must prove that (1) prison officials actually knew about the conditions challenged, and, (2) that despite the substantial risk to inmates caused by the conditions, the officials failed to do anything about them.

## REVIEW QUESTIONS AND ANSWERS

### Key Words to Define

- **Blanket assumptions**–Unlikely conclusions sometimes based on preconceptions.
- **Criminal procedure**–Set of rules the government (police and lawyers) must follow in order to maintain law and order, while protecting a citizen's rights.
- **Double jeopardy**–A person cannot be tried for the same crime twice; a guarantee in the Bill of Rights (Fifth Amendment)
- **Due process**–Procedural issues guaranteed to a defendant.
- **Eavesdropping**–A person does not have an expectation of privacy if his speech is overheard in a restaurant; often used as a tactic by investigative bodies.
- **Grand jury**–Not used in all states; A state jury who looks at all types of evidence and decides if there is enough reason to go to trial.
- **In absentia**–Defendant voluntarily fails to show and the trial continues without him.
- **Indigent**–A person who does not have enough money or property to hire a lawyer; without resources, income, etc.

- **Petit jury**–Hears a case at trial and makes a decision about it.
- **Pro se**–Self-representation in the courtroom.
- **Sequestration**–Rules that attempt to prevent witnesses from being influenced by testimony of others; news media, or other distractions.
- **Voir dire**–Means "to speak truly"; it's the questioning and qualifying of potential jurors.

### Question for Review and Discussion

1. *Question:* What is *taking* the Fifth Amendment? *Answer:* No person shall compelled to be a witness against his own best interests; cannot testify against himself.

2. *Question:* How does the Supreme Court define "interrogation"? *Answer:* Express questioning.

3. *Question:* Recite Miranda warnings. 1. You have a right to remain silent, 2. Anything you say can and will be used against you in a court of law, 3. You have a right to talk to a lawyer and have him present at questioning, 4. If you cannot afford a lawyer the state will appoint one for you, 5. You can decide at any time to exercise these rights and not answer questions or make statements.

4. *Question:* Name two things the accused does not get a government-appointed lawyer for. Discretionary appeal, blood sampling, handwriting sample, photo i.d., pre-charge investigative line-up, parole or probation revocation hearings, post-conviction "writ of habeous corpus."

5. *Question:* What is the difference between "privileged" and "confidential" communication? *Answer:* Privileged talk is protected by law such as with: attorney-client conferences, whereas confidential communications are ethical obligations on the behalf of a skilled specialist such as a

marriage counselor out of court only (they can be compelled to testify).

6. *Question:* When does the right to speedy trial begin? *Answer:* After arrest.

7. *Question:* Explain the term "bench trial." *Answer:* The defendant has a right to dispense with a jury trial and can request a trial and decision to be made by a judge.

8. *Question:* How do the prosecution and defense attorney remove jurors during voir dire? *Answer:* Preemptory challenges.

9. *Question:* If someone's trial ends in mistrial, can they be tried again? *Answer:* Yes.

10. *Question:* Does everyone get bail? *Answer:* No, if the crime is serious or heinous in nature or if there is the risk of the defendant leaving the country; or, if based on past behavior the defendant bolted, bail may be denied.

## *Essay Exploration*

What is the essence and importance of "confronting witnesses" for the defendant? If the student says any of these in their essay: Part of the Sixth Amendment; It requires that the witness take an oath, exposes the witness to further examination, allows the judge and jury to assess the witnesses' demeanor and credibility.

# Chapter 9

# MEN IN BLUE

Anarchism is a game at which
police can beat you.
       –George Bernard Shaw, *Misalliance*

## Police Models

Citizens generally form their idea of what police are and what they do by watching popular television shows or reading national newspaper headlines. The operations, size, and capabilities of their own police are assumed to be similar to those depicted on the screen. While these "model" composites are entertaining, they may have little to no resemblance to the function, procedure, and real human beings who inhabit the system in your home town or community. Each law enforcement agency, whether local or city police, a sheriff's department, state police, or one of the federal law enforcement agencies, has its own blueprint of hierarchy, jurisdiction, and operating procedures. For this reason, a citizen or even an interested career-minded individual should check out the policies of the agency he or she intends to learn about, for information specific to that organization.

## HISTORICAL OFFICERS

Because law enforcement did not spring full-blown from the breast of Lady Liberty, and because some law enforcement students may be interested in the historical underpinnings of how men became police officers, a few of the key classical figures who helped to shape law enforcement are featured below. The "historical" evolution of policing has important enforcement features which we still use today.

## England: Seventeenth and Eighteenth Centuries

In early England, every citizen was a police officer and every police officer was a citizen, marshalling other citizens together. With the growth of urbanization, a variety of buildings were grouped together, commerce developed and town guilds appointed a "watch and ward" brigade to rouse the citizens and protect them from fire and burglar-ies.

Constables were overseers for some communities and beadles (minor parish officials) were paid to clear vagrants, and preserve the peace at civil functions and within the church. In the late 1600s, certain citizens functioned as private investigators called thief-takers, but their behavior more aptly resembled the bounty hunters of yore. Although they possessed no official status or statutory authority, they received rewards from the crown for their service. Highway robbery was big business, making travel perilous and, in 1693, Parliament offered £40 for the capture of a highwayman, payable on conviction. The thief-taker who nabbed his man, also got the robber's assets, his horse, money, and weapons. It so happened that sometimes professional thief-takers were themselves criminals.

The gin riots, around 1720, were responsible for the modern police. Because inexpensive alcohol was available to the folks in urban ghettos, binges of drinking, rabble-rousing, and rioting lasted almost 100 years. Watch and ward bailiffs got beaten up during these skirmishes and often could not control the situation undertaken. As a consequence, citizens were read the "Riot Act" which was a call for the military to quell the riots—some believe this was the precursor of our present day National Guard.

In the early 1700s, a man named Jonathan Wild, and befitting his name, did just that—ran wild as an organized crime boss. Operating the largest crime faction in London, Wild controlled robbery, thieves, and fencing. His recruits "turned over" their loot by charging a ransom for it. Wild and his conspirators operated with a free hand until the efforts of Henry Fielding.

Henry Fielding is known as one of the greatest artists among English novelists of the eighteenth century, and is credited with the birth of the novel as a literary form. A liberal, Fielding was also appointed magistrate in 1748 and helped to lay the foundation for the first modern police force. The progressive Fielding advocated the release of petty thieves, issued reprimand instead of death for punishment, begged leniency for the poverty-stricken, and pushed for lower sentences. He urged local magistrates to pay salaries to their aids, instituted the publication of crime reportage and provided pawn brokers with frequent lists of stolen goods. Among these many contributions, Fielding formed the Bow Street Runners, an unpaid volunteer group, which was established to clean up the Bow Street area in London. The theory of crime prevention sprung up under Fielding's atmosphere of invention, and his core of "runners" espoused swift and fair justice; they were physically strong and able, and known for their incorruptible nature. Later, these constabulary features were refined and continued as Henry's half-brother, John Fielding, took over due to Henry's failing health.

Sir Robert Peel was a British statesman who served as home secretary in the 1820s. Known as the "father of modern policing," Peel advocated a partial return to the Anglo-Saxon policy of personal responsibility. In addition, the forward-thinking Peel was also largely responsible for the first salaried bureaucratic police force enacted under the Metropolitan Police Act of 1829. This London force comprised the first formally sanctioned police for order, prevention, and detection of crime. The familiar London "Bobbies" are named for him.

Later, under the tutelage of Charles Rowan, a former military man, and Richard Mayne, an attorney, a legally guided and more formal police force evolved. Some of their changes for reform were that: forces would be militarily organized with a hierarchy of command; they would utilize a centrally located division to be deployed by time and area; there would be appropriate disciplinary procedures for their own; along with strength and moral training, they would have a distinct, uniform look.

## POLICING IN EARLY AMERICA

August Vollmer, sometimes called the "father of modern police" in the United States, was a chief of police in Berkeley, California, and author of *The Police and Modern Society* (1936). Vollmer presented a paper called "Policeman as Social Worker," which recognized the importance of service. O.W. Wilson, a patrol officer serving under Vollmer, and whose career spanned several areas of enforcement and service as chief public safety officer in several European countries, instituted a sound management approach. Wilson's ideas specified a professional police separate from politics, with rigorous selection and training, and the use of technology. Oddly, even though Wilson called for professionalism, he did not like civil service tests and the rules of seniority that he felt boxed-in the leadership.

Later, works written by such leaders as Raymond B. Fosdick, *Municipal Police Administration*, and Bruce Smith's *Police Systems in the United States* stressed keeping the classic kernels of police management, but also talked about a synthesis of action, a succinct division of labor including a narrow span of control, and a centralization of authority.

William Henry Parker, a compadre of Colonel O.W. Wilson during WWII and a police officer who rose to captain in the Los Angeles Police Department, (1950–1968), discovered irregularities in the police promotion process in Los Angeles. Parker had concerns about personal accountability, which triggered his renewed interest in background investigation for new hires, accepting a particular IQ from recruits, along with requiring a thorough psychiatric examination of all his potential officers.

Soon after, another model appeared, providing impetus from 1925 to the present. Called the Human Relations and Participative Management Model, it is a synthesis with the personnel thrust of the scientific model, the democratization of the team policing approach and, is today, concerned mostly with stress management.

\* \* \*

## HIERARCHY OF POWER

At the national level, federal criminal law violations are investigated and enforced by the Federal Bureau of Investigation (FBI). Located in the Department of Justice, in Washington, D.C., the FBI is by far the most powerful of the federal law enforcement agencies. With nearly 25,000 people under its command, including more than 10,000 special FBI agents spread out over fifty-six field offices in the U.S. and twenty-one foreign offices, it uses its broad powers to enforce over 260 violations under their jurisdiction. An annual budget exceeding two billion dollars provides the FBI with the most sophisticated methods in crime prevention and investigation. They contribute a number of services to local law enforcement agencies including continued education, database system analyses, and advanced investigation techniques.

Other federal agencies have law enforcement authority in specific areas. Among them are the U.S. Marshals Service; the Bureau of Alcohol, Tobacco, Firearms and Explosives; the Bureau of Indian Affairs; the U.S. Drug Enforcement Administration; and the U.S. Postal Inspection Service. On March 1, 2003, services formerly provided by the Immigration and Naturalization Service transitioned into the Department of Homeland Security (DHS)[1] and became the U.S. Citizenship and Immigration Services (USCIS). Also under this new umbrella are the U.S. Customs and Border Protection (CBP), which is charged with regulating and facilitating international trade, collecting import duties, and enforcing U.S. trade laws; as well as the U.S. Secret Service, which was transferred from the Department of Treasury.

Many states have their own municipal agencies which mimic the role of enforcing specific areas of law, ranging from traffic safety to gambling, from agricultural importation to dispensing alcoholic licenses.

At the local level are county and city law enforcement agencies. Almost every rural county in America has a sheriff. In most states, sheriffs are elected to office and exercise a great deal of authority as the chief law enforcement officer. In Northeastern cities, however, many traditional powers have been granted to state or metropolitan police forces. More than 20,000 cities and towns have a police department.

Figure 6. Law enforcement training center.

Law enforcement agencies enforce criminal law and, as a consequence, have much discretion. Under the umbrella of this power, law enforcement personnel can investigate suspicious criminal activity, arrest suspected criminals, and detain arrested persons until their cases come before the appropriate courts of law. Two of the primary assumptions society makes in respect to their law enforcement are that officers should prevent crimes and maintain order. Altogether, 40,000 federal, state, and local agencies are involved in law enforcement.

## DISCRETION

Discretion is the exercise of individual choice or judgment concerning possible courses of action. The authority to exercise legitimate use of power is the most important characteristic of police action. For this reason, discretion is a significant concept to explore when choosing action for law enforcement problems. It is the crossroads of choice. It is the decentralization of hierarchy. It allows an officer power without having to check back with management. It is a trust given that implies officers will act in good faith. To begin, here is a list of "discretionary plateaus"—when internal and external pressures and influences are applied at each discretionary choice level. For example, these are the times when individual decisions are made, such as, to arrest or not? Will evidence support it? What is the choice of charges filed?

### Discretionary Plateaus

- When citizen reports crime to law enforcement
- When police investigate
- When police apprehend suspect

---

1. The Department of Homeland Security is established with the passage of (Public Law 107-296).

- When prosecutor makes charges
- When there is plea bargain or trial
- With a judge or jury sentence
- When suspect appeals
- When correctional decisions are made
- When convict reenters society
- Citizen acceptance of convict

## Discretion for the Police Officer Is Exercised During These Times

- When the officer determines the seriousness of the crime
- As victim requires
- With regard to a previous record
- According to the time of day and location
- When the law is vague

### Discretion Is Affected by

- Departmental policies
- Public expectation
- Precedents (previous court decisions)
- Current attitudes of the prosecutor and his or her relationship to the department
- Characteristics of behavior of the offender
- Disenchantment with the justice system

## OTHERS WEIGH IN

## What the Supreme Court Says About Officer Discretion

Recent Supreme Court Decisions Demand Police Discretion Because:
- Police officers are more knowledgeable than the average citizen
- Police are entrusted with badges and must strive to be more honest than citizens
- Special training and experience enable police to exercise actions not apparent to other people
- Police are constantly exposed to unusual danger and must at all times and circumstances act to protect themselves
- Key to effective policing is to allow officers the use of discretion

## Arguments Against the Use of Discretion

- Leads to unfair and unequal decisions
- Operates in conflict with rules, regulations, policy, and law
- Police should set the example to follow law to the fullest extent
- Discretion is affected by moods, weakness, and values
- Can have serious consequences
- Can diminish accountability

## THE LETTER OF THE LAW

All law enforcement officers must contend with the law in order to obtain a conviction. Everything points to a legal conclusion. Because of this dictum, law enforcement officers, no matter what division or level, must uphold and follow the law in order to obtain proof of guilt and the satisfactory result–a judgment against the perpetrator. Any egregious technicalities against the suspect's constitutional rights give rise to many problems, delays, mistrials. Any mistakes can result in a case's dismissal. The drama of dealing with these problems can add triumph and tragedy to your department. Just realize that not every mistake leads to a criminal's freedom, and not every encounter can end with a positive conclusion.

## CHARACTERIZING A POLICE OFFICER

To know police officers, it helps to remember they are first human beings. Everyday civilians view cops with a skewed perception. He is "the guy who gave me a ticket," or it is someone to complain to about an injustice or the problems with society, as if it is in their power to do something about it. It's a status that calls forth certain cliched images the media helps to perpetuate through news, books, and movies. The corrupt cop and the stupid cop stereotypes are usually the staples of any private eye story or anything involving a conspiracy theme. Society, in general, relies so instinctively on these character types and preconceptions they don't realize its presence most of the time.

It would behoove you then, if you are in law enforcement, to act as a role model. Since much of an officer's time is spent with fellow officers and their families, it is a good idea to expand your circle of friends. Try to cultivate and continue a positive outlook in life. Since officers most often bump up against the dregs of society, it can affect their outlook and demeanor. Find outlets for the stress and keep the job in the proper perspective. And just as doctors have their Latin prescriptions, scientists have their elements, so do police officers have their codes and calls–their *argot*–a unique system used to relay information in a smooth and studied manner, which also serves to insulate the speech from the common people involved. Speech is a powerful separator. Look to be a better communicator with those not involved in the system.

## PATROL OFFICER

The Patrol Division is the backbone of the agency. Regardless of where officers come from, they will experience some of what the patrol division offers. As the first assignment, a rookie officer is usually placed with a more senior member, who could be referred to as a field training officer or the more colloquial version, coach. The trend in law enforcement training is toward the use of field training programs, however, a substantial portion reported they now rely on on-the-job training combined with additional classroom instruction.

The community to which a new officer is assigned depends upon the personnel needs of the patrol bureau and the philosophy of the chief administrator. One chief may feel perhaps that the new officer should be directly challenged and evaluated, and will assign the rookie to a high-crime area to accelerate experience. Others opt for a slow-

Figure 7. Target and range practice are a must for law enforcement officers.

er approach, putting officers in a less hostile environment before the immersion into a highly charged region. A chief may boast about how his or her patrol bureau is the "backbone" of the agency and then proceed to transfer the best and brightest to other assignments or put them in select bureaus such as the detective squad, etc. Obviously, if this continues with any regularity, problems ensue. The practice will keep inexperienced men or women with little ability or motivation in the patrol division.

## Peer Pressure

An important human factor for the rookie is "belonging," or the peer pressure brought on the new recruit. Pressure from contemporaries is used to uphold loyalty for the profession and can be used as a weapon to sanction someone deemed a "hot dog" or one who may not know the division's unwritten rules. Treating someone as an outcast, and using every chance to get the rebel in trouble, are classic ways of manipulating behavior for the "good of the group." The propensity for conforming as required by the clique does serve its own purpose, though; it helps to bolster the officer against the slings and arrows of outrageous streets. The loss of autonomous values helps officers to remember where they stand, a kind of "us against them" mentality, and serves to shield them from an emotional reaction; a kind of failing some cops may argue, and too much of a human reaction.

The chain of command follows a discernible hard line and is referred to as "formal structure," whereas, the informal structure that subordinates set up, can be used for under-the-table advice, sand-bagging, or corruption. This is a phenomena that, in order to relate, needs a commander with his or her own pack of memories.

## THE LIFE

Another problem that plagues patrol is the fact that these divisions operate round-the-clock, seven days a week. The dangerous nights, coupled with an erratic schedule, can take its toll. Consequently, many officers wish to be transferred to other units. In addition to laborious shift-related duties, they must factor into their job court appearances and family conflicts.

Their days are spent on a lot of rather routine duties or patrol, with the odd occasion to perform noncriminal services for their community. It can pulse from sleepy time to adrenaline fear. They are subjected to having to respond to crimes in progress, or crimes that have been just committed. The potential for physical harm in these particular instances is high.

Also, in order to conduct many of their community responsibilities, they will often be expected to work with less desirable civilians: drunks, prostitutes, petty criminals, child abusers, and others with serious mental problems. Even domestic calls are dangerous because of the unpredictability of entering a volatile situation, and having to confront families with long-seated dysfunctional psyche.

## Underappreciation

The status of a police officer on patrol does not convey many financial rewards or those of the more appreciative variety. They may work for many years without glory, and their service goes relatively unrecognized by their community or sometimes even their department.

There is a lot of leeway for what activities patrol officers follow because there are no hard-and-fast rules. Some departments may consist of a lot of routine patrol and observation, and even that may also fall under different interpretation. For some, it could include traffic enforcement and citations, or it may mean patrolling a business district to deter burglaries or robberies.

Non-crime calls eat up between 80 and 90 percent of an officer's time. Calls for property eviction, animal control, disruption with parties, tenant disputes, and property-line disagreements are a few of these. Attendance at certain civic events may be required to help provide for peaceful assembly, and other event-related duties may be incorporated into their day, plus sometimes a summons comes down for help with a benevolent community charity such as helping people who are lost, informing loved ones about accidents, delivering blood from one hospital to another, or finding adolescent children.

Preliminary investigations are often begun by patrol officers since they are most likely the first people to arrive at the scene of a crime. They are responsible for preserving the integrity of the area, caring for the injured, and apprehending the offender if still in the area. He or she may continue in service by collecting evidence, cataloging and filing it, and preparing the necessary reports. The follow-up can be taken away from him or her by an investigative unit, or if it would take said officer out of the

Figure 8. A small lab within a station house does its share of investigation.

assigned district. Many small departments cannot afford the expense of another office and the patrol officer may act as a jack-of-all-trades in an extremely small community.

## Nontraditional Roles

For the nontraditional role of patrol, there may be groups comprised that perform park and walk patrol, bicycle patrol, horse patrol, and golf cart patrol. These are usually developed within departments that recognize the need for additional interaction between police and community residents and business persons.

## Police on Wheels

Police traffic problems are one of the most pervasive problems for law enforcement service. Responsibility for congestion control, traffic enforcement of laws, and accident prevention has a way of finding itself enmeshed in many other activities. Traffic duty then is almost always a shared duty unless there is some type of municipal sheriff's station, traffic bureau or other–but traffic still occurs as a job for everyone in law enforcement at one time or another.

## The Detective Role

Part image, part public relations, part god-awful job, the detective role responds to a lot of depictions in the public (and media's) mind. Some of the historical aspects of the freedoms given over to detectives are often highlighted in books and movies, and, now,

there is no failure of police literature to mention that a lot of these stereotypical duties are today not quite as freewheeling as the public assumes.

Usually investigators are dispatched after a patrol unit files its reports. There are some simultaneous dispatches but we're told that it's rare for simple allocation reasons. After receiving this documentation, detectives are usually responsible for developing potential leads, mapping out an investigation plan, and canvassing. The investigator will usually make calls and interview those closest to the victim. Since there are always cases pending, they are given individual priority according to the leads presented, the heinousness of the crime, or if the victim involved has received high-profile attention because of notoriety in the press or community.

Some of the investigator's other duties include reviewing new cases, paperwork, processing prisoners who may have been taken into custody the night before, court appearances, and more footwork.

A follow-up investigation may have to do with lineups, lots of digging through files and field interrogation records, but all require more paperwork for the prosecutor's office. Usually, huge databases of known offenders and intelligence files are maintained in this office. The larger and better financed departments have crime analysis bureaus, and others can initiate a special strike force or sting operation such as buying stolen property in an attempt to identify fences and burglars.

The daily operation includes incident reports, which have been prepared and assembled from the previous day and hand-

---

**FYI**—The main point about "operations" is that each police agency is different or distinctive from one another because of certain variables such as the size of the district, the population of the town, the needs of the people, the budget, qualified personnel, assignments, and other defining factors. Most police have public relations offices and those officers, will be happy to either answer your questions or refer you to a specific officer or agent who will help you with inquiries about methodology, a procedure, or a problem. The keen law student or police trainee will maintain a resource directory for future reference. Also, be sure to send a note of thanks to the individuals for their time when they help you.

ed out to the appropriate unit. Assignments may be by crime specialty, for example, robberies, sex offenses, and other, but often the reports are given over to the unit supervisor, who assigns his or her own individual(s). The first few hours (24-48) are always critical to a case's solvability.

## Evidence Technicians

Many departments use trained evidence technicians to collect and process fingerprints, blood evidence, and any other evidentiary materials (which can range from hair, to paper, wood, or cloth fibers, etc.) Some are crime scene investigators or criminalists. They help to preserve the scene, relay information to the medical examiner, and will sometimes check latent fingerprints against those of known criminals.

In Chapters Seven and Eight, we addressed the basic constitutional rights of criminal defendants as they pass through the criminal justice system and that affect the police.

## Limits on the Conduct of Police Officers and Prosecutors

• No unreasonable or unwarranted search and seizure
• No arrest except under probable cause
• No coerced confessions or illegal interrogation
• No entrapment
• A suspect must be informed of his or her rights under questioning

Now discussion will move to one of the most important elements of police work, surveillance.

## SURVEILLANCE

Much reflection on the part of law enforcement, prosecutors, and the courts in regard to the collection and use of evidence has been crammed down the throat of many who enter the profession, and for good reason. These are vitally important procedures that attempt to link evidence with those accused of the crime. Surveillance, which is the act of shadowing, tailing, photographing, or listening in on a suspect, is often used in order to detect criminal activity, obtain evidence, or prevent a crime. As an added bonus, surveillance may also lead to possible accomplices, witnesses, or other evidentiary pluses with which to build the case.

## Tailing a Suspect

Tailing or shadowing a person can run the gamut from a boring car observance to a footrace. A lot of manpower and significant downtime is required of surveillance in this up-close-and-personal endeavor, so it is reserved for those situations most likely to proffer information. Sources such as "streetwise" informants may point to a lead, or often a perpetrator will return to the crime scene out of anxiety, because of excitement, or to relive the event.

## Electronic Surveillance

These silent and invisible intrusions on the privacy of an individual can take many forms including the use of wiretaps, highly sensitive microphones, and other electronic devices. Since using electronic equipment skirts the protections of the Fourth Amendment, the Supreme Court has approved the use of searchlights, field glasses, aerial photography, and various other means of enhancing a police officer's power of observance. In the past, lower courts have allowed miniaturized television camera surveillance.

## LEGAL REASONING ABOUT SURVEILLANCE

The question of legality is always whether the surveillance methods infringe on a person's reasonable expectation of privacy. If police use binoculars to see what could otherwise be seen through the naked eye, then the use of binoculars as a sensory aid is not a search—the rationale here is that it results in exposure of that information which is otherwise visible. The same goes for the use of a flashlight, microphones—provided sound could be heard with the naked ear, and aerial surveillance.

## Beepers and Thermal Imaging Devices

Police have often used devices to track the movements of a defendant's vehicle. An electronic gadget which sends out radio beeping signals is easily attached to a car. In *United States v. Knotts*,[2] the Supreme Court said that the use of a beeper was not a search

in these circumstances because the information obtained only related to the movements of the suspect within society and, of this, he had no expectation of privacy. In essence, the defendant suffered "no prejudice."

Whereas thermal imaging devices passed muster a while ago, the Supreme Court just changed their minds. In *Kyllo v. United States*, decided June 11, 2001, they said a device which compares heat emanating from one object, in relation to the intensity of heat of surrounding objects, constitutes a search because that device is not in public use. Police used this tool for detecting marijuana plants in someone's house and, in the past, the courts have likened it to a canine sniff, which is not a search. Okay, basically a dog sniff of closed luggage is not a search, because it can only tell the officer whether the luggage contains contraband or not. There is no protectible privacy interest in contraband and, through the sniff, law enforcement really learns nothing about any personal or innocent information contained inside.

## Bank Records

In *United States v. Miller*[3] the government served a subpoena on Miller's bank in order to obtain copies of checks, deposit slips, and other financial statements. This activity was not a search said the Court, because Miller could not have had an expectation of privacy in information he conveyed to his bank. The bank has access to it, so the government could have equal access.

## Telephone Pen Registers

A pen register is a device that allows the police to access every number dialed from a

---

2. *United States v. Knotts*, 460 U.S. 276, 103 S.Ct. 1081, 75 L.Ed.2d 55 (1983).
3. *United States v. Miller*, 425 U.S. 435, 96 S.Ct. 1619, 48 L.Ed.2d 71 (1976).

specifically targeted phone. Does the owner expect that the telephone company will not use this information? Since the caller gives the numbers away freely in making the call, it is not a search for police to obtain these numbers, therefore equivalent government access is okay.

## Wiretapping and Pagers

Since electronic eavesdropping smacks of intrusion, Congress enacted Title III of the Omnibus Crime Control and Safe Streets Act.[4] This stroke prohibits interception of electronic communications without a court-ordered warrant unless one party to the conversation agrees. On sworn application, with considerable detailed information, and for a thirty-day period of time, a wiretap order can be executed.

There is some question in certain state courts currently about whether cordless and cellular phone interception is legal. The Florida Supreme Court held that nonconsensual interception of cordless phone calls without prior judicial approval violates a state statute protecting the privacy of communications. They based their decision on statutory grounds, however, so check your individual territory before using this type of surveillance.

## Dropsy

The results of a warrantless search do not justify the means. *Dropsy* is a slang term for recovering evidence during a search or patdown of a suspect. Word has it that in order for certain evidence (mainly drugs) to hold up in court, when a police officer is doing a search and finds incriminating drugs that may not withstand judicial scrutiny on

Fourth Amendment principles, the evidence gets dropped. Usually the officers will testify in court that the defendants dropped the contraband before the arrest. When it lands on the ground it becomes plain view. This activity skirts many issues, however, and is not advised.

## POLICE AND FORCE OF ARREST

There are those who think that police beating of civilians is inexcusable. With certain media enhancement, say, for example, when a particularly brutal beating comes to light like the one we witnessed in the Rodney King case, the cards are stacked against police methodology altogether. Possibly no aspect of police service evokes more passion or controversy than that and the use of deadly force.

A recent survey published by the National Institute of Justice[5] provides some answers. Out of a national sample of 900 officers interviewed, the majority of American police officers believe that it is unacceptable to use more force than legally allowable to control someone who physically assaults an officer. And although a substantial majority expressed the view that police should be permitted to use more force, the overwhelming majority did not believe that officers regularly engaged in the excessive use of force. However, in somewhat conflicting statements, almost 22 percent agreed or strongly agreed that officers in their departments sometimes used more force than was necessary. And in response to the "code of silence" question (keeping quiet in the face of misconduct by others), one-quarter of the sample agreed that whistle-

4. Title III, Omnibus Crime Control & Safe Streets Act, 18 U.S.C.A. § § 2510-20.
5. Police Attitudes Toward Abuse of Authority: Findings from a National Study, NCJ 181312.

blowing is not worth it and more than two-thirds reported that police officers who reported incidents of misconduct were like to be given a "cold shoulder" by fellow officers; and a majority agreed it is not unusual for officers to "turn a blind eye" to other officers' improper conduct.

Most states have laws or police regulations specifying the degree of force used to apprehend violators. Officers are usually permitted to use such force as is necessary to effect an arrest and are not required to retreat from an aggressor. The use of deadly force is authorized when apprehending felons, or when necessary to prevent the escape of a suspect who poses a significant threat of death or serious injury to the officer or others.

An officer who kills someone in the line of duty is sometimes charged with a criminal

Figure 9. Ammunition is too heavy to stock on regular shelves.

offense. As long as he or she acted reasonably and was not in violation of the Fourth Amendment, a state law, or some other police regulation, the defense of performing a public function available to the officer can be used.

## POLICE INTERROGATIONS

An interrogation under Supreme Court description is "express questioning or its functional equivalent," including any words or actions on the part of the police that the police know is reasonably likely to elicit an incriminating response from the suspect. And Miranda applies only to "custodial questioning."

Of course, interrogation is usually done at the stationhouse but there is no automatic custody rule for stationhouse interrogation, meaning, that just because someone is asked to come to the station and answer questions it's a voluntary move on the part of the suspect and does not imply custody. Custody also does not apply when a person is called to testify before a grand jury, or during a normal traffic stop. In other words, no warnings are required before questioning in these circumstances.

Interrogations can take many forms, including subtle psychological techniques. Miranda warnings must be issued though, and the subject must have either waived those rights or obtained counsel. Miranda is supposed to remove inherent pressures of the interrogation atmosphere, but police do employ techniques of their own.

### Delay Tactics

Sometimes a police officer will delay the arrest in order to question the suspect in a breezy, conversational manner, feeling they will gain more evidence that way. If an officer can convince a judge he or she was engaged in only general questioning and would have allowed the suspect to walk away when finished, when suddenly information came through, police can attempt to evade the Miranda mandate.

## Using Silence Against Them

If someone is arrested and chooses not to declare the statement, "I didn't do it," an officer can relay that information to the prosecution who will then ask in court, "Why didn't he tell the arresting officer that he really didn't do it immediately upon arrest?"

## Confronting a Suspect with Incriminating Evidence

In a Florida case[6] a confession hinged on an officer's claim that he had laboratory reports implicating the suspect. The appellate court upheld a trial judge's order holding the confession involuntary. The court expressed concern that false documents could wind up in police files as genuine.

## Physical Threats and Brutality

If the police obtain information by coercive means, it is not only illegal, but the information is not admissible, even if a Miranda warning was given prior to the confession. Not only that, but if any new evidence crops up as a result of a physical threat or brutality, it is considered "fruit of the poisonous tree" and equally inadmissible.

## Psychological Coercion

Actual police brutality is unusual and can be documented with photographs. But if an interrogation takes the form of swearing or a

screaming match it is harder to prove improper conduct. Since judges believe that defendants are motivated to lie in order to protect themselves, they are more inclined to side with police and conclude that no coercion took place.

## Mutt-and-Jeff Strategy

Sometimes referred to as the good cop/bad cop tactic, one officer is friendly and sympathetic while the other is rude and aggressive. The objective is to coerce the defendant into confessing to the good guy, and there is good reason to believe it works. The Supreme Court has alluded to the fact that Mutt-and-Jeff is a possible example of impermissible psychological coercion, yet courts have generally ignored the practice.

## Public Safety Exception

Police officers may ask arrested persons about weapons and other potential threats to society without Miranda warnings. The purpose of the rule was to up the likelihood of finding out the whereabouts of weapons or dangerous objects such as bombs, before they fall into the hands of co-conspirators or innocents.

## Promises of Leniency

Empty are the promises of leniency. Police may want to recommend a lighter sentence, but in the end, it is the prosecutors and judges who determine charges and sentencing on the basis of law and expediency.

## Tape Recording Statements

Anything put on tape means the defendant is likely to have it show up again at trial.

6. *State v. Cayward*, 552 So.2d. 971 (Fla. App. 1989).

If suspects are afraid their information will be distorted they can request to be taped, or at least have a written summary to sign, making minimal opportunity for police to distort facts.

\* \* \*

## Lie Detector Tests

## IDENTIFICATION PROCEDURES

Police officers will often ask suspects to take a lie detector test to "clear your name." It is often used as a ploy to get confessions, and they may falsely inform suspects they are "flunking," so they might as well come clean. These tests are usually never allowed in court and their results are in question. There have been many false-positives but it may prompt the police to make an arrest.

Here in Chapter Nine we investigate the procedures of law enforcement as they should be followed in order to collect further evidence, interrogate suspects, and address the legal ramifications of identification. There are two types of identification procedures. First, forensic science helps police to match physical evidence taken from the crime scene with suspects. Second, there are a variety of methods–lineups, showups and photographs–to find out if victims or witnesses can identify their perpetrators.

Figure 10. Using ink to roll fingerprints for a booking.

---

# PRESS HARD, MAKING FOUR COPIES

## ALL INFORMATION IS ESSENTIAL

TYPE OR PRINT WITH BLACK BALL POINT PEN

| LAST NAME | FIRST NAME | MIDDLE NAME | ARREST TRACK NO |
|---|---|---|---|

SIGNATURE OF PERSON FINGERPRINTED

**THIS DATA MAY BE COMPUTERIZED IN LOCAL, STATE & NATIONAL FILES**

SIGNATURE OF PERSON FINGERPRINTED

| DATE / / | ARRESTEE SOCIAL SECURITY NO. |
|---|---|

CHARGE AND CODE NUMBER | CHECK IF FELONY/MISDEMEANOR

1. _____ ❑ FEL ❑ MIS

2. _____ ❑ FEL ❑ MIS

3. _____ ❑ FEL ❑ MIS

**PLACE ALIASES ON BACK OF FINGERPRINT CARD**

| DATE OF BIRTH / / | PLACE OF BIRTH (CITY, STATE) |
|---|---|

| ARRESTING AGENCY ORI NO. | SEX | RACE | HGT | WGT | EYES | HAIR |
|---|---|---|---|---|---|---|

| DATE ARRESTED / / | AGENCY CASE NO. | ARRESTING OFFICER |
|---|---|---|

| SID NO. | FBI NO. | ARRESTING AGENCY |
|---|---|---|

| COUNTRY OF CITIZENSHIP | DRIVER LICENSE NO. AND STATE |
|---|---|

CAUTION

| 1. RIGHT THUMB | 2. RIGHT INDEX | 3. RIGHT MIDDLE | 4. RIGHT RING | 5. RIGHT LITTLE |
|---|---|---|---|---|

| 1. LEFT THUMB | 2. LEFT INDEX | 3. LEFT MIDDLE | 4. LEFT RING | 5. LEFT LITTLE |
|---|---|---|---|---|

| LEFT FOUR FINGERS TAKEN SIMULTANEOUSLY | LEFT THUMB | RIGHT THUMB | RIGHT FOUR FINGERS TAKEN SIMULTANEOUSLY |
|---|---|---|---|

PRIVACY ACT OF 1974 (P.L. 93-579) REQUIRES THAT FEDERAL, STATE, OR LOCAL AGENCIES INFORM INDIVIDUALS WHOSE SOCIAL SECURITY NUMBER IS REQUESTED WHETHER SUCH DISCLOSURE IS MANDATORY OR VOLUNTARY, BASIS OF AUTHORITY FOR SUCH SOLICITATION, AND USES WHICH WILL BE MADE OF IT.

Structure 4.

## FORENSIC SCIENCE

In the context of police work, the beginnings of forensic comparison begin. Without a warrant a suspect can be required to give fingerprints, a blood sample, hair and fingernail samples, and either clothing or fibers. As part of the booking process his or her photograph will be taken, they may ask him or her to provide his voice for tapes or her handwriting for exemplar comparison. The Supreme Court has held that providing handwriting can be compelled because it is not testimony but an identifying physical characteristic.[7] Some courts require "probable cause and necessity" before a blood sample, semen, or DNA may be taken without a warrant, in order to determine if the suspect is under the influence of alcohol or to otherwise compare his fluids to known sample from a crime scene. Other courts deem that the more intrusive test of collecting pubic hair must also carry a warrant. The two general conditions are that these methods are conducted by qualified persons, and that it does not violate the constitutional prohibition of compulsory self-incrimination. Typically situations are considered on a case-by-case basis; the Supreme Court denies any broad rules. Defendants can request their attorney be present during testing, but it is not legally required.

\* \* \*

## Lineups

An eyewitness identification method, lineups usually take place at police stations or county jails. In a lineup, a group of typically five or six people are displayed. A victim or witness, who is usually shielded from view is asked to pick out the person—beyond bright lights or through a one-way mirror—he or she saw commit the crime or noticed at the crime scene. Individuals in the lineup are often asked to step forward, turn sideways, wear certain types of clothing, or otherwise speak or assist the witness in identification. One person in the lineup is the suspect, the others may bear a close resemblance and are decoys.

The Supreme Court has sanctioned the use of lineups, saying there is no Fifth Amendment immunity against being placed in a lineup for identification purposes; lineups are considered nontestimonial.

Witnesses may be brought in separately or together to view the lineup. The only stipulation is that they do not confer or hear another's choice. If there is an indication of influence, the identification may be suppressed upon a motion or attacked as unreliable in court. Police officers and possibly the prosecutor and defense attorney will be present. Defense lawyers may also bring a private investigator or other employee to observe as protection against any unfair proceedings. It is a defendant's right to have a defense lawyer present at a post-charge lineup and the advocate may even take photos of the lineup.

## UNFAIR LINEUPS

An "impermissibly suggestive" lineup may be:
- The defendant stands out as the only person who resembles the witness' account, or if there is only one African American after the perpetrator has been described as African American.
- Witnesses have been allowed to talk to

---

7. *Gilbert v. California*, 388 U.S. 263, 87 S.Ct. 1951, 18 L.Ed.2d 1178 (1967).

FYI—A judge may require a person submit to a lineup as a condition of granting bail or a release on one's own recognizance. In reality, though, bailed-out defendants are less likely to be called up than are incarcerated ones. A refusal to cooperate may have the effect of making police think the person is hiding something and as a result may investigate the suspect more aggressively.

each other, either before entering the viewing room or when inside.

- Only one person is in handcuffs, or a handcuffed person was paraded through the waiting room.
- If police cannot resist speaking to the witness, such as saying, "Pay particular attention to suspect Number Four."

## RELIABILITY TEST OF AN IDENTIFICATION

Judges have standards[8] about whether impermissible suggestiveness has affected an identification that includes:

1. the degree of suggestiveness, for example, a one-on-one photo is more likely to effect a witness;
2. the opportunity to view, for example, coming face to face with the suspect versus seeing him or her forty feet away;
3. degree of attention, for example, if the witness was focused on other things at the time;
4. accuracy of the description, for example, if the witness describes a unique physical characteristic it is likely the specificity is accurate;
5. level of certainty, for example, the courts believe that the more certain the witness is about the identification, the more likely it comes from sources other than police suggestiveness;

6. the time between pre-identification opportunity to view and the identification itself, meaning, the "mental picture" of a perpetrator fades as time passes;
7. character of the witness, which suggests to the judge whether the person is easily led or has a need regardless of the accuracy.

If a defendant has not been in a lineup, there are other procedures and he or she may still be identified in court.

## IMPORTANT POLICE TOOLS

### Showups

A one-on-one identification procedure, the showup is different in character from a lineup in several distinct ways. Showups occur in police stations but they may also take place in the field, for example, a handcuffed suspect may be taken by police back to the scene of a crime, such as returning to a grocery store robbery to be identified by the clerk. It may also happen soon after a crime is committed. And although showups are thought to be more reliable because of the immediacy, it is inherently suggestive because it is obvious to the witness that police believe they have caught the offender. Also, since showups almost always take place before a suspect is charged, the right to an attorney's presence is not guaranteed. On the plus side, prompt identification helps to exonerate innocents rather quickly.

---

8. *Manson v. Brathwaite*, 432 U.S. 98, 97 S.Ct. 2243, 53 L.Ed.2d 140 (1977).

## Photo Identification

A photo pack–or six pack–is a set of "mug shots" that are shown to eyewitnesses or victims in the hopes they will be able to produce a reliable identification. The presentation should not emphasize one photo over another, and an attorney's presence is not required. In addition, police may display photos, or an individual photograph, to a witness in an attempt to "search for a suspect," meaning, they may have no evidence that persons whose photos displayed have committed the crime. But the fact that they may be mug shots tends to indicate a previous criminal record. Generally, persons whose photos were used do not know about it.

Police may try to trick the suspect into confessing by telling defendants they have already been identified in a photo array, even if they have not. Judges usually admit the resulting confessions, despite the lie. And the same unfair principles apply with photo IDs as with lineups and showups, although the prosecutor is generally required to keep records of what photos were displayed; absence of those records, and the judge can exclude the identification from trial.

## Warrants for Online Data

During the past few years, the number of search warrant requests for citizens' online data has gone up 800 percent. The searches typically involve cases ranging from harassment and child pornography to violent crime and fraud. The aim is to discover the identity and tracking activities of subscribers.

Congressional leaders informed of the increase, said they will examine legal standards and develop questions for police. Some of the information Congress will require is when, why, and how police perform electronic searches. While critics and privacy experts fear for abuse of electronic surveillance, the FBI's Thomas Gregory Motta says there is little reason for concern.

While the arrest power rule–the latitude police are given with searches incident to arrest–is strong, there are other times when police may conduct inquiry and search, namely, sobriety checkpoints, at roadblocks and on the border.

## Sobriety Checkpoints

In order to reduce the number of drunk driving accidents, police officers often set up sobriety checkpoints. All drivers must stop briefly at a designated point and are observed for signs of intoxication. The legality of sobriety stops has been challenged on Fourth Amendment grounds, mainly that the police have no probable cause to believe that any driver in particular has broken a law. The courts have upheld these measures as minor intrusion and inconvenience, saying as long as the procedures are not discriminating and apply to all motorists, the stop is reasonable.

## Roadblocks

Since roadblocks do constitute a restraint on the liberty of the motorist, they are susceptible to challenge under the Fourth Amendment. Because of the restrictive nature then, police agencies must take care that they are operated according to guidelines that help to constrain the exercise of discretion by its officers. Often they are set up to apprehend fleeing criminals or felons, but occasionally, they are used to perform safety checks or possession of insurance. The methodology requires a minimal length of stop, of somewhere in the area of thirty seconds, and, if the driver appears intoxicated, he or she is instructed to pull the vehicle over to the side of the road for a license and registration check. If indicated, a field sobriety test is administered.

## Field Sobriety Test (FST)

Police administer field sobriety tests to drivers they believe may be under the influence of alcohol or drugs. The driver may have slurred speech, smell of alcohol, have bloodshot eyes and an unsteady gaze. The officer typically asks the driver to perform field sobriety tests such as reciting the alphabet–forwards or backwards–walking a line heel-to-toe, making a one-legged stand or performing a blind nose touch test. In addition, the officer may conduct blood alcohol tests using a portable machine that analyzes a suspect's breath. This device supposedly measures blood alcohol concentration (BAC). The driver blows into a vial. From the breath, his or her blood alcohol concentration is computed. Most state statutes use 0.08 or 0.10 parts of 100 the standard for illegal driving. In most jurisdictions the driver can request a urinalysis or blood test; these will be conducted at the stationhouse.

There are three instruments for breath analyzer devices: the gas chromatograph, a beam of infrared radiation using a scientific principle called Beer's Law, and a photometric device.

## P.A.S. III Sniffer

A driver slows to a stop for a sobriety checkpoint, rolls down his window and the police officer thrusts the illuminated end of a flashlight six inches from his nose and starts asking questions. Impolite? No, a secret test. The motorist is unaware that a tiny, battery-powered device on the end of the flashlight is sucking in his breath and analyzing it for traces of alcohol.

Civil liberties groups do not like the Sniffer, saying it is an invasion of privacy and infringes on the Fourth Amendment's protection against search and seizure. Covert use amounts to entrapment, says John Whitehead, president of the Rutherford Institute, a civil liberties group based in Charlottesville, Virginia. Truth is, the constitutionality of the Sniffer has never been tested in court.

Jarel R. Kelsey, president of PAS Systems International thinks the Sniffer falls under the "plain sight doctrine," which holds that observations an officer makes with the senses do not violate the amendment. The doctrine applies whether the officer collects the air sample with his or her unaided nose or with the Sniffer, Kelsey says. For daylight use, the company also sells a clipboard containing an alcohol senser.

## Crip Kits

For years police officers have been able to run quick color tests to determine the possible presence of numerous drugs such as opiates, amphetamines and methamphetamine, cocaine, crack, cannabis, and LSD found both in the field and at the stationhouse. The Crip kit uses color reactions with reagent solutions to identify the drug in question. The same company also supplies explosive-incendiary residue test kits.

## Border Searches

Border searches are considered administrative, and the interest is in protecting American borders and regulating the flow of goods into the country. Since it involves special needs it is evaluated under Fourth Amendment principles, but is essentially found reasonable without a warrant or probable cause, and often without suspicion. Customs officials, at all border points in Canada, Mexico, and all ships of foreign port stations, may stop all entrants for routine investigation, questioning, and limited search of effects, vehicles, and clothing.

# REVIEW QUESTIONS AND ANSWERS

## *Key Words to Define*

- **Argot**–A unique system to relay information; lingo, jargon of the industry.
- **August Vollmer**–"Father of Modern Police" in the United States; from Berkeley, California, wrote *The Police and Modern Society* in 1936.
- **Crip kit**–Quick color tests police use to test and determine the presence of drugs.
- **Discretion**–The exercise of an individual choice or judgment concerning possible courses of action best based on experience; often linked to key positions of authority.
- **Dropsy**–Slang for evidence recovered during a search or pat down.
- **Evidence technician**–CSI, crime scene evidence collection officer.
- **"Father of Modern Policing"**–Sir Robert Peel, British statesman in the 1820s; set up first salaried bureaucratic police with the Metropolitan Police Act.
- **FBI**–Federal Bureau of Investigation, under the Department of Justice in Washington, D.C., federal law enforcement agency with offices in every state.
- **FST**–Acronym for Field Sobriety Test, given to drivers believed to be under the influence of alcohol or drugs.
- **Henry Fielding**–Novelist and magistrate (1748); Fielding laid the foundation for the first modern police force (England).
- **The letter of the law**–To uphold and follow the law, plus proof of guilt, put together should equal a satisfactory result for prosecution.
- **Line-up**–Five to six people displayed before a witness for identification.

- **Operations**–Each police jurisdiction is different and distinct from one another.
- **Pen register**–A device that allows access to every number dialed from a phone; cell data recording.
- **Promise of leniency**–A tactic used by police during questioning.
- **"Riot Act"**–A call for the military to quell riots brought on by inexpensive alcohol made available in urban ghettos (historical etymology).
- **Six-pack**–Set of mug shots.
- **Surveillance**–The act of shadowing, tailing, photographing, listening to the behavior of suspects.

## *Questions for Review and Discussion*

1. *Question:* Name three federal agencies with law enforcement authority. *Answer:* U.S. Marshals Service, Alcohol, Tobacco, Firearms and Explosives (ATF), Bureau of Indian Affairs, U.S. Drug Enforcement Administration (DEA), U.S. Customs and Border Protection (CBP), FBI, Immigration and Naturalization Service (INS) are now U.S. Citizenship & Immigration Services (USCIS), U.S. Postal Inspection Service.

2. *Question:* Name three times when law enforcement personnel (or others) may be required to use their own discretion. *Answer:* When a citizen reports a crime, when police investigate, when police apprehend a suspect, when prosecution makes charges, during a plea bargain, judge and jury sentencing, when suspect appeals, correctional decisions, when convict reenters society, a citizen's acceptance of the convict.

3. *Question:* What is the backbone of the police department? *Answer:* The patrol division.

4. *Question:* Name some types of peer pressure for a new rookie. *Answer:* "Belonging," upholding loyalty for the profession, being a "hot dog," as an outcast, under

manipulating behavior, an "us against them" mentality, drawing the hard-line, when under-the-table advice is presented, sandbagging, and under corruption within.

5. *Question:* List three things that plague patrol officers. *Answer:* Round-the-clock work, dangerous nights, transfers, shift-related duties, court appearances, family problems, erratic scheduling, stress, working with low-lifes, volatile situations.

6. *Question:* Who heads up an investigation? *Answer:* The detective. And what are a few of their duties? Heading up the scene, interviewing, canvassing the neighborhood, notifying families of a death, paperwork, processing prisoners, going to the morgue for reports and evidence, court dates, data filing, evidence follow-up.

7. *Question:* What is always the main legal question with surveillance? *Answer:* Whether the surveillance methods violate a person's reasonable expectation of privacy.

8. *Question:* Name a couple tactics police use with interrogations. *Answer:* Delays, using their silence against the interviewee, confronting them with evidence, photos; psychological coercion, Mutt and Jeff technique (good cop/bad cop), taping sessions, using a lie detector, suggesting leniency and so on.

9. *Question:* Does the Supreme Court sanction line-ups? *Answer:* Yes. Suspects have no Fifth Amendment right or immunity against being placed in a line-up for identification purposes.

### *Essay Exploration*

Write a short essay about the standards for the reliability test of identification. You will know if the student has an understanding of the identification principles if the student mentions any of the characteristics listed on page 175.

# Chapter 10

# RESUME OF A PROSECUTION

The true creator is necessity, which
is the mother of our invention.
            –Plato, *The Republic*

## THE PROSECUTION

*Assistant District Attorney Henry Cassin was well-studied and prepared. His opening statement was neither formal nor wordy. Using a clear, direct, and serious tone he began by introducing himself and his associates, and stressing how important the jury position was to the state, and state justice, and how he appreciated the juror's time and patience. He talked a little about the criminal justice system's objectives and how the jury played an important part in that process, both historically and today. He thanked the jurors for their appearance, and the subtle effect of this warm-up to the case we all knew, was to convince the jury that he was a nice man and doing his job. But he didn't hasten to remind us, that as a representative of the state—and the very people sitting in the jury box <u>were</u> the state—he had no compunctions about ". . . my dogged interest is in securing justice."*

## Who They Are

A prosecutor is recognized as the legal representative of the state, sometimes referred to as the district's attorney or state's attorney. Most often, they are elected officials, and this is a powerful political position because he or she is the chief law enforcement agent within a jurisdiction. Prosecutors instigate criminal charges against an accused person and represent the state at trial.

Prosecutors generally are or have been active members in bar associations, although, some may start out with little significant experience in the criminal justice system. Experience as a prosecutor is typically a stepping stone to a higher political office and, for that reason, the length of civil service is rather short and the turnover in office is quite high.

## ROLE OF THE PROSECUTOR

The role of the prosecutor spans the entire criminal justice process. Prosecutors often have a great deal of resources available to them that are not possessed by the defense. In addition to the great numbers of people on the prosecution staff, they also have the best "scientific tools" at their disposal–items and artifacts that have been examined by the state or county forensic examiners and scientists to help support their cases. And cooperative police have been known to chase an identified suspect relentlessly and, in the case of killers of police officers, with enthusiasm. The "protect and serve" mentality unfortunately sometimes means a lack of impartiality.

## AUTHORITY AND PRESTIGE

Some of the prosecution's power and influence occurs at every step in the system as follows:

- **Investigation:** Prosecutors often prepare search and arrest warrants and work with police to make sure that investigative reports are complete. They may, upon reports from citizens, initiate their own investigations independent of police but under a harried metropolitan schedule (possibly 200 cases or more a day) decisions will be based on a cursory review of the police report and criminal's history.
- **Arrest:** Following arrest, prosecutors screen their files to determine which cases should be prosecuted and which should be dropped. Police officers usually start the charging process with an arrest or citation.
- **Charges:** Since the prosecutor institutes and controls the case, he or she may file criminal charges even if the victim does not approve, or refuse to file certain others despite the victim's desire that criminal charges be brought to bear.
- **Initial appearance:** It is up to the prosecutor's office to ensure that all defendants are notified of the charges against them and that someone from their office is represented at the first court appearance. They can also influence bail decisions. An

important point to anyone accused of a crime–and this is the penultimate fact–prosecutors can also discontinue a prosecution by drafting a *nolle prosequi.* This is a formal document entered into the record that declares the state is unwilling to go forward.

- **Grand jury:** The prosecutor is for all intents and purposes the "judge and prosecutor" within the grand jury. He or she is usually the only major legal officer in the room when the citizens determine whether or not to indict. Plus, the prosecutor decides what evidence the grand jury will or will not hear.
- **Preliminary hearing:** Prosecutors establish probable cause and draft *nolle prosequi* where applicable. So, in jurisdictions where there is no initial appearance, they proceed directly to the preliminary hearing with the formal notice of charges and bail option.
- **Information indictment:** Prosecutors make ready information that establishes probable cause and binds over the accused for trial. In jurisdictions that use indictment rather than information, they establish probable cause for hearing by the grand jury.
- **Arraignment:** Prosecutors bring the accused to the court to answer to the matters charged in the information or indictment. Plea negotiations would normally take place during, before, or after this appearance. Plea negotiation is a method that allows the defendant to plead guilty to a reduced charge or charges. Most offenders choose this option rather than go to trial.
- **Pretrial motions:** As representatives of the state, prosecutors introduce and present the arguments for any pretrial motions.
- **Trial:** Prosecutors are the government's trial lawyers; they are sworn to argue the

case on behalf of the state. Since the accused is innocent until proven guilty, their job is to prove the guilt of the accused beyond a reasonable doubt, also called "burden of proof."

- **Sentencing:** Prosecutors make sentencing recommendations to the judge.
- **Appeal:** Through written and oral debate, prosecutors make certain that convictions were obtained properly and legally, and should not be reversed by the courts.
- **Parole:** In some jurisdictions, prosecutors make recommendations for or against parole when an inmate's records come up for review.
- **Probation and parole revocation hearing:** When a probationer or a parolee violates a condition of probation or parole, he or she is entitled to a hearing to see whether or not probation or parole will be revoked. Someone from the prosecutor's office may act as advocate for the state in these hearings.

## THE GAME OF LIFE

As Z.G. Standing Bear, Ph.D., Diplomate with the American Board of Forensic Examiners and one of the organization's chief authors on ethics says, "The problems faced by prosecution and defense are quite different and, some say, tend to even each other out given that each side had advantages and disadvantages. This 'game theory' approach in what may be a life or death situation for someone accused of crime is understandably often not appreciated by the individual looking at execution or long, hard time in prison. In many situations, criminal defendants are poorly educated, indigent individuals who may not understand how the 'game' is played. On such a playing field, often the innocent go to prison and the guilty

go free, depending upon the skill of the gladiator (lawyer) in the ring."

## THE PRESENTATION

The presentation of the case for the defense is similar to that of the prosecution in that the defense counsel calls witnesses, and directly examines them, then turns them over to the prosecutor for cross-examination. There are standards of behavior and considerations of procedure that apply to the defense as well as the prosecutor. Briefly they are:

- The defendant is not required by law to present witnesses. Instead, the defense can be based entirely on the evidence and testimony presented by the state.
- The defendant is not required to give personal testimony. A defendant's refusal to take the stand cannot be called to the attention of the jury by either the prosecutor or the judge. Any inference that would imply guilt, because of the defendant's lack of testimony, is prejudicial. If he or she does choose to take the witness stand though, a defendant faces the same hazards of cross-examination as any other witnesses.
- The defense lawyer is not obligated to prove the innocence of his or her client but merely to show that the state has failed to prove guilt beyond a reasonable doubt.

## THE WORK LIFE

Overworked and undervalued are two words to describe the caseload and rigor involved in the life of a prosecutor. For state purposes, there are generally two types of management for prosecutorial tasks: segmented prosecutorial function, or what is referred to as fluid prosecutorial function. If an office operates under segmented prosecutorial function, only a certain number of prosecutors perform duties during any one particular stage of the system. As an illustration, in large cities the younger or junior prosecutors fill the prosecutorial role at initial appearance and preliminary hearings because court appearances usually eat up a lot of time. The more senior officials are left to determine whether the facts warrant sufficient evidence to give rise to criminal charges, and, if so, it is up to them to decide what charges will be made. Other attorneys may be in charge of arraignments and pretrial motions. And still others–the most articulate–are used as state's trial litigators, the lions of the court. And finally, in another segment of the office, certain prosecutors will handle only cases on appeal.

In the other type of prosecutor's system– the fluid office–a state attorney will handle a case from beginning to end. More conducive to smaller offices and communities, in the fluid system prosecutors will take the case from its inception, get involved in investigation, and work it until the case is processed through the system. He or she will act as the jack-of-all-trades, from warrant to incarceration and even beyond.

In addition to the list of services provided in either one of these office systems, prosecutors must also maintain a certain media image. Since they are elected officials, they may appear in public service announcements on television or radio, or present themselves at highly publicized, justice-related media events.

## When Prosecutors and Police Butt Heads

The marriage of police with prosecutors is not always made in heaven. Insiders who study the system claim that there is a "cooperation gap" between certain police investigators and their legal partners. Policies between these two offices can prove very different, as well as the priorities one places on them. For this reason, case attrition–when an arrest is made but no charge is ever filed–is not out of the realm of possibility. Another difference that can rub raw is the fact that the officer is the one most knowledgeable about the case, yet usually lacks person-to-person contact with the state's attorney. They work different hours, have very different points of view, and do not socialize.

In more practical matters, prosecutors need certain types of quality evidence in order to build a case and the police may not always be able to deliver. Thus, when there is a shortage or mistake, a plea bargain or dismissal may be the only alternative, which tends to leave the officer involved quite unhappy. Another example is if the officer and the prosecutor do not coordinate on witness weaknesses, the defense may make them both look stupid in court. Unfortunately, time, additional investigation, and follow-up do not always coordinate for the best outcome.

## Bringing Charges

Prosecutors have what is frequently referred to as *prosecutorial discretion*. They look at all the factors of a case including the criminal's past record and decide whether to file charges on all the crimes police arrest for, or can file charges that are more or less severe than the charges proposed by police initially. In felony murder cases, it is the prosecutor, along with state statutes, who decide whether the defendant will face the death penalty.

If a crime is a misdemeanor, a prosecutor files an accusatory pleading directly in court. This pleading may be called a criminal complaint, an information, or a petition. On a felony, charges can use the same accusatory pleading format as with a misdemeanor, or the prosecutor can also rely on an indictment handed down by a grand jury.

> **Other Notes**—Sometimes behavior as defined in a statute can perch on the line between felony and misdemeanor. Such crimes are called "wobblers" and the prosecutor has the discretion to decide which charge to bring. The ambiguity of a situation can add angst to a prosecutor's decision over which way to go.

> **FYI**—How prosecutors decide to seek the death penalty varies widely. Prosecutors use a wide range of criteria running from visiting the crime scene, to seeking the death penalty for those who kill with an axe, knife, or in some other grisly way, with most coming down hard on multiple murderers. One Oklahoma prosecutor admits to taking the hard line on robbers who kill convenience store clerks and another may be bothered by husbands or wives who kill their spouses in anger.

## PROVING GUILT

This last point, proving guilt, lies at the very heart of a criminal trial. Because for the prosecutor, whether the defendant did it or not is not relevant to his or her prosecution. What is relevant is the prosecution's ability to produce admissible evidence to prove the defendant's guilt to the judge or jury beyond a reasonable doubt. Evidence is what the judge permits the jury to hear and consider. Evidence may take the form of physical exhibits, such as photographs, bullets, or a black-and-blue face. Answers to questions asked by the lawyers or by the judge are also evidence; as is the sworn testimony in written form of a witness who cannot appear personally in court.

## Me First

It is generally believed that the prosecution gets to go first in a trial because they have the burden of proof. This may not be an advantage. The prosecution, by presenting its case first, does not know much about the defendant's line of attack. Of course, this temporary setback is remedied by a part of the trial called the rebuttal.

## RULES OF EVIDENCE

In order to give the accused the opportunity to provide an informed defense, it is the state's duty to present evidence in the case initially. This presentation of evidence is governed essentially by the rules of evidence. These concepts are similar to the rules of a game, which governs the conduct of the players.

Evidence is made up of legal proofs presented to the court in the form of witnesses, records, documents, objects and other means for the purpose of influencing the opinions of the judge or jury toward the case of the prosecution or the defense. The rules of evidence control the content—what kind of information witnesses can provide—and the manner in which witnesses testify, that is, obtaining information through a series of questions and answers instead of long, uninterrupted narrative.

Evidence rules evolved through common law judicial decisions. Most judicial evidence rules are written into state statutes, for example, California has the California Evidence Code, which was adapted for the Federal Rules of Evidence[1] (FRE), a set of laws that governs federal trials. Nowadays, legislatures have taken over the development of evidence law but the judges are still the ones who interpret it. With this power, the judge can require more proof for allowing legally admissible evidence.

## Key Rules of Evidence

Relevance is the foundation for evidence rules. Some logical relationship must exist between the evidence and the factual issue it is supposed to prove in order for it to be relevant. Like a link in a chain, the importance of any single item of evidence needn't be so strong that it proves or disproves a fact. It's good enough if the piece of evidence establishes proof along with other pieces of evidence. Good examples of this are the *Matlock* shows that were broadcast on television with Andy Griffith as the country lawyer in the ubiquitous seersucker suit. The defense would always object to Matlock's dramatic and continuing stories as being irrelevant to the case. Of course, in the end, he was always given leeway in order to prove that this one single piece of apparently insignificant evidence, was the key to the case. The main limitation with relevance is that the connection must be based on reason and logic rather than on bias and emotion.

## Admissibility

Before evidence may be admitted in court, whether real, testimonial, direct, or circumstantial, it must meet certain legal requirements. To do this, a judge may have a witness questioned privately to determine whether the jury should be allowed to hear the same testimony. Information used to determine the admissibility of other evidence is called *foundational evidence* and is conducted in a phase of the trial called a *mini-trial.*

## Similar Fact Evidence

A very technical law of evidence, similar fact evidence presents facts similar to the facts of the crime charged. For example, the evidence might reveal the pattern of an additional or ancillary crime. To get similar fact evidence into court, however, one must show that the knowledge is both relevant and has probative value in establishing a material issue—in other words, the information must provide proof that this is a crucial or pivotal point. Although hemmed in by not being allowed to show bad character or a propensity to commit crime, still, some similar fact evidence may be introduced to show motive, identity, or absence of mistake.

A case involving sexual abuse of children might allow similar fact evidence. For example, if an older child testifies to a similar course of sexual misconduct such as what happened to a younger sibling by the father, who is being charged. A Wyoming Supreme Court upheld admission of the testimony[2] because the younger child's credibility was attacked and the evidence admitted at trial was inconclusive as to the younger sister's physical symptoms. In order to block the possibility of appeal, the court included in the brief a lengthy footnote showing that about half of the state courts now liberally admit the legality of introducing prior bad acts as evidence in sexual offenses for various purposes.

---

1. Title 28 of the United States Code Annotated.
2. *Gezzi v. State,* 780 P.2d 972 (Wyo. 1989).

## TYPES OF EVIDENCE

The four types of evidence are real evidence, testimony, direct evidence, and circumstantial evidence.

- **Real evidence** is made up of tangible objects such as maps, stolen goods, photographs, blood samples or fingerprints, knives, guns or other weapons, etc. Sometimes reasonable facsimiles of objects like photographs, reproductions, or videos may stand in place of real objects for practical purposes.
- **Testimonial evidence** is the statement given by sworn witnesses. In a trial, after opening statements are made, the prosecution calls its first witness. The witness takes an oath or affirmation to tell the truth by raising his or her hand and swearing to do so. The prosecutor then begins to present evidence by using questions and answers called *direct examination.*
- **Direct evidence** refers to the observations of eyewitnesses. Indirect evidence, on the other hand, usually consists of circumstantial evidence.
- **Circumstantial evidence** is information that tends to prove or disprove a point at issue. Circumstantial evidence may be admissible as a result of being inferred, for example, a forensic technician gives testimony in court that the defendant's fingerprints were found on the drawer that held the murder weapon. It may be inferred that the defendant opened the drawer to get the knife.

Figure 11. Calling up fingerprints using the Automated Fingerprint Identification System (AFIS).

## OTHER KINDS OF EVIDENCE AND THEIR MEANINGS

### Judicial Notice

Commonly held knowledge or what one might call "conventional wisdom" is accepted without proof by the courts. Either party can ask that judicial notice be taken as evidence without question. An example of this would be agreeing not to require proof that whiskey is an intoxicating liquor, because to do so would demand the testimony of a trained medical technician. So, for expediency, the court can decide to dispense with the laborious testimony because we all know what happens when someone imbibes alcohol.

### Admission

Admission is when either party willingly admits the truth of any matter during the course of discovery or trial. This frees the other party from the trouble of introducing evidence to prove the matter.

### Stipulation

During a trial you may hear "The defense stipulates that the day in question was Sunday, your Honor" or something to that effect. When both sides agree that particular matters or events are true, no further evidence need be offered. This is another time-saving device with introducing evidence.

### Hearsay

Hearsay is a statement or assertion of conduct that was made outside the courtroom by someone other than the witness and is offered for the truth. In other words, hearsay is knowledge or information the witness acquires secondhand, that is to say, facts he or she was told by someone else. The hearsay rule governs the admissibility of the statements, for example, whether something said by an absentee individual can be heard. Despite this rule–or an objection made by defense–out-of-court statements are often heard because the rule is riddled with exceptions. To figure out if a statement is admissible, ask yourself "What is the statement offered to prove?" If the statement is offered to prove something other than its truth, it is nonhearsay.

## SOME EXCEPTIONS TO THE HEARSAY RULE (at least ten exist)

### Dying Declarations

Because people want to believe that a dying person's last words will be the truth, this exception admits into evidence statements made by someone who senses imminent death and presents dying declarations. The dying declaration must be that of the victim, not a third person.

### Excited Utterances

The excited utterance exception to hearsay admits evidence statements made under the stress of excitement of perceiving an unusual event. The defining words here being "unusual event." For example, after witnessing a shooting, someone might say to the police, "That man with the scar over his eye just shot that woman!" and that witness then runs away and is never found again. The policeman in court may testify to the stranger's comments.

### Admission of Guilt or a Confession

If an accused tells the investigator that he

was at the apartment when the shooting took place, that admission will tie the defendant to the crime scene and may be admitted as evidence. This does not defy the Fourth Amendment protection against self-incrimination because the testimony of the law enforcement officer is that he heard the defendant say that outside the courtroom.

## Assertions of State of Mind

The mental state of a defendant is often germane to his or her behavior and goes to help prove motive and intent in a criminal case. The assertions of state of mind exception admits into evidence accounts describing and characterizing people's emotions, beliefs, and intent as it may hold influence over other criminal elements. These statements can be key elements for the prosecution.

## Prior Inconsistent Statements

If a witness's testimony varies in some important way from prior out-of-court statements made by that witness, the prior statements are admissible in evidence. Contradictions or a change of fact, before and after, usually indicate dishonesty or fudging with facts. For example, say an officer observes some type of conduct or writes down a statement from a witness, puts it in the report,

and then finds the statement is changed markedly in fact at trial, the prior statement can be admitted and will usually cast doubt on the testimony provided.

## Business and Government Records

Since businesses and government offices alike often keep records with some regularity and must rely on them for accurate reports, these documents can be admitted as evidence because they are presumed trustworthy indicators reflecting regular business practices and activities.

## 9-1-1 Calls

In Supreme Court case 05-5224[3], a 911 operator ascertained from Michelle McCottry that she had been assaulted by her former boyfriend petitioner Davis, who had just fled the scene. McCottry did not testify at Davis's trial for felony violation of a domestic no-contact order, but the 911 call, *inter alia*, was offered as evidence of the connection between Davis and McCottry's injuries. Davis objected, arguing that presenting the recording without giving him the opportunity to cross-examine McCottry violated his Sixth Amendment right to confront his accuser as interpreted by the U.S.

---

**Inter Alia** (in-tur eh-lee-ah) is Latin meaning, "among other things". This phrase is often found in legal pleadings and writings to specify one example out of many possibilities. Example: "The judge said, inter alia, that the time to file the action had passed." Legal drafters would use it to precede a list of examples or samples covered by a more general descriptive statement. Sometimes they use an inter alia list to make absolutely sure that users of the document understand that the general description covers a certain element without, in any way, restricting the scope.

---

3. *Davis v. Washington*, U.S. 05-5224, 154 Wash. 2d 291, 111 P. 3d 844, affirmed; No. 05-5705, 829 N. E. 2d 444, reversed and remanded.

Supreme Court in *Crawford v. Washington.* The Washington Supreme Court disagreed, finding that the call was not "testimonial" and was therefore different from the statements at issue in Crawford. He was convicted. The Washington Court of Appeals affirmed, as did the State Supreme Court, which concluded that, *inter alia,* the portion of the 911 conversation in which McCottry identified Davis as her assailant was not testimonial.

When police responded to a reported domestic disturbance at the home of Amy and Hershel Hammon, Amy told them that nothing was wrong, but gave them permission to enter. Once inside, one officer kept petitioner Hershel in the kitchen while the other interviewed Amy elsewhere and had her complete and sign a battery affidavit. Amy did not appear at Hershel's bench trial for domestic battery, but her affidavit and testimony from the officer who questioned her were admitted over Hershel's objection that he had no opportunity to cross-examine her. Hershel was convicted, and the Indiana Court of Appeals affirmed it. The State Supreme Court also affirmed, concluding that, although Amy's affidavit was testimonial and wrongly admitted, it was harmless beyond a reasonable doubt.

In a 9–0 decision, the Court ruled that the Confrontation Clause of the Sixth Amendment, as interpreted in *Crawford v. Washington,*[4] does not apply to "non-testimonial" statements not intended to be preserved as evidence at trial. Although McCottry identified her attacker to the 911 operator, she provided the information intending to help the police resolve an "ongoing emergency," not to testify to a past crime. The Court reasoned that under the circumstances, McCottry was not acting as a "witness," and the 911 transcript was not "testimony." Therefore, the Sixth Amendment did not require her to appear at trial and be cross-examined.

## STATE'S EVIDENCE

A phrase used for testimony given by an accomplice or mutual associate in the commission of a crime is referred to as *state's evidence.* The testimony usually tends to incriminate or convict others and is usually provided as the result of a promise of immunity or a lesser charge.

## Expert Evidence

Expert witnesses do not have to have any firsthand knowledge of the crime and they are not restricted from expressing their opinions. Their testimony is given in relation to some scientific, technical, or professional matter and they are allowed to speak with authority because of their special training, ability, or familiarity with the subject.

## Opinion Evidence

This is reserved for witnesses who are called upon for the specific purpose of expressing their opinion. The court can

---

**FYI**—Although the hearsay rule implies the information is based on an "oral statement," it applies to written statements as well. Statements made in letters, faxes, and business reports or other documents may be hearsay or not, depending on their usage. And just as hearsay may be admissible because of an exception, so may the contents of a document.

---

4. *Crawford v. Washington,* 541 U.S. 36 (2004).

accept anyone as an expert who has credentials that establish him or her as an expert in that field.

## Material Evidence

Material evidence relates to the crime charged or has a legitimate bearing or effective influence on the decision of the case.

## Prima Facie Evidence

This is evidence, which, in the judgment of the law, is adequate to establish a given fact—"on its face." The phrase may be mentioned in respect to a prima facie case, meaning, if a grand jury is convinced by the prosecutor's evidence that a prima facie case has been made (so far as can be judged on its face value) the evidence will prevail as proof of facts until it can be contradicted or overcome by other evidence.

## Noncharacter "Bad Person" Evidence

As a general principle, evidence rules do not allow prosecutors to charge someone with a crime and then attack his or her character—it would be too damning. For example, a jury might convict someone because he or she is a "bad person" and should be punished, regardless if the case presented was a strong one or not. To avoid the rule, a prosecutor may argue that "bad person evidence" is relevant on a noncharacter theory. For an example of this, a judge might allow more latitude if a prosecutor were to try to convict a defendant charged with assault, and wanted to offer up evidence that the defendant had assaulted the same person in the past in front of witnesses. Even though there is the risk that jury members might believe the defendant just naturally had a violent character, the judge would allow it as

Figure 12. The ubiquitous crime scene preservation tape.

> **FYI**—A new state's evidence rule is on the books for many jurisdictions. With the alarming increase in sexual assault crimes comes a new character evidence rule that allows prosecutors to offer evidence that defendants charged with sexual assault crimes have committed previous sexual assaults.

noncharacter evidence on the principle that the evidence would show the defendant had a grudge against the victim (making this more evidence of motive). To use the information, the judge would need to issue a limiting instruction to the jury, warning them to not think of this as forbidden character use.

The same tactic is used by prosecutors to introduce evidence of "priors." By using the defendant's past misdeeds as *modus operandi*, the prosecutor can introduce evidence of methodology, proving the defendant used the same method previously, which was almost nearly identical to the one allegedly used to commit the present crime. Again the judge would institute limiting instruction, in order to differentiate between past criminal charges and what could be called the defendant's "m.o."

## Witness Character Evidence

Both the prosecution and the defense are allowed to attack the credibility of adverse witnesses according to the rules of evidence. The only stipulation is that the traits attacked must be concerning honesty. They can offer evidence of past misdeeds or anything involving dishonesty, evidence of deceit given by another witness, and evidence of specific acts such as dodging the IRS and refusing to pay taxes.

## DIFFERENT TYPES OF EVIDENCE

Evidence may take many forms including:

- Identification
- Seen leaving the crime scene
- Forensic or crime scene evidence
- Weather
- Animals
- Wounds
- Weapons
- Motive
- Time of death
- Pathology reports
- Exhibits
- Confessions, excited utterances
- Statements of family, friends
- Statements of police, witnesses, experts, victim
- Noncharacter "bad person" evidence
- Documents such as wills, letters, plans, diary
- Prior record
- Government and business records
- Electronic surveillance such as video-tapes, cameras, or audio tapes
- Receipts, records of rental or purchase
- Personal habits
- Personal electronics such as answering machines, beepers, cell phones, etc.

There are, however, many things that must not be considered as evidence. For instance, what a lawyer says or claims to have proven is not evidence. Nor is testimony that the jury has heard but that the judge has ordered stricken from the record. Although difficult, the jury must treat all such testimony as though it had never been given. Similarly, matters that a lawyer offers to prove, but that the judge will not allow to be presented, are not to be considered as evi-

FYI—Here are two important factors about certain types of testimony and the prosecutor's responsibility. First, a defendant can never be compelled to be a witness by being called on by the prosecutor without consent. But if so agreed, testifying must always be in a question-and-answer format. This process gives the prosecutor a high manipulation factor, and can be used to the state's advantage when conveying trial testimony.

Also, it is rare that a prosecutor will bring charges for perjury (lying under oath). It's difficult to prove an actual knowledge of false testimony, so it is not generally pursued. The only way perjury must be charged is when the prosecutor has no choice, such as when a high-profile person lies in full view of millions, on televised court proceedings, or when the media makes issue of it.

dence. A juror is not allowed to consider any information about the witnesses, parties or lawyers present, nor anything connected with the case other than the evidence seen or heard in the courtroom.

## SCIENTIFIC EVIDENCE AND THE FRYE TEST

Because of the evolution of new technology, new procedures and forensic services are becoming available to police at every turn. Evidence realized through scientific and technological discoveries can be both relevant and probative in a criminal case. The only stumbling block is to ensure that the new method can be supported by research.

In the past, federal and state courts followed the criterion that was formulated as a result of a case *Frye v. United States*[5] in which the admissibility of a polygraph (lie detector test) was brought into evidence. The major consideration was whether experts in that field accepted the new scientific technique.

Over the years, this test has been broadened and modified such as in a New York Court of Appeals which said the technique's

acceptance need not be unanimous, but just accepted as reliable.

The result of the wavering interpretation has reached a consensus where both sides present as many expert witnesses they think can shoot down the other side's experts. Juries are often confused because both sides can hold honest opinions and, if one looks hard enough, can secure dishonest opinions for a price.

## GRAND JURY

Similar to regular petit juries, grand juries are made up of individuals randomly selected for jury duty. (In our community they come from the registered voter database.) They are charged with the duty of indictment, meaning they decide from the evidence provided whether the person or persons should be charged with a crime. All proceedings for grand juries are held in secret. Their term of service can be as long as a term of court, which can run from six to eighteen months. There are between fifteen and twenty-three people called for service to a grand jury, and a federal grand jury unit

---

5. *Frye v. U.S.*, 293 F. 1013 (D.C. Cir. 1923).

has sixteen to twenty-three people. While petit juries must have unanimity to convict, grand juries need not be unanimous to indict, for example, in federal situations, needing twelve or more to agree to indict. Readers can obtain a copy of the "Handbook for Virginia Grand Jurors" on the Internet at: http://www.courts.state.va.us/text/gjury/cover.htm.

## Grand Jury Process

Several states operate under the grand jury system which means a prosecutor must obtain an indictment, also called a true bill from the grand jury in addition to, or instead of, the preliminary hearing. The Fifth Amendment carries with it the words "No person shall be held to answer for a capital, or otherwise infamous crime, unless on a presentment or indictment of a grand jury." The Supreme Court has allowed states to defer from this somewhat, based on the concept that they are not bound by the Fourteenth Amendment as the federal courts are. Just the same, about half the states have constitutional provisions obligating the use of grand juries as either an investigatory or supervisory board.

## Grand Jury Power

Investigative grand juries have the aid of subpoena power. This ability gives the grand jury the right to require the possessions of the accused to be brought forward. These then, may be obtained without probable cause, which is a necessary staple for police, who have to use the search warrant system.

While defendants are usually warned that they are suspected of committing a crime, the grand jury prosecutor need not tell the accused that he or she is a target. As a consequence, they may only be told of the general subject matter of the proceeding. In fact, the accused does not even have to be present at the proceeding. And most states do not allow the accused to have counsel in attendance, and, in federal situations, a witness must step outside the courtroom to speak with his or her attorney.

With respect to witnesses, anyone who fails to show under subpoena or refuses to cooperate with the investigation can face possible jail time for contempt. A target witness is given no warnings of any kind, yet, if found giving false testimony before the grand jury he or she may be prosecuted for perjury. A contempt order also may be issued for anyone who fails to keep the details of the proceedings secret. The sheer power of the coerciveness of the court's demeanor puts a great pall over the entire interrogation process.

## BURDEN OF PROOF

It's been bandied about, used as a title for novels and films, but what is the burden of

---

**Other Notes**—There are great possibilities for oppression with the federal grand jury system. The insults to "due process" fairly scream out for exposure. Believed to act as a buffer between the accused and an overzealous prosecutor, the grand jury system really cancels out the accused's constitutional rights to due process, an open and public trial, the ability to face his or her accusers, the right against self-incrimination, the right to counsel and cross-examination, and the lack of advisement rights so inherent in police interrogation.

proof and who is to judge this elusive concept? The burden of proof is a fundamental legal principle placed on the prosecutor, who must prove the defendant's guilt beyond a reasonable doubt. Remember that the defendant is presumed innocent to start, and remains so, up to the time the judge or jury finds him or her guilty. The prosecutor's job is to provide enough evidence to convince either the judge or jury that the defendant is guilty.

We have defined crimes–that means, broken them down into their elements. For a refresher on those elements, refer back to Chapters Two, Three, and Four. For example, if someone is accused of simple burglary, a burglary occurs when: a culprit (1) breaks into, (2) and enters, (3) the dwelling, (4) of another, without consent, (5) with the intent to commit a felony or steal property. If the prosecutor wants the defendant convicted for those charges, all elements must be proved to the reasonable satisfaction of the judge or jury.

Reasonable doubt, it has been said, ". . . is not a mere possible doubt, because everything relates to human affairs, and depending on moral evidence, is open to some possible or imaginary doubt. It is that state of the case which, after the entire comparison and consideration of all the evidence, leaves the minds of the jurors in that condition that they cannot say that they feel an abiding conviction, to a moral certainty, of the truth of the charge."

## OTHER STANDARDS OF PROOF

### Preponderance of the Evidence

Civil law uses preponderance of evidence as its standard of proof. A much lower stan-

dard than beyond a reasonable doubt, one side must merely produce slightly more convincing evidence than the other side in order to win.

### Clear and Convincing Evidence

The clear and convincing evidence standard is higher than the usual civil preponderance but somewhat lower than beyond a reasonable doubt. For an insanity defense, it is up to the defendant to prove it by clear and convincing evidence.[6]

## THE PLEA

### Plea Bargains or Negotiated Plea

Since more than 90 percent of felony suspects arraigned plead guilty, everyone should know more about plea bargains. A plea bargain is by its very nomenclature an agreement. The defendant agrees to plead guilty or no contest in exchange for an agreement by the prosecutor to drop some charges, reduce a charge to a less serious offense, or recommend a reduced sentence to the judge which is acceptable to the defense. Bargaining is between the prosecutor and the defendant–but it also must be sanctioned by the court–and can take place anytime, generally, from the moment a defendant speaks to his lawyer for the first time, right up to the time a jury walks in with a verdict. In fact, it's been said that looking into the eyes of jurors has made more than one defendant choose a deal.

### State's Advantage

Despite being unpopular with citizens, there are several good reasons for the plea

6. Insanity Defense Reform Act of 1984 18 U.S.C.A. § 17 (b).

bargain procedure: It saves time and gets the matter over with quickly; it saves money for the courts; those who are not likely to receive much jail time are processed out of jail; there are less problems with prison over-crowding; there is less frequency that serious offenders will be let go before their full sentence; to lighten the state's caseloads; it beats the uncertainty of a trial with an assured conviction.

## Defendant's Advantage

The principle benefit for defendants taking pleas is he or she may receive a lighter sentence for a less severe charge than might be gotten from a judge or jury. Other benefits are: getting out of jail immediately following the judge's acceptance; a quick disposition is less stressful; a less serious offense is on record; there is less social stigmatizing with reduced charges; it saves on lawyer fees; there is less publicity; it protects someone else.

## Victims Point of View

The benefit to victims is also numerous in that it moves the situation on rather quickly, with less publicity and stress of a trial. Since the victim may feel the defendant was "let off" too easily, many judges and prosecutors are consulting with the victims before accepting any final pleas. In some jurisdictions, the victim or victim's family can address the judge directly before sentencing takes place, in an effort to influence the probation terms or sentencing recommendations. The pendulum is swinging away from the defendant with this new determination.

## A TWIST OF THE STATE SCREW

## Confiscation and Forfeiture

Taking a defendant's property as part of a civil forfeiture proceeding is actually a separate proceeding from the criminal case. The government takes property as part of criminal activities, such as confiscating a boat that transported drugs, or holding an airplane or conveyance vehicle used to transport controlled substances. The federal law for this can be found generally under 18 U.S.C.A. §§ 981-982. In 1996, the U.S. Supreme Court held that civil forfeiture is not "punishment" and as a consequence, the forfeiture does not

---

**FYI**—Certain jurisdictions have enacted mandatory sentencing laws for certain crimes. This movement takes away any discretion on the part of the judge to adjudicate lower sentences and is the ultimate deal-breaker. Check your jurisdiction's sentencing guidelines.

---

**Other Notes**—It's not at all unusual for an innocent person to take a plea. Sometimes the pressure of the justice system will make accused persons so nervous that when told the judge will be harsher on them if they go to trial, or that the prospect of losing looks bad, they succumb to a quick negotiation. In reality, the "good deal" that the prosecutor offers may happen simply because the evidence against the defendant is weak.

violate the prohibition against double jeopardy.

Cars that are taken because the owner sold narcotics from them are technically forfeited rights, in favor of the government, and, in some instances, it does not matter that the car belongs to someone else. The theory is that the owner has the responsibility to see to it that his or her property is only used under legal conditions.

There is an interesting case you may want to look up. It concerns a home that was purchased with drug money and taken away as part of a bust. The Supreme Court ruled that, although proceeds traceable to an unlawful drug transaction are subject to forfeiture, an owner's "lack of knowledge" that her home had been purchased with the proceeds of illegal drug money constitutes a defense to a forfeiture proceeding under federal law (*United States v. A Parcel of Land*, 507 U.S. 111, 113 S.Ct. 1126, 122 L.Ed.2d 469 [1993]).

*Confiscation* is the seizure of personal property and usually takes the shape of contraband, or property that citizens have no right to possess such as drugs, pornography, illegal guns, or illegal cigarettes. This type of property often becomes evidence at trial and the citizen does not get it back. No one talks about it very much and word has it that illegal narcotics sometimes find their way back out onto the street, after being taken from the police evidence room. However, much of it is destroyed.

It has been found that an entire farm was confiscated because the owner grew marijuana on the land. The sale of the farm for forfeiture reasons put money into the coffers of the law enforcement agency that seized it in the first place. Not only that, but a fight against forfeiture is both cumbersome and expensive. Rumor has it that the government will drop a civil complaint upon seizing the property, and the owner must then respond within a certain number of days. If not, the property is irretrievably lost. If the property is seized, no matter the outcome, the owner can contest but may never get it back.

## Fines

The most common form of criminal punishment is the monetary fine. If you've spent anytime in the courthouse, you will see the registrar's office taking checks and assessing penalties (the cash register sings!). Most misdemeanors carry fines, especially for first offenses. Serious economic crimes, as defined by federal law, will also carry quite heavy monetary fines as part of the penalty phase.

In state courts, defendants are often required to pay court costs in addition to a sentence of probation or imprisonment. The effectiveness of assessing minimum and maximum fines sometimes seems ridiculous as the defendants who commit these crimes may also be classified as indigents or very poor indeed.

## OTHER COURT PENALTIES

### Perjury

The Mosaic Code—the codes from Moses in the Old Testament—had a stipulation about bearing false witness. Progressing through the ages since Biblical times, the taking of an oath during a judicial proceeding grew into the common law offense of false swearing.

Today's federal law[7] has proscribed the elements of perjury as: taking an oath to tell

---

7. 18 U.S.C.A. § 1621.

**Other Notes**—A common scenario of compounding a crime occurs when a crime victim whose goods have been stolen agrees with the thief to take back the goods in exchange for not prosecuting. In some courts, the dismissal of this kind of behavior may be granted because of the restitution to the victim, but an agreement cannot always be reached without prior court approval.

the truth before a competent tribunal, officer, or person in which the law of the United States requires an oath and he testifies or swears about documents, or declarations, plus, he willfully contributes as true any material matter which he does not believe to be true is guilty of perjury. Most states follow this basic principle and have laws against perjury. Difficult to prove, perjury is made more difficult to prosecute by the two-witness rule that predominates in most jurisdictions. Under this rule, the prosecution must prove the deceitfulness of the defendant's statements by utilizing two witnesses or by the testimony of one witness and corroborating–read this as validating–documents or circumstances.

## Defense Against Perjury

If someone makes a false statement under oath, he or she may recant that statement and tell the truth. Federal law makes a defense exception called *recantation* for people who decide to "'fess up," provided the perjury has not substantially affected the proceedings or if it has not become evident that the deception has or will be exposed. The untruthfulness must be repudiated, which means retracted in the prior testimony, and it must take place before prejudice or damage has occurred.

## Obstruction of Justice

Anytime someone interferes with the course of justice, he or she can be charged

with obstructing justice. Many states have laws defining obstruction and it can take numerous different forms such as, giving false information, knowingly giving a false alarm, impersonating an officer, intimidating a witness, tampering with a juror, and destroying public records. These charges occur frequently in federal law as well, and although this is a rather modern statutory development, it is taken very seriously when the prosecution begins stockpiling charges.

## Compounding a Crime

A person compounds a crime when he or she accepts money or something else of value in exchange for agreeing not to prosecute a felony. Turning a "blind eye" to wrongdoing is just as bad as committing the crime in some people's viewpoint. There is a modern statutory approach to the offense of compounding a crime and many states have designed their own policies but, basically, any benefit given under an agreement for refraining from initiating or aiding in a criminal prosecution is illegal.

## PROSECUTORIAL STANDARDS

It's probably no surprise that the American Bar Association–the largest professional organization of United States lawyers–has a list of standards for criminal justice and prosecutor function in particular. Conduct such as misrepresenting facts; using illegal means to secure evidence or employ others to do so is "unprofessional conduct" and subject to sanctions.

For a list of the standards, there is a web site with some information. The URL is: http://www.november.org/ABAstandards.html.

# REVIEW QUESTIONS AND ANSWERS

## *Key Words to Define*

- **Arraignment**–The accused appears in court to answer to the charges, that is: guilty or not guilty plea; also completed within 48 hours in most states.
- **Circumstantial evidence**–Information that tends to prove a point at issue; evidence that can be inferred from what is presented.
- **Direct evidence**–Observation of eye-witness(es).
- **Excited utterances**–Evidence made by statements under the stress of the event and is used as an exception to hearsay.
- **Foundational evidence**–Witness questioned to determine admissibility of other evidence.
- **Frye v. U.S.**–The admissibility of a polygraph was brought into evidence in this case; it poses the question of whether evidence is accepted as a new scientific technique or reliable test of evidence.
- **Hearsay**–A statement made outside of court by someone other than the witness; a repeated story.
- **Information indictment**–Information that establishes probable cause and binds the accused over for trial.
- **Initial appearance**–First court appearance; notification of charges.
- **Nolle prosequi**–A document prepared

by the prosecution stating that the state is unwilling to go forward with the charges.
- **Perjury**–Taking an oath to provide the truth, which is then violated; historical underpinnings.
- **Preliminary hearing**–Formal notice of charges is conducted here along with bail option.
- **Prior inconsistent statements**–A witness's testimony that varies from a prior, out-of-court statement that has been testified to by another and is now admissible as evidence.
- **Prosecutor**–Legal representative of the state; state's attorney.
- **Real evidence**–Tangible objects such as maps, fingerprints, guns, etc.; may be found at the crime scene, the home of the accused or otherwise; artifacts; hard evidence.
- **Relevance**–A logical relationship between the evidence and the factual issue it is supposed to prove.
- **Rules of evidence**–Controls the content, what kind of information witness can provide or offer up, and the manner employed for questioning.
- **Similar fact evidence**–Information that provides proof that is crucial or pivotal to the case at hand.
- **Stipulation**–Both sides, prosecution and defense, agree that a particular event or matter is true; no dispute; i.e., an expert is qualified.

## *Questions for Review and Discussion*

1. *Question:* Is the district attorney appointed or elected? *Answer:* An elected official.

2. *Question:* Name three things the defendant is not required in presentation. *Answer:* (1) Defendant is not required to present witnesses, (2) not required to testify, (3) defen-

dant's lawyer is not required to prove his client's innocence.

3. *Question:* What is a prosecutor's power called? *Answer:* Prosecutorial discretion—looks at all factors and decides whether to move forward with a case.

4. *Question:* What is *most relevant* to a prosecutor? *Answer:* His ability to produce admissible evidence with which to prove the defendant's guilt to the judge and jury beyond a reasonable doubt.

5. *Question:* Name the four "types" of evidence. *Answer:* Real, testimonial, direct and circumstantial.

6. *Question:* Are there exceptions to hearsay evidence? *Answer:* Yes. Name two. Dying declarations, excited utterances, admission of guilt or confession, assertions of the state of mind.

7. *Question:* Name ten different types of evidence. *Answer:* Identification, forensic, weather, animals, wounds, weapons, motive, time of death, pathology report, exhibits, statements from family, friends, police, victims, witnesses; "bad person" evidence, documents, prior record, business records, government documents, surveillance evidence, electronics, etc.

8. *Question:* Do all states operate under the grand jury system? *Answer:* No. Is the grand jury system secret? Yes. They have subpoena powers to bring forth possessions and evidence of the accused without probable cause; they defendant need not be told he is being investigated; and defense need not be present; contempt order powers, and can compel witnesses.

9. *Question:* Why are plea bargains good for the state? *Answer:* Saves time and money, less jail time means less jail overcrowding; less prison overcrowding, lightens everyone's case load, beats the uncertainty of a trial.

10. *Question:* What is compounding a crime? *Answer:* He accepts money or something of value in exchange for agreeing to not prosecute a felony; state's individual right; benefit gained is illegal.

## *Essay*

Explain burden of proof as best you can. If student uses these terms or writes any of these facts: a legal principle, prosecutor's burden, defendant is presumed innocent until proved guilty; prosecutor defines the crime—shows evidence, proves intent and motive beyond a reasonable doubt to a judge and jury so that they can accept the truth of the charge.

# PART THREE

# A Walk Through the Justice System

# Chapter 11

# ARREST, CHARGES, AND BOOKING

The road to ruin is always
kept in good repair.

–Anonymous

In order to better understand the steps the accused–soon to be the defendant–goes through, we will follow the criminal offender on the descent from arrest to trial. Many criminal justice scholars maintain that if one is processed all the way through the criminal justice system, he or she will encounter eighteen steps or processes. In this chapter we will designate each as discussed, beginning with reporting the crime and moving sequentially toward the time of the trial.

## THE REPORTED CRIME

Police are either alerted to the possible commission of a crime by members of the community or an observant citizen, or, officers will discover an offense on their own or from a fellow police officer's investigative or intelligence work. Studies indicate that less than half of all crimes are actually reported. The most often reported crimes are theft or destruction of property and crimes involving drugs or alcohol and assaults, with less than 5 percent the more violent offenses of robbery, rape, and homicide.

## FELONIES AND MISDEMEANORS

The fundamental distinction between a major crime, a felony, and a minor offense, a misdemeanor, are the types of offenses committed and the consequences of committing them. Major crimes are those that cause serious damage to another person or property. These are called felonies. Traditionally, the punishment for felonies was forfeiture of land, property, or life. In modern times, the felony is occasionally punishable by forfeiture, such as what is done with drug crimes, but primarily, results in more than one year in jail and the loss of certain civil rights; for example, the right to vote, the right to bear arms, etc. Sentences of more than one year are served in a state penitentiary, whereas misdemeanor sentences are usually served in county jails or workhouses, or may result in some type of diversion program or community service.

Misdemeanors then, are lesser crimes where the punishment is a year or less in jail and, most likely, some type of fine or court costs. To help further distinguish the differences between misdemeanors, many states have other classifications that correlate with the amount of punishment that is possible. The higher classifications are called *gross misdemeanors* or *high misdemeanors*. Those infractions on the lower end of the scale, are referred to as *petit crimes* or *simple misdemeanors*. These petit crimes will generally not result in a jail sentence and are usually offenses involving a traffic ticket or some type of disorderly conduct. The trial for a misdemeanor is almost always done before a local magistrate and is relatively swift although there are serious misdemeanor trials completed with either twelve- or six-person juries. Generally, in most states the right to a jury trial is an option for any crime which can result in jail time, or what may exist with multiple convictions, or serious repeated offenses.

## INVESTIGATE

Police procedures will vary depending on whether they are investigating a newly discovered crime, past crimes still open on the books, crimes involving anticipatory offenses, sting operations, or conducting investigations under the aegis of the prosecutor, using direction and power based on subpoena. For our purposes we are using a newly discovered crime, so the first two questions will be "Was a crime committed?" and "Who did it?"

In these types of circumstances, police will attempt to answer these questions and collect evidence in order to prove guilt at a later trial. Investigations may involve one or more of these functions: locating the offender, interviewing suspects and asking for identification, interviewing the victim and any witnesses, canvassing the neighborhood, preserving and examining the scene, collect-

ing physical evidence, checking department records and files, contacting informants, surveying the scene, and performing undercover work, if necessary.

## ARREST

Arrest is based on probable cause and the accused is taken into custody for transport to police facilities for booking, charging, and detention. Although interrogation usually occurs at the stationhouse after arrest, it may occur anywhere. Miranda warnings must be given if the accused is subjected to express questioning, or any questioning if suspicion has found a suspect is not free to go. For misdemeanors or certain traffic crimes, offenders may be issued a citation that they sign, which is a notice to appear, allowing immediate release without bail until a specified court date. Some suspects who are given citations in lieu of being taken to jail because of overcrowding or other considerations, must go through the booking process within a few days of their arrest. Weapons, contraband, or evidence will be collected from those arrested and may result in additional charges.

## JAILS

Although the word "jail" is adapted from the French/Norman word gaol, the concept of incarceration has existed for centuries. All ancient civilizations had designated confinement areas.

### Diversion

Certain cases may be averted out of the criminal justice system by using diversion. Defendants typically have to attend a treatment or rehabilitation program. This alter-

**Caution**—Arrest reports in criminal cases play a huge role in the many proceedings after their initial making. First, they are used to help determine what charges the prosecutor will file, they influence the judge with how much bail is required, they leave their stamp on the aftermath of preliminary hearings where hearsay evidence is permitted, and they affect the willingness of the prosecutor to plea bargain. Likewise, in a strange twist of fate, arrest reports can also be used to discredit the police officer who testifies in court, called *impeachment*, if later testimony varies from that which is inscribed in the report.

native allows the defendant who successfully completes the program to avoid the taint of a criminal conviction. Eligibility rules vary from one locality to another and are most often available to those charged with misdemeanors or nonviolent felonies involving drugs or alcohol.

## Jailhouse Informants

The accused should never assume that a fellow inmate is a friend, confidant, or brother (sister). Incarceration may have many effects on the accused, the least of which is to consider the bunkmate as a "soul brother" or someone who will side with him or her at being "set up" or put in jail on "trumped up charges." Baring the soul or explaining the details of the case could put the accused into deeper water. The person confided in may be looking for his or her own way out and the prospect of exchanging information for some type of deal is not out of bounds–this person is a prisoner too after all!

## Types of Facilities

Today there are three types of jails, or short-term facilities as distinguished from prisons. In the United States there are pretrial detention facilities, sentenced facilities, or a combination of the two. And in keeping with all things in threes, jails serve three functions. First, they serve by segregating offenders from the general public and ensuring that those persons charged with crimes will appear at trial. Second, jails are used with the hope that some type of attitude or behavioral change will occur, that is to say, the rehabilitative function. Third, they also act as a form of punishment. In law, the functions of incarceration are: deterrence–to stop; incapacitation–to isolate; retribution–to punish, and rehabilitation-to save.

It's interesting to note that no one really knows how many jails there are in the United States. The reason for this is that some administrators count their work farms or work-release centers as jails. Lock-ups used specifically for drunk tanks or drug abuse are often counted separately. The fed-

**FYI**—The first paragraph in a handout called the "Garland County Detention Center Inmate Rules and Regulations" states: You are now an inmate within the Garland County Detention Facility. We did not catch you, convict you, nor sentence you; but we are charged with the responsibility of confining you.

eral agency's number of facilities does not add up against the Law Enforcement Assistance Administration, which also does not coordinate with the Advisory Commission on Intergovernmental Relations. We think there are between 3,500 and 4,000 short-term facilities.

One thing we do know for certain is that between 1950 and 1986, the jail population more than tripled.

## JAIL FUNCTIONS

Although originally set up as short-term facilities, jails have had to provide additional functions over the years. Various agencies prevail on the "good spirit" of local jails to provide room for a motley crew; hence, some of those who are in any jail's population include

- Pretrial detainees;
- federal defendants held according to the Bail Reform Act of 1966;
- witnesses in protective custody;
- convicted offenders awaiting sentencing;
- sometimes segregated juvenile offenders (perhaps, those being charged as adults);
- indigents, vagrants, and the mentally ill, the latter of whom suffer many problems including being "lost" within the system;
- prisoners wanted in other states on warrants;
- persons on contracts between the state and federal prisons for overflows;
- alleged probation and parole violators.

## Administration and Pitfalls

Unfortunately, administration of jails is the unpopular tail that wags the dog. Usually jails are the province of county sheriffs— those elected with no special qualifications,

previous law enforcement experience, and no national standards for professionalism. The pay structure for chief jailers and staff is generally poor, and, in some cases, the position is appointed as a punishment for officers who have committed infractions or for disciplinary purposes, making them [deputies] no more than custodians.

Often, officers have no special education or training for dealing with inmates, and the budgeting constraints make for poor career opportunities as well as poor conditions. In the past, the selection of correctional officers placed an emphasis on physical attributes rather than behavioral or educational skills. In general, jail operations are underfunded and inadequate. Little accountability for jail improvements or upkeep is woven into the system, and sometimes monies are diverted to the sheriff's other responsibilities such as keeping the peace within county lines and assuring that traffic flows smoothly. Sometimes, money is often redirected toward new patrol cars or other large-ticket items.

## Jail Overcrowding

Much has been said recently and loudly about jail overcrowding. According to *Crime and Justice in America*, "A government report published several years ago notes that 22% of the nation's 621 largest jails (those with a capacity of more than 100) were under court order to either expand capacity or reduce the number of inmates housed, and 24% were under court order to improve one or more conditions of confinement." As a consequence, overcrowding creates tension among prisoners and staff, increased wear and tear on the buildings and equipment, problems with overtime for officers, and the inability to meet program standards and services.

FYI—The onus of arrest is far-reaching. In addition to having an official arrest record, the arrest may have to be reported to employers and any licensing agencies such as a state board of medical practices or a professional banking affiliation.

FYI—Prosecution for a misdemeanor—a less serious offense than a felony—if initiated by a prosecutor, comes in the form of a complaint. The term *complaint* gives the impression that it is an action taken by an injured party or the victim of a crime. Not so. Although the victim of a crime may be the complainor, the plaintiff, meaning, the person who brings the case to the court for remedy, is actually the *people of the state*, acting through their local representative who is the district attorney.

## BOOKING

Upon arrival at the holding facility, booking begins. Booking records provide information about the people detained, and create an official arrest record. It is a highly impersonal process. The name, arrival, and offenses are put into the police log, which is strictly a clerical function, and suspects are re-informed of the charges. Most everything nowadays is put into a computer system. The arrested person will then be photographed, sometimes called a mug shot. The photograph, albeit unflattering, serves several purposes in addition to the most obvious purpose of identification; one other purpose is to document the suspect's physical condition on arrival.

Next, personal belongings such as keys, wallet, or a purse are held for safekeeping and a receipt is furnished. Contraband, evidence, or any illegal substances will not be returned. At booking, police can search the contents of the accused's wallet, read any papers on his or her person, or push pager triggers to discover the names and numbers of persons who have most recently contacted the suspect.

Taking fingerprints is a regular part of the booking record. Many of today's newer precincts have dispensed with the messy inking and blotters of old, and the suspect places fingers and palms on an electronic plate which scans the fingerprints and automatically logs them (somewhat like a copy machine). Any fingerprint or handprint impressions are also, as a matter of record, entered into a nationwide federal database which is accessible to local, state, and federal agencies. With the AFIS (Automated Fingerprint Identification System), fingerprints can be compared with a countrywide database in the hopes of identifying wanted suspects.

In addition to the basics, arrestees may also be required to provide voice, hair, and fingernail samples, or to act as a "possible" in a lineup for identification purposes. The legal standard of probable cause precedes the taking of the suspect's blood without a warrant. Blood samples are usually wanted for the purpose of determining whether the suspect is under the influence of alcohol or drugs; but it requires consent or a warrant and may also be used for a comparison to blood found at crime scenes. Collection of pubic hair or other evidentiary minutiae generally requires a warrant on the premise that such material is an intrusion of personal privacy.

## Full Body Search

The booking can get lengthier and more humiliating. Courts have generally held that a suspect can be subjected to a strip search as part of the booking process. A full-body search, including the cavities of the body, can be conducted with a warrant by medical professionals in order to determine if the person is hiding a weapon or contraband.

Some jurisdictions have allowed the police to use reasonable force to prevent someone from destroying evidence by swallowing it. Police cannot choke, threaten, or cut off air passages, but they may force a suspect's chin to the chest, making it difficult to swallow.

Finally, the booking process may include health screening for the safety of jail officials and the well-being of other inmates. X-rays used to detect tuberculosis are common, and blood tests for a determination of sexually transmitted diseases are sometimes conducted. Note: This is not without a warrant in most, if not all, states.

## Decision to Charge

The initial decision to arrest the suspect lies with the arresting officer to begin. The decision to charge is up to the district attorney and will be again reviewed by both police and prosecutor, although, prosecutorial review is an ongoing process. Simultaneous with this is a procedure called checking the warrant, which means the booking officer will check to see if the arrested person has any outstanding warrants from other states or is wanted for other crimes ranging from parking tickets to murder charges.

## Pre-filing Screening

Prosecutors can adjust charges, require more evidence, or even release the arrestee until obtaining more evidence and then re-arresting them at a later date. They may interview the arresting officer–at least try to do so with felony charges–and some will insist on interviewing the victim in certain cases.

Some common reasons for the decision not to proceed–also called "no paper" decision or *nolo prosequi*–are because of:
- insufficient evidence;
- witness difficulties such as loss of desire to proceed, fear of reprisal, or witness can no longer be found;
- criminal proceedings in other processes such as prosecution given over to another jurisdiction, probation revocation, or pending charges for a different offense;
- in the interest of justice, meaning prosecution is not appropriate even though proof of guilt is not the problem;

---

**FYI**—All states do have mandates allowing suspects one or more telephone calls after being booked. Arrestees often phone their attorneys, friends, and family in order to obtain bail money and advice. And since eavesdropping is not disallowed on the premises, suspects should be careful about what they say because police officers and other administrative officials are known to sometimes monitor calls. On the other hand, transmissions between the accused and their attorneys, or for pretrial detainees, should be guarded and private.

**FYI**—We are told that the formal filing of *nolo prosequi* is now abolished in almost all states.

- anticipated use of a diversion program, such as enrolling in treatment programs, providing restitution, or participating in some other corrections program.

## Motion for Joinder of Offenses

When a defendant is accused of several distinct offenses arising from one related crime, instead of prosecuting each offense separately, they are prosecuted jointly and this is called *joinder*. Two or more offenses may be charged in the same indictment or information in a separate count for each offense, if the offenses charged are the same or similar in character and based on the same act.

## Severance

In cases where a defendant can show that a joint trial of two or more charges would unfairly prejudice the defense, a motion for severance of the charges is filed. Trial judges have the discretion in this matter and the defendant bears the burden of proving prejudice. When would this work? If a defendant is willing to testify in one case, but does not want to testify about another charge, a severance might be the remedy. Or say, for example, a defendant has two charges: one is a convicted person in possession of a firearm, the other is a case of robbery. To support the charge in the firearm case, the prosecution would have to show the defendant's prior

---

5. MOTION FOR JOINDER OF OFFENSES.

_____, Defendant, in support of his motion for joinder of offenses, states:

1. That the Defendant is charges with the offense of [specify offense] in Docket No. _____, and is charged with the offense of [specify offense] in Docket No. _____.

2. That both offenses are within the jurisdiction and venue of this Court and are [based on the same conduct] [arise out of the same alleged criminal episode].

3. That the prosecuting attorney has sufficient evidence to warrant trying both of the offenses at the same time.

4. That the ends of justice would be served by joinder of such offenses.

WHEREFORE, the Defendant, _____, prays that the Court grant his motion for joinder of offenses.

Respectfully submitted,

By _____
Attorney for Defendant

Address:_____

**NOTE**

See Rule 21.3, Arkansas Rules of Criminal Procedure.

Structure 5.

**Other Notes**—In order to process multiple criminal charges jointly, or separately, a prosecutor must consider the Double Jeopardy Clause of the Fifth Amendment. The basic test given by the Supreme Court is to determine whether there are two separate offenses and whether each provision of the criminal law requires proof of an additional fact that the other does not. The Blockberger test compares the elements of the crimes in question. In 1980 though, the Supreme Court reviewed a case where the defendant was first convicted of failing to slow his car in order to avoid an accident. Later, he was charged with manslaughter arising from the same accident. Vitale,[1] the defendant, was told he would have a substantial claim of double jeopardy. Now the Blockberger test is not the exclusive method of determination for the principle of double jeopardy, and some courts look also to the evidence presented with something known as the same evidence test. The criteria here bars a second prosecution based on the same conduct by the defendant that was at issue in the first prosecution. This, too, has come and gone and the Blockberger test is back in vogue. One important thing to remember though, the dual sovereignty of the federal government and the states allow separate trials of a defendant for the same offense. Not a problem in the past, but a new wrinkle for the future.

bad acts, or previous conviction of a felony. Obviously, such a showing would be prejudicial to the defense of the robbery charge if heard by the same jury.

## FILING THE COMPLAINT

In Arkansas, the prosecutor files a document called an information with the general trial court. In felony cases the complaint serves to set forth the charges only before the magistrate court, because an information or indictment will replace the complaint as the charging instrument when the case reaches the trial court.

## Complaint Contents

A fairly brief document, the complaint will set forth a statement that the accused, at a particular time and place, committed specific acts constituting a violation of a particular criminal law. The complaint will be signed by a person, usually the victim, who swears under oath that the factual allegations are true. If a police officer is the complainant and did not personally witness the crime but relied on information received from witnesses or others, he or she will note that the allegations are based on information and belief. After the filing of the complaint, the accused officially becomes the defendant in a criminal proceeding.

## THE FIRST APPEARANCE

Once the complaint is filed, the case is before a magistrate court, and the defendant must appear within a specified period of time. This appearance of the accused has

---

1. *Illinois v. Vitale*, 447 U.S. 410, 420, 100 S.Ct. 2260, 2267, 65 L.Ed.2d 228, 238 (1980).

**COVER SHEET**

**STATE OF ARKANSAS**

**CRIMINAL INFORMATION**

This criminal information cover sheet or the standard criminal information form is required by Supreme Court Administrative Order Number 8 to be completed for every defendant and filed by the prosecutor. The data contained herein shall not be admissible as evidence in any court proceeding or replace or supplement the filing and service of pleadings, orders, or other papers as required by law or Supreme Court rule. Instructions are located on the back of the form.

County   **Garland**                    District _____   Case Number   **CR-2000-**_____

Judge _____   Division _____   Filing Date _____

Style of Case _____

Prosecutor Providing Information _____

| | | | |
|---|---|---|---|
| Is this an Amended Information? | ☐ Yes | Is D being charged as a Habitual? | ☐ Yes |
| If yes, are you | | Are multiple D's charged in the information? | ☐ Yes |
| Adding Offense(s)? | ☐ Yes | | |
| Dropping Offense(s)? | ☐ Yes | | |
| Changing Offense(s)? | ☐ Yes | | |

| Defendant's Full Name | Date of Birth | Race | Sex | SID # | Arrest Date |
|---|---|---|---|---|---|
| | | | | | |

| Address (Street, City, State, Zip) | SS# | Driver's License No. |
|---|---|---|
| | Arrest Tracking # | Prosecutor's File # |
| | | |

| Alias 1 | Alias 2 | Alias 3 |
|---|---|---|
| | | |

The attached information accuses the above named defendant of the following crime(s):

| Code # | Offense | A/S/C | Offense Date | Counts | F/M | Class |
|---|---|---|---|---|---|---|
| | | | | | | |
| | | | | | | |
| | | | | | | |
| | | | | | | |
| | | | | | | |
| | | | | | | |

Structure 6.

```
                                      MC:   99-00000
                                      ARR:  6-20-00
                                      B/O:  Direct
                                      SID:  123456
                                      ATN:  567890
```

             IN THE CIRCUIT COURT OF GARLAND COUNTY, ARKANSAS

THE STATE OF ARKANSAS                                    PLAINTIFF

VS.                          Case No. CR 2000-

JOHN DOE                                                 DEFENDANT

                                INFORMATION

INFORMATION FOR:

**Possession of a Firearm by Certain Persons**
**Class D Felony**
**NMT 6 yrs. ADC and/or a fine NMT $10,000.00**

CODE NO:   5-73-103

     I, GEORGE WASHINGTON, Prosecuting Attorney within and for the
Eighteenth Judicial District of the State of Arkansas, of which
Garland County is a part, in the name and by the authority of the
State of Arkansas, on oath, accuse the defendant, **JOHN DOE (W/M
DOB: 1-6-81)**, of the crime **Possession of a Firearm by Certain
Persons**, committed as follows, to-wit: The said defendant on or
about June 20, 2000, in Garland County, Arkansas, did unlawfully
and felonisouly: **possess a firearm, having been previously
determined by a jury or court that he committed a felony, to-wit:
Defendant was convicted in Garland County on 10-11-99 for the
charge of Possession of a Controlled Substance**, against the
peace and dignity of the State of Arkansas.

                         GEORGE WASHINGTON
                         PROSECUTING ATTORNEY

                    BY: _____
                         THOMAS JEFFERSON
                         DEPUTY PROSECUTING ATTORNEY

Filed this _____ day of June, 2000.

                         BENJAMIN FRANKLIN, CIRCUIT CLERK
                    BY: _____
                         DEPUTY

Endorsed Witnesses:

_____

Structure 7.

many names: preliminary appearance, arraignment on the complaint, initial presentment, or preliminary arraignment. The exact timing of the arraignment usually coincides with the custodial status of the accused, which means that if the person was released on a citation, or if a stationhouse bail was posted there is likely to be an interval of a few days or weeks because he or she has not been pacing in jail. On the other hand, if the accused was arrested and remains in jail, this must be attended to rather quickly, for example, within several hours to forty-eight to seventy-two hours after arrest, and can be sent to an evening or night court. Most arraignments though, are conducted as the first business on the court calendar, for example, they are heard the first thing in the morning, sometimes starting as early as 8:30 A.M.

In some cases which involve a plea and arraignment for felony, the case is bound over to a circuit court, meaning, this type of statute is either out of this court's jurisdiction or level of experience.

## Arraignment Specifics

Usually this first appearance will be brief. The accused will usually be dressed in jail attire (in this area of Arkansas, that means an orange jumpsuit), he or she will be escorted from the holding cell, walked or driven over to the courthouse with either shackles or cuffs on either, or both, legs and hands, paraded down the courthouse halls, and made to sit on a bench under the watchful eye of a deputy or bailiff or both. If the accused is out on bail, he or she will appear in a suit, or at least business attire with hair cut or trimmed. The magistrate will certify the identity of the accused, inform him or her of the charges, read his or her rights, and one of the most important functions for the accused, set bail.

For a misdemeanor, if the defendant enters a guilty plea, the magistrate will provide a sentence which could include jail time, restitution, diversion to a different program, community service, and a fine along with leveling court costs (everyone pays court costs!). For a felony charge, the defendant will stand together with his or her attorney and enter a plea, most likely "not guilty." After hearing the plea, the magistrate will set a date for the preliminary hearing, give advise on any rules or admonitions about timeliness, and set a cutoff date for motions.

## RIGHTS ADMINISTERED AT ARRAIGNMENT

- You have a right to an attorney, if you cannot afford one, one will be appointed to you.
- You have a right to a trial by a jury of your peers.
- You have the right to not incriminate yourself.
- You have the right to a speedy trial.
- You have a right to cross-examination.
- You have a right to confront accusers.
- You have a right to subpoena witnesses.
- If you plead guilty, you could be sentenced to death (for a capital case) or serve life in prison without the possibility of parole.

Do you understand these rights?

## ABOUT THE ATTORNEY

If the defendant does not have a private attorney, the magistrate will inform him or her of the right to be represented by counsel, and, if indigent, the right to court-appointed counsel. The counsel right is applicable in all jurisdictions for all felonies and serious misdemeanors. The magistrate determines if the defendant is indigent, based on a financial statement that will be completed, and a public defender will be assigned–this person is usually in court. If so, the accused will talk to the attorney before entering a plea.

If the defendant decides not to take representation, he or she will have to sign a waiver. This is serious business because representation of counsel is based on our Sixth Constitutional Amendment.

Public defenders are held suspect by many different groups. People generally believe they are not very good because they are not in private practice, but work for the state. It's because of this government position that defendants don't trust them either. It is also thought that the quality of service is determined by the money, meaning, public defenders typically receive a set county or municipal fee no matter how many hours they put in the case–and their caseloads are deep. More money is available for a capital case naturally, but investigative work and interviewing is expensive, and usually out of the purview of a city employee's salary.

## Panel Attorneys

In states that have not set up public defender offices, there will be panel attorneys sometimes called an assigned counsel system. Panel attorneys handle most of the criminal cases in a kind of round-robin affair. They are pooled from a group of private attorneys who devote either part or all of their practice to representing indigent defendants at government expense.

A "conflict of interest" may take the public defender out of the game so to speak, and the judge would then appoint private counsel from the panel attorney roster, or appoint private counsel in general. Some of the following situations may result in a conflict of interest: If two defendants are charged jointly with committing a crime, it's likely the

public defender will not take on both clients because later, each defendant may attempt to assign blame to the other. If the victim is a former public defender client, conflict of interest is pretty evident. Since crime has a tendency to repeat itself like a bad penny turning up again and again, this situation presents a double conflict. The public defender would be sworn to zealously represent the current client's interests over any personal inclinations, plus, he or she would have to agree to not disclose any confidential information learned through their previous dealings. Too much to ask for.

There is something called a "don't peek" or "Chinese wall" policy among public defenders which unofficially states that a public defender will not use information or any prior evidence against a former client. The term don't peek refers to keeping honor by not looking into old public defender files for damaging information. Note: This practice is outlawed in almost all jurisdictions.

The judge has an interest in accepting such promises from a public defender–a fiscal incentive. It will almost always be less expensive to appoint a second public defender than it will be to seek out a private attorney for indigent representation.

## COMPETENT COUNSEL

Public defender stories abound. Some say public defenders are young lawyers trying to gain experience, others claim they are old dogs, not competent enough to support themselves in private practice, and still others say the public defender's office is simply a stepping stone to politics, entrance into private firms, or even an easing into retirement.

Even though public defenders rack up more guilty pleas than private attorneys do, one must consider the type of clientele that is thrust upon them. They handle clients who are often guilty, repeat offenders some-times called *recidivists,* or rightly, they may be just starting out. A couple of advantages to starting out, however, may be that newly appointed attorneys have the zeal to repre-sent clients to the best ability possible, and the nature of their young minds is such that the criminal law statutes, rules, and new reg-ulations will be very fresh in their minds. Whatever one may think about this misrep-resented and misunderstood sect of criminal justice society, they are sorely needed.

Some common complaints with respect to their inefficiency are that they may sacrifice justice in the interest of cutting their over-whelming caseloads. Others believe they may not be sufficiently independent of the system who hires them, meaning, in the day-to-day dealings with either opposing counsel or the judge, they may not want to alienate themselves, offend, or, "rock the boat." In any event, all public defenders want a suc-cessful case record.

The assigned private counsel or panel attorney also has its benefits and peccadil-loes. Lawyers who are pulled out of private practice to defend an indigent may acquire fees that are too small to cover expenses and will not want to exhaust themselves or their staff to further the investigation. On the other hand, if he or she is a defender of right, he or she may go broke trying! Another dis-advantage of their service is that there is no guarantee that attorneys from a pool will have the necessary experience if their back-ground lies primarily in corporate law. This means that the newbie will have to "study up" quickly in order to hold his or her own.

## BAIL

Apart from the obvious desire to get out of jail quickly, the accused person has a bet-ter chance of aiding defense counsel from "the outside." While out on bail, he or she can help locate witnesses, puzzle out details, and confer with counsel without the incon-venience and stigma a jail cell carries. Dur-ing this interval of freedom, the accused can also pursue gainful employment (a plus in the eyes of the court), get a haircut and bet-ter clothes, and take care of family responsi-bilities while awaiting the disposition of criminal charges.

Getting a pretrial release is commonly referred to as granting bail. Bail comes in the form of cash or its equivalent, called a bail /bond, which is tendered by the defendant in exchange for release from jail and continued liberty until the conclusion of the case. From the court's viewpoint, bail is a financial incen-tive for defendants to show up for all court appearances. Most state statutes or court rules have provisions for bail and the amount gen-erally follows a schedule, though the court is the ultimate decision maker as to who gets bail and how much. The criteria used to determine whether the defendant is eligible for bail is typically based on the accused's prior convictions, character, employment his-tory, history of showing up for court, and ties to family and community, while weighing these factors against the seriousness of the crime, which could also be called the nature and scope of the criminal charges

## TYPES OF PRETRIAL RELEASE

There are generally four types of pretrial release: personal recognizance, release to the custody of another, posting an individual bond, posting a surety bond. Being released on your own recognizance is akin to pulling the "Get out of jail free" card in Monopoly. Sometimes called O.R. Release–own recog-nizance release–this type of pretrial release is no-cost bail. To get one, defendants sign a written promise to appear when needed as required. Even though no amount of money is exchanged, the judge can place conditions on the defendant such as, meeting with the parole officer regularly, or refraining from the use of alcohol or drugs. Some communities have O.R. officers who will help the court decide who gets O.R. by running a check on the defendant's background and current activities.

In special circumstances, the magistrate may decide, with encouragement from the defendant's attorney, to release the person into the custody of some responsible person, usually the defendant's own attorney, but it can also be a priest, private counselor or some other designee.

Posting an individual bond puts the defendant in the position of posting an amount of cash or other security in order to guarantee all future appearances. And posting a surety bond is similar in that the magistrate sets an amount of bail, the defendant signs the bond, which is a type of insurance that he or she will appear, but the company granting the bond is required to pay the court the amount of bond. After a forfeiture of bail (read this as a failure to appear), any amount over $50 is reported to the bondsman and he has 180 days to adjust the forfeiture. Adjustment can be accomplished by the bondsman appearing in court: either with the defendant–along with a good reason for the failure to show up on time–with notice that the defendant is either dead or physically ill and unable to appear in the time allowed, or the defendant may be turned over to the court and subsequently, the police.

## Show Me the Money

The courts will accept cash or a check for the full amount and, if it is in the vicinity of $1,000, some defendants will pay their own way. For others not so fortunate, surety bonds purchased from a bail bond seller– referred to as a bail bondsman–means that the defendant can purchase that same $1000 bond at about 10 percent, or $100. And it's important to note that bail bond sellers often refuse to do business with someone who lacks collateral. Collateral is personal property, such as a house or car, that can be used to cover the bond seller's loss should the defendant fail to appear in court–also called "jumping bail." The bondsmen are hard-wired to the system, however, and can collect by hiring a bounty hunter, also called "skip tracers," someone to either collect the goods or bring the defendant into court. When a surety employee promptly produces a defendant, any money forfeited to the court because of the defendant's failure to appear can usually be recovered, ample incentive to "get their man!"

## SELF-REPRESENTATION

## A Defendant's Best Friend

For those defendants who are brave enough to represent themselves, they may also try to convince the judge to lower the bail or release them on O.R. They will have to assert certain facts to get it, however, and here are some of the factors they can use to prove they are worthy. The defendant– *"Me, Your Honor"*–does not pose a physical danger to the community. (Now, if the crime is especially grisly, this will not hold up.) What else? The defendant does not have a criminal record and has shown up at all required appearances. For good measure, the defendant can drag a family member or employer into court in order to better illustrate close family ties and employment.

**FYI**—Many people think the bondsman has stuck his neck out for the defendant, but truth is, the court-demanded payment of bond is made by an insurance company. So the bail bondsman is not really dipping into his own personal assets to pay, and the risk is spread out among all bail bondsmen in the form of an insurance policy.

**FYI**—In some states courts also offer court-financed bail. Sometimes described as a hybrid between posting full cash bail and buying a bond from a private seller, under the hybrid system the defendant pays a fee of 10 percent directly to the court. Collateral may or may not be required under these circumstances. The major difference between this and the surety company system is that when the defendant fails to appear at a required hearing, he or she will be re-arrested and, usually, a new criminal charge of bail jumping will be tacked onto the previous offenses listed on the complaint.

## The Sky's the Limit

The Eighth Amendment to the Constitution, which is about our rights against cruel and unusual punishment, also has a clause that states "excessive bail shall not be required." The Supreme Court has made it clear more than once that the purpose of bail is not to raise money for the state and it is not a way of punishing the accused, but it does leave the discretion of how much to charge, and the terms of enforcement with the individual states.

## Federal Law: Appeal and Bail

The Federal Bail Reform Act of 1966 asserted that the defendant in a federal court was entitled to bail pending appeal, unless there was reason to believe that any condition of release would produce a failure to appear. The Act didn't last. The Bail Reform Act of 1984,[2] put the burden of the presumption of bail entitlement right back onto the defendant. Now, before granting bail pending an appeal, the court must find, basically, that the defendant is not likely to flee,

**FYI**—*"Hurt them in the pocketbook,"* the cop replied. One of the reasons police tend to report the most serious criminal charge possible—provided the facts support it—is that it hurts the accused in the pocketbook. Escalating a misdemeanor to a felony charge, for example, by taking a small amount of marijuana and classifying it as "possession with intent to sell," means the bail schedule will jump up accordingly.

---

2. 18 U.S.C.A. §§ 3141–3150.

that the appeal is not for the purpose of de-lay, that the appeal raises a substantial ques-tion of law or fact, and that the final decision in a new trial is likely to result in a reversal.

## Bail Story = Conflict

Bail bondsmen accept the persona that they are agents of justice and sometimes act as if they do the court system a big favor in finding criminals and bringing them back to justice. Many people believe this is a myth. Those who advocate bail reform argue that the interest of the bail bondsman is not in retrieving fugitives for justice reasons, but strictly for financial gain. They believe the system cultivates abuse and criminality. For instance, if bondsmen are willing to loan bail to thieves and they lack the cash to pay it back, the bond money is not always come by honestly.

Reformers also contend that bail bonds-men have unlimited powers of arrest and custody, and that the corresponding loss of civil liberty for the accused is worse than what is socially acceptable by even police officers. Reformers claim that, in a large number of cases, the bounty hunters who look for bail jumpers are simply criminals themselves. They go on to explain that the bail bondsmen's system of enforcing the law means that bail jumpers are often: shackled for long periods of time, beaten, and, no matter what happens, the defendant is still out the 10 to 20 percent of interest—and that this form of strong-arming tends to put the accused under pressure to obtain the money owed by illegal means.

## PRELIMINARY HEARING

A preliminary hearing should not be con-fused with the initial appearance. A prelimi-nary hearing has several other names such as "probable cause hearing," "preliminary examination," "PX" or "prelim." Generally held within ten days of arrest, the prelimi-nary hearing is the next scheduled step in a felony case and is conducted in the court-house. It is only directed where the defen-dant has pleaded "not guilty" at a felony arraignment. The Supreme Court has ruled that when an arrest is made, a preliminary hearing is constitutionally required to deter-mine the adequacy of the charges. At a pre-lim, the judge will decide whether there is "probable cause" to bind the accused over for a trial. A kind of mini-trial, most states provide for open hearings in semi-adversari-al fashion. If the state still uses the grand jury system, sometimes called an "indictment jurisdiction," the case is bound over after a secret grand jury hearing instead of a public prelim.

## Prelim Function

Coming before a judge only, the prelimi-nary hearing provides an independent (read this as neutral) judicial review of the prose-cutor's decision to prosecute. Check the laws of your own state to figure out exactly what type of system it uses. In some states, pre-liminary hearings are held in every criminal case. In others, they are only used for felony cases; in still others, the defense may have to request them. On the other hand, the defense may decide to waive the right to a preliminary hearing altogether, which is not uncommon. A substantial percentage of de-fendants, about 30 to 50 percent, choose to waive their hearings because they intend to plead guilty and know they will go straight to the court where they can so plead, without much delay.

The objective of a preliminary hearing is to screen—to guard against unfounded prose-cution which stands to harm the accused unjustly, and clogs up the court calendar with weak cases. There are usually three consequences as the result of a preliminary hearing. Most often, the defendant is bound over, or instructed to stand trial, where he or she will be adjudicated on the original charges. The judge may opt to reduce the charges if the evidence is weak and the defendant will be charged with a lesser crime(s). Finally, a small percentage of cases, about 5 to 10 percent, result in dismissal at the preliminary hearing phase.[3]

## Preview of Coming Attractions

Still conducted in an adversarial context, the preliminary hearing is a nutshell version of what the trial will be like. The prosecutor starts by calling witnesses who will testify to what they saw or heard. If the prosecutor has a witness, say, a female who might balk at testifying at a later trial, he or she will bring the witness into the preliminary because this is another way of preserving her testimony. It is all taken down as a matter of record. At this time, the prosecutor may introduce certain pieces of physical evidence, but will never present the whole case, reserving some witnesses and other types of evidence; showing just enough to convince the judge that the trial should go forward. The burden of proof in a preliminary hearing is reduced to "probable cause that the defendant did it," so the evidence proving each criminal element is minimal.

The procedural rules of evidence in this hearing mimic what's given in a real trial, such that the witnesses cannot give opinions and the defense may both cross-examine and object to testimony. Hearsay evidence though, is often a staple at preliminary hearings and some witnesses need not appear– instead, relying on the testimony of the arresting officer or the arrest reports.

## Now What?

The preliminary hearing is over, the judge has signed his or her name to the complaint and the prosecutor files this information. Defendants may be free on bail, or, if not, can request bail again at this hearing. (They may get it if the case just presented is not as bad or as strong as first reported.) If the court system in the jurisdiction is multileveled, the defendant can be arraigned a second time. But, generally, now the parties will either proceed to some type of plea offer and negotiation, or if the prosecution is unwilling, the case awaits the trial phase.

## GRAND JURY REVIEW

Even though all American jurisdictions still have the option of authorizing grand jury screening of felony charges, it is mandatory only in those areas that require an

---

**Caution**—Even though a defendant will want to participate heartily at the preliminary hearing, he or she and the attorney need to bide their time. Cross-examining a witness or two to try to figure out their weakness is all right, but don't present evidence! Conventional defense strategy advises against helping the prosecution prepare for trial by presenting witnesses and subjecting them to cross-examination at this pre-trial stage. This is an opportunity to hear the prosecutor's case and then prepare an approach to thwart it.

---

3. The prosecution can seek to re-file cases dismissed at a prelim, provided there is more information.

> **FYI**—Be aware that the preliminary hearing can be a substitute for a trial if both the prosecutors and the defense attorneys agree to "submit on the record." This means the disposition of the case rests in the decision of the judge and not a jury, because the defense has either waived the right to a public trial, or opted out of jury trial for other reasons. Sometimes, the prosecutor knows it's a losing battle and instead of facing a poorly executed trial, will decide to put it into the judge's hands. In the other extreme, the defendant may realize that a guilty verdict is all but written, and he or she simply accepts: it's the end. If the accused is more hard-headed than that, he or she may ask that the attorney submit on the record in order to move the case right onto appellate court, making this a short-cut route to continued hope.

indictment, which is a charging instrument issued by a grand jury specifically. Currently, slightly less than half the states require a grand jury indictment for at least some classes of felony prosecutions. Nevertheless, in several of these indictment states, prosecution by indictment is ordered only for felonies dependent on the most severe punishment such as life imprisonment and capital punishment. In the federal system, all federal offenses require either a felony preliminary hearing or a grand jury indictment unless it is waived by the defendant. If an indictment is delivered, it will be filed with the general trial court, and will replace the complaint as the accusatory pleading in the case.

The grand jury process is frustrating, dangerous, and a foreboding question mark for the accused. Because of its closed screening, the prosecution is the only side able to put forth evidence. The defendant has no such rights and may not even be present. The secretive atmosphere surrounding this process, and the incongruity for the defense in terms of due process, can provide trepidation. Typically the jury consists of twenty-three persons, but in smaller jurisdictions there may be as few as twelve people and some will only require a small majority to indict.

Will seven private citizens find the evidence compelling enough to proceed? More likely than not. Grand juries refuse to indict in only 3 to 5 percent of the cases presented before them. They are generally the prosecution's little darlings.

## Summons

In cases such as minor misdemeanors, traffic violations, or motor vehicle infractions, the offender is simply issued a summons. In many cases, the person can waive a court appearance by paying a predetermined fine. If a court appearance is required, it is typically resolved by entering a plea, evidence is taken, and a verdict is rendered right then and there by a judge. Defendants can always provide their own counsel, but the expense is probably not worth it and at any rate a summons usually walks hand-in-hand with some type of fine or court costs.

## JURISDICTION

In order to hear and decide a case, the court must have jurisdiction over the subject matter and the parties living in the district. State courts, of course, have jurisdiction over criminal offenses that take place in their state. An individual cannot be tried for a crime unless the court has jurisdiction over that person, for example, a resident of the state. An arrest warrant or *capias* is issued. The term capias is used when the prosecutor has already filed an information.

## Venue

Venue is often confused with the terminology and meaning of "jurisdiction." It need not. The venue refers to the place of the trial. In fact, Article III in the Constitution tries to make that distinction for us. It states:

> *Trial shall be held in the State where the said crimes shall have been committed; but when not committed within the State, the Trial shall be at such Place or Places as the Congress may by law have directed.*

There are federal courts in all fifty states, as well as federal territories. A federal offense is normally tried in the particular district where the crime was committed. Also, federal land means federal courts and this can even mean territory such as a federal state park system.

State courts often take in two or more counties and, like the federal mandate, offenses touching upon those counties are held in that particular county's court. Sometimes the federal jurisdiction will overlap that of the states if, to cite an instance, the crime was perpetrated and committed in both territories, for example, as with a kidnapping. In the past, the conflicts between courts have been resolved according to precedents set.

## Extradition

If you have a suspect that flees the state seeking asylum or for other reasons you may have a candidate for extradition. Extradition is the demand, or surrender, of an individual accused or convicted of an offense in another territorial jurisdiction, whether it be a state or a country. The purpose of extradition is to bring the offender back to the jurisdiction he or she fled to be adjudicated. Any hearings in the asylum country are for identification purposes only. Be aware though, many countries will not return someone if the crime carries the death penalty. Likewise, some other countries will not extradite someone who is accused of committing a crime that is not a crime in the asylum country. There are various extradition treaties and the smart lawyer would need to consult with the individual jurisdictions before preceding. Generally, if the crime is quite serious, most countries will try to cooperate. If the extradition is agreed upon, a law enforcement official will travel to that country to escort the offender back.

Most states have adopted the Uniform Criminal Extradition Law that sets out procedural rules for handling interstate extradition and transport. Congress has enacted statutes for this in accordance with Article IV, section 2 of the Constitution.[4] Usually the governor of the asylum state issues a warrant for the fugitive's arrest. The person sought as a fugitive can contest the extradition—with a petition for a writ of habeas corpus—by returning to a court of law in the asylum state and challenging whether in fact the petitioner is the person charged or attacking the method of the proceedings. Under this umbrella, the judge would seek to determine

---

4. 18 U.S.C.A. § 3182.

release but would not adjudicate on the issue of guilt or innocence.

## Bench Warrant

An arrest warrant issued by a judge, the bench warrant is usually the result of the accused showing up previously in court, and then failing to show again at a later time as ordered. This "no-show" behavior angers the judge and usually this is how it is dealt with. It is cause for re-arrest.

IN THE CIRCUIT COURT OF GARLAND COUNTY, ARKANSAS

THE STATE OF ARKANSAS                                  PLAINTIFF

VS.                          Case No. CR 2000-

JOHN DOE                                               DEFENDANT

## BENCH WARRANT

    The State of Arkansas, to any Sheriff, Constable, Coroner, or Policeman, in the States:

    YOU ARE COMMANDED forthwith to arrest **JOHN DOE (W/M DOB: 1-6-81) address unknown** _____

(Bond: _____)

and bring him before the Garland County Circuit Court to answer an information in that Court against him for the offense of __Possession of a Firearm by Certain Persons, Class D Felony _____

of if the Court be adjourned for the Term, that you deliver him to the Jailer of Garland County.

    The Defendant is to be admitted to bail in the sum of _____

_____

Dollars ($_____), [ secured by cash   professional surety property with surety's affidavit   signature   Clerk's 10% depsoit]

The undersigned finds reasonable and probable cause for issuance of this Bench Warrant from:

__XXX_    Sworn affidavit of ___(arresting officer)_____ dated ___6-20-00_____.

_____    Sworn Violation Report of the Garland County Circuit Court Adult Probation Office dated _____.

_____    Probable cause finding by Hot Springs Municipal Court after hearing, dated _____.

_____    Opportunity for probably cause hearing in the Hot Springs Municipal Court, Waiver and thereafter, bound to the Grand Jury.

_____    Other: _____

        _____

    DATED this _____ day of _____, 2000.

                _____

                CIRCUIT JUDGE
                18th Judicial Circuit East
                State of Arkansas

Structure 8.

# REVIEW QUESTIONS AND ANSWERS

## *Key Words to Define*

- **Bench warrant**–Issued by a judge when a defendant fails to show up for a court date, hearing or trial.
- **Booking**–Information about the detained that creates an official police record; I.D. photo and other documents are made; belongings of the accused are taken; possible exemplars or bodily samples created; strip search or body search may be conducted.
- **Complaint**–Document that sets forth the charges before a magistrate, to be replaced with an information or indictment.
- **Diversion**–A treatment or rehabilitation program that diverts the offender out of the typical criminal justice system of charging, prosecution and sentencing.
- **Extradition**–The demand or surrender of an individual accused or convicted of an offense who ran to another territory and needs to be returned; flight-risk type of individual who took off.
- **Felony**–Major crimes that cause serious injury to people or property or both.
- **Jurisdiction**–Area of government; for example, a state court has a jurisdiction over criminal offenses committed in that state.
- **Misdemeanor**–Lesser crimes where punishment is less than one year in jail and court fines or restitution.
- **Motion for joinder of offenses**–When multiple offenses are prosecuted jointly.
- **Preliminary hearing**–Probable cause hearing; prelim, "PX", the next scheduled step in a felony where the defendant has pleaded "not guilty" to determine the adequacy of the charges.
- **Public defender**–State- or court-appointed attorney for the defendant.
- **Surety bond**–An amount of cash or property or other security to guarantee all future appearances of the accused (defendant).
- **Venue**–Not to be confused with jurisdiction; the place of the trial.

## *Questions for Review and Discussion*

1. *Questions:* Are all crimes reported? *Answer:* No, estimates are less than half of the crimes committed are reported.

2. *Questions:* Arrest is based on _____ _____. *Answer:* Probable cause.

3. *Questions:* What three functions do jails serve? *Answer:* (1) To segregate offenders from society and to ensure they will show at trial, (2) to scare the accused or frustrate them in the hopes that some rehabilitative efforts make their mark; (3) to act as a form of punishment.

4. *Questions:* Name the four functions of incarceration as indicated by the criminal justice system of principles. *Answer:* Deterrence–to stop; incapacitation–to isolate; retribution–to punish; and rehabilitate–to save.

5. *Questions:* Name two pitfalls of jail administration. *Answer:* Province of city sheriffs with no special qualifications or standards for professionalism; the pay structure is poor so you may not get the best people; it can actually be a punishment for officers; dealing with inmates is difficult and responses may be inadequate because of lack of training. Jails are often underfunded and sometimes inadequate in terms of facility and other upkeep factors.

6. *Questions:* What are a couple reasons why the prosecutor may file a nolle prosequi? *Answer:* Because of insufficient evidence, witness difficulties, victim is frightened or uncooperative; proceedings may be moved to another jurisdiction; not appropri-

ate justice solution, a diversion program is preferred.

*7. Questions:* What is the objective of a preliminary hearing? *Answer:* To guard against unfounded prosecution which stands to harm the accused, or clog the court calendar with weak or ill-supported cases.

### Essay Exploration

Write a few paragraphs on what it means to have incompetent counsel. The lawyer may be too young and inexperienced; or too old and incompetent; not interested or have no zeal; not enough time spent with the client; not aware of key law statutes, rules and new regulations, in a hurry to close the case–any of these written in essay form should be acceptable.

# Chapter 12

# JUVENILE JUSTICE: DIFFERENCES

Youth is quick in feeling
but weak in judgment.
–Homer, *Illiad*

Damion, a three-year-old in diapers, managed to wiggle free of the two older girls, one five-year-old and the other age six, when they pushed his face into a muddy puddle, in back of their grandma's house. Then the girls decided they could do better. One of them ran into the house and came back with a pillow. They put the pillow over Damion's face and one girl straddled the boy, while the other sat on the pillow until Damion stopped struggling once and for all. Damion was pronounced dead before he reached the hospital. It was just around 11 o'clock on a hot Sunday morning.

Investigators and police eventually concluded the girls "intended to kill Damion with the pillow," according to a spokesperson for the Riverside County Sheriff's Office in California. He went on to say, "We really don't have a motive."

District Attorney Grover Trask commented that as the California law is written, children under age fourteen can be charged only if there is clear proof that at the time of committing the act, they knew its wrongfulness. It is clear the criminal justice system is not

prepared to do anything with little girls five and six years old. Most states consider children under age seven to be legally incapable of forming *mens rea*, that is, guilty mind, which is necessary to be morally guilty of a crime and thus, subject to criminal punishment.

Research is telling us that aggression in children is escalating and taking place at earlier ages. Studies indicate that anywhere from 7 to 25 percent of preschool and early school-age children meet the diagnostic criteria for a scientific-sounding disorder called Oppositional Defiant Disorder (ODD) or, in other words, conduct problems akin to aggression, noncompliance, and defiance. Clearly, the Justice Department and current legislation within all states have not prepared for these developments. The current policy is to agree with child-development experts who contend that children of that age cannot understand the irreversibility of killing. One innovative training program called "The Incredible Years Parents, Teachers, and Children Training Series" is designed to prevent, reduce, and treat conduct problems in children aged two to ten, and has been adopted by hundreds of youth-serving agencies in forty-three states. We can only hope more programs such as this will address this particular and often startling cause for concern.

## ". . . more problems than solutions"

*Variance* is a term used to describe the actuality that no one seems to agree on what exactly juvenile delinquency is, when the criminal justice system should get involved, or to what extent. As a consequence, a juvenile is any person below a certain age that any given jurisdiction uses to define an adult. It varies from state-to-state, and while eighteen years old is the most common age for an adult, some states may be different.

## JUVENILE DELINQUENT–WHOSE CONCEPT IS CORRECT?

Police officials often adopt a general opinion about juvenile delinquents and, through their work, discover they are youngsters who are impulsive, immature first-time offenders who very likely will get a break. Many police officers with extensive juvenile experience believe that juvenile delinquents are those involved in a series of antisocial acts who do so as a result of personality disorder and, as such, will usually be repeat offenders and the most likely to be processed into the criminal justice system.

The school concept begins with their academic record and thereby, a juvenile delinquent to them is someone who is not working to capacity. School counselors often see the behavioral angle and a juvenile delinquent to them is someone who is either unable or unwilling to respond to school rules, teacher demands, and who sometimes creates altercations. For those who work within special education, a juvenile delinquent is a handicapped or disabled person, either mentally or physically, and the school system puts the struggling students into situations where they are unable to compete which makes them hostile or frustrated, for example, earning them the designation learning disabled. Cruel connotations often come from their peers, who consider them to be "retards."

The family notion of a juvenile delinquent child as perceived from the viewpoint of parents and siblings is a child who is "out of control" or incorrigible; he or she does not obey parents, guardians, or the demands and reciprocal exchange of home life in general.

The official juvenile delinquent legal viewpoint is that this is an underage offender who violates the law and, as a result, the courts can exercise paternalism. This court paternalism is rooted in history and stems from a legal concept called *parens patriae*, meaning, "parent of the country." The philosophy behind it is that parents are merely custodians of the child and it is up to the juvenile and family courts to uphold the ultimate responsibility for its minors and minor offenders.

Social services sees a child who has been petitioned through the system for breaking the law and he or she is either a JINS–a juvenile in need of supervision–or the situation may present as FINS–families in need of supervision. In other words, "juvenile delinquency" is an obscure term and means different things to different states, communities, and individuals.

## CRUEL HISTORY

Two thousand years ago, the Code of Hammurabi, one of the first written surviving codes of law, had over 300 legal provisions pertaining to the family and its youth. There were edicts about witchcraft, wages, and loans, with a particular reference to the motto, the "Strong shall not injure the weak." *Lex Talionis*, a social order based on individual rights, formalized into law a legal practice referred to as the "law of retaliation." Rebellion against the father was not tolerated and, as an example, decree and punishment number 195 said: "If a son strike his father, one shall cut off his hands." During western civilization's heyday and ancient Rome's period of greatness, it was primarily a patriarchal society and the father of the home exercised unlimited authority and corporal punishment. As the absolute owner of the whole family, which included children, land, other property, animals, and slaves, if a child was unwanted, he or she was sold into slavery. This, in turn, influenced Anglo-Saxon common law.

In thirteenth century England, the tenet of *parens patriae* was spawned. This meant the King was father of his country, and an overseer of the behavior and property of minors. This entitlement policy sanctioned the right of government to take care of minors and assume the role of parents; for example, the state could take children away from their parents for any number of reasons.

The Hospital of St. Michael was the first institution for the treatment of juvenile offenders. The hospital had work areas, cells for resting, and the Pope's stated purpose for the facility was: "For the correction and instruction to *prevent idle and injurious behavior* so that they may become useful to the state when taught."

## Middle Ages (700-1500 A.D.)

The poor juvenile behavior of the time closely resembles what can be seen today with juvenile delinquents in that there was bad language, drinking, sexual trysts, and severe school attendance problems. Similar to today's gangs, the wayward youth of the Middle Ages sometimes armed themselves and fought duels.

Academics were important—school was conducted all day and into the night and the posture of industriousness was required among students. Values, generally, advocated no vagrancy, no interest in material wealth, and one was almost certain to follow in their father's footsteps.

Among the peasants, life was tied to the soil and their feudal obligation was to serve the lord of the manor. Since life evolved around agricultural duties, physically able children became serfs and were apprenticed out to the estates. Girls learned to prepare food, mend clothes, and complete other domestic chores, while boys learned physical skills, farming, and other related duties.

For the aristocracy, landholders generally had a small nuclear family, but tended to foster an extended family interaction with others who shared a common heritage and tradition. This union of families extended their power and holdings by intermarriage. Girls were educated at home to manage estates, supervise servants, and order supplies. They often married in their teens and jointure (the formal term for the marital arrangement) promised her family financial assistance. Marriage was kept within social classes and newborns were given over to "wet nurses," and the parents and children were often apart for long periods of time. Because of this separateness, child care in the Middle Ages meant a lack of parental affection and emotional remoteness. If too many girls were born into the family they were sent to a convent or abandoned. Punishment of children was severe and the rigid social class structure meant there was much conflict, suspicion, and hostility.

Boys were sent to monastery or cathedral

school and the warrior class, acted as apprentices called squires. Most were in the service of a rich relative until they reached age twenty-one. The young nobles then aspired to knighthood where they inherited titles and an estate of their own. Usually there was only one married couple in a castle. Bored young adult males entered tournaments, jousted, and joined in the traditional melee in order to acclaim themselves and win fame and fortune. Primogeniture required that the oldest surviving male child inherited the father's property and could divide it up among his brothers, but, if he didn't, there was often rebellion and fratricide.

## Seventeenth and Eighteenth Century: Change for Youth

The major social development of the time was one of structure and saw families moving from an extended family back into a smaller, nuclear family. Marriage was based on love now, although parents were still hard disciplinarians. A scholastic movement took place that saw an emergence of boarding and grammar schools which required distinct preparation for children in order to become adults. This curriculum included intelligence and moral training while restricting physical movements and activities. Flogging from teachers was an accepted practice and this system was sanctioned by upper classes until the nineteenth century.

A children's court movement signaled the appearance of laws for more state control over children. English poor laws called for the appointment of church wardens and overseers, appointed by the Justice of the Peace, which allowed for poor kids to be apprenticed as servants–throughout their minority years–and ushered in the advent of the poor house and the work house. The

masters of the business industry within the county had authority over all tasks and punished children severely. Incarcerated youth apprentices were often placed in workshops of isolation, which is a precursor for a classification of our penal system today.

## Role of Chancery Court

The Chancery Court of this time protected property rights under the umbrella of patrial supervision. This meant that under protective order of the King, children could be taken away from parents, but it was essentially used to "control the parents." This type of coercion fixed on families of the lower class and it was said to be for the protection of the young and incompetent, or those who shied away from normal crimes.

## United States Youth

In the period from approximately 1646-1824, the Puritans stressed moral discipline for their children which was strictly enforced in the colonies. A child's behavior was often seen as evil, and parents were responsible for controlling their property, their child, and their child's spiritual development. In the mid-1600s, Stubborn Child Laws sprung up that required children to obey their parents or be whipped in public by their parents. Other neighboring children were required to attend the public beatings and executions, probably in an attempt to further control them.

The Child Protection Laws became popular in 1639. Although the concept sounds like one of merit, the laws were full of hypocrisy and largely symbolic in nature, because families still beat their children as they pleased and child labor was integral in helping to support the family.

## 1800s Concern For Youth and Social Reform

The Society for Prevention of Pauperism was an organization formed by a group of rich, New York women early in this era. The social reformers under its banner focused on the needs of the underclass and attacked taverns, brothels, and gambling, while advocating considerable "moral training" of children. Later, all sorts of movements got lumped together and were called the Child Savers. Child Savers were usually presented as a moralist group, people who felt that poor children presented a threat to the moral fiber of America and must be controlled or they would hasten the destruction of the nation and the economic system. They influenced state legislature so much so, that, in turn, the states created laws that committed runaways and delinquents to the same institutions that included those who were deemed out of control (read this as insane asylums).

The New York House of Refuge ran from 1823–1825, and was created by the Society for Prevention of Pauperism. This was the first place established to take crime off the street and place the youth into a family-like environment. The New York House of Refuge took in vagrant kids and status offenders–conduct that is illegal because of age. It was run like a prison with rigid schedules, discipline, and separation of sexes. There were so many runaways by 1860 that twenty more programs shot up under this model. The institutionalization of deviants, delinquent, and dependent children was in full swing. A New York philanthropist, Charles Brace, was instrumental in forming the Children's Aid Society in 1853, which provided temporary shelter for neglected children in private homes and became the forerunner of today's concept of foster homes.

## Ex Parte Crouse

In 1838, the Pennsylvania Supreme Court said the right of a parent is not inalienable, meaning it can be transferred to another or taken away, which is what they did here. The court claimed the right to retain custody over a twelve-year-old girl because her father was poor, although she had committed no offense. This special treatment was justified legally by the power of the state to act in *loco parentis*–in place of the parents–for the purpose of "protecting the property interests and the person of the child." Children were seen as helpless, in need of state intervention, and the family was considered to be a major cause of juvenile delinquency.

## Illinois, a Leader

It wasn't until 1831 that the penalties for juveniles were different from adults. And in 1899, in Cook County, Illinois, the first juvenile court[1] was formed establishing a separate legal system for children which used reform and rehabilitation as their ideology. Although a bona fide court, its proceedings were dramatically different from adult court operations. The court's primary purpose was to help the wayward child become a productive member of society. Guilt or innocence using the rules of evidence was not of principal importance. The aim was prevention and rehabilitation of behavior and character, not punishment. Disposition of all cases was based on the child's special circumstances and needs. This was the first time the courts would look at the individual and assess their background. Judicial decisions were often aided by social workers and psychologists.

---

1. Illinois Juvenile Court Act of 1899.

In 1900, the Progressive Reformers of Cook County, Illinois, undertook a ten-year study of juvenile court cases. Through their research and interviews, they concluded that the girls coming before the court were largely there as a result of morality issues, and that most of the youth brought before court were the children of poor immigrants.

## JUVENILE RIGHTS

The era of social jurisprudence in the juvenile court system lasted from the 1950s to the 1970s under a philosophical bent which provided assessment, rehabilitation, and a protective nature like that of the parent for the juvenile. Finally, though, experts began to recognize that this model did little or nothing to affect or prevent delinquency. Juvenile court hearings were conducted in an informal atmosphere with a different set of words used to describe criminal situations. Any testimony and background information for a case was introduced without regard to rules of evidence and was usually provided by counselors or child behavior experts. In addition, the juvenile was denied many of the constitutional rights commonly given over to adults such as representation by counsel, confrontation with one's accuser, cross-examination of witnesses, and the right to invoke the privilege against self-incrimination.

Judges, with the help of social workers, psychologists, and psychiatrists would determine facts; for example, Who is he? How did he become this way? What can we do to help him? Focusing on the offender and not the crime; it had a clearly diagnostic feel. Some of the major considerations given weight went to the environment, the physical well-being of the youth, and the resulting course of action was to prevent, rehabilitate, and counsel. Youngsters were not criminals,

but juvenile delinquents. They were wayward children in need of assistance. The court took on the role as superparent until about 1967.

In *Kent v. United States* (1966), sixteen-year-old Morris Kent was arrested for housebreaking, robbery, and rape. At the time, juveniles were under the jurisdiction of the District of Columbia Juvenile Court. Their statute though, said that Kent could be transferred to U.S. District Court. After being admitted to a receiving home for children, Kent's mother, his attorney, and a social worker discussed the possibility that the juvenile court might waive its jurisdiction. Following a week's detainment, there was no arraignment, no hearing, and no hearing for the petitioner's apprehension. Kent's lawyer arranged for a psychiatric examination and a motion requesting a hearing on the waiver. The juvenile court judge ignored the motion and directed the trial to be held under regular proceedings in criminal court. Kent was indicted by a grand jury, found guilty of housebreaking and robbery, and not guilty by reason of insanity for the rape. He was sentenced to a period of 30 to 90 years on his conviction.

On appeal, Justice Abe Fortas of the U.S. Supreme Court said that the guiding philosophy of the juvenile system under *parens patriae* had not been fulfilled, and that youngsters were getting the worst of both worlds. They were not only denied rights normally accorded adults, but they did not receive the care and treatment promised under the *parens patriae* doctrine. He wrote, "under our Constitution, the condition of being a boy does not justify a kangaroo court." From then on, the Supreme Court set up criteria concerning a waiver of jurisdiction. What courts needed to consider before transferring a juvenile to adult court were:

1. the seriousness of offense;

2. nature of the offense in terms of violence, willfulness;
3. if the offense was committed against persons or property;
4. the merits of the complaint;
5. the desirability of a trial;
6. the sophistication and maturity of the juvenile;
7. his record and previous history;
8. protection of public and likelihood of rehabilitation.

Plus, the decision must also be based on an amenability to treatment, grounds to believe the complaint, and a statement of the reason for waiver.

### *In Re: Gault v. Arizona* (1967)

Fifteen-year-old Gerald Gault was sentenced to a correctional school for six years, until age twenty-one, for making lewd phone calls. The Supreme Court of Arizona claimed they followed a due process in the juvenile courts which was "implied." Reasonably, if they were adjudicating an adult, the sentence would have been a $5 to $50 fine and less than two months in jail. The Arizona court did not explain the charges to Gault, did not allow him to confront his accuser, and did not allow him counsel. The Supreme Court in hearing his appeal took exception to this and said that the courts had violated the family's rights, and that the juvenile court system should use more common sense with its sentencing. The sentence was reversed.

### WHERE WE ARE TODAY

Under the influence of *Kent*, *Gault*, and others cases like *In re Winship* (1970), the juvenile court was transformed. Congress passed the Juvenile Justice and Delinquency Prevention (JJDP) Act in 1974, which established the Office of Juvenile Justice and Delinquency Prevention (OJJDP) within the sheltering arms of the Department of Justice. Plus, the juvenile court system now has two distinct facets: an adjudication phase, which accords juveniles the same due process rights as adults–omitting the public trial requirement; and a disposition phase in which, following a determination of guilt, a treatment or rehabilitation plan is drawn up.

Also, today the juvenile justice system exists in all states by statute. Ordinarily, juvenile court is simply another division of general jurisdiction, similar to a superior court. Most of the nation's 20,000 police agencies have a juvenile component. There are thousands of juvenile police officers, juvenile court judges, juvenile probation officers, and juvenile correctional employees accounting for hundreds of millions of dollars. Some of them are professionals, some are part-time social workers, and some have no certified training–it is a varied and unusual heterogeneous crew of people and interests.

The juvenile justice system of today still provides a legal setting in which youth can account for their wrongs and receive official protection and assistance, including community diversion and mental health programs, as well as having jurisdiction over those children who are neglected, abandoned, or abused. There has also been a movement referred to as the deinstitutionalization of status offenders, which means youths who are caught running away, in truancy, accused of incorrigible behaviors, or under curfew violation are not necessarily subject to detention or confinement.

Police still need probable cause to search and arrest a minor, but public officers (read this as "quasi-parental situations" like school officials and counselors) do not need probable cause to detain or search a minor, or check the minor's property such as would be within a school backpack or locker.

## WHAT JUVENILES
## DO AND WHY

Twenty-five acts are identified in state statutes that apply to juvenile delinquent behavior, including those referred to as status offenses. Problems with truancy, smoking, underage drinking, or sometimes even carrying beepers are some of the examples of status laws. Basically, it boils down to what a particular community will tolerate because all states have crimes committed by juveniles that would not be crimes if they were committed by adults. It is behavior that disturbs or "is offensive." Sometimes the language within different state codes is ambiguous but it is behavior which state law generally forbids for people under a specific age.

Figure 13. Stolen bikes and music components— common booty from juveniles who steal.

ally forbids for people under a specific age.

Through research studies, juvenile experts have come to a consensus about what creates a juvenile delinquent. Some of the more common theories of the cause for juvenile delinquency are boredom, hopelessness, personality defects, parental influence or the lack of it, the complexity of life, and fear of the future.

## JUVENILE JUSTICE PROCESS

There are generally six components within the juvenile justice process: (1) intake and investigation, (2) detention, (3) court, (4) probation services, (5) rehabilitation services, and (6) aftercare.

### Intake and Investigation

The juvenile justice process typically begins with the youngster encountering the police as the result of just being out and about. Their involvement can include serious offenses, disturbances, status offenses, or, because they move in groups, their congregating can become the object of complaints. Of course, reports come in from parents and school officials, and law enforcement receive more referrals than any other agency.

Although police discretion seems haphazard to many people, police are predisposed to help and their power of discretion–sometimes called "street corner" or "stationhouse adjustments"–often come in the form of reality-planned diversions or alternatives to formal charges are common. To that end, the basic procedures of the police officer when first encountering a juvenile are: to warn and release with no report, release and prepare a report, call parents to come and get the child with no charges filed, locate an agency for help such as a community-based social service agency or a welfare agency, proceed with formal charges, transport the juvenile to juvenile hall or a shelter, and process the offender through the juvenile court system.

## Detention

As part of the screening, if law enforcement has filed a petition, parents are notified, and the youth is officially referred to juvenile court. One of the first decisions to get through is one of jurisdiction. Three requirements must be met: the youth must be within the age of jurisdiction for juvenile court; in Arkansas it is ages ten to eighteen. The youth must be involved with an act covered by state law. And because of the times, there has been an increase in demand for hard evidence to be presented by police; *prima facie* evidence, or evidence of youth involvement meaning, evidence adequate enough to establish a fact.

Also, as a general rule, unless the screening determines that the youth is a threat to him- or herself, others, or property, the primary issue now is whether a juvenile should remain in custody and stay at a detention facility, or be returned to the home. A detention hearing is what is used to determine whether to remand the child to a facility or return to home.

## Pretrial Functions

This pretrial function decides whether minors should go to court. The procedures are just recently being modified, because the juvenile court system is applying a more adversary methodology which is focused on conviction instead of the offender, more like the traditional screening role assumed by a prosecutor with an adult. Officials study court reports and interrogate youth as to their previous history along with a school inquiry—either a simple cursory or full-

blown investigation of records. It asks the juvenile for a plea. If the child denies the allegation of delinquency, an adjudicatory hearing or a true-type trial is scheduled. In the event of extraordinary circumstances, a juvenile who commits a serious crime may be transferred to an adult court, instead of being adjudicated.

## Juvenile Court Intake Screening Objectives

The following are types of procedures made possible through an initial hearing. These steps permit the court to screen out its own intake on jurisdiction and social grounds, for example, a particular social environment may dictate that the child needs to go someplace else, perhaps he or she is in need of medical evaluation. The juvenile court system also has tremendous power and can actually remove a child from the parents for days, months, or years depending on their competency.

Intake screening provides an immediate test of jurisdiction; it makes clear contested areas before an actual court proceeding, and answers any questions the defense or defendant has. It also serves to cull out cases not worthy or that may otherwise be deemed too petty. The exposure a hearing offers also provides a mechanism for referrals to other agencies. Plus, intake screening is the best way to discover the attitude of the parents, the child, and other involved persons. These preliminaries are engineered with the objective of saving time and limited resources. Finally, intake screening helps local government control the court's caseload.

## Adjudication

Adjudication is what is normally referred to as the trial process, only in juvenile court terminology. The judge will have already solicited the juvenile's "plea" in the initial hearing and this adjudication is usually the place to ascertain the facts, double-check the outcome, and add any further information pertaining to the case. At this stage, the juvenile is given many of the same privileges and guarantees entitled to adult offenders such as representation by an attorney (either state-provided or otherwise), freedom of self-incrimination and involuntary confessions, the right to both confront and cross-examine witnesses, and, in exceptional situations, the right to a jury trial. Different states have different ideals regarding rules of evidence, and some exert powers including finding out the competency of witnesses, discussing various pleading options, and entertaining certain pretrial motions. In closing this session, the court (a juvenile court judge) will render a judgment, often called a *disposition.*

### Differences in Language Between:

| Adult System | Juvenile System |
|---|---|
| Criminal | Delinquent child |
| Crime | Delinquent act |
| Arrest | Take into custody |
| Halfway house | Residential facility |

### Terminology Differences

| | |
|---|---|
| File a complaint | File a petition |
| Warrant | Summons |
| Jail | Detention |
| Arraignment | Detention hearing |
| Reduction of charges | Substitution |
| Trial | Adjudicatory hearing |
| Guilty | Involved |
| Plead guilty | Agree to a finding |
| Sentence | Dispositional hearing |
| Parole | Aftercare |
| Incarceration | Commitment |
| Prison | Youth development center, boot camp, training school |

### Court Procedure

| | |
|---|---|
| Trial is public | Juvenile court is private |
| Juries | Nine states with juries |
| Probation officer at end | Probation at front end |
| Right to bail | No right to bail |
| Penalties clearly defined | Broad range of discretion |
| Records permanent | Records destroyed (expunged, physically destroyed) |

## Probation

The probation plan is tailored to each individual and, generally, it is not specifically written in a book but falls within court guidelines. Juvenile probation officers are held responsible for the development and implementation of a trial period plan—we could think of this as an experimental plan. The two major approaches to juvenile probation services are a hybridization of social work and probation, with an emphasis placed on the protective parent role, or instead, they will outline probation services or diversion, for the protection of the community. The final stage in probation requires a crystal ball—it is in determining future problems.

## Diversion

There are many alternatives to the formal application of the petition. Diversion, sometimes called early delinquency intervention, attempts to divert the juvenile from the juvenile justice system. Diversionary programs are numerous and take the guise of boot camps, community service, special schools, institutional counseling, or vocational opportunities.

**FYI**—A juvenile probation officer is a person with many layers of obligation. Usually staffed by social workers or child psychologists, they are charged with the responsibility of knowing a little about everything; creating social studies investigations, writing diagnostic reports, and making decisions involving a child's life. As a consequence, they analyze six important areas in a juvenile's world: their peers, family, neighborhood, school, value system, and attitude, which must be brought together in meaningful report. Any decision here has a profound effect on a child's current existence, lifestyle, and future.

## THREE FACTORS TO JUVENILE PROBATION

Juvenile probation is based on supervision and treatment has three main elements attached to it:

**Surveillance**–Keeping in touch with the individual, making him or her aware of their responsibilities and promises to the court; giving assurance to the child that says, "Society is aware of your situation and is interested in you."

**Casework services**–Attempting to determine the extent of the problem between the juvenile and the family. Analysis makes use of every available community service, deciding what organization is best for the child's development; a complicated stage, families usually don't want someone messing in their lives.

**Counseling**–Bringing service and surveillance together by mobilizing everyone's energies to solve a problem or series of problems for both the parents and the children, the counselor enables them to turn in a different direction. The minimum goal of probation is to prevent delinquent behavior.

In order to do this, probation officers wear three hats: They must be *social diagnosticians* who identifies factors that cause delinquent behavior. They need to develop and implement a program to eliminate delinquent behavior, and prepare the juvenile and his or her family for the outcome. Social diagnosticians must also have and pass on adequate information, so that a referral to a social agency can be a successful alternative. And, most important, they need to make this social study a positive experience for the child and the family based upon the key philosophy of social work, which is to strengthen their relationships.

Probation officers also have to be controlling in order to prove the ultimate goal, which is to restore the juvenile's freedom from restrictive status. In addition, they must simultaneously convince the child on the front end, that the goal is to "free you," but that it can only be accomplished through a combination of control and help; to develop socially accepted standards and socially accepted controls.

The most common problem at this stage is in denying them access to other delinquent social relationships. How far to go in restricting friends? In restricting jurisdiction? In restricting activities?

As agents of change, good juvenile probation officers map out possible relations to both the court and the community. They must identify what can be done to bring the change about, but, the unique problem here is that judges in the juvenile courtroom are case-conscious and don't often see the child's problems at the same ground level a probation officer sees them.

# Juvenile Court Controversy

Although the ultimate goal of the juvenile court system is to help, care, and protect a child offender, there is much controversy. People wonder how the courts can assume responsibility beyond its resources. Typically, in most any system, there is not enough time, staff, or money. The juvenile court cannot take the place of a failing educational system, it cannot take the place of a broken home, it cannot take the place of the formal social community such as was available with neighborhoods of the past, and it cannot deal with serious and violent offenders.

Conventional wisdom says there are may weaknesses in the juvenile court system, such as: laws that are unclear and vague; juvenile judges and staff who are socially directed rather than legally-minded and where the workers hold social degrees rather than specific law degrees; many workers are part-time officials; staff members are undertrained, undercompetent, and it is said they contribute to delinquency because the cards are stacked in their favor.

Critics point out that the juvenile court system's focus on the rights of kids is weakening serious offenses, and that court fosters a belief in them that they can beat the system, for example, gang leaders often use youngsters to run their dirty work because they know the juvenile will get off if caught.

Also, many pundits wonder if incarceration is a such a good idea for someone so young. They claim that more than half go through the system, and, the longer they are jailed, the more they get corrupted. Some opponents of the courts even hold onto a popular social belief that says a juvenile has a better chance of turning out okay if he or she doesn't get caught.

# JUVENILES AND CASE LAW EXAMPLES

*Wellesley v. Wellesley* (1827)–Set the tone for the court to take over custody of a child. A Duke loses his child despite resistance.

*O'Connell v. Turner* (1870)–Chicago reform school took a child vagrant. Question: whether children could be committed because of acts of misfortune versus criminal acts (Note: this is the opposite of *Ex parte Crouse*).

*Reynolds v. Howe* (1884)–Connecticut Supreme Court has authority to place neglected children in an institution.

*Commonwealth v. Fisher* (1905)–Pennsylvania Supreme Court upheld constitutionality to commit a child to House of Refuge until his twenty-first birthday.

*Ex parte Sharpe* (1908)–Right of a state juvenile court to operate under *parens patriae*; development of juvenile court movement.

*Pierce v. Society of Sisters* (1925)–Supreme Court said compulsory education did not have to be within public schools alone, parochial schools were qualified (considered a reasonable substitute for public schools, still needed to attend).

*Ginsberg v. New York* (1968)–Unlawful to sell pornography to minors.

*Tinker v. DesMoines Independent Community School District* (1969)–Students' right to passive speech; ability to wear political protest shirts or black armbands. School suspended the boys in protest. Court said the school needed more than the desire to not deal with the problem because it offended them. Free speech is allowed in school but it must not interfere with school requirements.

*In Re: Winship* (1970)–Stole $115 from a purse. Question: whether proof beyond a reasonable doubt applied and not a preponderance of evidence. One result was that a greater degree of safety is required in delinquency cases (previously reserved only for adults).

*McKeiver v. Pennsylvania* (1971)–The result of *McKeiver* is that jury trials were not to be a constitutional right afforded juveniles in a delinquency proceeding. The Court felt that this aspect of the adversarial process was not appropriate for the juvenile justice system.

*Breed v. Jones* (1975)–Robbery. Would have been charged and processed as a juvenile, then as an adult; "double jeopardy" was finally attached to juvenile proceedings.

*Fare v. Michael C.* (1979)–Boy arrested, suspected of murder; wanted to speak with his probation officer during interrogation. He confessed, then appealed. Court suggested that the juvenile division consider the totality of circumstances and indicated that police should make an effort to inform juveniles of their right to remain silent; that a probation officer is not an attorney. Juvenile went back to jail.

*Wisconsin v. Yoder* (1972)–Said traditional Amish culture was able to provide skills for their own Amish society. They could remove children from public school after eighth grade. Choice between compulsory school and freedom of religion.

*In Re: Snyder* (1973)–Minor's right to proceedings against parents.

*Baker v. Owen* (1975)–Supreme Court told Baker that corporal punishment is sanctioned, as long as there is due process with it. Student and parents must be given reason for punishment.

*Goss v. Lopez* (1975-76)–Ohio; disturbance in school lunchroom; suspended with others. No one was allowed to testify, which violated the due process clause. Schools must provide a rudimentary hearing and list of charges for students to understand. Needs to be established on a case-by-case

basis.

*Wood v. Strickland* (1975-76)–Three sixteen-year-old girls in Mena, Arkansas, drinking intoxicating beverage at school; student received a new trial and reinstatement of student's rights. Students can sue the school board members for violations of constitutional rights.

*Ingraham v. Wright* (1977)–Question: The right of teachers to administer corporal punishment. Received injuries from paddling and challenged severe punishment referring to the Eighth Amendment and the Fourteenth Amendment of due process. Court said that neither the Eighth nor Fourteenth Amendments were violated and that schools can establish reasonable discipline as long as the right is no more restrictive than a parental right.

*California v. Prysock* (1981)–Murder. Miranda, advised of rights and convicted of first-degree murder; allowed a new trial without incriminating statements.

*Schall v. Martin* (1984)–Robbery and assault with a weapon. Detained before the trial; had a weapon, gave false address, judge considered the hour of the crime (due to lack of supervision); was sentenced to two years in jail; appealed on writ. Result: State's right to place juveniles in preventive detention.

*New Jersey v. T.L.O.* (1985–Two girls smoking in restroom, claimed they did nothing wrong. Administrator examined girl's purse. Found smoking paraphernalia; informed mother, and subject confessed to dealing drugs. Motion to suppress evidence because of school search. New Jersey Supreme Court decision overturned the search decision as not justified. Supreme Court said "No"–students do not give up rights when walking onto school property, however, school needs to provide an educational environment. Because of this school officials need "reasonable suspicion" for scope of search, age consideration, and questionable activity. School won out.

*Bethel School District No. 403 v. Fraser* (1986)– Question: Free speech. School's right to discipline a student who uses obscene words or gestures. School can control lewd speech that undermines the nature of the school's mission: civilized order of society.

*Hazelwood School District v. Kuhlmeier* (1988)– School official could censor active speech in a school publication; any publication should be part of the curriculum and with the school's knowledge.

*Maryland v. Craig* (1990)–Allows child abuse victims to testify on closed circuit television.

## CHILDREN AS VICTIMS

According to reports prepared by the Office of Juvenile Justice, juveniles are twice as likely to be victims of serious violent crime and three times as likely to be victims of assault. Between 1908 and 1997, nearly 38,000 juveniles were murdered in the United States. Many victims are quite young, and child protective services has received reports on more than 3 million maltreated children. In 80 percent of these reported cases, the alleged perpetrator was a parent. The United States does not have a good record when it comes to child victimization.

## Missing Children

Juvenile services are often the venue for many different groups of needy children. A list and a description of each group follows:

**Runaways**–Life on the streets looks good but usually only temporarily; females comprise almost one-half of the total numbers. (Two-thirds are between sixteen and seventeen years of age.) They have left parents or guardians without consent; not all want to leave home, a large majority are running from abuse, some estimated 50,000 per year.

**Throwaways**–Children who are pushed out, they may be perceived as too troublesome to parents or ignored; they come and go as they please.

**Walkaways**–A growing category, most juveniles in this group leave because of an unbearable situation or parental abuse. Typically it is not reported because parents know where the kids are. Parents and guardians either don't care or are resigned to the situation; they may live with others or relatives. If not for economic reasons, they would be gone.

**Abducted children**–400,000 per year, many abducted children are because of parental kidnappings or pickups by a family member, but there are also numbers of stranger abductions. Children taken by parents are usually the victims of a couple who are divorced or separated. Sometimes the mother or father simply fails to return the child after a scheduled visitation period. Girl victims account for 74 percent; one in seven is found.

**Homeless youth**–This group comprises all the combinations of above but it usually applies to runaways or those who have been exiled from a family group.

**Lost/injured children**–Children injured or trapped, they didn't intend to run away. Usually happens because of an extraordinary, but daily circumstance such as being lost in a park, wandering when away from the neighborhood.

## TYPICAL RUNAWAY

These children are victims of multiple abuses, most likely unemployed or unemployable. They have no plans, are vulnerable and despite this, may seem cocky or defensive. Juveniles in this category are usually frightened and do have potential but fall through the cracks. They do not "feel important" to their families and, as a consequence, learn survival tactics of the street and get involved in activity criminal in nature.

## Runaway Shelters, Halfway House, Crisis Center

Intended as a safe haven, frightened kids may go there on their own but police will often take certain individuals to various facilities as well. And, most times, law enforcement expect to see them back on the streets. Juveniles will often run away from a shelter if they think they will be sent home. Policies are typically to return them to their home, so, this often helps to foster a chronic runaway syndrome.

## Government Response

- Missing Children Act of 1984
- Missing Children Assistance Act: 1984
- National Center for Missing and Exploited Children, 1-800-THE-LOST

## GANG LIFE

Lt. Willie McCoy has invested more than twenty-one years in law enforcement, bringing himself up through the ranks. McCoy has done it all, patrol, traffic, bike patrol, and liaison. He is often called to speak to various groups and is a key member in the Hot Springs, Arkansas, Police Department while working at public and community relations. A tireless advocate for children he even works at the local Boys Club and has won national awards for his efforts in preventing and subduing youth gang activity. He holds a bachelor's degree and has lectured at numerous schools. Below is a chart that McCoy uses to show his listeners the difference between a school offense in the 1940s, against a typical school offense today.

## What's Happening in Our Schools?

| Top Offenses in the Year 1940 | and Today |
|---|---|
| 1. Talking out of turn | 1. Drug abuse |
| 2. Chewing gum | 2. Alcohol |
| 3. Making noise | 3. Pregnancy |
| 4. Running in the hall | 4. Suicide |
| | 5. Rape |
| | 6. Robbery |

## SOME STATISTICS ASSOCIATED WITH JUVENILES

**Teen Suicide:**
5% have tried
12% have come close}  **Reasons for:**
1. Problems growing up
2. Drug abuse
3. Peer pressure
4. Can't get along with parents

## *#1 Reason Child Is Removed From the Home:*

Poverty

## *2 Main Reasons for Gangs:*

1. Poverty
2. Racism

## *Definition of a Gang:*

A group of three or more who:
- has a turf or territory
- has a unique name
- has identifying mark or symbol
- associates regularly
- engages in criminal or antisocial conduct

| Safe Cities | Dangerous Cities |
| --- | --- |
| Irvine, CA | Atlanta |
| Amhearst, NY | Miami |
| Livonia, MI | St. Louis |
| Simi Valley, CA | Little Rock |

## *A Dr. Walter B. Miller 25-Year Study From 1979-1995:*

| City | Number of Gangs |
| --- | --- |
| 1. California | 293 |
| 2. Illinois | 232 |
| 3. Texas | 95 |
| 4. Florida | 67 |
| 5. New Jersey | 55 |
| 6. Massachusetts | 39 |

| Gangs in America | What Gangs Offer Youth |
| --- | --- |
| Hispanic | Status |
| Mexican | Sense of self-worth |
| Puerto Rico | Place of acceptance |
| Blacks | Personal protection |
| Latinos | Affection (Love) |
| Asians | Money |
| Whites | |

Most states have quite specific laws about criminal gang activity, committing crimes to profit the gang, and using a facility or building for gang purposes.

## *More Gang Facts*

- Gangs evolved from immigrant groups
- Gangs and Hollywoodism—a skewed spotlight
- In excess of 1,100 communities have gangs
- Gang victims are each other
- Once in a gang, extremely difficult to get out
- Leading cause of death for black males ages 15 to 34 is homicide
- Arrest rate of female offenders growing faster than that of males
- Juvenile violence up over 50 percent in last decade
- One in four adults will be a victim of gang offender
- Ages thirteen to eighteen largest group to shoot others

---

**FYI**—For those who are interested in gang culture, the information is out there. Details such as the fact that black gangs are becoming more profit-oriented now, and Asian gangs are completing more techno-crime with computers, for example, with making money orders, is fundamental. Details about gang life are fascinating and unique. For example, one group in Arkansas has names for popular brand-name clothing like: "REEBOK" is **R**espect **E**ach and **E**very **B**lood **O**kay. They also have their own language and euphemisms such as, a bill is $100 dollars; "BWPs" are Bitches with Problems, and "Beam me up" means a person who is hooked on cocaine, looking for a high. Hand signs and clothing are prevalent symbols as well. The biggest gang businesses are drugs, prostitution, and robbery.

## New Breed

1. More violent
2. Younger
3. Increasingly female
4. Increasing minority involvement

## Gangsta Rap

A number of antisocial encouragements with rap music:
1. Violence
2. Anti-female
3. Promiscuity
4. Drug use
5. Profanity
6. Sexual prowess
7. Anti-police
8. Racism
9. Rebellion and anger

## Juveniles Top Crimes in 2003

The 2.2 million arrests of juveniles in 2003 was 11 percent fewer than the number of arrests in 1999.

| Most Serious Offense | 2003 Est. # of Juvenile Arrests |
| --- | --- |
| Violent Crime Index[2] | |
| Murder and nonnegligent manslaughter | 1,130 |
| Forcible rape | 4,240 |
| Robbery | 25,440 |
| Aggravated assault | 61,490 |

The juvenile arrest rate for Violent Crime Index offenses declined in 2003, falling 48 percent from its 1994 peak and reaching its lowest level since 1980. The rate for each of the Violent Crime Index offenses–murder, forcible rape, robbery, and aggravated assault–has declined steadily since the mid-1990s. Juvenile arrest rates for Property Crime Index offenses also declined in 2003, reaching their lowest level in at least three decades.

Although the numbers in juvenile crime trend downward, problems remain. For example, between 1980 and 2003, juvenile arrest rates for simple assault increased 269% for females and 102 percent for males. During the same period, juvenile arrest rates for drug abuse violations increased 51 percent for females and 52 percent for males.

## A TYPICAL JUVENILE DETENTION CENTER

Sgt. Bill Livingston hadn't always worked with kids. He was in manufacturing and automotive work and earned a degree in agricultural engineering. He has worked for the Garland County Sheriff's Department as a bailiff and is now an instructor at the County Juvenile Detention Center in Hot Springs, Arkansas. Livingston says the juvenile detention facility has certain standards and their key responsibility to juveniles is first their rights, how to take care of them, and further training. "Everything works according to our guidelines," says Livingston.

The center where Livingston works opened November 25, 1996, and has admitted well over 300 juveniles. Just recently, the operations are now used to detain and house truancy offenders under court order. The Sergeant says that there are three major differences between the adult system and juvenile justice: confidentiality, intake approvals,

---

2. Crime in the United States 2003, Washington, DC: U.S.Government Printing Office, 2004.

and punishment. "In our facility, punishment is interactive, met with one-to-one counseling," says Livingston.

## What Does It Take To Be a Caseworker?

"It's an education every day, but the number one thing is to be open-minded. To listen and react to their needs," says Livingston. Forty hours of juvenile certification, conducted at the facility, is required in order to work there and that also includes 140 hours of continuing education every year just to remain certified.

There are three people on each shift, minimum, and the house has a maximum of twenty kids. (The community population is 36,000-plus.)

Behavior changes, building relationships, and confidence are the objectives. Juveniles are restricted from activities for acting out. The personnel often go one-on-one with the juveniles, listening to each one, and they do not ridicule or correct them in front of anybody else. We ask them, "What do you think would be appropriate to do?" We ask *them*. They ask, "Are you going to turn this [poor behavior report] into the court? It's amazing what we can get out of them when they are apprised of the situation," says the sergeant.

## Getting Processed

There are 7,000 square feet encompassing the detention main facility building. A "sally port" is engineered in order to allow an arriving vehicle to drive in–to enter the building. Weapons are placed in a gun locker before entering (unless approved by the Sheriff to do otherwise). They shackle one hand and, if needed, cuff them together, then do a pat-down. It's unlawful to take pictures of juveniles so no typical mug shot is taken. Males do male body searches, females do the female searches and Livingston said they try to ". . . touch the body as little as possible."

Paperwork is completed and they have their first contact with the intake officer. Livingston says they start building a relationship here with a medical history report, and try to diagnose if the newly admitted are possible suicide victims. They ask parental-type questions and the process takes about an hour and a half for intake, allowing for communication and explaining to the juvenile what is to take place.

Arrivals then shower and delouse. The staff washes their clothes for reissue; if they've not been to court, they can wear street clothes. When they go to court they wear green hospital garb and if they're sentenced, it's orange jumpsuits. (A deterrent, the ones dressed in orange do not get the same privileges as the others.)

Every night, all residents' clothes are washed by staff. "We do all the janitorial service ourselves, everything. The first hour is the most critical time," says Livingston, "they cry, and are sometimes scared to death."

## Control

The control room is monitored visually twenty-four hours a day. It allows the staff to see confrontations and gang signs (which are not tolerated). There are closure system locks for all the doors. The outside doors are always locked, and one must have credentials to some through. The intercom system is always on. "We listen to what's happening in sleeping rooms and others cannot enter. Anyone approaching must have a picture ID and be family members or guardians," says Sgt. Livingston. No purses are allowed in the facility.

Families visit in one of two visitation rooms, according to specific hours: 5-7 P.M.

Monday to Friday/5:30-7:30 P.M. Saturday and Sunday. The staff encourages family visits and they have fifteen minutes but employees don't rush them. There are holding cells and one rubber room for suicides and drug users. Each location is monitored every five minutes and the holding cells are only for incorrigibles and for isolation.

In the barracks are sleeping areas that accommodate between one to four people. A staff member stays in the barracks area with them. There is a mini-library. All personal property is taken and put into a milk crate. The only items they get to keep are: one religious reading, soap, towels, linens, shoes, and clothes. The facility provides all their hygiene items.

Staff are on walkie-talkies at all times and Livingston says it is amazing what it does for their behavior to have an adult interacting with them constantly. There are TVs in each barracks but they can only watch religious shows, learning programs, and Nickelodeon (approved shows only). Sometimes they'll see a sports event. Each area has a telephone which is cut off at 9 P.M., and it is for collect calls only.

An outdoor recreation yard exists and the staff does a mesh wire check occasionally for contraband. Outside, a staff member is present with one to five residents and the entirety of the rec area is on monitor too. A conference room is handy for private talks and the residents receive twenty-four-hour counseling through the Department of Youth Services, which is state-funded. Juveniles have a required school curriculum with classes credited toward their high school diploma and the school runs all year. There are special rooms here, and the only place to write letters.

## DETENTION LIFE

"By law, juveniles can only be told to clean their surrounding area, and they don't leave the facility except for the doctor, dentist, and going to court. And we don't want them to like it well enough to come back."

Juveniles must go to court within seventy-two hours of arrival in detention. And, of course, they can be bound over to a circuit court and tried as an adult. Livingston said, "We had one in for murder. The Department of Youth Services in Little Rock sent the juvenile to us because they do not have enough facilities. People are on waiting lists and they don't have anywhere to put them. Fifty percent of our visitors come from five other counties."

When asked about the work, Livingston said, "I'll tell you our goal. Our goal is to keep juveniles out of the big system. That's what's important."

## REVIEW QUESTIONS AND ANSWERS

### *Key Words to Define*

- **Adjudication phase**-Accord juveniles the same due process as adults get but omits the public trial.
- **Caseworker**–A person with juvenile certification status appointed to work with children, juveniles; typically within a detention center.
- **Child Protection Laws**–(1639) This required children to obey their parents or get whipped or disciplined in public; often required watching for other children.

- **Child Savers**–They affected laws in the 1800s New York; it was a moral movement for state's laws to commit runaways and delinquents to insane asylums.
- **Children's Aid Society**–Started by philanthropist Charles Brace in 1853, to provide temporary shelter for neglected children in private homes; the forerunner for the foster care system.
- **Cook County, IL**–1831, the first juvenile court; penalties different than for adults.
- **Detention**–Facility set up to house delinquents awaiting adjudication.
- **Disposition phase**–Determination of guilt, and a treatment or rehabilitation program is drawn up.
- **In loco parentis**–Means "in lieu of parents" or in place of parents; a claim over a child who is poor as witnessed in the case: ex parte Crouse.
- **In Re: Snyder**–In 1973, this case established a minor's right to proceedings against their parents.
- **Juvenile Justice and Delinquency Protection Act**–1974, Established The Office of Juvenile Justice Protection (OJJDP) within the Department of Justice.
- **Parens Patriae**–The King was father of his country, and an overseer in the behavior and property of minors.
- **Patens patriae**–similar to its previous historical underpinnings, which stated that the juvenile system's guiding philosophy was for juvenile treatment.
- **Throwaways**–Children who are pushed out of their homes because they are too troublesome; they come and go as they please; ignored by parents or guardian.
- **Variance**–No one agrees on what juvenile delinquency is, when the criminal justice system should get involved, or to what extent.

## *Questions for Review and Discussion*

1. *Question:* What is JINS? Social science term for "Juveniles in need of supervision" FINS? *Answer:* "Families in need of supervision."

2. *Question:* How did the era of social jurisprudence in the juvenile court system operate from 1950 through 1970-1979? *Answer:* It operated under the philosophy that provided for assessment, rehabilitation, and a protective nature like that of parents, but did nothing to prevent or affect delinquency.

3. *Question:* Why was In Re: *Gault v. Arizona* (1967) significant? *Answer:* It recognized that Gault was not afforded the same due process in the court system given over to an adult; the beginning of common sense with sentencing.

4. *Question:* What are the six components with the juvenile justice process? *Answer:* (1) Intake and investigation, (2) Detention, (3) Court, (4) Probation services, (5) Rehabilitation services, and (6) Aftercare.

5. *Question:* Name four differences in terminology between the adult system and the juvenile system. *Answer:* For example: (1) "Jail" for adult, "detention" for child; (2) "Criminal" for adult, "delinquent" for child; (3) "Arrest" versus "taken into custody"; and (4) "Trial" for adult and "adjudication hearing" for child, etc. (list on page 265).

6. *Question:* What are the three factors to juvenile probation? *Answer:* (1) Surveillance, (2) Casework services, (3) Counseling, (4) And on what is it based? Based on supervision and treatment.

7. *Question:* Pick one juvenile case law example and be prepared to explain it to the class (lists on pages 207–209).

## *Essay Exploration*

Look up one of the government web sites for missing children on the Internet and explain its mission, operations and goals.
- Missing Child Act of 1984
- Missing Children Assistance Act: 1984
- National Center for Missing and
  Exploited Children, 1-800-THE-LOST

# Chapter 13

# PRELIMINARIES

Life is just one damn
thing after another.
–Elbert Hubbard,
*Thousand and One Epigrams*

A defendant is someone you don't want to be. Defendants are someone formally charged by either the prosecutor or the grand jury with committing a crime. Their defense is information stating why they are not guilty. The defense attorney is the person who speaks and acts on the defendant's behalf, a legal champion, if I may say it, a counselor who will use all his resources to see that the defendant receives a fair trial. The defense attorney's objective is to win cases. His or her very livelihood and reputation depends on an ability to present a better case.

The reality of a criminal trial, and the script of what is "true-to-life," occupy a relatively different position and viewpoint in the scheme of what is generally portrayed on film or in a novel. In any given year, less than 10 percent of suspects apprehended for serious crimes go through the formal steps of a criminal trial. No matter. The drama of pitting a man against the law in a struggle for either his freedom or his life is one of the most compelling scenarios in fiction. It's been the grist for stories since man first raised his hand to kill, and it will be a story line as long as time continues. In this chapter we will look at the criminal process through the eyes of the defendant and the defense attorney.

## PROSECUTION OFFENSE

In addition to the arrest and search powers of law enforcement, the courts have allowed searches of businesses. A search warrant is still required, of course, but the general attitude is that a business holds a lesser privacy interest for the defendant and written records reflecting regular business and government activities are admissible in court. An investigator must be careful though, a search of a newspaper office or a television station must follow certain protocol because of the First Amendment's right to free expression and media's vehemence with protecting it.

Also, the prosecution is not allowed

access to the defense attorney's office because of the attorney-client privilege that applies to all clients' files. If the defense counsel were involved in other criminal activity, however, a search warrant with specific and narrow delineation as to what items could be recovered is allowed.

## DEFENDANT'S
## PRETRIAL RIGHTS

- To be informed of charges
- To remain silent
- Writ of habeas corpus
- Prompt arraignment
- Benefit of legal counsel; if indigent, attorney provided
- Reasonable bail

## RIGHT TO COUNSEL

The Sixth Amendment's framers wanted to ensure that criminal defendants could be represented at trial by their retained counsel. Under English law, attorneys were prohibited from appearing on behalf of defendants in felony cases. The Sixth Amendment reversed this rule and made counsel's assistance available to all who could afford to hire a lawyer.

The primary responsibility of the defense attorney is to represent his or her client, who has the constitutional right to counsel. If there is one credo most defenders live by, this is the ritualized speech most often heard: *The rights of the accused were designed to protect the innocent, and if the guilty are freed as a result of some technical issue, then that is the price that must be paid in order to ensure that the scales of justice remain balanced.* And today, it almost goes without saying, defendants facing criminal charges often need a lawyer to assist them. The law and its procedures are con-

fusing, and the tasks required to facilitate fairness require a level of expertise most criminal defendants do not have. In order to understand the nature and consequences of the proceedings against them and to be able to navigate the intricacies of courtroom operations, calls for someone from inside the system.

According to an article published by the University of Illinois, Urbana-Champaign, graduate Meredith Halama believes that subtle shifts have reduced a criminal defendant's right to counsel. Halama criticized a 1995 decision by the Supreme Court of Louisiana that introduced hairsplitting distinctions in order to permit police to interrogate a suspect alone after indictment. Now a clerk for U.S. District Judge James F. Holderman, Halama says the Supreme Court needs to "strike an appropriate balance between obtaining reliable confessions and safeguarding fundamental rights."

## A Twist

An interesting twist on the legal representation guarantee lies in the case *Caplin & Drysdale, Chartered v. United States.*[1] Apparently Caplin and Drysdale used illegal monies and collateral to fund their defense. The court, responding to this situation, said that retaining a private lawyer was a qualified right if the defendant used forfeited assets to obtain him. The Supreme Court said that the right to retain counsel has a major qualification in that, if the defendant has the ability to pay, fine. But the defendant in this particular instance had his assets forfeited constitutionally as a result of illegal activity, and had no right to offer them as payment for his attorney.

A second override on this qualified right of chosen counsel rests with the prosecutor's right to object to the defendant appointing counsel who has a potential for a conflict of

---

1. *Coplin & Drysdale, Chartered v. U.S.*, 491 U.S. 617 (1989).

**FYI**—The Supreme Court adopted a two-part test to determine when a person can receive counsel—just what events are covered in regard to a criminal prosecution and actually when counsel can enter the picture. First, the event must be an "adversarial judicial proceeding" meaning, this is the time marked by the appearance of a prosecutor and a judge. Filing a charging document such as a complaint or an information is enough to start the proceeding, including the arraignment and certain other appearances.

Secondly, the proceeding must qualify as a "critical stage," meaning, any trial-like event, including a preliminary hearing, a postindictment lineup, a guilty plea negotiation, and a sentencing hearing. These are the situations under which a person is entitled to right to counsel.

interest. A trial judge can disallow representation in such cases, even if the defendant wants to proceed with his retained counsel of choice and take his chances.[2]

## Counsel For Noncritical Stages

Since there are always exceptions to the rules in law, sometimes defense counsel can be appointed for a noncritical stage according to due process. For instance, counsel may be required to appear at parole or probation revocation hearings—and this is judged on a case-by-case basis—which usually takes place when there are substantial reasons for not revoking (read this as *canceling*) the client's parole or probation. The lawyer's appearance is sanctioned because the reasons for the client's release may be complicated or difficult to present without counsel.

## Right to Counsel on Appeal

Also, there is something called a *per se* due process clause on the right to counsel when the first appeal from a criminal conviction is presented. (*Per se* means "by itself" or "in itself.") This is because an indigent defendant would need the assistance of someone who is law-savvy to present an effective appeal which generally calls for combing the records, preparing the arguments, and looking for loopholes, etc.

A condition of per se due process is that the courts expect defense counsel to provide "effective assistance" on this first appeal. There must be something concrete with which to bring the case up for review. In order to not pursue frivolous functions and tie up the resources of the courts, if defense counsel believes the re-evaluation of the case has no merits, he or she can request permission to withdraw. A brief, often called an Anders[3] brief, would be filed.

## Ethical Problems of Defense?

The American Bar Association has defined the defense attorney's job as representing and defending clients to the best of his or her ability and doing everything possible, within the Canon of Ethics, to ensure that the client is acquitted. Let's explain it another way. Say, for example, an attorney were to hear something he does not want to hear, an admission of guilt perhaps. As an officer

---

2. *Wheat v. United States*, 486 U.S. 153, 108 S.Ct. 1692, 100 L.Ed.2d 140 (1988).
3. *Anders v. California*, 386 U.S. 738, 87 S.Ct. 1396, 18 L.Ed.2d 493 (1967).

of the court, he is bound to reveal his client's admission to the District Attorney, except for the fact that the client-attorney relationship of confidentiality would forbid him from doing so. The only way defense counsel can divulge something the defendant says is if the defendant gives him express permission.

For the defense lawyer, the premise is, and always has been, that a defendant is not guilty until a jury says so. A lawyer is not required to believe the client. Perhaps if the attorney is troubled by the guilt of a defendant, a good way to continue would be to consider that the client may be protecting someone else or has an irrational need to confess. Also, the attorney may actually believe–as a result of training and oath-taking–that a guilty person deserves due process just like any other citizen. Whatever methodology is used, it is the defense attorney's job to come up with an alternate scenario of the crime if possible, so as to explain the evidence in another more compelling way. He or she does not have the job of proving anything–that is the prosecution's job.

And, often, a defense attorney will suggest that the client not attempt to tell his or her side of the story–that the client is not, and never will be, obligated to do so. If the attorney knows the defendant is guilty, he or she will be kept from testifying because of two reasons. One, that would be allowing the client to lie under oath and the attorney will not be party to perjury, and two, because the defendant would be left open to cross-examination and impeachment. All that is needed to make it an "adversarial process" is for the defense to demystify and debunk the prosecution's scenario. If good enough at recreating the prosecutor's scheme, only one member of a jury can turn things around. The defense attorney is not bound by any moral or ethical code other than whatever can be done in favor of this client.

No one may really know the truth. The prosecution may put forth the testimony of someone who is lying. He or she is not allowed to knowingly do that, but if it is presented as bona fide evidence believed to be true, he or she also, is doing his or her job.

## DEFENSE COUNSEL FUNCTIONS

According to the American Bar Association (ABA), the defense, much like the prosecution, performs a multitude of functions while representing a client throughout the entire criminal proceeding. Some of these functions are:

- Represent the accused immediately after arrest in order to provide advice during interrogation and to ensure constitutional safeguards during pretrial procedures.
- Review police reports and conduct further investigation.
- Interview the police, the accused, and any other witnesses to find additional evidence.
- Discuss the unfolding events with the prosecutor with the intention of gaining insight into the strength of the case against them.
- Represent the accused at all bail hearings and plea negotiations.
- Prepare, file, and argue various pretrial motions.
- Prepare the case and alternate scenario for trial.
- Participate in jury selection.
- Represent the accused at trial.
- Provide advice and assistance at sentencing.
- Determine and pursue a legitimate basis for appeal.
- Present written or oral arguments for appeal.

## Criminal Defense Costs

A private defense attorney is an expensive proposition. An attorney will set fees according to the likely complexity of the case, his or her experience, and geography, meaning generally, the cost of living is different in different regions of the country and so will be the subsequent fees. Since no standard legal fees exist, it is whatever the market will bear. Obviously, a misdemeanor offense will cost less than a murder trial and if the suspect if famous, the trial could cost millions.

Criminal defense attorneys will typically charge by the hour, called a billable hour, or by the case. In addition, some hidden costs may be passed on to the defendant such as fees for copies, subpoena fees, filing fees, and any extras incurred with, say, the footwork completed by a private investigator or other subcontractor services. People retaining lawyers often feel intimidated by hourly fees, especially if the case becomes unusually complicated. They feel it may give the attorney a reason to spend more time on a case than it requires, or to work slower because of the advantage the clock affords.

Case billing means a lawyer may charge by the case according to the offense. Say, for example, it is a drunk driving charge, a lawyer make have a set charge of service fees for defendants charged with this crime.

A retainer is a portion of money that is paid up front. It is the equivalent of a down payment on services. Perhaps the client will pay in advance for twenty hours of the lawyer's time. That amount will be set against the bill and the accused will receive regular statements outlining the balance, until it eventually reaches zero, when negotiations of money will need to be set again.

Contingency fees are most commonly used in civil litigation, such as personal injury cases where the client stands to receive an award from the court's decision. The lawyer's fee will be a percentage of what monies are recovered for damages, so if the client recovers no money, the attorney won't either. Contingency fees do not apply in criminal cases and are disallowed and considered unethical[4] by the ABA.

## LAW OFFICE SETTING

### Large Law Firm

Welcome to the legal mall. Probably located in a high-rise with an upscale address, and the roster reads like the collegiate-elite alumnae newsletter; everyone's from Princeton, Yale, Harvard, or Stanford. There are the young startups in the basement checking research; mid-level wannabe top-dogs are working the minor nuisance

---

FYI—Lawyers who are hired and are members of a firm have a tendency to delegate work to others. For example, a law student may be asked to conduct legal research, an associate lawyer may be delegated to handle the pretrial conference, and a paralegal might pinch-hit in preparing the defendant for trial. Of course, for the defendant it makes the costs less expensive, but he or she would need to get used to a lot of different faces and the frustration of a changing hierarchy.

---

4. See the ABA Model Rules of Professional Conduct.

cases en masse; upper-level counselors are hitting the streets on their way to court to file and argue motions; and the senior level partners are romancing the big money corporate, insurance, and foreign government clients with off-shore accounts.

The surroundings are plush with oriental carpets, large wooden or leather doors opening on paneled rooms with wing chairs, mahogany desks, art, and oh, those glorious, expensive legal books ringing the walls. There may be dozens of secretaries (with their own hierarchy), mailroom clerks, telephone operators, receptionists, and computer technicians all tucked away on floors with less fancy carpeting and more efficient décor.

## Medium-sized Law Firm

A more close-knit group, they have a well thought out division of labor. This way to insurance, family court here, personal injury through the white door, and estate planning by appointment only. The area of expertise is all over the board and the twenty to fifty members either choose their own area or are assigned to work for a partner.

It is a busy place with more utilitarian surroundings and maybe a modern bent. Floors are oak or painted colors and the walls donned with this year's competent color. Smooth round edges and the occasional plastic molding but still tasteful–a nouveau look for the up-and-coming.

Not as quiet as the uptown place, phones ring and secretaries are typing and talking, checking calendars and the food cart as it passes through the foyer. Everyone is working and the place is abuzz. The salaries are lower but they are closer to the clients, some of whom may use them for years.

## Small Legal Office

From three to up to twenty, these lawyers are probably friends from college or at least, legal contemporaries. A little more laid back, the wait in the traditional lobby is quiet and friendly.

Even though there is a sophisticated phone and intercom system you may hear the county attorney beckon an aide from the small conference room at the end of the hall. An air of camaraderie exists throughout and the hustling, independent sole practitioner days are either a long-ago memory or a thing of the past.

## PRO SE OR PRO PER

Self-representation is a tricky proposition but some will do it. A Latin term *pro se*, meaning "for himself" or, *pro per* defendant or even "in propria persona" meaning, "in one's own proper person" are all saying the same thing–a client representing him- or herself. The best known story of this is a high-profile defendant named Colin Ferguson. Ferguson was tried in 1995, and was dubbed the "Long Island Railroad Killer" by the press. Despite the fact he was facing life in prison without the possibility for parole for his gunning down six commuters on the Long Island Railroad, he insisted on leading his own parade.

The judge ruled that Ferguson was legally capable of participating in his own trial, but there were many who saw it as a complete folly and a cruel blow to the survivors of the attack. The jury held up in defiance of Ferguson's often long, rambling dissertations of unintelligible babble, just long enough to convict him on all counts after a quite brief deliberation.

## Writ of Habeas Corpus

This is a petition, a writ of *habeas corpus*, sent to the court, to seek a remedy against an illegal arrest. In Latin it means, "you must have the body" or "bring the body forth" and technically, it is an application for discharge. The police are to bring the person into court and determine if he or she is being held improperly. If the court sides in the accused person's favor, there may be cause to bring a civil suit or civil action for either false imprisonment or violation of civil rights and there could be remuneration in the form of damages. Then, too, if this proves to be the case, the arresting officers may be subject to some criminal liability of their own, especially if excessive force was used during the arrest.

## Lawyers at Lineups

Sometimes the police will make an effort to push through a lineup before the suspect has been charged, in order to avoid the appearance of his or her lawyer. If the accused asks the police to delay long enough for a lawyer to arrive, it may work, and some agencies even have attorneys on "lineup duty," a twenty-four-hour client service.

Not only will the attorney's presence be an assurance to someone who is a first-timer, but lawyers often bring cameras or a blank seating chart to make sure the procedure is on the up-and-up. By knowing who the witnesses and other suspects are, they can add invaluable details to the defense case.

The lawyer at lineup will also keep an eye open for any questionable behavior on behalf of the police such as, coaching a witness, having the attendees dress differently in a manner that might set them out from the pack, or giving subtle signals. A wise defense attorney will also watch for clues to witness credibility and if they say something to the effect, "It was pretty dark and I was distracted" or, "I can't tell, he was wearing a cowboy hat," or, "I was coming around the corner, 40 feet away . . ." then those statements can be used later on in court.

In addition, where witnesses might otherwise not want to speak with an attorney, the presence of the police in a safe environment may make them more approachable and they may consent to an open interview or answer questions in this cooperative setting. Then, too, if they are nervous, they may divulge some clue or attitude that may prove helpful later on. By the way, any refusal to cooperate in a lineup by the defendant is considered circumstantial evidence of the suspect's "consciousness of guilt."

## Lawyers at Arraignment

The arraignment, which is usually held within forty-eight hours, sets the arrangements for everything that follows. Remember, during an arraignment the suspect becomes the accused and is presented with the charges against him or her; the defendant can apply for court-appointed counsel; the defendant's plea is asked for; the judge sets a schedule for either a pretrial conference, a preliminary hearing, a hearing on pretrial motions, or the trial date itself. Then, this is when any unresolved bail issues are answered in regards to either setting bail, raising or lowering bail, or releasing defendant on own recognizance.

A defense lawyer may use the tactical advantage of either trying to delay the trial date or, in other cases, pushing it through at the first available moment. The advantage of delay is almost always in favor of the defendant. Why? Because the passage of time serves to give adequate time for the witnesses to forget what they've seen or heard. Law enforcement believes that important cases must generally be worked right away. The first forty-eight hours of a case are critical. After that, the potency of evidence starts to diminish, the crime scene becomes polluted, and prosecutors may lose track of evidence. And because of factors that cannot be controlled such as human nature, people will have a tendency to lose interest and momentum.

For the defendant, the extra time allows an opportunity to receive counseling, find employment, or otherwise establish a course of behavior more favorable to the courts, and seek out other witnesses. If released on bail, defendants can literally makeover their appearance by dressing more appropriate to court appearances, getting a haircut or restyling, shaving facial hair, and just generally becoming more presentable. Defendant's counsel can choose to formally delay the preliminary hearing by filing a motion to postpone the event using a document called a "Motion for Continuance." This type of

motion also can be made orally and involves a simple rescheduling.

In terms of the defense wanting to speed the trial through, a perfect example of that is the 1995 O.J. Simpson case, when Orenthal James Simpson was charged with the murder of his wife, Nicole Brown Simpson, and another unrelated individual, Ronald Goldman. Simpson's defense team pushed for an early adjudication of this case so that the prosecution was unable to rally all the component people and evidence together and prepare and present in a timely manner an especially complex case.

And likewise, a "waiving of time," that is, giving up the right to a speedy trial, at a preliminary hearing, is still another way to place time between the event and the trial.

Another good idea for the defense team is to construct a logical, believable story. They must be able to weave in the evidence, and create a scenario that the prosecution and,

---

21. MOTION FOR CONTINUANCE.

_____, Defendant, moves the Court to grant a motion for continuance for the following reasons:

1. That the Defendant, _____, is charged with the offense of

_____.

2. That a continuance is needed for the following reasons: [Describe].

3. That the [specify number] continuances have been previously granted for the following parties: [names].

4. That manifest in justice would result by requiring the trial of this cause to commence as scheduled.

WHEREFORE, the Defendant, _____, prays that the Court grant continuance for [specify time needed].

Respectfully submitted,

By _____
                        Attorney for Defendant

Structure 9.

later, ordinary people–the jury–will accept. This story will obviously run counter to the prosecution's theory because he or she must paint the defendant as a bad person, with ugly motives who is capable of committing the crime. The defendant and his or her attorney will have to put their heads together prior to plea bargaining in order to answer the charges by contrasting it with a defense, and be able to answer to the motive by using a counterclaim of some sort, before a plea bargain.

## PRELIMINARY HEARING

Remember, preliminary hearings are the best way to get a preview of the trial. And, in order to get one, the defendant must plead "not guilty" at the arraignment. (Also, check independently Dear Lawyer, the state you are in may not have a law allowing for preliminary hearings or may only allow them under certain conditions.) Here the judge decides whether there is enough evidence to move further, or whether to reduce the charges, and it is the best way to provide an overall judicial review–some cases do get dismissed!

The defendants' biggest gain from attending this event (even though they most likely will lose and the case will go forward) is the ability to be privy to the other side's evidence for the first time in a legal context. The defendant and counsel must listen very carefully to any witness stories put forth at this time, because any variation in the telling at trial, is cause for impeachment. There is also an opportunity for the defense counsel to vigorously (or politely, depending on the

Figure 14. The Honorable Judge Ralph Ohm (one of the authors) listens to testimony regarding a civil case in the Municipal Court of Hot Springs.

tact) cross-examine prosecution witnesses. The defendant should make notes as to: How are they holding up? Do they sound credible? What do you know about them that is going unsaid that may help your case?

Most importantly, there are rules of evidence where defense lawyers are required to object to inadmissible evidence during a prelim, otherwise, they may not be able to assert the right to object to that evidence later at trial. In the absence of such a rule, however, the defense may opt to remain silent and let the prosecution think it has a strong case, only to derail it later in court with its inaccuracies and misinformation.

## PLEA BARGAIN

A plea bargain could also be called a mutual concession. In many cases, the guilty plea comes as the result of the prosecution and the defense striking a deal. At least 90 percent of felony suspects arraigned plead guilty or no contest, so that means that less than 10 percent of criminal cases actually end up in trials. The deal involves an understanding that the accused agrees to plead guilty in exchange for either a reduction in the number or severity of charges, or a promise on behalf of the prosecutor to not ask for the maximum penalty for the offense charged.

Since most prosecutors overcharge, that is, they file more charges than they expect to explain and win on, this tactic also gives them more power at the bargaining table. Because there is more to give away and because most likely the prosecution would not have been able to demonstrate those charges to the court, the state loses little by reducing the number of charges. Most defense lawyers know this and take that into consideration before they let their client-defendant cry "Uncle!"

If the prosecutor feels confident about pursuing the case and the defense sees no alternative, rather than to face a judge who may have a tendency to administer the strictest sentence, the defense attorney may suggest the client make a deal for a lower sentence. Since any outcome under a jury trial is always the unknown, a plea bargain does allow some control over the result.

In all jurisdictions, plea negotiations need the approval of the trial court to go through and, in certain areas, judges participate directly in plea-bargain discussions. The invited judge practice is supposed to ensure that the parties agree jointly in an equal and quick resolution, but many courts feel that the presence of the judge may unduly influence the defendant and the outcome, making the presence of a knowledgeable defense attorney all the more important. And another issue of note: a contingency with accepting a plea is that the defendant must accept the plea on the basis of guilt. If he or she pleads guilty while still maintaining innocence, a judge does not have to approve the transaction.

## Reneging on a Plea

A couple episodes of *Law & Order* have seen Executive Assistant District Attorney Jack McCoy withdrawing a deal. He may have agreed to a reduction in charges only to find that the defendant has manipulated the state, making him look like a fool in court and, that in turn, makes Jack a very angry man. McCoy actually changed his mind in front of the judge in this particular case, and used the testimony told him at the bargaining table against him in court. A defendant caught up in the throws of this situation, would have the right to simply withdraw his plea of guilty and take his chances on the verdict. In some cases, the prosecution will only make a "promise" toward recommend-

FYI—One of the best moves the defense attorney can make in plea negotiations is to start with the attorneys at the bottom of the ladder in the prosecutor's office. A new fledgling may be the best bet for a better deal.

ing a reduction in sentence. In that case, the defendant's plea would stand. For the man who caved in in court? He wound up with a conspiracy charge of murder, and went down with his lovely paramour glaring at him as they were both led off to jail. Both elephants and district attorneys have long memories and are willing to take revenge.

And finally, there is another instance regarding mandatory sentencing laws that affect plea bargaining tactics. In some states, judges have no say over what sentences they can impose, meaning, a bargaining chip is sorely missing from the game regardless of how they feel. So unless the defense attorney can finagle a reduction in charges, the defendant may have to take his or her chances with the jury after all.

## The Competent Client

Defendants who help their attorneys present the most effective defense possible are competent clients. They share the responsibility of defense by understanding the attorneys' role and ethical duties; by participating in important case decisions; and by following through with appointments with counselors and supporting activities that display rehabilitation. It would be in the clients' best interest to attend similar court sessions to learn from a real procedure. They can use it as an example, noting the demeanor and dress of witnesses, along with any other details that either impress or "turn off" the jury.

Defendants should not try to play "second-chair" to the attorney, but instead, learn

as much about their charges and their previous interpretations in order to see and understand local statute variations and sentencing.

## Defendant Competency

Competence to stand trial is a complicated issue depending on more than just the defendant's current comportment. If, at the time of a trial, a defendant's sanity is in question, other measures must be taken because a defendant cannot be put on trial if suffering from a mental disease. The defendant needs to be able to understand the proceedings, and to assist in his or her own defense. If not, a judge will hold a hearing and take evidence concerning the defendant's current competence. As mentioned previously in the information about the insanity defense, the defendant has the responsibility of proving incompetence by a preponderance of the evidence. If the judge determines the defendant unstable, he or she will be placed in a mental institution until sanity is reestablished. At that time, a trial will be held.

## Proximate Cause

Proximate cause, sometimes called attenuation, is a term most commonly associated with homicides. You may hear it defined as the "legal causation," meaning, that death is a natural, continuous chain, unbroken by any other disruptive causes, that produces the consequences that occur. In other words, if the result that occurs was the proximate

**Other Notes**—The defense of insanity is a relatively rare plea, and doctors make little use of the idiom "insanity," except for law-related purposes. For example, Loreena Bobbitt could have gone to jail for twenty years for cutting off her husband's penis. Instead, as one physician put it, ". . . she broke from reality last June 23 and was unable to control her impulses—the definition of temporary insanity." Over forty-eight witnesses testified on her behalf, filing one by one to the stand, many with alarming versions of accounts where John Bobbitt had beaten, punched, kicked, and choked his wife. He was ruthless, often breaking down doors to get to her or dragging her by the hair.

cause, it was foreseeable. Legal eagles use the "but for" test here, meaning that "but for" the accused person's actions, the harm would not have happened. For example, if a victim was injured by the defendant's bullet to her shoulder and the victim dies in the hospital later as a result of the hospital's negligence, the perpetrator could not be charged with her murder but with a lesser offense such as assault with a deadly weapon.

## DEFENSE-SPEAK

### Depositions

Since it is in the defendant's best interest to investigate his or her own case, there are some techniques for gathering evidence in preparation for the trial. Interviewing prosecution witnesses through deposition is one such technique. Sometimes referred to as the *compulsory process*, this is tied into the Sixth Amendment guarantee. By using depositions

the defense can find out what prosecution witnesses think, their credibility and their ability to connect with people in expressing those beliefs, and whether the testimony rings true or differs greatly from previous testimony (facts established at the preliminary hearing). By studying these testaments, the defense team can develop a tactic that will help them to poke holes in the prosecution witness testimony at trial.

It is completely legal to speak with and interview prosecution witnesses prior to the trial, as the testimony is not controlled by the prosecution. It is up to each individual witness to agree to be interviewed, however, and the defendant should make no attempts to contact the victim who may interpret contact as a threat and the defendant may lose bail and face other criminal charges as a result. The attorney should make all arrangements for contact in this instance. And although prosecutors, by rule, cannot advise their witnesses to keep to themselves, they will often tell said witness, "You are not

**Caution**—Tension is often a component of proximate cause. Say the offender is charged with homicide, but he or she is certain his or her bullet is not the one that killed the person whom he or she may have shot at. In order to save their butt from long-time sentencing, you need to consult an expert in forensic scene recreation—and with the help of physics—prove your client is not a killer.

required to talk with the defendant."

For the defense to secure a witness interview, there are two alternatives: the private investigator and the deposition. Provided the money is there, a private investigator will find and interview reluctant witnesses for a fee, often charging between $75 to $150 per hour for their services.

In most jurisdictions, interviews are possible through a subpoena, which is a court order compelling the witness to attend an interview and answer questions in order to prepare a deposition. Most commonly used in civil cases, the deposition is a record of testimony, given under oath, and transcribed into a booklet for use. The process is expensive because not only is the attorney's time required for the development of questions and the interview, but the court reporter also receives a fee for the take-down and transcription.

## Other Pretrial Motions

Finally, a deposition can preserve the testimony of an infirm witness or someone who may not be available for trial. It can also be issued to inspect the minutes of a grand jury proceeding, and finally, it might be used to disqualify a judge based on various grounds including a relationship to parties, demonstrated bias, or using the judge as a material witness.

## Subpoena Duces Tecum

These three magic words can compel uncooperative people or offices to cough up their records, documents, or objects. A subpoena duces tecum is relatively easy to get; they are pre-stamped forms and the defense attorney need only fill in the blanks to generate a court-ordered directive.

## DEFENSE STRATEGY

Communication between the defendant and his or her attorney helps to establish the "account" of events from the defendant's viewpoint. The attorney is not expecting to fabricate a story to present as evidence, but the telling of the story—the actual account—may differ markedly from what the prosecution has said. For example, fingerprints at the scene can be explained in any number of ways, such as, the defendant was there the week before, had performed some service for the victim, or had even come in to use the phone.

In the defendant's version of the story, things may look different if the defendant tried to leave the premises before the criminal activity took place. If the defendant had claimed an "alibi" and was out of town at the time of the crime, the account of what he or she was doing adds credence to the story. In essence, the ultimate defense strategy grows out of, but is not the same as, a defendant's version of events. The theory of the case will include such highpoints as moral culpability and the defendant's attitude toward crime. All of these factors must be pieced together with provable facts and hard evidence.

## Confidentiality

Because of the rule of confidentiality between the defendant and lawyer, only certain things need be relayed to the prosecution in preparation for a trial. Normally, the prosecution will know if the defendant's version hangs on an alibi or an insanity defense. The identities of defense witnesses and their written statements are divulged, and the general outline of the case is imparted early, in the event a plea bargain is possible. One very important rule to note here; the defendant's version of the story, as relayed to counsel, is the one he or she must stick with. Any alternate version from the first would constitute perjury if submitted in court. Ethical rules forbid defense attorneys from calling witnesses whom they know will perjure themselves. Now this does not mean that the story will not get modified with other important details or even some inaccuracies; it does mean the story cannot be a continual infringement against professional ethics. The ethical conduct of the lawyer and the moral principles of counsel have been stretched by some, we have no doubt. What determines if this is successful or not relies heavily upon the matter of "getting caught." Lawyers are not sworn in, nor are they under the same oath as their witnesses. But the ABA frowns on marginal behavior.

## Pretrial Discovery

Before we leave communication evidence and what can be allowed, every jurisdiction has a procedure where the prosecution has to tell the accused what evidence it intends to use. This is information included in pretrial discovery. The accused may make a Motion for Discovery—a written request—or file a pleading to obtain it, or the prosecution may just turn it over for the asking. Since prosecutors have a legal duty to turn over any information that might help the defendant, it's often unnecessary to file even if the defendant fails to ask for it.

The file should include the names of witnesses and their addresses (this part is optional), and any prior criminal activity on their part. Also, a list of documents or other exhibits to be used against the defendant as evidence in court will be in the discovery generally, including hard evidence such as fingerprints, bullets, photographs, specimens taking from the body, etc. All statements made by the defendant, either oral or written, should be provided. And, all the reports prepared by prosecution experts who have conducted examinations of the evidence, any type of physical or mental analyses, and other scientific tests or comparisons, must be turned over.

The defendant should take this process seriously because the prosecution is also obligated to turn over any evidence it has that might establish the defendant's innocence or at least point to other options, called *exculpatory evidence.* How could that be? Maybe something turned up accidentally, or maybe the police failed to follow another path that has recently come up–and the accused has a right to examine those records, police reports, and other scientific matters. Most prosecutors will reveal this evidence to the extent required by local rules without objection.

## Due Process Right to Tools (Indigents)

Aside from the right to counsel, the Court has confirmed that certain types of technical support must be available for an indigent's counsel. For example, in order for a defendant to have adequate access to the appellate process, a trial transcript must be provided by the state. They also have the right to receive the basic tools of adequate defense at trial, including expert witnesses if necessary for an effective presentation.

## 4. MOTION FOR DISCOVERY.

_____, Defendant, for his motion for discovery states:

1. That the Defendant is charged with the offense of _____.

2. That the prosecuting attorney is obligated to disclose to defense counsel the following material and information which is within the possession, control, or knowledge of the prosecuting attorney:

A. The names and addresses of persons whom the prosecuting attorney intends to call as witnesses at any hearing or at trial;

B. Any written or recorded statements and the substance of any oral statements made by the Defendant [and _____, Co-Defendant];

C. Those portions of Grand Jury minutes containing testimony of the Defendant;

D. Any reports or statements of experts, made in connection with this case, including results of physical or mental examinations, scientific tests, experiments or comparisons;

E. Any books, papers, documents, photographs or tangible objects, which the prosecuting attorney intends to use in any hearing or at trial or which were obtained from or belong to the Defendant;

F. Any record of prior criminal convictions of persons whom the prosecuting attorney intends to call as witnesses at any hearing or at trial;

G. The substance of any relevant Grand Jury testimony;

H. Whether, in connection with this case, there has been any electronic surveillance of the Defendant's premises or of conversations to which the Defendant was a party;

I. The relationship to the prosecuting attorney of persons to whom the prosecuting attorney intends to call as witnesses;

3. That the prosecuting attorney should disclose and permit inspection, testing, copying, and photocopying of any relevant information regarding:

A. Any searches and seizures resulting from a warrant to search the premises at [address] issued on [date] by [court] and executed on or about [date];

B. The acquisition of a statement from the Defendant on or about [date] at [address] by [law enforcement agency].

4. That the prosecuting attorney should disclose to the defense counsel any material or information within his knowledge, possession, or control, which tends to negate the guilt of the Defendant as to the offense charged or which would tend to reduce the punishment therefor.

5. That this Court in its discretion may require disclosure to defense counsel the following relevant material and information which is material to the preparation of the defense: [List relevant material and information] [to be used when discovery is discretionary under Rule 17 of the Arkansas Rules of Criminal Procedure].

WHEREFORE, the Defendant, _____, prays that the Court grant his motion for discovery and order the prosecuting attorney to disclose the material and information described herein.

Respectfully submitted,

By _____
Attorney for Defendant

Address:_____

**NOTE**

**See Rule 17, Arkansas Rules of Criminal Procedure.**

Structure 10.

## PRETRIAL PROCESS

Important negotiation usually obscured to the public, notions like pretrial motions, the suppression hearing, habeas corpus, and other expressions are part of the pretrial process.

## Pretrial Motions

Motions can be made before, during, or after a trial. Some are more confusing than others, but basically, the motion is a procedure, whether written or oral, requesting the court to make a ruling with regard to most any legal issue surrounding the case. In extremely involved cases, a motion could consist of a written brief, something that raises complex legal issues that only a judge can respond to fairly.

## Three-Step Process

Motions are ordinarily a three-step process. First, the defense attorney must give notice that an adversary motion will be made. A written notice is prepared called a Notice of Motion and the notice is then filed with the court and another copy is presented to the prosecution. Inside the notice are papers that state what specific request the party is asking for; an explanation of facts for the request, usually in the form of an affidavit; and the legal basis for the request in a document referred to as the Memorandum of Points and Authorities.

The next step is a hearing of the motion, where each party has a right to present their oral arguments with the express purpose of getting the judge to agree to their side. The judge will decide to sustain–support–the motion or deny it. This meeting can take place in the judge's chambers or can even be avoided by having the prosecutor agree to a new court date or some other calendar matter. This would be called "stipulating" to a continuance, whereby the written stipulation would be filed with the court, awaiting the approval of the judge in order for the request to take effect, while dodging yet another meeting.

Finally, the judge may make no immediate ruling but rather, "take the matter under submission," meaning, the ruling will be conveyed in good time whether that be the next day, the next week, or even months later. At this time the judge can also ask the requesting party to make further written arguments to simplify a complex situation.

---

**Caution**—Dear Lawyer, it would behoove you to know how to prepare and use motions. To begin, a motion made as a legal brief carries more weight simply because the preparation is more exhaustive than that of a simple oral declaration of need. Judges often like to read these arguments and consult other records of precedence before deciding. And, finally, the defendant will have a record of the motion should an appeal somewhere down the line be needed.

If motions are deemed to be frivolous documents and viewed as tying up both the good nature of the judge and the time of the court though, his Honor can fine the offending party. This is not a defense tactic to be abused.

## COMMON PRETRIAL MOTIONS

### Motion to Reduce Bail

Even if a judge has already set bail, new circumstances may bring to the judge's attention the need for a reduction, which may vary from the standard measure.

### Motion to Dismiss

If there are mistakes on the document used to charge the crime, a defendant can attack the improper complaint with a Motion to Dismiss Complaint filing. A correct complaint specifies all the elements of the crime, the defendant charged, and the authority for such charges. Technically, the failure of the complaint to allege all these elements could result in a dismissal if not for the fact that prosecutors use templates and often toss out the defective forms. In addition, the state's team is usually allowed to amend the mistakes, so motions of this nature are unlikely to work but, if it is a motion to dismiss based on double jeopardy, granted immunity, or some other violation, it will be taken in for review. Also–a loophole–if

---

3. MOTION TO REDUCE BAIL.

_____, Defendant, for his motion to reduce bail states:

1. That the Defendant is charged with the offense of _____.

2. That pretrial release inquiry was conducted by [judicial officer], on _____, 19_____, at which time such judicial officer set bail in the amount of $_____ to insure the appearance of the Defendant in Court.

3. That such bail is excessive taking into account all facts relevant to the risk of willful nonappearance by the Defendant, including the following:

    (a) Defendant has been a resident of the City of _____ for _____ years.

    (b) Defendant has been employed at _____ as _____ for _____ years.

    (c) Defendant has strong family ties to the community in that defendant's [parents] [family] [husband] [wife] [children] reside at _____.

    (d) Defendant's reputation, character and mental condition are good.

    (e) Defendant has no past history of failure to respond to legal process.

    [(f) Defendant has no prior criminal record.]

    (g) _____ and _____, who are responsible members of the community, are prepared to vouch for the Defendant's reliability.

    (h) Defendant is not charged with a serious offense and the apparent probability of [conviction] [the likely sentence] reduces the risk of nonappearance.

WHEREFORE, the Defendant prays that the Court grant his motion to reduce bail.

Respectfully submitted,

By _____
                    Attorney for Defendant

Address:_____

Structure 11.

the prosecution fails to re-file erroneous charges within the time period specified for the "statute of limitations" the charges may be dismissed.

## Motion for Bill of Particulars

This filing is used in order to learn the basis of the formal charge the defendant faces. Upon granting a Motion for Bill of Particulars, the judge will order the prosecutor to specify with particularity just what the defendant did wrong. The return of a document like this helps the defense plan a strategy, but it is usually unnecessary because defense counsel is, as a matter of course, given a copy of the police report and other essential paperwork.

## Motion to Reduce Charges

An uncommon filing simply by virtue of one going through a preliminary hearing, where the judge decides whether the prosecution's felony case is sufficiently supported by evidence. Still, this is a motion where a defender can ask that charges be reduced and may be used if substantial circumstances change or new evidence comes up. Plea bargaining, based on an equitable exchange of either information or a confession, is typically the vehicle used for reduction of charges.

---

2. APPLICATION FOR CHANGE OF VENUE.

_____, Defendant, petitions the Court for a change of venue and in support of such petition states:

    1. That the Defendant, _____, is charged with the offense of

_____.

    2. That the minds of the inhabitants of this County are so prejudiced against the Defendant that a fair and impartial trial cannot be held in this County.

    3. That attached hereto in support of such allegations are the affidavits of _____ and _____, two credible persons who are qualified electors and actual residents of this County and who are not related to the Defendant in any way.

    4. That this Court has the authority and discretion to change venue pursuant to Arkansas law.

    WHEREFORE, the Defendant, _____, prays that the Court grant this petition and issue its order removing this case to [specify desired jurisdiction].

Respectfully submitted,

By _____
              Attorney for Defendant

Address:_____

**NOTE**

**See Arkansas Statutes Annotated §43-1501 et seq.**

---

Structure 12.

## Application for a Change of Venue

A jury trial is most often conducted in the county where the crime took place. If because of adverse publicity or difficulty with finding unbiased jurors, a motion asking for a change of venue is requested. For the defendant, a change in jurisdiction is not always the best move. What if the case goes to a more undesirable location? The distance may put the defense far away from the office, and, for the defendant's family and friends, it may be a stretch for them to attend. In addition, court costs may be restrictive away from defense counsel's home base. Something to think about: The O.J. Simpson case may have had a markedly different outcome if the trial had taken place in its original jurisdiction of Brentwood, California, instead of South Los Angeles county.

## Motion to Strike a Prior Conviction

Oftentimes records of conviction have mistakes. Prior bad "rap sheets" can have a negative connotation when it comes to sentencing. Defendants with priors are usually handled more severely and may be charged with more serious charges as a consequence. Judges also sentence repeat offenders much more harshly. Also, if a procedural irregularity such as a denial of counsel took place and the case resulted in a prior conviction, the defendant would not want that record to reflect on his or her present circumstances so a Motion to Strike a Prior Conviction would be a positive move. The judge would then strike the information—instruct the prior record to be disregarded, in all manner and forms.

## Motion to Preserve Evidence

This is most often used for perishable evidence. It will force a prosecutor to keep evidence safe long enough for the defense to obtain its own experts and run its own tests. The Motion to Preserve Evidence would most likely be used for evidence on blood alcohol tests and drunk-driving offenses.

## Motion to Disclose Identity of a Confidential Informant

It is in the defense attorney's interest to find out if the prosecution is relying on the testimony of a government informant. If so, an attack on the informant's credibility is an option, as well as finding out if he or she is an active participant in the offense. If he or she is a paid informant or has something to gain by testifying against the defense client, knowing that, is another strategy development and a way to curb the damage with his or her testimony. The judge's decision to grant the motion is based on balancing the public's interest toward the free flow of information to the police, versus the defendant's right to prepare a defense free of bias. Similar to this is a Motion to Examine the Police Officer's Personnel File. The benefit of doing this is one of distraction. If the police officer has reprimands in his or her record for planting evidence, racial prejudice, or excessive force, his or her credibility may be at issue and stands to weaken the prosecution's case. Note: these both will be hard to get without good reason.

## Motion to Suppress Evidence

Evidence obtained illegally cannot be used in a criminal trial; also called exclusionary evidence. And, evidence which was taken as a result of the exclusionary evidence–fruit of the poisonous tree–is also illegal. If the motion to suppress evidence comes through, that generates an evidentiary hearing. The details of the motion will be brought forward, including all charges pertaining to Fourth Amendment grounds of search and seizure and a granting of the motion will undermine the government's case considerably.

## Motion in Limine

Likewise, a Motion in Limine–Latin, meaning "at the very beginning"–means that evidence is inadmissible before the prosecution introduces it at trial. By using this early on in a trial, it prevents the jury from ever hearing it. A critical move, a motion in limine must be timed perfectly, or the judge would have to issue an order to the jurors to "disregard" the evidence as stated. If I said the evidence involved a "white bear," do you know how difficult it would be to forget the white bear? For example, say two boys were being tried for killing their parents, they may want evidence of their spending spree after the deaths to be excluded. Another point, this motion action may trigger another legal brief called a Memorandum of Points and Authorities, or, a document that describes the legal basis for a request.

## Motion to Suppress Confessions, Admissions, or Other Statements Made to Police

Since the accused is constitutionally protected from giving involuntary confessions, the way to bring that forward for determination is to file the motion to suppress. A number of related questions can arise as the

result of this seeking such as whether the confession was obtained in violation of Miranda rules or under self-incrimination.

## Motion to Suppress a Pretrial Identification of the Accused

If, during a lineup or showup the process was impressively suggestive to a witness, it would violate due process standards and this motion would be used to generate an inquiry into the practices of police during pretrial identifications.

## Motion to Sequester Witnesses

The defense can request that witnesses be physically barred from the courtroom. They must sit outside and cannot hear another witness's testimony until it's their turn to testify. The reasoning here is that the prosecution witnesses will not have the benefit of hearing anybody else's words and at the very least, it will frustrate or irritate them. They will surely not be influenced by what others say. They can be kept out from all phases of the trial such as jury selection, arguments of the counsel, and other witness examinations.

## Stipulations

The term *corpus delicti* is Latin for "the body of the crime" and means the prosecution must show a crime is committed before going further. Often this phraseology is used incorrectly, making people think that in order to charge murder, the corpus delicti has to do with the body of the victim, when, in fact, murder cases have been won without a corpse. It's rare, but it has happened.

The corpus delicti or basic elements of the crime may be stipulated. Stipulations are a kind of shorthand. A stipulation is a fact agreed upon by both sides, and accepted by

20. MOTION TO SUPPRESS EVIDENCE.

_____, Defendant, for his motion to suppress evidence states:

1. That the Defendant is charged with the offense of _____.

2. That the is scheduled to be tried on _____, 19____.

3. That the prosecuting attorney plans to introduce evidence, namely [describe evidence], seized in violation of the Defendant's constitutional right to be free from unreasonable searches and seizures under the 4th and 14th Amendments to the United States Constitution [and in violation of Rule _____ of the Arkansas Rules of Criminal Procedure] in that:

[A. The evidence seized was not subject to seizure.

B. The seizure was based on the authority of a search warrant issued _____, 19____, by [issuing judicial officer], and the issuing judicial officer was not authorized to issue warrants.

C. The seizure was based on the authority of a search warrant issue on _____, 19____, by [issuing judicial officer], and on the record before the issuing judicial officer, there was no reasonable cause to believe that the search would discover the individual or things specified in the application for the search warrant.

D. The seizure was based on the authority of a search warrant issued on _____, 19____, by [issuing judicial officer], and the warrant was invalid for failure to describe with sufficient particularly the place to be searched or the persons or things to be seized.

E. The seizure was based on the authority of a search warrant issued on _____, 19____, by [issuing judicial officer], and the warrant was executed on _____, 19____, at approximately [time of day], a time not authorized therein.

F. The seizure was based on the authority of a search warrant issued on_____, 19____, by [issuing judicial officer], and the scope of the search by which the things seized were discovered exceeded that authorized by the warrant.

G. The seizure was based on the authority of an arrest of Defendant on or about _____, 19____, and the arrest was invalid.

H. The seizure was based on the authority of an arrest of Defendant on or about _____, 19____, and the search by which the things seized were discovered, or the seizure, was not authorized.

I. The seizure was based on the consent of _____, and the consent was not voluntary.

J. The seizure was based on the consent of _____, and such person was not authorized to give consent.

K. The seizure was based on consent, and a warning required prior to such consent was not given.

L. The seizure was based on consent, and the scope of the search by which the things seized were discovered exceeded the scope of the consent.

WHEREFORE, the Defendant, _____, prays that the Court grant his motion to suppress the evidence.

Respectfully submitted,

By _____
Attorney for Defendant

**NOTE**
See Rule 16.2 and Comment thereto, Arkansas Rules of Criminal Procedure.

Structure 13.

the jury without further proof. For example, if the prosecution called the medical examiner in to testify, the judge would stipulate that the M.E. was, indeed, an expert on death and the cause of death.

## OTHER DEFENSE STRATEGIES

In addition to hiring a private investigator, taking depositions of prosecution witnesses, and developing a plan of action, the defense has the option of bringing in his or her own scientific experts to review the work of forensic lab technicians and others. The costs associated with expert witness testimony is prohibitive, meaning it may be very expensive and out of the reach of those with moderate incomes. Keep this in mind. A defendant may be forced into doing his or her own photography (of the crime scene); his or her own documentation (gathering records or other court documents), and finding a safety net (either someone to substantiate an alibi or others interested in justice) in order to save his or her own skin.

### Alibi Defense

This is a classic practice, consisting of evidence the defense was somewhere other than the scene of the crime at the time it was committed. Although subject to a poor connotation—jurors may be loathe to accept an alibi—it is a viable reason for innocence and, with corroboration—someone to affirm the alibi—the best piece of evidence possible. If there is no corroborating testimony possible, the prosecution has the burden of proving that the defendant was at the scene at the time of the crime as suggested.

## Character Witnesses

Putting a character witness forward to testify to the strengths, disposition, and positive traits of the defendant may backfire instead of help the case. Evidence rules allows that witnesses can be attacked as to their credibility, past misdeeds, or honesty. Because of this cross-examination right, a witness testifying for the defense must be of truly exemplary character. Note: Due to the sharp increase in sexual crimes, assaults, and molestation against children, many states have enacted legislature that mandates new character evidence. The new rule gives prosecutors the right to offer proof that defendants charged with sexual crimes have committed previous sexual infractions.

## Hypnotically Enhanced Testimony

Hypnotically enhanced testimony is an area of expert testimony that has yet to gain credibility and its admissibility in court in questionable. An early 1980s Maryland court admitted such evidence, and a later California Supreme Court did not. The Utah Supreme Court once published an exhaustive opinion and took a look at that overall status of the law at the time, but decided that any testimony regarding anything recalled from the time of a hypnotic session forward, is inadmissible as evidence.

Around the same time, the United States Supreme Court qualified their position and held that to exclude hypnotically enhanced testimony when it pertained to a defendant testifying about his or her own posthypnotic recall violated his or her constitutional right.[5] Most of the other courts have now taken this position.

---

5. *Rock v. Arkansas*, 483 U.S. 44, 107 S.Ct. 2704, 97 L.Ed.2d 37 (1987).

## SOME FUNDAMENTAL RIGHTS OF DEFENSE TRIALS

- It is up to the state to convince a judge or jury that the defendant is guilty. This is tied into the concept of "burden of proof."
- The prosecution has to prove the elements of the crime to meet its burden of proof. Look to the statute to find the elements. For example: A robbery is: 1) entering a 2) dwelling or structure, 3) belonging to another 4) without permission, 5) with the intent to commit a crime. Those are the elements.
- The strength of the proof must be "beyond a reasonable doubt." This has no definitive wording–it simply means that the jurors must be convinced of guilt to a "moral certainty."
- The defense does have to prove a notion called "affirmative defenses." For example, if the lawyer claims the defendant is not guilty by reason of insanity, he or she may have to have statements from doctors or evidence of unstableness.
- An innocent defendant runs the risk of hurting his or her case if he or she testifies on his or her own behalf, but he or she does have the right. Some commons reasons against testifying are: the jury may not like the defendant's demeanor; on cross-examination the defendant is sworn to tell the truth; it opens up the possibility to show something in the defendant's past; it gives the jurors an opportunity to weigh the prosecution's story against the defendant's story.
- The defense is allowed to cross-examine the prosecution's witnesses.
- A trial cannot usually be tried in the absence of the defendant. If they voluntarily fail to show up, the case may move forward "in absentia."

- Judges can prevent the media from televising a trial.
- Every jurisdiction has statutes that specify time limits for moving cases from the charge stage to trial.
- The defendant has a right to know the evidence against him or her.

## INEFFECTIVE LAWYERS

Under the Sixth Amendment, a claim can be made that involves the habeas review of certain claims that there was ineffective assistance of counsel. It is a fundamental right given to criminal defendants that they should receive counsel which assures them a fair defense throughout the trial procedure, and represents for them, a legitimate player in the adversarial process. The lawyer must show a deficient performance, with prejudice, and adhere to a strict test, often called the *Strickland*[6] review, which for Strickland, was about effectiveness standards applied at capital sentencing. The elements of competence in Strickland are that effective representation should entail both a reasonably thorough investigation, and a reasonably competent presentation of the defendant's case. Some examples of incompetence follow.

## What Are Ineffective Lawyers?

- When a lawyer **fails to prepare** such as, contact witnesses, interview the primary witnesses, and other required paperwork but they also must have prejudice. In this instance, prejudice would mean that this failure to prepare caused a significant problem for the case.
- If the defense counsel was **appointed late**, with prejudice. For example, a

---

6. *Strickland v. Washington*, 466 U.S. 668, 104 S.Ct. 2052, 80 L.Ed.2d 674 (1984).

lawyer coming onto the case at the last minute, perhaps while already at trial, would not be able to prepare adequate defense or a cogent closing argument.

- If there is evidence of a **material misrepresentation** by a lawyer which "induces a guilty plea." For example, say an attorney solicits a guilty plea in order to clear his or her caseload; however, to be merely disappointed or hoping for an expectation of leniency is not ineffective assistance. Simple disappointment with the outcome doesn't qualify.
- **Conflict of interest.** Defendant is entitled to automatic reversal, if, for instance, the defense counsel shows favoritism. Suppose there are two defendants tried for the same case, and the attorney services the second client over the needs of the other.
- **Failure to know** the law, with prejudice. When a lawyer would take on a case out of his or her level of expertise that results in a gross neglect of the knowledge required to represent the case.
- **Lack of experience** or youthfulness of counsel is another reason for an ineffective lawyer claim. The defendant would have to show examples of gross negligence and prejudice.

## Contempt

We mention contempt here because people who are accused of a crime have a tendency not only to mistrust the system, but to rail against it by speaking out. The offender of the court is called a contemnor and it is a crime. The power to punish persons whose conduct interferes with the orderly functions of the court or the administration of justice (say, acting boisterous during a hearing), embarrassing the court, or degrading a judicial officer is punishable under contempt.

Criminal contempt has two different classifications: it's either direct or indirect. *Direct contempt* is disrespectful behavior that takes place in the courts. An interruption or any hindering of proceedings are consider contemptuous.

The *indirect contempt* order, sometimes called *constructive contempt*, are comprised of acts that take place outside the courtroom but that serve to either denigrate the court or ignore their instructions. For example, if a juror were instructed to avoid the media and he or she decides to speak out on television, he or she is intentionally committing indirect contempt.

## REVIEW QUESTIONS AND ANSWERS

### *Key Words to Define*

- **ABA**–The American Bar Association; organization for professional lawyers, sets ethics.
- **Adversarial judicial proceedings**– Time marked by the appearance of a prosecutor and judge; such as with filing a charging complaint, including arraignment and other appearances.
- **Alibi**–Evidence that defendant was somewhere else at the time of the crime.
- **Attenuation**–"Proximate cause" means that death is a natural, continuous chain; also "legal causation" meaning that death was foreseeable.
- **Corpus delicti**–Latin for "the body of the crime"; prosecutor must show a crime was committed; sometimes confused as a body in a crime, not so.
- **Contempt**–The power to punish persons who interfere with the orderly functions of the court.

- **Defense counsel**–The attorney for the defendant.
- **Depositions**–Formal statements for interviewing prosecution's witnesses; compulsory process request.
- **Material misrepresentation**–Lawyer induces a guilty plea in order to clear caseload or hoping for leniency, and is not ineffective counsel.
- **Motion for Bill of Particulars**–Used in order to learn the basis of the formal charge the defendant faces; helps for defense strategy.
- **Motion for Continuance**–A document to formally request a delay on the proceedings; postpone motion.
- **Motion for Discovery**–Document and written request for the prosecution to turn over anything they have collected in the way of evidence, statements.
- **Motion in Limine**–"At the very beginning" in Latin; Evidence is inadmissible before the prosecution introduces it at trial.
- **Motion to Strike a Prior Conviction**–Defendant with a prior record requests that prior record to be disregarded.
- **Motion to Suppress**–Document used to pull information out of the trial such as confessions, admissions made to police, or even line-up proceedings.
- **Per se**–Means "by itself"; Due process clause on the right to counsel at the first appeal after a criminal conviction.
- **Plea bargain**–Mutual concession; guilty plea as the result of the prosecution and defense striking a deal.
- **Stipulation**–A fact agreed upon by both sides and accepted by the jury without further proof.
- **Subpoena Duces Tecum**–To compel uncooperative people to present records, documents or other objects.
- **Transcript**–A document of everything said in court.
- **Writ of habeas corpus**–Literally means, "to bring the body forth" and is a petition sent to the court to seek legal remedy for an illegal arrest.

## *Questions for Review and Discussion*

1. *Question:* List all six of the defendant's pretrial rights. *Answer:* (1) To be informed of charges, (2) To remain silent, (3) Writ of habeas corpus, (4) Prompt arraignment, (5) Benefit of legal counsel, and (6) Reasonable bail.

2. *Question:* For the defense lawyer, what is the first premise he should operate under? *Answer:* A defendant is not guilty until a jury says so.

3. *Question:* Is it wise for the defense to tell his side of the story? *Answer:* No. That leaves him open to questioning; cross-examination; and juries may not accept his version.

4. *Question:* Name just three of the many defense counsel functions. *Answer:* (1) Represent the accused immediately after trial to provide advice and continue safeguards and ensure constitutional rights for his client, (2) Review police reports and conduct further investigation, (3) Interview the police, the accused and any other witnesses, more found on list on page 218.

5. *Question:* Private criminal attorneys will typically charge a client by _____ _____. *Answer:* Billable hours or by the case.

6. *Question:* Why is extra time good for the defense? *Answer:* Witnesses forget, more time to investigate, allows time to establish a better course, allows for a change in appearance and behavior preparation.

7. *Question:* What is the defense's biggest gain from a prelim? *Answer:* Ability to know the prosecution's evidence.

8. *Question:* Defendant competency is what? *Answer:* A defendant's sanity with regard to proceeding toward a trial and at trial.

9. *Question:* Explain the three-step motion process. *Answer:* (1) Defense attorney gives notice of a prepared notice called Notice of Motion, gives one to court, one to prosecutor; (2) Hearing of the motion, each party can present oral arguments and judge decides to support or deny it, (3) The judge may also take no immediate ruling until later.

10. *Question:* Name four fundamental rights of defendant trials. *Answer:* List on page ???; (1) Burden of proof, (2) Prosecution must prove all elements of the crime, (3) Beyond a reasonable doubt, (4) Affirmative defense options, (5) Does not have to testify, (6) Defense attorney may cross-examine all witnesses, (7) Usually a trial must have the defendant present, (8) Media can be barred from courtroom, (9) Time limits for any stage to trial, and (10) Defendant right to know evidence against him.

## *Essay Exploration*

Pick one motion from pages 254, 259, 260-261, and 263-267 and explain it in-depth.

# Chapter 14

# ANATOMY OF A TRIAL

For who can be secure of private right,
If sovereign sway may be dissolved by might?
Nor is the people's judgement always true:
The most may err as grossly as the few.
　　　　　–John Dryden, *Absalom and Achitophel*

Everything has been building up to this point. All the information presented previously will come together at this junction. The criminal justice system, consisting of three parts–police, courts, and corrections–is decided upon in court, heard under this tribunal. The findings made here will alter significantly what happens for each component and the people involved in criminal conduct: law enforcement, the victim, witnesses, the jurors, counsel, and the defendant.

The authority given over to the courts is established by legal limits called jurisdiction. Jurisdiction then, is competent standardized local, state, or federal law, invested with the power to punish, try and sentence the accused for the crime committed. You are summoned to court. Here you will see the legal machinations of the adversarial process. Here is where the drama of decisions and testimony can change a life forever.

## State Jurisdiction Is What Exactly?

The United States has a dual court system. There are state courts and federal courts. We'd like to make things easy and tell you about the standard state court system, but there is no generic court system in the United States. Even the name designation varies. While Supreme Courts are usually thought of as the courts of last resort, in New York the name "supreme" is assigned to the main trial court, while their N.Y. Court of Appeals is the real state's court of last resort.

To begin, we'll start with the state court system and a simplified three-part hierarchy to help explain jurisdiction. First, there are courts with limited jurisdiction sometimes called municipal court, small claims court, traffic court, and justice of the peace. These lower courts have the least amount of power. Most often misdemeanors will show up here rather than felony cases. Sentences are typically less than one year in jail, plus a fine of not more than one thousand dollars.

Because of its limitations, no exact records of the proceedings are needed. These courts can also include family court, probate court, and juvenile court. There is no trial process at this level and there exists an informality in proceedings not seen in the higher courts. It was once common practice to appoint magistrates with no formal training and little judicial attitude. Typically the police report acts as the prosecutor, and the accused defend themselves. Speed is the watchword.

The next level holds courts of general jurisdiction or the primary venue for trial courts in the criminal justice system. Sometimes called circuit court, district court, state court, or county court, these courts have the power to try and conclude major criminal cases. This is the original jurisdiction for felonies, and also serves as a court appellate jurisdiction for misdemeanor convictions that have been adjudicated in the lower, limited court.

And last there are the courts of appellate jurisdictions. Sometimes called superior court, appellate court, district court of appeals, or state supreme court. These are the appeals courts in the United States. They deal specifically with questions of law arising from the trials and handle appeals coming from the courts of general jurisdiction. In other words, they answer questions about constitutional or legal violations.

## TYPES OF STATE COURTS

### Lower Courts

Starting at the bottom and working up, the lower courts are ones with limited and special jurisdiction. Numbering over thirteen thousand, they handle all minor criminal offenses—also called petty crimes or misdemeanors, such as traffic offenses; drunk driving; petty theft; and violation of community, county, and city ordinances.

### Trial Courts

Because each state has its own independent judicial system, it can be tidy and streamlined or extremely complex according to its state constitutional structure. One thing is certain, however, these state trial courts handled more than 90 percent of the criminal prosecutions in the United States. Being a court of general jurisdiction, they are the lowest courts of record at the state level.

Some systems within larger communities provide for separate criminal and civil divi-

Figure 15. The Garland County Courthouse in Hot Springs, Arkansas is referred to as a "circuit court."

sions. A few have chancery or equity tribunals specifically for estate or property dispositions called probate, and others have domestic relations courts. Only important civil litigation shows up here, and persons accused of crimes governed by a *de novo* trial–crimes heard and tried for the first time–answer for their deeds here, and, if an appeal is possible, it will be bumped up to a higher court for a hearing.

Occasionally, these trial courts may serve as appellate courts for cases that started out in courts of limited jurisdiction, usually civil in nature.

## Intermediate Appellate Courts

These types of courts often undertake a review of the case presented by using a panel of three or more judges. The facts of the case are not in question, they are looking for judicial error. Since an appellate court cannot typically reverse the factual findings of the trial court, they are working from transcripts and oral arguments. Usually, if an immediate appellate court refuses to hear an appeal, the court's ruling is the same as upholding the lower court's decision.

The intermediate appellate court is a more contemporary institution and has locations in thirty-six states, providing relief for overburdened state supreme courts and acting as the court of last resort for a majority of appeals that come up from the courts of original jurisdiction. Other state appellate courts travel *en banc*, meaning, all the judges of an appellate court come together–at various locations, to hear oral arguments in a case.

## Courts of Last Resort

Each state has an appellate judiciary court and it is commonly called the state court of appeals, or sometimes is referred to as the _____ (fill in the state) Supreme Court of

Appeals. It represents the final authority in issues involving state law. In almost every state the court is established through the state constitution, and its judges are most often elected. A deep background of law and law practice is one of stipulations for a candidate of judge. As a comparison, the state court of appeals is similar to the way the United States Supreme Court relates to lower federal courts. In states such as Mississippi, though, who does not have an intermediate appellate division, they are not allowed to choose which cases they decide to hear.

Following a loss at the state supreme court level, the only other alternative to going on is to get a hearing from the United States Supreme Court. Usually only those cases involving constitutional law go forward. It is a difficult weeding out process, and fewer and fewer appellate court cases reach the U.S. Supreme Court every year.

## FEDERAL COURT HIERARCHY

The difference between federal courts and state courts is in what they are allowed to hear. Federal courts deal primarily with federal laws or laws made by the Senate which govern all the country and were established under legislative powers expressly granted to it by the United States Constitution. Since the Bill of Rights guarantees certain liberties for its people, any violations against those rights are a concern for the federal courts.

A four-tier federal system has the U.S. magistrates at the bottom, followed by the district courts, then the U.S. court of appeals, and finally, the U.S. Supreme Court at the top. The federal system also includes military law for their armed forces, and has exclusive jurisdiction over other federal affairs such as the federal banking system

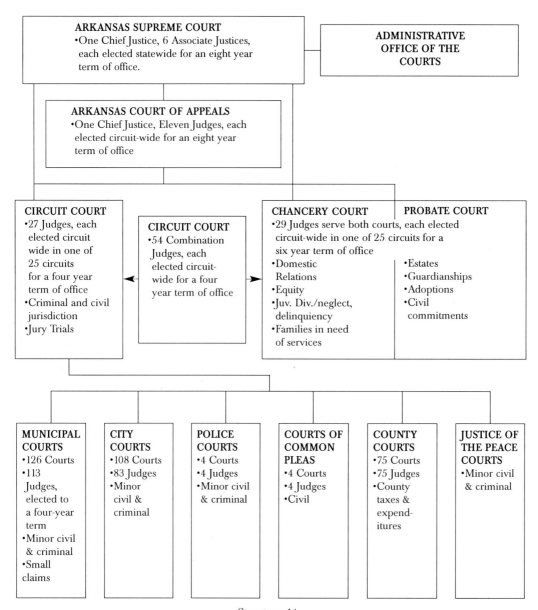

Structure 14.

and the Bureau of Printing and Engraving, the U.S. Postal Service, international trade, and any crimes committed on federal or tribal grounds, sometimes called territorial courts.

## U.S. Magistrates

Not actually a court system, U.S. magistrates, formerly called U.S. commissioners, are federal judges who assist the district courts and handle duties such as hearing misdemeanors, setting bail for more serious offenses, reviewing civil rights petitions and issuing search and arrest warrants.

## U.S. District Courts

Created first by the Federal Judiciary Act passed by Congress on September 24, 1789, today there are more than ninety district courts. These are tribunals of original jurisdiction and the U.S. District Courts typically try noncriminal, or civil cases under federal law. Some examples of these are: patent rights, copyright violations, postal problems, bankruptcy, and those crimes prohibited by Congress and punishable by the federal government.

Each state has at least one territorial district to delineate the district court boundaries and some larger states have more, for example, Texas and New York have four each. District court judges who are nominated by the president are confirmed by the U.S. Senate and serve for life. Most districts have

at least five judges, and some have up to twenty-four. A single judge conducts the trials in the lower tribunals, except in cases that involve the constitutionality of national or state statutes.

## The U.S. Courts of Appeal

Hovering above the U.S. District Courts and the U.S. Magistrates–federal judges with limited powers such as trying lesser misdemeanors, setting bail for more serious cases, and assisting district courts–are the U.S. Courts of Appeal. Next to them we could group the specialized federal courts, and the U.S. Supreme Court is at the top. Any decision being contested from a district court is handled here. They, like their state counterparts, accept no new evidence. Decisions are based upon the original transcript of the case along with possible oral arguments.

The number of judges authorized to sit in on each district ranges from six to twenty-eight, but normally three adjudicate a case. There are twelve U.S. Courts of Appeal including the District of Columbia, each with a jurisdiction over a particular geographical area called a *judicial circuit.*

## U.S. Supreme Court

The United States Supreme Court is the court of last resort for all courts, and its powers are mandated by the Constitution. In 1996, more than 7,600 individuals and companies went "all the way to the Supreme

---

**FYI**—In recent years, there has been a boom in habeas corpus jurisdiction of U.S. District Courts. Inmates who have been tried, sentenced, and confined in and by state courts are contesting their incarceration by state authorities. This type of postconviction remedy is allowed under federal law. The prisoners must contend that some aspect of their federal rights have been violated.

Court" seeking to overturn a decision made by a lower court. The justices that year agreed to hear only eighty-four cases. The issues ranged from physician-assisted suicide to indecency on the Internet. They are usually issues that will affect large numbers of people. About one-half of these decisions are announced in full-published opinions. For the rest of the unheard cases, the lower court decisions will stand. An important point here: A Supreme Court decision that reverses or overturns a defendant's conviction or sentence does not necessarily free the appellant or impose a lighter penalty. What happens is the Court remands or returns the case to the court of original jurisdiction for a new trial. In those rare instances where the Court allows the defendant to go free, the case is considered to be reversed and rendered.

The justices—there are nine of them to help avoid a tie vote—are appointed by the president and subject to confirmation by the Senate. One of the members is the chief justice. The Supreme Court considers itself a discretionary court and that has been borne out over the years as less and less cases receive hearings. Cases usually proceed to the Supreme Court through a *writ of certiorari*, which is an order sent to the lower courts instructing them to prepare records so the Supreme Court can decide if the law has been correctly applied.

## FEDERAL OR STATE?

Sometimes a person will commit an offense involving both state and federal statutes. A common example of this is if someone assaulted an FBI officer. If the officer was on duty, the federal courts want to punish him. If it was done in the state of Ohio, the state courts may want to charge him with assault and battery as if he were one of their citizens. If the crime is especially heinous, such as was the Rodney King beating, the offenders (in this case police officers) were subject to both courts' charges. Some other federal offenses may be terroristic behavior such as "bombing a federal building," for example, the Oklahoma bombing and its perpetrator, Timothy McVeigh; robbing a bank, which is a federally funded entity; environmental pollution; counterfeiting money; and so on. (The federal system has a separate jurisdiction over the military, as well as on American Indian reservations.)

---

**Other Notes**—To get the inside skinny on how the Supreme Court works, there is a controversial book written by a former Supreme Court law clerk. *Closed Chambers* (1999) by Edward Lazarus, describes infighting among justices and clerks a decade ago and asserts the politicization over certain issues. Lazarus was seen as violating an obligation to keep court matters confidential. David Garrow, a law professor at Emory University in Atlanta read Lazarus's book very carefully and says *Closed Chambers* contains little that was not already available from other books and the late Justice Thurgood Marshall's papers at the Library of Congress.

A far more revealing and excellent book about the Supreme Court and its history is *A People's History of the Supreme Court* by Peter Irons (1999).

## COURTHOUSE AS A SETTING

Even though much of the work completed in courthouses is both solemn and serious, courthouses in large metropolitan areas can be bustling, confusing and noisy. A lot happens out in the halls and many people in the elevator look nervous, tired, and scared.

Often located within a community in the center of town, courthouses can be venerable looking buildings and have pillars, stairs, or large cement blocks holding up their principles. And most every downtown worker will know where it's located.

Once inside will be a reception area, a directory, or guards at the main entrance. Some courthouses have taken measures against violence and disruption and many are equipped with magnetometers or other devices used to detect metal or metal objects on people entering. Occasionally guards will spot-check briefcases of unknown participants and ask to look inside packages or bags. No search warrant is needed for this and judges can request a search of anyone acting suspicious.

In addition to the rooms where trial proceedings are held, there will generally be other courthouse employee offices, holding areas for prisoners, rooms where the press convenes, jury assembly rooms, a law library is possible, and temporary rooms for other court-related activities. The watchwords to entering any room are be observant and nonobtrusive. The spectator area is always behind the prosecution and defense tables somewhere in the gallery. And no one is allowed to enter the gated area often referred to as the "bar" or the area surrounding the judge.

For those who want to study the process or find out what goes on at various proceedings, they should call the courthouse clerk's office to determine the schedule and ask about being a visitor. One note though, check just before you leave for the courthouse; jury members usually have to call in the night before to find out if they are required and things can change rapidly and often.

## The "R" Rulings

Judges make final rulings and, coincidentally, they all begin with the letter "r." For example:

**Remands**–this means a case is returned to its court of original jurisdiction for a retrial; it also means the defendant is returned to custody.

**Reversed** and **rendered**–when the case is reversed and rendered, the defendant goes free. Reverse rulings in two-thirds of cases are due to "rightness" and involve specific issues the court wishes to address; most of the time they involve constitutional questions.

When the Supreme Court reaches a majority decision and rules on a case, its rule becomes precedent that must be honored by all lower courts. The application of precedent in the legal system is a giant wielding of power for the Supreme Court. Their influence helps to shape the everyday operating procedures of the police, corrections departments, and other trial courts.

## COURTROOM PERSONAE

Many different people with different responsibilities serve the courts or are the key players in cases. Briefly, here are their positions:

**Defendant:** the accused. His or her guilt or innocence rests with the criminal justice system, the police, the courts, and corrections. If acquitted, the defendant will go free and may not be tried for the same offense again according to the Fifth Amendment guarantee of double jeopardy. If found guilty, the defendant will lose his or her liberty, and perhaps even his or her life.

**Defense attorney:** a person or group of lawyers who will defend the accused. They make sure the defendant receives a fair trial, and will use all the powers and resources at their disposal to free their client. Those who work with the Public Defender's office often represent indigent clients and face seriously crowded court calendars.

**Prosecuting Attorney:** the person representing the state who brings charges against the defendant. They have much discretion and power in that they can reduce the charges, offer a plea bargain, or pursue prosecution to the full extent of the law. Their office commands much respect.

**Judge:** also called a **magistrate** or **justice**. The judge acts as an impartial referee or arbiter. Judges conduct hearings and make rulings on any pretrial business such as motions. It is up to the judge to decide what evidence will be allowed into court. He or she can confer "expert" status onto those who provide forensic science testimony, and he or she will rule on all questions regarding substantive law and procedure. A judge will also give the jury instructions and answer any questions for them during the proceedings. Judges also sentence defendants in situations absent a jury, often called a bench trial.

**Court clerk:** the court clerk handles all the paperwork and documentation such as, issuing subpoenas, safeguarding evidence, handling business forms and fines, and keeping track of all case records also called case files—file folders with all the pertinent documents needed for public record. They also keep track of the dates and times for trials on a court calendar, sometimes referred to as the "docket." Their office is located conveniently close to the judge's chambers and they answer questions on behalf of His Honor and sometimes handle the judge's court calendar. The handyman for judicial paperwork, the court clerk will maintain the roster of jury members, call roll, and keep track of who has been selected for *voir dire* questioning, and who will get paid for their services. If a defendant fails to show, the clerk may assist the judge in preparing a bench warrant for his or her arrest. Occasionally the clerk will be put in charge of marking, admitting, and controlling evidentiary material.

**Court reporter:** an employee of the court who takes down testimony using a stenotype machine or recorder. Every word is recorded and later transcripts of each day's proceedings become an official record of the trial. Usually there is some type of signal to alert the judge to the fact that testimony may not be heard, or, if two people are speaking at once, the process may need to be slowed or reviewed. Electronic technology has replaced some court reporters with audio or video recordings or computer-generated hook-ups for on-the-spot courtroom monitoring and recording.

**Bailiff:** the court's police officer and peace keeper. The bailiff is responsible for safeguarding all who appear in court, and guards the defendant against escape or misconduct. He or she is also known as the arbiter of etiquette and language. A recent trip to municipal court found the bailiff admonishing a visitor for his watch sounding off every half hour. They can remove anyone they deem disruptive.

The bailiff may also signal the proceedings by issuing the crier's archaic invocation of "Oyez-Oyez-Oyez, All Stand, the Honorable Judge Simon Wheedel for the Court, the proceedings are now in session." The baliff telegraphs to the courtroom attendees that a performance is about to begin and takes the trial across a threshold into consecrated legal space. Later, he or she will also help to shepherd visitors and jurors to where they belong, making sure they do not encroach on the judge's bench or counsel's table. He or she will also respond to any questions and/or responses from the jury room, whether summoned by a buzzer or a knock.

**Court police:** Usually, and often in high-profile cases, there will be additional uniformed and armed police or a peace officer assigned to court duty.

**Jury:** a community composite of registered voters, licensed drivers, or some other such system, who are called in for jury duty on behalf of the state. A jury consists of twelve men and women–along with, usually, two alternates, in case of illness of a principal juror. Jurors promise to listen to the facts and testimony, and then render an impartial and fair decision based on the law's guidelines.

**Witnesses:** those attendees who are sworn in to tell the truth. Witnesses will provide additional information and evidence according to their own knowledge of the events of the case. There are two other types of witnesses: character witnesses who attest to the character of the accused; and expert witnesses who give opinions regarding medical, scientific, or specialized evidence.

**Court interpreter:** these people are language translators whose services depend on court demands. They can be called in on an "as needed" basis to interpret and explain court proceedings, interviews, or any other court-related events, including deciphering language-specific documents.

**Law clerks** or **Research attorneys:** are usually employed by the judge. They may be law students who are waiting to take the bar exam, paralegals, or full-time licensed attorneys providing a service. Often they review motions, pleadings, and help to prepare paperwork submitted to the court for review. If further research or precedents need looking up, the law clerk is at the ready.

**Clerk of the Court:** a behind-the-scenes employee who works under the direction of the judge to handle administrative duties in regard to courtroom function. He or she will hire and prepare reports on personnel, coordinate caseloads, and help with accounting.

**Jury commissioner:** may be appointed by the judge to oversee all duties required as a result of putting together a jury, compiling jury lists and rosters, reviewing requests for postponement from potential jury candidates, and keeping the registers full by issuing jury duty summons and managing the daily operations needed to handle jury availability, and other requests.

## *The Basic Trial Rights of Criminal Defendants as They Pass Through the Criminal Justice System*

- Speedy and public trial before a judge or jury
- Impartial jury selection
- Trial venue must be free of prejudice, fear, and outside interference
- No compulsory self-incrimination
- Adequate counsel
- No cruel and unusual punishment
- Ability to appeal convictions
- No double jeopardy

## THE COURT

*"All rise. The Honorable Judge Simon Wheedel presiding," the sober-looking court bailiff recited. The buttonholes in his khaki shirt were spread open like smiles, fighting to hold back a midriff that looked like a roasting wiener splitting its casing on a hot grill. He was wearing a gun that'd make any little kid's eyes pop open with keen anticipation; a personal-sized cannon wrapped in a black leather holster.*

*The judge opened the door to the usual fanfare: everyone in the courtroom was jostled out of their stupor, out of their seats, and onto their feet in homage. Then Judge Wheedel swept in wearing a stereotypical flow of black Antron nylon like an aging Zorro, sans mask. The Justice has flyaway, thinning, red curly hair if there were such a combination, and when he applied pince-nez glasses on his nose behind a prodigious hump, his countenance was severe.*

*I was fixed on the court reporter to the judge's left, my right. She was a big-boned girl, blond, with full pink lips that came to rounded points like rose hips with the little dips in them. Soon those lips were hidden behind the cone of silence. As the proceedings go on, the court reporter dictates a word-for-word account of everything uttered, by anyone, into this soft mask. It's connected to machinery with a cord like a curly umbilical, and the private receiver that envelops her mouth is contoured to fit over the lay of the cheeks. I'm not sure if the tape gets transcribed later or what happens if she has germs from a terrible cold? But once the drama starts, you never so much as see a tooth from her again.*

## Court Proceedings

This hypothetical court scene describes what, for many of us, is an unknown alternate world. In legal vernacular a court is the location where a trial is held, but it can also mean the body holding the trial, and the presiding judge. That is precisely why people

often say that "the court is handing down a decision."

It is important for the accused to know what type of court he or she will be tried in, what the parameters of the court's power are, and what the charges are. The charges will be written out in a document called the "complaint." If there have been grand jury proceedings, the charges will be written out in a similar document known as an "indictment." Those accused of a crime have a right to a copy of this complaint or indictment. Even though it may not make much sense or may be embarrassing to hear read aloud, the accused can insist the judge read it at the first appearance and have it explained.

\* \* \*

*"In the matter of the State of Ohio versus Derrick Borehead," the clerk called out, "the charge being one count of murder in the first degree with special circumstances. A plea of not guilty has been entered."*

*"Are we ready?" Judge Wheedel asked, peering over the top of his spectacles from one table to the other.*

*The people at both tables stood up. "Ready for the prosecution, your Honor." Assistant District Attorney Henry Cassin said.*

*"Ready for the defense," attorney Jensen declared. His assistant, a young man with thick hair and generous eyebrows was shaking his head in the affirmative, bobbing his head all round like a fake toy terrier in the rear window of a car.*

*"Good," the judge said, "Let's impanel a jury and get underway."*

## JURY IDEALS

The primary phase of any criminal trial is the selection of a jury. For the accused, now the defendant, it is probably the most important procedure. The right to a trial by jury is a distinctive feature in the system of jurisprudence, dating back more than seven centuries. The English Magna Carta of 1215 contained the stipulation that no freeholder would be deprived of life or property except by judgment of his peers. Article III of the Constitution incorporates this principle with the following statement: "A trial of all crimes except in cases of impeachment shall be by jury." The Sixth Amendment holds that, "in all criminal prosecutions the accused shall enjoy the right to a speedy trial by an impartial jury."

The accused also has a right to dispense with a jury and can request to be tried by a judge alone. These trials are called *bench trials*. Sometimes defendants choose bench trials in the hope that a judge will be subconsciously influenced by information that is technically inadmissible. In some states, defendants must file a request for a jury trial either when they enter a plea, or at some time before the beginning of a court term in which a jury would be impaneled. Failure to file constitutes a waiver of the right. In all criminal matters in which jail is a potential penalty, though, the accused have an absolute right to a jury trial.

## Speak To Me Nice

When addressing the judge, "Your Honor" is the most popular, neutral greeting and the one they most likely want to hear. It is not proper to call him or her "Sir" or "Yes, M'am" but "Your Honor" and they do expect everyone to stand (or sit in the witness box), address the microphone, speak slowly and clearly and not talk unless asked. Any talking over or interrupting is considered disrespectful and, if continued and unbridled, is subject to contempt of court.

## JURY OBJECTIVE

The primary purpose of a jury is to serve as a check against arbitrary or vindictive law enforcement. In *Duncan v. Louisiana* (1968) the U.S. Supreme Court recognized that juries advance the means needed for a fact-finding process: they are selected by law and sworn in to determine matters of fact and, sometimes, matters pertaining to sentencing in a criminal action. But in reality, most often, the judge is both the fact-finder and the person who decides what law to apply to those facts. It is almost unique to the American system that ordinary citizens have the responsibility to decide a criminal defendant's ultimate fate. The judge's power—and the power of precedent or previous law—help in defining the rules of law and the sentencing guidelines, and thus, provide him or her certain amounts of discretionary authority.

It is important for the accused to know what size jury he or she is entitled to. Over the years, jury costs have forced states to limit jury size and in many states a litigant is likely to get a six-person jury if he or she is not charged with a felony. Given the choice,

---

**FYI**—A little known fact called "jury trial penalty" means that sometimes juries impose harsher sentences than a judge might consider rendering. If judges suggest, in an aside or off-the-record conversation, that the defense attorney should opt for a bench trial and save the added time and expense of a trial, the defense should take note of this remark or the client may pay for the ignorance by having time added onto the sentence.

the twelve-person panel would be to the accused's advantage. Since the prosecution needs a unanimous jury to convict, it makes sense that he or she is more likely to find sympathetic individuals within a larger group.

A *venire facias*, also referred to as an *array*, is a writ summoning the jurors to court.

## JURY SELECTION

Out of all the members who received a letter from the county to report for jury duty, a winnowing of numbers must take place. As they report in, the bailiff will take their juror summons—usually an official letter or jury ticket—and check off their names. They will generally be seated together along the back of the courtroom. After they are assembled, the bailiff instructs jurors that there will be no more talking, eating, drinking, or otherwise casual behavior in the court. He calls the court to order and the judge enters and takes his seat at the bench.

To begin the thinning process, members of the venire are sometimes asked questions in open court to determine their general qualifications. If they do not understand and speak English, they may be dismissed. Other reasons for dismissal are problems involving health, poor hearing, or any personal hardship that might keep them from returning. They must be citizens of the state and have never been involved in and convicted of a felony offense. (Certain states will disqualify a convicted felon from jury duty.) In addition, most lawyers and doctors are automatically exempted from the jury in order to continue with the service of their clients and patients, respectively.

Your Honor will introduce him- or herself and thank the civilians for responding to their civic duty call. He will explain that they will be asked questions and they should answer carefully and truthfully so as to find an impartial jury panel. The bailiff administers an oath and the jurors respond, "I will" or "I do."

After reading a short summary of the case, the judge introduces the attorneys, the parties involved—he or she may read a list of the witnesses—and gives a guesstimate as to the length of time expected for the trial. Afterwards, the clerk, who has put all the juror names into a bin, mixes the container and pulls them out much like lottery numbers. When the juror's name is called, he or she marches to the jury box until all members are selected. The attorneys are carefully watching this procession, making note of any outstanding or inconspicuous characteristics or attributes, as much as one can tell from body language, dress, and demeanor.

### Voir Dire

Each side in a case is given a list of the potential jurors. There are perhaps one hundred twenty names on the original call-up list, so an initial examination of them is difficult. A much smaller percentage will be represented in court on the day of the trial through attrition, and nearing the end of the term of service, the numbers will be smaller still. From this pool, fourteen names (twelve jurors and two alternates), will be drawn at random from the attendees. This first batch will undergo a *voir dire* (pronounced VWAR deer) examination by the judge and the attorneys for both sides.

*Voir dire*, French for "to speak truly" is the questioning of the jurors by both opposing attorneys. The process is meant to ferret out those who will, in their administration, act fairly, and remain unbiased beyond any reason. The prosecution and the defense are each allowed a specific number of preemptory challenges, the ability to remove prospective jurors from their duty with no explanation given. They usually work from numbered charts.

There exists a constitutional check on the use of preemptory challenges by the prosecutor. The Supreme Court has upheld the use of preemptory challenges to exclude jurors by reason of racial or other group affiliation in isolated cases.[1] Later, *Swain* was struck down as condoning discrimination against minority groups when they ruled again in a case involving a black defendant named Batson, whose lawyer established a prima facie case of racial discrimination in selection of a petit jury on the basis of a prosecution's use of preemptory challenges.

Jurors can also be removed for "cause"—this occurs when there is some fact that is disclosed which would make the prospective juror unfit to serve. Some common reasons for removal may be: if there is relationship between one of the jurors and a witness; if they are conscientious objectors when it comes to alcohol, religion, or guns, which would render a prejudice; or if the potential juror is a member of a specific race or ethnic group of which someone involved is a member.

## Death Qualification

In cases involving a capital offense such as murder, jurors are often subjected to complex questions about their attitudes toward the death penalty. A juror who could never vote to put a defendant to death is likely to be excused for cause, as is one who would always vote for death for any defendant convicted of murder. People generally have very definite feelings about the death penalty, and the absence of moral or religious convictions in favor or against, plus an open mind is essential.

Some typical questions that a defense lawyer might ask a jury member are: Do you recognize the defendant or have you ever had any business dealings with the defendant? Is anyone in your family affiliated with the court, law enforcement, or a member of the Bar Association? Have you read the publicity associated with this case? Can you follow the judge's instructions to remain fair and impartial in this case? Do you have any strong feelings about the defendant or the explanation of the case thus far? Etc.

The jury, when in session, will sit in a specially provided jury box located within short walking distance to the witness box—so as to better hear the testimony, usually to the left of the judge—and the judge's bench. No one goes near the bench, including attorneys, unless asked to come forward or to "approach the bench."

## Juror Opposes Death Sentencing

On the morning of February 14, 1978, a gift shop-service station in Camden, Arkansas, was robbed, and Evelyn Boughton, the owner, was shot and killed. Ardia McCree was later arrested in Hot Springs, Arkansas, after a police officer saw him driving a maroon and white Lincoln Continental matching an eyewitness' description of the getaway car. McCree admitted to police that he had been at Boughton's shop at the time of the murder. He claimed, however, that a tall black stranger wearing an overcoat asked him for a ride, took a rifle out of the back of the car and used it to kill Boughton. McCree also said that, after the murder, the stranger rode with McCree to a nearby dirt road, got out of the car, and walked away with the rifle. Two eyewitnesses who saw McCree's car at the time of the murder contradicted his story and said they saw only

---

1. *Swain v. Alabama*, 380 U.S. 202, 85 S.Ct. 824, 13 L.Ed.2d 759 (1965).

one person in the car. Police found McCree's rifle and a bank bag from Boughton's shop alongside the dirt road. Based on ballistics tests, an FBI officer testified that the bullet that killed Boughton had been fired from McCree's rifle.

McCree was charged with capital felony murder[2], convicted and sentenced to life without parole. Because the State originally sought the death penalty, eight prospective jurors were excluded from McCree's jury because they revealed they would not impose the death penalty under any circumstances. McCree sought a writ of habeas corpus from the federal district court. He argued that social science data proved that the death-qualified jury that convicted him was *conviction prone*, in violation of his constitutional rights. The district court granted the petition and ordered the State to retry McCree. The Eighth Circuit Court of Appeals affirmed, spending several pages of the opinion reviewing the social science literature and the testimony of the expert psychological witnesses from the habeas hearing.

The Supreme Court granted review. The question became: during a capital trial does the Constitution prohibit the removal of prospective jurors whose opposition to the death penalty is so strong that it would prevent or substantially impair the performance of their duties at the sentencing phase of the trial?

The Court[3] found that excluding people who are unwilling under any circumstances to impose the death penalty during sentencing did not violate a defendant's Sixth and Fourteenth Amendment rights. Justice Rehnquist argued that the state has a legitimate interest to impanel jurors who "can properly and impartially apply the law to the

facts of the case at both the guilt and sentencing phases of a capital trial." As long as a jury is selected from a fair cross-section of the community, is impartial, and can properly apply the law to a case's circumstances, then a defendant's constitutional right to a fair trial is protected.

## Teen Killer's Executions Weighed

In 1993 in Missouri, Christopher Simmons, 17, concocted a plan to murder Shirley Crook, bringing two younger friends, Charles Benjamin and John Tessmer, into the plot. They were to commit burglary, and then murder—by tying up a victim, and tossing them off a bridge. The three met in the middle of the night but Tessmer dropped out. Simmons and Benjamin broke into Mrs. Crook's home, bound her hands and covered her eyes, drove her to a state park and threw her off a bridge.

At trial, the evidence against Simmons was overwhelming. He confessed to the murder, performed a videotaped reenactment at the crime scene; and testimony from Tessmer against Simmons showed premeditation and that he had later bragged about the crime.

The jury returned a guilty verdict. Even considering mitigating factors: no prior criminal history, sympathy from Simmons' family, and most significantly for a later appeal— his age, the jury nonetheless recommended a death sentence, which the trial court imposed.

Simmons first moved for the trial court to set aside the conviction and sentence, citing, in part, ineffective assistance of counsel. His age, and thus impulsiveness, along with a troubled background were brought up as issues that Simmon's claimed should have

---

2. Ark.Stat.Ann. § 41-1501(1)(a) (1977).
3. Lockhart v. McCree 476 U.S. 162 (1986)

been raised at the sentencing phase. The trial court rejected the motion, and Simmons appealed.

The case worked its way up the court system, continuing to uphold the death sentence. Then, in 2002, the Missouri Supreme Court stayed Simmon's execution in light of a U.S. Supreme Court ruling, *Atkins v. Virginia*[4], which overturned the death penalty for the mentally retarded. Simmons filed a new petition for state post conviction relief, and the Missouri Supreme Court concluded that "a national consensus has developed against the execution of juvenile offenders" and sentenced Simmons to life imprisonment without parole.

The State of Missouri appealed the decision to the U.S. Supreme Court, which agreed to hear the case. On appeal to the Supreme Court[5], the government argued that allowing a state court to overturn a Supreme Court decision by looking at "evolving standards" would be dangerous, because state courts could just as easily decide that executions prohibited by the Supreme Court (such as the execution of the mentally ill in *Atkins v. Virginia*) were now permissible due to a change in the beliefs of the American people.

The question then presented: Does the execution of minors violate the prohibition of "cruel and unusual punishment" found in the Eighth Amendment and applied to the states through the incorporation doctrine of the 14th Amendment?

Yes. In a narrow 5-4 opinion the Court ruled that standards of decency have evolved so that executing minors is "cruel and unusual punishment" prohibited by the Eighth Amendment. The majority cited a consensus against the juvenile death penalty

among state legislatures, and its own determination that the death penalty is a disproportionate punishment for minors. Finally the Court pointed to "overwhelming" international opinion against the juvenile death penalty.

According to the Death Penalty Information Center[6] in Washington, D.C., only the USA, Somalia, Iran and Congo permit executions for juvenile's crimes.

## JURY MYTHS ABOUT SELECTION

Since picking a jury may be one of the most important elements of winning a case, many lawyers have both strange and sensible ideas about their choices. Along with intuition, some of their "less studied hunches" can prove ridiculous or even superstitious. A few of the more common juror ideas surrounding jury selection are that older people are more tolerant and, as a consequence, may be indulgent. Females are thought to be hard with sentencing other females, whereas college-educated females under the age of thirty-five are thought to be defendant-favorable. And because most law enforcement employees feel that blacks from inner city developments have built-in prejudice toward cops, many defense attorneys believe that as well. Certain groups are labeled as too intelligent, so writers, editors, and publishers are looked at with caution (thanks!).

Jo-Ellan Dimitrius, a jury consultant who has worked on more than six hundred jury trials including Rodney King, McMartin Preschool and the O.J. Simpson case says, "Each courtroom is a microcosm of life, filled

4. *Atkins v. Virginia*, 536 U.S. 304(2002).
5. *Roper v. Simmons* (03-633) 543 U.S. 551 (2005), S. W. 3d 397.
6. http://web.amnesty.org/library/print/engact500042003

> **Other Notes**—Often jury consultants use what's called "focus groups" in order to see how potential jurors may react if this fact were asked, or if thus and so were true. Very little has been written about this process, and some additional research might net some insightful viewpoints for a legal paper or report.

with anger, nervousness, prejudice, fear, greed, deceit, and every other conceivable human emotion and trait. There, and everywhere, every person reveals his emotions and beliefs in many ways." For an idea of how Dimitrius works, writers can read her book *Reading People: How to Understand People and Predict Their Behavior-Anytime, Anyplace* (1998).

## Swearing In

The jurors have been weedled down to the twelve regulars along with two to four alternates. The judge will ask that they not discuss the case outside of the jurors' room, avoid all media—either reading, listening, or speaking to—and not take it upon themselves to visit or view the crime scene. They will then take an oath to show up, pay attention, and render a verdict based on the evidence presented.

## Grand Jury

Before we leave this information on juries, a few notes about grand juries. A grand jury is made up of a number of private citizens selected either to review or investigate felony cases for terms lasting periods of time. Traditionally, a grand jury consists of twenty-three persons and requires a majority vote to indict. At this time, two-thirds of American states do not use grand juries.

The grand jury system and due process rights generally are recognized as two of the great checks—of the checks and balances principle—charged with protecting private citizens from the dangers of an overzealous

prosecutor and a person's due process rights. In the case, *United States v. Dionisio* the Supreme Court proclaimed that the purpose of the grand jury is to stand between government agents and the suspect as an unbiased evaluator of evidence. Thus, in theory, the grand jury should protect suspects from indictments based on unsubstantiated information presented to it by the prosecutor.

Over the years, a build-up of constitutional restraints have been placed on traditional, crime investigation agencies. As a consequence, there has been an increase in the popularity for using investigative grand juries. In grand jury proceedings the target of the investigation is not afforded the normal due process rights that a criminal suspect receives at the stationhouse because of its very nature—its coercive behavior. For example, in a federal grand jury proceeding, a witness is only allowed to speak with counsel by stepping outside the courtroom.

## Sequestration and Other Notes

Sequestration is used for high-profile cases so as not to allow any tampering with the jurors or their opinions. Based on a judge's decision, the jury and all alternates will be escorted to a hotel, where rooms and meals will be provided, away from any publicity or incoming phone calls.

And since the jurors are supposed to listen very carefully to the evidence as presented by prosecution and defense in court, many trial judges have avoided allowing jurors to take notes. In recent years the notepad rule has changed, however, and the judge does provide notepads and pencils, provided the jurors leave them behind at night before adjourning and returning to home. Often the jurors will be able to ask questions of the judge during deliberation by presenting them to the bailiff for disposition.

## OPENING STATEMENTS

We've come to the trial's beginnings–the centerpiece of this book, if you will–and now you are going to find out what is exactly meant by the term adversarial proceedings.

The jury has been impaneled. The trial opens with a reading of the indictment or information. It is time now for the prosecution to give an opening statement. (Generally the prosecution goes first in most states.) This is the opportunity to present an overview of the case to the jury. He or she will most likely introduce himself or herself again (and any staff accompanying), and, after these niceties, he or she will explain the charges–the major elements of the crime– describe the crime the defendant is alleged to have committed, and point out how the state will prove their case against the defendant "beyond a reasonable doubt." In addition, he or she may mention what witnesses he or she is going to call who will testify for the state, along with what evidence will be presented. One very important point here: what is said during opening statements is not evidence. The prosecutor may say something like, "You will hear the defendant's next door neighbor tell you she saw him enter the house angry on the night in question." Now, if state's witness does not show at a later date, the defense can use that opening statement against the prosecution in the closing argument by saying something like, ". . . and the prosecution failed to deliver the evidence promised by the defendant's neigh-

bor, . . . why is that?" thereby setting up some doubt. This is a very unique game of hint, gesture and verbal communication, and all must be carefully calculated lest the attorneys dig themselves a hole they cannot cover over later.

In the opening statement the prosecution may even explain the rules of evidence somewhat–talk to the jury about foundation evidence, hearsay evidence, and its relevancy–a type of quick-course in court semantics. He or she may also reiterate the judge's instructions, and remind the jury of their duty to deliberate and decide the case based on the evidence–not on emotions, not on the look of the witnesses, not on speculation, but simply, the evidence presented.

By going over these specifics, the prosecution is trying to establish rapport with the jurors, educate them as to the lawful requirements needed for assigning guilt, and make sure they are able to follow the case. In essence, he or she is setting forth a drama, there's a story to tell the jury and the evidence has to be selectively turned into a believable plot. Like a good movie, each scene that the state unfolds will disclose some piece of the story that the audience needs to learn in order to make an effective decision. One thing the prosecution cannot do, however, is to promise evidence it cannot deliver. And, in regard to rules of evidence, he or she may not make references to any evidence he or she knows is inadmissible and may not make reference to the defendant's prior criminal record. (Because remember, everyone is presumed innocent until proven guilty and for the prosecution, that means proven beyond a reasonable doubt–the state's burden of proof.) It is not unusual for the prosecution to describe fully what "beyond a reasonable doubt" means. For example, he or she may say something like, "Reasonable doubt means that the State's account of the crime, supported by testimony and evidence, must convince you that it is the most plausible, the most reasonable recreation of the case involving the murder of _____ on _____ by _____ using _____ in an unlawful manner and with intent (fill in the blanks). That the evidence, witnesses, and artifacts fit the facts and leave no reasonable doubt that the defendant committed the crime. It does not mean "no doubt whatsoever." It does not mean our version must be the only possible scenario because after all, we were not there. A shadow of doubt can always be raised by a skillful defense attorney, perhaps it was all a plot made by the defendant's enemies. Don't allow their story version to cloud the evidence. . . ."

Professional rules of conduct dictate that the prosecutor must not be argumentative in the opening statement, as he or she is just trying to orient the jury to the proceedings, and will make no disparaging remarks against defendant's counsel. Be sure your notes reflect that premise.

Then the prosecution thanks the jurors for their attention, patience, and sits down.

## Defense Counsel Opening Statement

Now the defense counsel is entitled to present an opening statement. He or she may decide to counter what the prosecution has just said, or, at the very least, stop his or her momentum. It is his or her choice. It is typically a good move to get the jurors' minds back to square one by reminding them the defense counsel has another version of the events and that his or her facts will bear out what really happened. He or

she may indicate that the weakness of the state's case will soon come to light, preparing them for another version.

In no state is the defense compelled to make an opening statement however, and he or she may opt out of doing so and decide to make the opening statement at the beginning of the defense's case.

## RULES OF EVIDENCE

We talked about rules of evidence such as real evidence, objects and weapons or documents; testimony, statements from witnesses; direct evidence or the observations of eyewitnesses, and circumstantial evidence or any information that tends to prove or disprove a point at issue–a fact that can be inferred, in other words–but let's go over some other terms so you will be in complete command of the obstacles that must be overcome for evidence to be admissible.

### Hearsay

Hearsay is a statement made by someone not in the courtroom, which is offered up as truth. This type of evidence is inadmissible, because no one is there to be cross-examined so it is one-sided and disallowed. There are exceptions to the hearsay rule, however, such as a dying declaration, a statement concerning people's emotions called an assertion of mind, excited utterances or something said under the stress of excitement, etc.

### Privileged Evidence

Attorney-client privilege are confidential

---

**FYI**—Either side can request that the witnesses be excluded from the opening statements, so that the oration does not affect or influence them.

communications that must be excluded as evidence because it is protecting certain relationships. There are other privileged comments such as what is given between patient and physician, clergy and confessor, and a newspaper journalist and source.

## Foundation

Foundation evidence is what must be secured in order to present something as reliable. For example, for a document to be admissible, the writer of the evidence must be authenticated before it can be used as truth.

## Relevancy

Relevancy has to be evidence that relates in a material way to the fact, for example, it must be something that either proves or disproves a disputed fact and has some real connection. Say, the prosecution wants to prove that Terrell Moore was driving drunk when he hit poor old Mr. Geezer. The state wants to offer up a witness that will testify that Terrell is a member of a street gang. This would not be relevant, unless the prosecution can prove that part of the gang's initiation is to commit a hit-and-run.

## THE WHOLE TRUTH

It would be naïve of us to think that witnesses have not undergone preparation. It is a poor and incompetent attorney who does not take steps to prepare witnesses for what is, what may be, and what may come up. The attorneys will know how to frame their questions in order to elicit the types of response that will most likely help their case. They will not encourage deception, and cannot "tamper" with witnesses, getting them to change their testimony or their particular slant. That is illegal.

When an attorney does prepare his or her witness, however, he or she must be extremely careful what he or she asks for, because the defense attorney can question the witness about what was discussed in preparation. Unlike the privilege between an attorney and his or her client, there is no client-attorney privilege between a witness and the attorneys.

All witnesses will be sworn in to tell the truth on the witness stand. If they have a religious objection to the procedure, they will be asked to affirm their testimony. They will generally raise their right hand, with their left on a Bible (or some variant–Moslems have the Koran, for example) and recite in response to "Do you solemnly swear that the testimony you give as evidence is the truth, the whole truth, and nothing but the truth, so help me God." (Occasionally the words "so help me God" may be omitted; check with your local jurisdiction but the effect is the same.) This is also a legal warning, so to speak, that if the truth is not told, the witnesses will subject themselves to perjury.

## PRESENTATION OF THE STATE'S EVIDENCE

The opening statements are over, and now it's time for the presentation of the state's evidence, also called the "Prosecution's case-in-chief." The first witness has been sworn in and the prosecution begins a presentation of evidence by direct examination. He or she will attempt to prove everything he or she asserted in the opening statement and a wise prosecution will time the most important evidence to come early in the morning when the jurors are fresh and at their most attentive.

Remember, the format for witnesses is very strict. Testimony will only emerge in a question-and-answer format, not unbroken

**FYI**—The Federal Rules of Evidence are flexible on the question of oath, specifying that the witness be required to declare their allegiance to the truth, by oath or affirmation, a process calculated to awaken the witnesses' conscience, duty, and the seriousness of the justice system. The possibility of prosecution is rare, and is not high priority because it is difficult to prove actual knowledge of falsity. In high-profile cases however, prosecutors feel compelled to file charges.

narrative, rambling stories, or opinion. The attorney will generally establish who the witness is, his or her occupation, background, or qualifications (for an "expert" witness usually) and how he or she is involved in the case. After these preliminaries he or she will inquire as to what the witness saw, heard, did, or found, in terms of evidence. Questions typically follow the who, what, where, when variety, excluding the "why" which would be more speculation that fact. He or she is trying to establish the chronological order of events leading up to the crime, or, establish each and every element of the case.

Leading questions–ones that inherently suggest to the witness how he or she should answer–will most likely be objected to, and an example of this would be, "Didn't you hear two shots?" The premise here is that the attorney is not allowed to testify.

## Hostile Witness

If the prosecution calls a witness and he or she is cooperative, only questions by direct examination can be asked. If the defense attorney cross-examines that witness who acts "hostile" toward the defendant–he or she can cross-examine the witness and ask leading questions. And leading questions are so pointed that the questioner does most of the talking during the question, that the witness is subjected to answering "Yes" or "No,"

in response; for example, "You won't deny to this jury that you had just been to the doctor and your eyes were dilated, sensitive to light, and you were more than 100 yards away, would you?"

## Argumentative Questions

Some questions just don't ask for information. These are argumentative questions and are sometimes referred to as "badgering the witness." Derisive questions such as, "You don't expect the jury to believe that do you?" is typical. Defense can either object, or they can turn this around and answer this question in order to induce favorable testimony, such as what might be considered a good rejoinder in reply to the above question, "I am not looking to convince the jury, I am just telling you what happened."

## The ABA Weighs In

The American Bar Association[7] has specific rules of conduct for both the prosecution and defense function, along with published standards. Within this document about prosecution presentation of evidence it states: A prosecutor should not knowingly offer false evidence, whether by documents, tangible evidence, or the testimony of witnesses, or fail to seek withdrawal thereof upon discovery of its falsity. The ABA carries additional requirements as well, stating

---

7. ABA Model Rule of Professional Conduct 3.3 (a)(4); 3.4 (e).

**Caution**—A wise attorney will never ask questions he or she does not know the answers to; because he or she is not prepared to deal with "surprises." The prosecution may then have to ask for a recess, in order to take in what he or she has heard, regroup, and go on to Plan B.

that the prosecutor should not bring inadmissible evidence, ask legally objectionable questions, or make other impermissible comments or arguments. They cannot allow tangible evidence to be displayed that would prejudice fair consideration, unless there is a reasonable basis for its admission in evidence.

The false testimony is clear, and the only exception is if the prosecutor is taken by surprise and someone pulls a fast one—but he or she is still obligated to see that it is corrected and, in certain instances, the courts have granted new trials, despite the prosecutor's ignorance of the false statements.

The inadmissible evidence statement is an interesting one. The ABA believes that the "mere offer of known inadmissible evidence or asking a known improper question may be sufficient to communicate to the trier of fact the very material the rules of evidence are designed to keep from the fact finder." In other words, comments made cavalierly or "off the record" do damage in their airing which cannot be undone. The showing of evidence before it is formally offered for admission is also grounds for trial dismissal (whereas it may have been okay to present that evidence at a later time in good faith). The Bar suggests that an immature or inexperienced lawyer confer with senior members before trying such tactics. To sum it up, anything unduly inflammatory is verboten.

## Expert Testimony

Expert witnesses, people who have special training, education, or experience, give testimony pertaining to their area of expertise whether that be a medical examiner (who will speak of the autopsy), the evidence technician (who may talk about evidence collection), or a forensic lab technician (who could explain DNA and its individual characteristics). In high-profile murder cases, the procession of forensic experts can entail the entire criminalistics community including forensic pathologists, crime scene technicians, fingerprints experts, blood splatter analysts, trace evidence lab technicians who deal with hair and fiber analyses, and firearms specialists, etc. Unlike other testimonials, expert witnesses are supposed to give opinion based on the facts as they know them. They will often refer to published reports, information provided by other witnesses, or their own written reports.

## Offering Exhibits

An integral part of examining witnesses, offering exhibits is an extremely important visual backup to testimony. For what is the talk of a gun without the instrument to look at and how are we even supposed to know that that particular hole was made by a bullet otherwise? How good is a verbal walk through the scene, when a map or diagram could show the logistics so much better, and, better still, that the scene was not contaminated by false evidence? A document might clearly indicate the intent of the offender, or it may wind up as exculpatory evidence if it is a letter of love. Anything, other than words, needs to be offered as an exhibit and this is a four-step process, the ignorance of which, may render the material inadmissible.

The first step is to have the object marked as an exhibit and usually this happens sometime before a trial begins, although sometimes it is done during the trial. A tag or some type of stick-on paper will be attached to the evidence along with an identifying number or marker. (This is another argument for chain-of-command, meaning, knowing who had the evidence before. . . .) Usually the court reporter will attend to this process.

Next, is having the evidence identified. That in turn means asking that the witness identify it. Dialogue would be something along the lines of, "Miss Teaburn, can you identify what has been marked as Exhibit #3?" If the answer is "No" it needs to be asked of another. If the witness says "Yes," then the procedure would be, "Please identify Exhibit #3 for the jury." She may answer, "This is the letter the victim showed me on September 3rd."

The exhibit should then be handed to the opponent along with dialogue for the record such as, "Will the record show I am handing Exhibit #3 to the prosecutor for identification purposes." The opponent is allowed to examine the object and may question the witness about its identification. The next step is to offer it to the Judge by saying, "I offer this into the record as Exhibit #3 Your Honor." If there is no objection, he or she will accept that. If, on the other hand, the opposing counsel has a problem, there will be some objection, perhaps to its relevance and any lengthy arguments will take place out of the presence of the jury.

Only after the exhibit has been marked, identified, shown to opposing counsel and offered up to the judge, will it become an official exhibit. And it is only then that the witness will be given the opportunity to explain it, read from it, or otherwise describe it.

# Defense Motion to Dismiss

Picture this: it's the middle of the trial. Say the prosecution has presented its case-in-chief and rested. The defense can make a Motion For Dismissal, also referred to as a *directed verdict*, and ask the judge to rule on whether the prosecution has provided enough evidence to justify a conviction. If the judge believes the prosecution's case by itself is too weak to support a guilty verdict, the case can be dismissed which in essence is the legal equivalent of an acquittal. The defendant can never be tried for the same crime again. If the motion is denied, the defense proceeds with its case. Since this motion is made out of the jury's presence– they may be sent out of the courtroom–there is nothing to lose even if the judge denies the motion.

These motions are typically based on one of four grounds: the prosecution failed to show that a crime was committed; the prosecutor failed to show that the defendant had anything to do with the commission of the crime; prosecution witness testimony was not credible; and the conduct of the prosecutor was improper.

There is an interesting loophole here, although we must mention that this motion is rarely met because prosecutors will not take a case to trial unless they believe they can win. Nevertheless, when this motion is made, a judge cannot direct a jury to convict the accused. Since the motion to dismiss is brought by the defense who is looking for a directed verdict of not guilty, if the case results in a finding of guilt, it can later be appealed to a higher court. By the judge's refusal to grant the motion, his or her decision can be one of the items for the defense on appeal. On appeal then, the defendant declares the judge did not use proper procedural care in making the decision. In addition, if the judge grants a directed verdict, he or she issues an order finding the defendant not guilty of the charges, but this is not a final decision. This kind of order is an exception to the rule, however, because now the prosecution can appeal a criminal case in which the defendant was acquitted.

## Defense Motion for Mistrial

If the prosecution has done anything that trampled the defendant's rights, the defense attorney can make a motion and ask for a mistrial. What he or she is seeking is a termination of the trial before it reaches a verdict. If the improper conduct cannot be corrected by jury instructions to disregard, or if the act was so prejudicial as to keep them from making a fair verdict, the judge has no choice but to grant the motion and most likely the trial will be rescheduled. This span of time then, serves to help the defendant by increasing the chance that important evidence will be dissolved, lost, or forgotten. The second trial though, does not count as double jeopardy because a verdict was never rendered—an important point.

If the misconduct came from a juror or if the jury is in hopeless deadlock, that is also reason for mistrial. In addition, illness of a judge or the removal of too many jurors because of an accident or flu epidemic or something out of the court's control which would make them short of full count, and a mistrial can result.

## DEFENDANT'S CASE-IN-CHIEF

Similar to the prosecution, the defense calls its own witnesses. The defense attorney must abide by the same rules of conduct, issuing questions in a Q & A format, refraining from leading the witness, and allowing for cross-examination.

## Objections

For an attorney, raising an objection is a delicate pas de deux between himself or herself and the judge. To begin, an attorney will put forth an objection when he or she recognizes that the opposition is about to introduce evidence or testimony that he or she believes the jury should not see or hear; something that may damage his or her client or case. It is up to the judge to decide to sustain—approve or consent to—the objection, or overrule—cancel, undo, or decide against the objection. But the decision to object is fraught with risk just for the very fact that by objecting, the attorney may be drawing the jury's attention to a bit of problematic evidence.

The trial judge on the other hand, needs to rule correctly on the objection, in split-second time, and if his or her ruling is questionable, it may be the basis for appeal. And because everything is a matter of record, attorneys often scour the court record for judgment mistakes made in haste.

## EXAMPLES OF OBJECTIONS AND WHAT THEY MEAN

### *Objection! Question assumes facts not in evidence, Your Honor.*

There is a way to phrase questions that makes it impossible for a witness to respond such as saying, "Most people go blank at the sight of a weapon, still you claim to have been calm when the gunmen entered." This is not a question and the prosecutor is not supposed to testify or assume facts. A savvy defendant's witness could counter the statement posed by saying, "I can't assume to tell you how other people would or wouldn't react to a gun, I can only tell you I wasn't rattled."

## *Objection, Your Honor, that calls for speculation on the part of the witness.*

Similar to the previous statement, an example of this would be: How many people do you think Edmond would have killed?" No one can tell what is in Edmond's mind and it is improper to expect a witness to either.

## *Objection! The prosecutor is misquoting the witness, Your Honor.*

Say a witness claims to be in the lounge drinking a beer when the shooting took place. The prosecutor might counter with, "So you say that you were a little high when the shots were fired."

## *Objection, Your Honor, that is beyond the scope of the direct examination.*

If a witness is being cross-examined and a question comes up that does not relate to the previous testimony, it is out of bounds. Cross-examination is limited to a scrutiny of the direct examination.

## *Objection, no proper foundation has been laid, Judge.*

The opposing attorney uses this objection to force his or her opponent to introduce evidence in its appropriate order. For example, for a gun to be exhibited, some attempt must be made to show that it is the murder weapon or has some relation to the crime before it can be traced to an owner.

## *Objection, asked and answered, Your Honor.*

This is to curb the examining attorney from going after the same point, only in another manner. It is a subtle form of harassment.

## *Objection! Irrelevant.*

The subject matter has slipped and the testimony is uncalled for or not relevant to the discourse (perhaps some event or character issue not specified).

## *Objection, immaterial, Judge.*

Another way of restating the previous objection that something is irrelevant; for example, something immaterial is besides the point.

### Cross-examination

Cross-examination is the process by which a witness has already been called and given testimony under direct examination, and the opposing side gets to re-examine or ask questions about that testimony. For a trial attorney, cross-examination is an essential art. The defense attorney will try to put the prosecution's witnesses on trial themselves. This is his or her opportunity to plant the seeds for an alternative version of the crime; he or she will have to shine here and know when to push, when to stop. One question too many may kill the case. She or he will try to unnerve the witnesses and undermine their credibility. Generally, people will not deliberately lie, but they will follow the lead given by the prosecution attorney. Likewise, the prosecution will try to show inconsistencies between the witness's testimony and will often have the same statements given over to police as reference.

When the defendant asks to testify, he or she is left open for cross-examination and no wily prosecutor will pass up the chance to impeach the defendant (using any prior convictions he or she may have had, pointing up the fact that the defendant has a problem with telling the truth), hammering the defendant as to the motive to commit the crime (suggesting that he or she had bills and ask questions about how he or she needed the insurance money), or will question the defendant's physical ability (such as would he or s he have been able to see a particular person in the yard so late at night).

A sly trick for the defense to ask during cross-examination is: "Have you discussed your testimony with anyone from the prosecutor's office?" Of course, the answer will be "Yes," but for some reason, it sets up the onus of impropriety. Many witnesses think it's wrong to discuss their testimony, so they will stutter, look worried, or attempt to deny it, when it is simply okay. It is not okay to be told what to say, however.

## Rebuttal

After the defense rests (has finished presenting his or her own evidence), the prosecutor has another shot. He or s he can offer rebuttal evidence which is evidence used to attack what has been offered during the defense case. Two important points: prosecutors may not used this as a device to rehash their own case-in-chief, nor are they able to put in new evidence that is unrelated to what the defense has shown.

## Surrebuttal

One last shot for the defense to put on evidence after the prosecution's rebuttal. If the prosecution lays low and does not rebut any testimony or evidence, there will be no surrebuttal.

## CLOSING ARGUMENTS

A famous credo with up-and-coming defense attorneys follows along these lines, "If you've got a good case, hammer the evidence; if you have a weak one, hammer the People's witnesses; and if you have no case at all, hammer the prosecutors.[8]

Closing arguments, also referred to as *summations*, present the prosecutor and defense counsel with an opportunity to convince the jury that the evidence and testimony previously shown supports their theory of the case. Again, the prosecutor goes first in most instances, and argues the burden of proof explanation and the defense will follow with his or her version of events. Certain jurisdictions allow the prosecutor another shot at rebutting defense arguments (lawyers

---

**Other Notes**—The best way for the defense attorney to prepare the defendant for cross-examination requires some role playing, for example, helping the defendant to see what he or she is up against by rehearsing what the prosecutor is likely to ask. The accused can vent and explain things not previously mentioned, which may serve to unearth additional problems.

---

8. Another version of the adage from old trial lawyers is: If the law is against you, pound the facts; if the facts are against you, pound the law; if both the law and facts are against you, pound the table.

should check their particular state's court guidelines). Judges who allow the prosecutor only one argument often allow the prosecutor to choose whether to argue first or second. Typically, though, the defense has the final word–the last chance to articulate clearly his or her defendant's "not guilty" posture.

Even though much emphasis is put on the decision-making process coming before them, some studies show that jurors have already made up their minds before the closing speeches. Just the same, the lawyers will reiterate which law is at question and what the requirements are to convict someone for it; they will remind the jury what was shown and said in testimony; they will evaluate the weight of that evidence and the credibility of the witnesses, and finally, they will make an inference as to how this fits into their version of the case better than opposing counsel's version of the case, which was weak and had holes.

The attorneys may even employ the use of emotional pleas, begging for the jury's mercy on the one hand if for the defendant, begging for justice on behalf of the victim on the other. There is some latitude given over to the defendant if he or she is representing themselves–a pro se defense–and the judge will allow such talk as "The prosecutor said the person who did this was an animal. I am not an animal, I am a human being just like you are."

Some attorneys famous for their elocution may quote from the Bible, Shakespeare, and even current song lyrics in their closing arguments. Others are known for their dramatic oration or emphasis, or their ability to appeal to the common man through parallel stories or experiences. One author describes it as "The reworking of a life in a trial is the lawyer's handiwork."[9]

## Judge's Instructions to the Jury

Both the prosecution and the defense attorney meet with the judge out of court to submit their instructions for the jurors. These instructions typically incorporate the legal theories which are routine and drawn from books of approved jury instructions. Sometimes the instructions are based on appellate court opinions, where the court justices define the crimes or other legal principles, for example, how to best explain "beyond a reasonable doubt." The prosecutor or the defense attorney can also craft their own version if they feel the published versions lack appeal or have shortcomings, or if they want to develop a new instruction for which no pre-approved direction exists.

## CHARGING THE JURY

The judge will create his or her instructions to the jurors, also called *charging the jury*, based on these submissions, in addition to adding in his or her own take on things. Typically the jury instructions will contain:

---

**FYI**—What if the defense realizes during the summations that he or she forgot to offer some important evidence? It happens! The defense attorney can ask the judge to "reopen the case-in-chief." Of course, the evidence must be important and relevant to the case, but it is not out of the realm of possibility that the judge can and will grant such measures as within his or her power to do so.

---

9. *The Trial Lawyer's Art* by Sam Schrager.

- The definition of crime and the elements needed to convict someone of that crime
- The definition of "reasonable doubt" is almost always given as it is usually a sticking point among jurors
- The presumption of innocence principle
- The fact that the burden of proof is on the prosecution
- Factors the jurors should consider when evaluating the credibility of witnesses
- How to select a foreperson, how the deliberations should be conducted, and rules on returning a verdict
- And, if after considering all the evidence, there remains some reasonable doubt as to the defendant's guilt, how he or she must be acquitted.

Sometimes judges will also suggest to jurors that anything said by the attorneys is not evidence (the attorneys are technically never sworn in). And if they find a defendant guilty of murder, they must determine as part of the verdict whether they find it to be of the first or second degree and, possibly, the judge will talk about the unanimous agreement required for a decision.

To avoid confusion, often the court reporter will make copies of the judge's instructions so the jurors have something to refer to during their deliberations.

## Jury Deliberations and Verdict

After the judge has given jurors their instructions, they will retire to the jury room to begin deliberations. Oftentimes they will have been allowed to take notes during the trial as they listen to testimony. The only communication available to them now is between the bailiff and themselves. After getting settled, their first business at hand is to elect a foreperson. The foreperson will usually be given a copy of the judge's printed instructions along with two forms for each

crime charged, one each for the "guilty" or "not guilty" decision.

Coffee and other drinks are available to them and, if necessary, they may break for lunch where meals will be provided, or some other arrangement specified within that jurisdiction. Several stipulations are always the same: they are not allowed to discuss the case outside deliberations, read newspaper articles pertaining to the case, or communicate with nonjurors. In addition, they must not attempt to conduct any investigation or experiments pertaining to the case on their own. They are encouraged to judge the worth of testimony and documentation in the light of their own common sense and experience. Generally the jurors will be allowed to spend their nights at home but, if necessary, they will be sequestered–which usually only happens for high-profile cases–where they be will escorted to dinner and a hotel where they will remain together until a decision is made. The decision to sequester the jury is left to the discretion of the judge.

During the discussions, which is a closed-room environment, they may ask the bailiff to have testimony reread, to view the crime scene, or to look at objects of evidence. Anything they need, even a reiteration or written note to the judge, is provided to them through the bailiff who is sworn to take charge of the jury and their needs. The attorneys of will usually be notified of any communication between the judge and the jurors.

Early on, it is suggested to the jurors that they hold a preliminary secret ballot to determine if they are far apart in thinking, or are close to making a decision. They will write a choice on a slip of paper which will be collected and tallied by the foreperson. It is rare to agree at the first go-round, and discussions about the case and its finer points will take place.

A unanimous verdict–everyone agree-ing–has been a basic requirement of com-mon law since the fourteenth century. The foreperson will notify the bailiff who in turn tells the judge a decision is in. The judge will reconvene court, the attorneys come back, and the jurors enter once again. The foreper-son will speak on behalf of the jury. The result of their decision is handed to the bailiff who will give it to the judge. He or she reads it and hands it back to the bailiff or clerk who presents it to the foreperson for a read-ing. A guilty verdict means the defendant is returned to jail pending sentencing. A not guilty decision will be logged by the court clerk, and the defendant is free to go. Occa-sionally, one or both of the attorneys will ask for a polling of the jury. Each juror will be asked, "Is this your verdict?" or some such question, the reason for this being, to check to see if a juror has been intimidated into his or her decision. In most cases the juror will restate his or her vote and the jury is dis-missed with thanks from the court for their service. If a juror dissents from his or her vote, the judge will dismiss the panel and declare a mistrial.

Sometimes, though, a jury becomes "hung," meaning they cannot agree on a ver-dict. In this instance, a judge will usually encourage them to reconvene and discuss the facts again until they can come to a con-sensus. Jury deliberations are not subject to fixed time limits and the judge will some-times continue to hear other cases. If the jury reports that it is hopelessly deadlocked, the trial judge will declare a mistrial, dismiss these jurors, and new trial proceedings will be scheduled using a new jury, essentially, starting the process all over again. It is at this point that many such cases are resolved by the attorneys and the defendant through some type of plea bargaining.

Juries have been known to disregard the evidence and the judge's instructions on the law and either acquit or convict the defen-dant for a lesser offense than charged. This is referred to as *jury nullification.*

Over the years, juror misconduct has taken many forms such as falling asleep dur-ing testimony, coming into court under the influence of illegal substances or alcohol, lying about their backgrounds or allegiance to get on a jury panel, discussing the case with counsel, talking to a friend about their decision, and conducting independent inves-tigations. Jurors who fail to obey any admo-nition from the judge will be removed from the jury and upon discussion with the attor-neys, may even cause a mistrial. A mistrial is the same as no trial at all and the proceed-ings will begin again at a later time.

## Post-Trial Motion

A convicted defendant frequently files a motion for a new trial. The motion will allege errors committed at trial. Sometimes the judge will rectify mistakes made during the process and award the defendant a new trial. In reality, though, it is a way for the defendant to open the way–a pro forma–to an appeal. At this time the defendant will also seek bail pending appeal. If the trial judge rules against or disposes of these motions, the defendant is up for sentencing next.

## SENTENCING

In misdemeanor convictions, sentences usually occur immediately upon conviction and within the guidelines of the statute. The judge will determine and deliver punish-ment. Nowadays there are many alternatives to incarceration. Community service, mone-tary fines, boot camp, house arrest–using electronic monitoring bracelets–and probation are some of the options versus serving jail time.

## The Presentence Report

In federal courts, as well as in many states, the court is obligated to order a presentence report, sometimes referred to as a presentence investigation (PSI), where the offender is sentenced as a first offender, or is under a certain age. Generally there is a rule that makes the reports available only to the judge, counsel for the state and defense, and any experts appointed to the court in order to assist in sentencing, all within the discretion of the sentencing judge. For those who may be sentenced to death, the Supreme Court requires the release of the presentence report to the defendant.

This document details the defendant's criminal history, details of the offense, medical history, family background, economic status or tax return, education, employment history, and any interviews conducted by probation officers assigned to the court. The interviews most likely will be with the spouse, employer, or any significant other. There also may be copies of court-instructed physical or mental examinations conducted on the defendant over the course of his or her entry into the criminal justice system. The idea is for the judge to have a fuller view of the defendant and his or her circumstances before imposing a sentence.

## Sentencing Guidelines

Looking like a mileage grid that comes with most maps, the sentencing guidelines are supposed to standardize criminal sentences and eliminate factors such as race, age, or socioeconomic level. The grid carries the seriousness of the offense, the degree level written in letters A, B, C class or 1st degree, 2nd degree and so forth, and the dangerousness of the offender, the criminal history or the number of counts, on the other. Chart the left-hand side of the grid with the opposite axis and find where these two figures meet. This number is the one the judge uses to decide the length of the sentence, whether it is probationary or commitment, and is written as the number of months of sentence applicable, low and high. Points are also given for other areas of misbehavior such as prior offenses, DWIs and others, calculated into the total score. Judges do have the authority to deviate from guidelines and impose harsher or lesser sentences when there are factors to justify the change.

## The Long-Awaited Day: Sentencing Hearing

Sentencing is obviously a critical stage in the defendant's life. After the judge has gone over the presentence report, weighed evidence offered by either party in the way of aggravation or mitigation of sentence, in most jurisdictions the convicted offender has a right to address the judge personally before any sentence is imposed. This statement on his or her own behalf is called *allocution* or sometimes called the *right of allocution*. It is simply another way to identify the convicted as persons, and they can plead for mercy, ask for a reduced sentence, a pardon, leniency, explain why they did what they did, or take responsibility for their actions.

## Victim Impact Statements

Victim Impact Statements[10] (VIS) are either written or oral accounts of the effect

---

10. Copyright © 1999 by the National Center for Victims of Crime.

the crime has had on the victim or his family. One of the legacies of thirteenth century English common law,[11] victim impact statements permitted the Crown to stand in the shoes of the victim in English adversarial proceedings. Victims spoke in support of "keeping the King's peace"–and as punishment of the perpetrator replaced restitution to the victim, backing the government's primary objective.

Most commonly used at sentencing today, oral statements give a human side to the cost of crime. It's an explanation about the emotional, physical and financial consequence the victim has faced as a consequence of the crime. For example, Texas law[12] allows victims of kidnapping, sexual assault, aggravated robbery, or any crime in which death or bodily injury occurs to provide victim impact information. Close relatives of deceased victims and guardians of victims can also exercise this privilege.

Not a legal right, the completed statement is given to a victim assistance coordinator–generally someone in the prosecutor's office–and it is seen by a number of people in the criminal justice process. The prosecutor may use information to help present the case at trial. Facts about expenses incurred as a result of the crime gives the prosecutor a better idea about the amount of restitution to request as a part of the sentence.

Sometimes the information is used to start the pre-sentencing document. Community supervision officers–probation officers, prepare these reports. After the defendant's guilt is determined, recommendations for sentencing are forwarded to the judge in a form called a pre-sentencing investigation report. These statements are *not* sent to a jury.

After the sentence has been pronounced, most states allow victims to make an oral statement to the court. The statement will not have an effect on the sentence because the sentence has already been determined. In the case of a plea bargain though, the judge must ask whether a VIS has been returned, and if one has, must consider the statement before accepting the plea.

In Texas, the VIS becomes a formal part of the court record and can be seen by the defendant and his attorney. If the defendant's attorney objects to anything in the VIS, the judge may decide to discuss the statement in court. If the defendant gets probation, the community supervision officer will have access to the VIS. If the defendant is sentenced to state prison, the statement goes with his commitment papers to the department of corrections. When the offender becomes eligible for parole, the statement is one of the items the Board of Pardons and Paroles considers before voting to release him. If the accused is a juvenile, the court may consider the statement to help determine the outcome of the case.

In a recent survey by the National Center for Victims of Crime, over 1,300 victims were asked to rate the importance of various legal rights. Over 80 percent stated that their ability to make a victim impact statement at sentencing and at parole was "very important."

Moments after the judge will give a pronouncement of sentence. Felonies are punishable by fines and prison time. The convicted can be sentenced for a determinate term or an indeterminate term, or a combination. Indeterminate sentencing is pretty much outmoded, it was designed to hold

---

11. Richard E. Laster, *Criminal Restitution: A Survey of its Past History and An Analysis of its Present Usefulness*, 5 U. Rich. L. Rev. 71 (1970).

12. *"IT'S YOUR TURN"* Texas Crime Victim Clearinghouse, Victim Services Division, December 1997. This booklet may be reproduced without written permission.

criminals in custody until the prison authorities determined that he or she was rehabili-
tated, and then the subject was paroled.
Determinate sentencing takes into consideration a variation of the definite sentence,
meaning the judge sets a fixed term of years
within statutory parameters, and the offender is required to serve that term without possibility of parole. You will also run into a
term called *definite sentencing.* The idea here
is to eliminate discretion, and all offenders
who commit the same crimes are punished
equally.

## Mandatory Minimum Sentencing

Legislatures have updated many state's
statutes that compel offenders who have
completed certain crimes to be sentenced to
prison terms for minimum periods. This
means that judges have no option with
which to place offenders on probation. Most
often, mandatory sentences take in heinous
or the most violent crimes, especially those
using firearms. In a similar vein, is the plight
of habitual offenders. These are automatic
increased crimes for persons convicted of
repeated felonies. And a variation of the
habitual offender tenet is the "three strikes
and you're out rule." Persons convicted of a
serious felony or third violent crime would
be incarcerated for twenty-five years to life.
Currently, the federal government and more
than half the states have some form of either
the habitual or three strikes statute.

## Sentencing Questions

Ralph Howard Blakely Jr. married his
wife Yolanda in 1973. He was evidently a difficult man to live with, having been diag-

nosed at various times with psychological
and personality disorders including paranoid
schizophrenia. His wife ultimately filed for
divorce. In 1998, he abducted her from their
orchard home in Grant County, Washington, binding her with duct tape and forcing
her at knifepoint into a wooden box in the
bed of his pickup truck. In the process, he
implored her to dismiss the divorce suit and
related trust proceedings.

When the couple's 13-year-old son
Ralphy returned home from school, Blakely
ordered him to follow in another car, threatening to harm Yolanda with a shotgun if he
did not do so. Ralphy escaped and sought
help when they stopped at a gas station, but
Blakely continued on with Yolanda to a
friend's house in Montana. He was finally
arrested after the friend called the police.

The State[13] charged Blakely with first-
degree kidnapping but a plea agreement,
reduced the charge to second-degree kid-
naping involving domestic violence and use
of a firearm; and the facts admitted in his
plea supported a maximum sentence of 53
months. Washington state law allows a judge
to impose a sentence above the standard
range if he finds "substantial and compelling
reasons" for doing so that were not computed into the standard range sentence. The
judge in this case imposed an "exceptional"
sentence of 90 months after determining
Blakely had acted with "deliberate cruelty."
Blakely appealed, arguing that this sentencing procedure deprived him of his federal
Sixth Amendment right to have a jury determine beyond a reasonable doubt all facts
legally essential to his sentence. A state
appellate court affirmed the sentence and
the state supreme court denied review.

The Supreme Court had this question to
grapple with: does a fact (other than a prior

13. *Blakely v. Washington* (02-1632) 542 U.S. 296 (2004) 111 Wash. App. 851, 47 P.3d 149

conviction) necessary to increase a sentence beyond the statutory standard range need to be proved by a jury and beyond a reasonable doubt?

In a 5–4 decision delivered by Justice Antonin Scalia, the Court held that an exceptional sentence increase based on the judge's determination that Blakely had acted with "deliberate cruelty" violated Blakely's Sixth Amendment right to trial by jury. Citing its decision in *Apprendi v. New Jersey*, the Court ruled that facts increasing the penalty for a crime beyond the prescribed statutory maximum must be submitted to a jury and and proved beyond a reasonable doubt.

## Concurrent and Consecutive Sentences

When someone commits multiple crimes and is charged with more than one, that leaves them open to receiving a separate sentence for each offense. These sentences can run concurrently or consecutively, at the discretion of the trial judge. Serving the terms concurrently means all of the various sentences are served simultaneously. If the judge orders a consecutive sentence, time will be served on the second sentence after the first sentence is completed.

## Death Penalty Cases

In states that allow capital punishment, the prosecutor has the initial charging decision on whether to seek the death penalty. He or she will either seek life without the possibility of parole or death and, if he or she does choose the former, that is the maximum punishment a defendant can receive.

If a prosecutor seeks capital punishment

in a jury trial, the jury will recommend to the judge whether to sentence a defendant to death. This jury recommendation often follows in what's called a separate, *penalty phase* hearing. The second phase is where the defendant has already been convicted and the jury listens to evidence concerning the defendant's background, interviews, and other reported matters. If the jury recommends death, the judge still has the power to impose a lesser sentence. If the jury recommends life without the possibility of parole, however, the judge cannot impose death.

## APPEALS AND THE WRIT

Appeals are subject to strict time limits. Within seven to ten days after the entry of a final judgment is the most likely window of time to file a paper called a Notice of Appeal. The appeals process is lengthy, taking many months, and cases may go through two or more levels of appellate courts.

A writ on the other hand is an extraordinary remedy, and is considered a last-ditch effort. These are usually reserved for cases where the defendant feels wronged by the actions of a trial judge, or there is a concern that goes beyond the trial record such as an incompetent lawyer charge, any challenge to the legality of their imprisonment or any new evidence. There is a writ of habeas corpus, literally meaning "bring the body to court," or a writ of prohibition–an order from an appellate court to stop some particular action–and the writ of mandamus, which orders a lower court to do something. These postconviction proceedings are remedies that must be proven by the defendant in order to overturn a sentence.

# REVIEW QUESTIONS AND ANSWERS

## *Key Words to Define*

- **Bailiff**–The court's police officer; safeguards the premises and announces the arrival of the judge or any other movement of the principal players.
- **Charging the jury**–The judge's instructions to the jury before they leave the courtroom for their discussion and decision; prior to deliberations.
- **Concurrent and consecutive sentences**–Multiple crimes committed means the defendant may be charged with more than one and each receive a separate sentence; concurrent means the sentences are served simultaneously, consecutive means the second sentences begins after the first sentence is finished.
- **Exhibits**–A document, gun, or any type of real evidence collected from the crime scene or defendant's home or possessions; follows "chain of custody" and is marked with a tag and signature of the person who processed it; also called exemplars.
- **Foundation evidence**–A document or something that can be authenticated.
- **Jury trial penalty**–When the jury wants to impose a harsher sentence than the judge has offered.
- **Lower courts**–Courts that handle the minor criminal offenses, also called petty court or misdemeanor court; issues may be related to traffic violations, driving drunk, petty theft, or violations of community, county and city ordinances.
- **Relevancy**–Material must relate to the fact or have some real connection to the point.
- **Remand**–A case is returned to its court of original jurisdiction for retrial.
- **Reversed and rendered**–The defendant goes free; the case sentencing is reversed and the decision is rendered.
- **Sequestration**–Jurors are sheltered together so as not to be affected by the outside world; usually high-profile cases.
- **Surrebuttal**–The last time the defendant can put on evidence following the prosecutor's rebuttal. Usually followed by the "defense rests, Your Honor."
- **Trial courts**–90% of criminal prosecutions are conducted here; that, and important civil litigation.
- **U.S. Supreme Court**–"The court of last resort"; court of final appeal, highest court in the land; usually hears cases involving constitutional law.
- **Voir dire**–"To speak truly"; the important process for questioning jurors by opposing attorneys to make a group of 12 (often with 2 alternates).

## *Questions for Review and Discussion*

1. *Question:* Does the United States have a dual court system? *Answer:* Yes. Federal courts and state courts.

2. *Question:* Does each state have a supreme court? *Answer:* Yes. It's the final authority in issues involving the state.

3. *Question:* What is on the four-tier Federal system of courts? *Answer:* U.S. Magistrates, then District Courts, the U.S. Court of Appeals, and finally the U.S. Supreme Court; military law in the armed forces is separate.

4. *Question:* What or who are U.S. magistrates? *Answer:* Formerly called U.S. Commissioners, they are federal judges who assist the state district courts and hear misdemeanors, for example, set bail, review civil petitions, and issue arrest and search warrants.

5. *Question:* Name the basic trial rights of a criminal as he moves through the criminal justice system. *Answer:* (1) Speedy and public trial, (2) Impartial jury, (3) A trial venue free from prejudice, fear and outside interference, (4) No self-incrimination, (5) Adequate counsel, (6) No cruel or unusual punishment, (7) No double jeopardy.

6. *Question:* Name a few things that opening statements accomplish. *Answer:* Presents an overview of the case, introduces the defendant, talks about the crime committed, suggests how the case will unfold, mentions future witnesses, establishes rapport.

7. *Question:* What makes a witness hostile? *Answer:* They are uncooperative, avoid, or refuse to answer the question asked.

8. *Question:* What will the ABA do if the prosecution used false evidence? *Answer:* They would probably sanction him; hold him over for disbarment if egregious.

9. *Question:* Why would the defense attorney ask for a Motion to Dismiss? *Answer:* Also called a "directed verdict"?; to ask the judge if they feel enough evidence has been given for a conviction; they may get an acquittal if the prosecution's case was too weak and they have nothing to lose as it is done out of court.

10. *Question:* What are objections? *Answer:* They are tactics to raise attention for an issue they feel is unworthy, not relevant or some other problem, and to have the judge cancel, undo, or decide against the current questioning; could be future basis for appeal.

## Essay Exploration

Each student will choose an objection and create a scenario they believe best fits its use, to be presented to the class orally for discussion. List on pages 295-296.

# AFTER THE TRIAL

# RIGHTS OF PRISONERS AFTER CONVICTION

After conviction, convicted persons are not completely stripped of their rights:

**"Right to access the courts"** is theirs which means they have to have reasonable access to pens, paper, stamps, and items that allow them to correspond with the judicial system. Additionally, inmates cannot be prevented from counseling with each other unless a reasonable substitute is provided such as a law library.

**"The right of uncensored mail."** Law enforcement cannot exercise broad censorship, however, they can censor mail if they can show that it furthers an important government interest and that inmate's censorship is not broad—for example, guards cannot open legal mail but if the warden suspects something is awry, they may open it in the convict's presence. Other letters can be scanned to prevent escape plans or contraband.

**"The right to access the press."** Corrections can only place restrictions on this according to the inconvenience or in order to maintain peace, etc.

**"The right to adequate medical care."** This means that deliberate indifference to a serious medical need or condition constitutes cruel and unusual punishment (Eighth Amendment). Simple negligence does not establish deliberate indifference.

## Rights Prisoners *Do Not* Have

They **do not have the right to do their time in any specific location** and may be transferred at any time for any reason.

They **do not have the right to unionize**. Prison officials can prohibit prisoners from soliciting other inmates for membership in a prisoners' union and from conducting union-type activities.

They **do not have the right to parole** (serving your time outside the walls).

**Prisoners do not have the right to be free from disabilities upon the completion of a prison sentence.** For instance, even if a prisoner has paid his or her debt to society (completed the sentence), a felony conviction is serious. In most states felons may not possess a firearm. In some jurisdictions they permanently disenfranchise the felon from the state and federal elections, they may terminate parenting rights on the conviction, they permit divorce for conviction or imprisonment of a felon, they may not be a part of public employment, and may not serve jury duty. Also, certain states require felons to register as former offenders.

# APPENDICES

# Appendix A

# THE BILL OF RIGHTS AND EXPLANATION

Government can easily exist without law,
but law cannot exist without government.
–Thomas Paine

## BILL OF RIGHTS

### Amendment I.
*Religion, Speech, Assembly and Politics*
*Congress shall make no law respecting an establishment of religion, or prohibiting the free exercise thereof; or abridging the freedom of speech, or of the press; or the right of the people peaceably to assembly, and to petition the Government for a redress of grievances.*

Congress is not allowed to declare an official church or to make into law any limits on the freedom of religion, speech, and the press. They may not restrict the right of groups to assemble or to present their petitions. These guarantees are not absolute–each may be exercised only with consideration to the rights of other persons.

### Amendment II.
*Militia and the Right to Bear Arms*
*A well regulated Militia, being necessary to the security of a free State, the right of the people to keep and bear Arms, shall not be infringed.*

Each state has a right to protect itself by maintaining a volunteer armed force. States and the federal government will regulate the possession and use of firearms by individuals.

### Amendment III.
*The Quartering of Soldiers*
*No Soldier shall, in time of peace be quartered in any house, without the consent of the Owner, nor in time of war, but in a manner to be prescribed by law.*

Before the Revolutionary War, British practice allowed soldiers to take lodgings in colonists' homes. Now military troops do not have the power to take over private houses during peacetime.

### Amendment IV.
*Searches and Seizures*
*The right of the people to be secure in their persons, houses, papers, and effects, against unreasonable searches and seizures, shall not be violated, and no Warrants shall issue, but upon probable cause,*

311

*supported by Oath or affirmation, and particularly describing the place to be searched, and the persons or things to be seized.*

The word "warrant" in this context means justification and refers to a document issued by a judge or magistrate which must indicate the name, address, and possible offenses committed by that person. In addition, anyone requesting the warrant, such as a police officer, must be able to convince the judge or magistrate that an offense most likely has been committed by this person (this is the basis for "probable cause").

---

## Amendment V.
### Grand Juries, Self-incrimination, Double Jeopardy, Due Process, and Eminent Domain.
*No person shall be held to answer for a capital, or otherwise infamous crime, unless on a presentment or indictment of a Grand Jury, except in cases arising in the land or naval forces, or in the Militia, when in actual service in time of War or public danger; nor shall any person be subject for the same offence to be twice put in jeopardy of life or limb; nor shall be compelled in any criminal case to be a witness against himself, nor be deprived of life, liberty, or property, without due process of law; nor shall private property be taken for public use, without just compensation.*

There are two types of juries. A grand jury looks at physical evidence and listens to the testimony of witnesses and then decides whether there is sufficient reason to bring a case to trial. A petit jury hears the case at trial and makes a decision about it. ". . . [T]o be twice put in jeopardy" means a person cannot be tried twice for the same crime and cannot be forced to give evidence or testimony against himself or herself. Plus, no person's right to life, liberty or property may be taken away except by following lawful means, called the due process of law. Private

property taken for use in public purposes must be paid for by the government.

---

## Amendment VI.
### Criminal Court Procedures
*In all criminal prosecutions, the accused shall enjoy the right to a speedy and public trial, by an impartial jury of the State and district wherein the crime shall have been committed, which district shall have been previously ascertained by law, and to be informed of the nature and cause of the accusation; to be confronted with the witnesses against him; to have compulsory process for obtaining witnesses in his favor, and to have the assistance of counsel for his defence.*

Any person accused of a crime has a right to a fair and public trial by a jury in the state in which the crime took place. The charges against the person must be spelled out and any accused person has the right to know who his or her accusers are. The accused also has a right to a lawyer to defend him or her, and to question those who testify against the defense. His or her attorney may also call people to speak in favor of the client at trial.

---

## Amendment VII.
### Trial by Jury in Civil Cases
*In Suits at common law, where the value in controversy shall exceed twenty dollars, the right of trial by jury shall be preserved, and no fact tried by jury, shall be otherwise re-examined in any Court of the United States, than according to the rules of the common law.*

A jury trial may be requested by either party in a dispute involving more than $20 in a civil case. If both parties agree to a trial by a judge without a jury, the right to a jury trial may be set aside.

---

*Amendment VIII.*
*Bail, Cruel and Unusual Punishment*
*Excessive bail shall not be required, nor excessive fines imposed, nor cruel and unusual punishments inflicted.*

Usually an amount of money is requested by the court to ensure that an accused person will return for his or her court case and final judgment and this is called bail. The amount of bail or the fine imposed as punishment for a crime must be reasonable compared with the seriousness of the crime involved. Any punishment deemed too harsh or too severe for a crime is prohibited.

*Amendment IX.*
*The Rights Retained by the People*
*The enumeration in the Constitution, or certain rights, shall not be construed to deny or disparage other retained by the people.*

Many civil rights that are not explicitly enumerated in the Constitution are still held by the people.

*Amendment X.*
*Reserved Powers of the States*
*The powers no delegated to the United States by the Constitution, nor prohibited by it to the States, are reserved to the States respectively, or to the people.*

Powers that are not expressly delegated by the Constitution for the federal government or are not specifically denied to the states belong to the states and to the people. This clause fundamentally allows the states to pass laws under its "police powers."

## QUICK NOTES:
## THE LIVING CONSTITUTION

Our Constitution is located at the National Archives and Records Administration (NARA) and is stored under glass for public display. It is located at Seventh St. and Pennsylvania Ave., N.W., in Washington, D.C.

# Appendix B

# WEB SITES

The National Criminal Justice Reference Service (NCJRS) is one of the world's most extensive networks of criminal and juvenile justice information. NCJRS provides a range of services and outreach activities to respond to the criminal and juvenile justice needs of professionals, practitioners, administrators, policy makers, and the general public. NCJRS carries reports with:
The National Institute of Justice
The Office of Juvenile Justice and
   Delinquency Program
The Office for Victims of Crime
The Bureau of Justice Statistics
The Bureau of Justice Assistance, and
The Office of National Drug Control Policy
http://www.ncjrs.org

For information on political and social-science research papers sponsored by the Bureau of Justice Statistics and the U.S. Department of Justice and compiled by **The National Archive of Criminal Justice Data**, go to:
http://www.icpsr.umich.edu/NACJD

**Clarence Gideon**'s main problem was lack of counsel and that is taken up in the Sixth Amendment. By the way, I did find a small sample of Gideon's handwritten appeal to the Supreme Court on the Internet. If you want to see it, go to: http://www.aclumontana.org/rights/gideon.html

To see **Police Test Kits**:
http://www.cripkit.com

For a partial translation on the **Code of Hammurabi**, go to:
http://www.commonlaw.com/Hammurabi.html

**Standards for Criminal Justice: Prosecution Function**:
http://www.november.org/ABAstandards.html

For articles, statistics, a prisoner's dictionary, court rulings–for example, on dreadlocks, and body cavity searches–a primer on prisoners' rights, and other pertinent news and information, go to:

**The Other Side of the Wall: Prisons and Prison Law**:
http://www.prisonwall.com

Also of interest is **Lock Down USA** at:
http://www.igc.apc.org/deepdish/lock down/ which compares the media portrayal of crime, justice, and incarceration with some different perceptions.

The **International Association of Correctional Officers** is at:
http://www.acsp.uic.edu/iaco/about.htm

This site is posted by the **National Association of Crime Defense Lawyers**, go to:
http://www.criminaljustice.org/public.nsf/ FreeFrom/PublicWelcome?OpenDocument

The **American Bar Association** and its site for their publications. Their goal is to provide publications designed to further a better understanding of criminal law Check out:
http://www.abanet.org/

These sites are great for additional information pertaining to **Federal Courts**:
http://www.uscourts.gov

This is the **Federal Judiciary Homepage** (check out the most "frequently asked questions"):
http://www.uscourts.gov/faq.html

The **Association of Federal Defense Attorneys**:
http://www.afda.org

FBI–**Freedom of Information Act Electronic Reading Room**:
http://foia.fbi.gov/

The *FBI Law Enforcement Bulletin*, a monthly publication:
http://www.fbi.gov/publications/leb/leb. htm

The **National Center for the Analysis of Violent Crime** (NCAVC):
http://www.fbi.gov/hq/isd/cirg/ncavc.htm

This page has some interesting links to provide you with the **rules and regulations governing the Supreme Court**:
http://www.law.cornell.edu/rules/supct/ove rview.html

This is a wonderful site and even has a **virtual tour**:
http://oyez.nwu.edu/

This page has a **list of historic decisions** that may help you with historic cases:
http://www.fedworld.gov/supcourt/

The **Supreme Court Historical Society** presents new ideas:
http://www.supremecourthistory.org/

An official government site that presents the **docket and public information**:
http://www.supremecourtus.gov/

# BIBLIOGRAPHY

## *Books*

American Bar Association, *ABA Standards for Criminal Justice: Prosecution Function and Defense Function* (3rd ed.). Boston: Little Brown,1993.

Bergman, Paul, and Sara J. Berman-Barrett. *The Criminal Law Handbook: Know Your Rights, Survive the System.* Berkeley: Nolo Press, 1999.

Boyce, Ronald, and Rollin M. Perkinds. *Cases and Materials on Criminal Law and Procedure* (8th ed.). New York: Foundation Press, 1999.

Burton, William C. *Burton's Legal Thesaurus* (3rd ed.). New York: Macmillan Library Reference, 1998.

Campbell, Andrea. *Forensic Science: Evidence, Clues and Investigation,* Philadelphia: Chelsea House Publishers, 2000.

———, *Rights of the Accused.* Philadelphia: Chelsea House Publishers, 2001.

Chambers, Mortimer, et al. *The Western Experience: Vol. 1 To the Eighteenth Century,* New York: McGraw Hill, 1995.

Dimitirus, Jo-Ellan, and Mark Mazzarella. *Reading People: How to Understand People and Predict Their Behavior–Anytime, Anyplace.* New York: Random House, 1998.

Dix, George E., and M. Michael Sharlot. *Basic Criminal Law: Cases and Materials.* St. Paul: West Publishing Co., 1987.

Elias, Stephen, and Susan Levinkind. *Legal Research: How to Find & Understand the Law* (6th ed.). Berkeley: Nolo Press, 1999.

Elsevier, Reed. *The New American Desk Encyclopedia* (4th ed.). New York: Penguin Putnam Inc., 1997.

Irons, Peter. *A People's History of the Supreme Court.* New York: Viking, 1999.

Kamisar, Yale, Wayne R. LaFave, and Jerold H. Israel. *Basic Criminal Procedure: Cases, Comments and Questions* (8th ed.). St. Paul: West Publishing Co., 1994.

Knowles, Elizabeth, ed. *The Oxford Dictionary of Quotations* (5th ed.). New York: Oxford University Press, 1999.

Kurland, Michael. *How to Try a Murder.* New York: Macmillan, 1997.

Lazarus, Edward. *Closed Chambers: The Rise, Fall, and Future of the Modern Supreme Court.* New York: Penguin, 1999.

Mullally, David S. *Order in the Court.* Cincinnati: Writer's Digest Books, 2000.

Roth, Martin. *The Writer's Complete Crime Reference Book.* Cincinnati: Writer's Digest, 1990.

Saeger, Michael. *Defend Yourself Against Criminal Charges.* Naperville, IL: Sourcebooks Inc., 1997.

Saltzburg, Stephen A., and Daniel J. Capra. *Basic Criminal Procedure* (2nd ed.). St. Paul, MN: West Publishing Co., 1997.

Scheb, John M., and John M. Scheb II. *Criminal Law and Procedure.* Belmont, CA: Wadsworth Publishing Co., 1999.

Schmidt, Steffen W., et al. *American Government and Politics Today*, 1997–98 edition. Belmont, CA: West Publishing Co., 1997.

Siegel, Larry J., and Joseph J. Senna. *Juvenile Delinquency, Theory, Practice and Law.* St. Paul, MN: West Publishing Co., 1997.

Territo, Leonard, James B. Halsted, and Max L. Bromley. *Crime and Justice in America: A Human Perspective.* St. Paul, MN: West Publishing Co., 1995.

Thibault, A., Lynch, et al. (eds.). *Proactive Police Management.* Englewood Cliffs, CA: Prentice Hall, Inc., 1995.

Trojanowicz, Robert, et al. *Community Policing: A Contemporary Perspective.* Cincinnati, OH: Anderson Pub. Co., 1990.

## Articles

The American Arbitration Association. "Alternative Dispute Resolution" http://www.lectlaw.com, The 'Lectric Law Library.

The Associated Press. "Bill Making It a Federal Crime to Harm Fetus in Assault OK'd," April, 2001.

The Associated Press. "Supreme Court Allows Police to Arrest, Handcuff for Minor Traffic Citations," *The Sentinel-Record*, p. 3A, April 25, 2001.

Biskupic, Joan. "5-4 Ruling Gives Wider Leeway in Interrogations," *USA Today*, p. 6A, April 3, 2001.

"Case before High Court Threatens Suspects' Rights," *USA Today*, p. 18A, April 18, 2000.

Hampson, Rick. "Men Run through Central Park Stripping and Groping Women," *USA Today*, June 12, 2000.

–––"The Supreme Court: The High Court: How It Works," *USA Today*, p. 14A, October 6, 1997.

Methvin, Eugene H. "Will the Supreme Court Arrest Miranda?" *Readers Digest*, pp. 161–168, May 2000.

Murr, Andrew, and Karen Springen. "Death at a Very Early Age," *Newsweek*, p. 32, August 28, 2000.

Parker, Laura, and Gary Fields. "Unsolved Killings on the rise," *USA Today*, p. 1A, February 22, 2000.

Reutter, Mark. "Courts Have Reduced Criminal Defendant's Right to Lawyer," University of Illinois Urbana-Champaign, April 2000.

Rodger, Will. "Warrants for Online Data Soar," *USA Today*, p. 1A, July 28, 2000.

Willing, Richard. "Justices Appear Split on 'Miranda,'" *USA Today*, p. 6A, April 20, 2000.

———"Prosecutor Often Determines Which Way a Case Will Go," *USA Today*, p. 6A, December 20, 1999.

## Government Pamphlets

1999 National Report Series, Juvenile Justice Bulletin. *Children as Victims*, Washington DC: U.S. Department of Justice, NCJ178257, May 2000.

Bureau of Justice Statistics. *Sourcebook of Criminal Justice Statistics 1995*, "Offenses known to police and percent cleared by arrest," NCJ-158900, p. 426, 1996.

Connors, Edward, et. al. *Convicted by Juries, Exonerated by Science: Case Studies in the Use of DNA Evidence to Establish Innocence After Trial.* Washington, D.C.: U.S. Department of Justice, NCJ 161258, June 1996.

*Eyewitness Evidence: A Guide for Law Enforcement.* Washington, D.C.: U.S. Department of Justice, NCJ 178240, October 1999.

Rottman, David B. et al. *State Court Organization 1998.* NCJ 178932, Washington, D.C.: U.S. Department of Justice, June 2000.

Webster-Stratton, Carolyn. *The Incredible Years Training Series.* Washington, D.C.: Office of Juvenile Justice and Delinquency Prevention, NCJ 173422, June 2000.

Weisburd, David, and Rosann Greenspan, et al. *Police Attitude Toward Abuse of Authority: Findings From a National Study.* Washington, D.C.: U.S. Department of Justice, NCJ 181312, May 2000.

## Internet

"Virginia's 21-day Rule," found at: http://www.vadp.org/21day.htm.

DiGregory, Kevin, Deputy Assistant Attorney General, U.S. Department of Justice. "*The Fourth Amendment and the Internet,*" Before the House Committee, April 6, 2000. http://www.usdoj.gov/criminal/cybercrime/inter4th.htm.

"Handbook for Virginia Grand Jurors," located at: http://www.courts.state.va.us/text/gjury/cover.htm

# LIST OF CASES INDEX

*N.Y. v. Quarles,* 467 U.S. 649, 104 S.Ct. 2626, 81 L.Ed.3d 550 (1984)

*Neal v. State,* 597 P.2d 334, 337 (Okl. App. 1979)

*New York v. Ferber,* 458 U.S. 747, 102 S.Ct. 3348, 73 L.Ed.2d 1113 (1982)

*People v. Eatman,* 91 N.E. 2d at 390 (Ill. 1950)

*People v. Merhige,* 1800 N.W. 419 (Mich. 1920)

*People v. Roe,* 542 N.E. 2d 610 (NY 1989)

*People v. Williams,* 318 N.W.2d 671 (Mich. App. 1982)

*Rhode Island v. Innis,* 416 U.S. 291, 301, 100 S.Ct. 1682, 1693, 64 L.Ed.2d 297, 308 (1980)

*Robinson v. United States,* 506 A.2d 572, 575 (D.C.. App. 1986)

*Rochin v. California,* 342 U.S. 165, 72 S.Ct. 205, 96 L.Ed. 183 (1952)

*Rock v. Arkansas,* 483 U.S. 44, 107 S.Ct. 2704, 97 L.Ed.2d 37 (1987)

*Roper v. Simmons* (03-633) 543 U.S. 551 (2005)112 S. W. 3d 397

*Roth v. United States,* 354 U.S. 476, 77 S.Ct. 1304, 1 L.Ed.2d 1498 (1957)

*State v. Anonymous,* 377 A.2d 1342 (Conn. Super. 1977)

*State v. Bingham,* 40 Wn. App. 553, 699 P.2d 262 (Wash. 1985)

*State v. Cayward,* 552 So.2d 971 (Fla. App. 1989)

*State v. Cole,* 403 S.E.2d 117 (S.C. 1991)

*State v. Grier,* 609 S.W. 2d 201, 203 (Mo App. 1980)

*State v. Harrison,* 846 P.2d 1082 (N.M. App. 1992)

*State v. Kennamore,* 604 S.W.2d 856, 860 (Tenn. 1980)

*State v. Rooks,* 468 S.E. 2d 354 (Ga. 1996)

*State v. Sainz,* 84 N.M. 259, 261, 501 P.2d 1247, 1249, (App. 1972)

*State v. Scheifer,* 121 A.805, 809 (Conn. 1923)

*State v. Tonnisen,* 92 N.J. Super. 452, 224 A2d. 21 (N.J. 1966)

*State v. Werner,* 609 So.2d 585 (Fla 1992)

*Strickland v. Washington,* 466 U.S. 668, 104 S.Ct. 2052, 80 L.Ed.2d 674 (1984)

*Swain v. Alabama,* 380 U.S. 202, 85 S.Ct. 824, 13 L.Ed.2d 759 (1965)

*Terry v. Ohio,* 392 U.S. 1, 88 S.Ct. 1868, 20 L.Ed.2d 899 (1968)

*U.S. v. Singleton,* 144 F.3d 1343 (10th Circuit 1998)

*U.S. v. Watson,* 423 U.S. 411, 96 S.Ct. 820, 46 L.Ed.2d 598 (1976)

*United States v. Armstrong,* 517 U.S. 456, 116 S.Ct. 1480, 134 L.Ed.2d 687 (1996)

*United States v. Booker* (04-104) 543 U.S. 220 (2005) No. 04-104, 375 F.3d 508, affirmed and remanded; and No. 04-105, vacated and remanded.

*United States v. Dionisio,* 410 U.S. 1, 93 S.Ct. 764, 35 L.Ed.2d 67 (1973)

*United States v. Knotts,* 460 U.S. 276, 103 S.Ct. 1081, 75 L.Ed.2d 55 (1983)

*United States v. Miller,* 425 U.S. 435, 96 S.Ct. 1619, 48 L.Ed.2d 71 (1976)

*United States v. Parcel of Land,* 507 U.S. 111, 113 S.Ct. 1126, 122 L.Ed.2d 469 (1993)

*United States v. Patane* (02-1183) 542 U.S. 630 (2004) 304 F.3d 1013

*United States v. Riley,* 968 F.2d 422 (5th Cir. 1992)

*Webb v. Texas,* 409 U.S. 95 (1972)

*Wheat v. United States,* 486 U.S. 153, 108 S.Ct. 1692, 100 L.Ed.2d 140 (1988)

# SUBJECT INDEX

## A

Abduction, death and, 44
Abscam, 128
Abuse
  excuse, 81, 92
  family life and, 42
  of the elderly, 42, 45
  spousal, child, 42
Accessory
  after the fact, 20
  punishment and, 20
Accomplice, 19
  activities of an, 30
  testimony of, 21, 26, 189
  testimony, remedy and need for, 31
Accusatory pleading, 183
Accused, 282
  guilt of the, 182
Accusers, 145-146
Acquisition crimes, 49
Acquittal, 98, 294, 299
Acts of criminal law, 11
Actus reus, 13
  defined, 15
Actus reus and mens rea, concurrence of, 13
*Adams v. Williams*, 120
Adjudication phase, 232
  definition of, 244
Administration of justice, 146
Administration, laws of, 12
Administrative law, definition of, 12
Admissibility, 185
  evidence, 185
Admissible evidence, 184, 293
Admission, 187

Adultery, 59
Adversarial judicial proceedings, 249, 289
  definition of, 270
  process, 269
Advisory Commission on Intergovernmental
  Relations, 206
Affidavit, 107, 262
  definition of, 133
  elements of, 133
  for search warrant, 108
  testimonial, 189
Affirmative defense, 82, 96
  defenses, categories of, 82, 269
  definition of, 99
"Against the king's peace," 10
Aggravated crime, 45
  battery, mayhem and, 40
  first-degree murder, case of, 34
  instrument for, 38
  robbery, 52
  versus simple, non-aggravated, 38
Aguilar-Spinelli test, 107-108
Aided and abetted, 20
  different from inchoate, 30
Aiding, weapons and, 20
Airport searches, 129
Alcohol, 72, 86-87, 159
  defense of, 86-88
Alfred the Great, 54
ALI Standard, 84
  definition of, 99
Alibi, 259
  defense, 268
  definition of, 270
Allocution, 301
Alternatives to incarceration, 300

list, 191
no-knock warrant and, 114
on record, 294
opinion, 189-190
other types of, 187
physical, 184
plain view, 124
preliminary hearing, 255
preponderance of the, 194
prima facie, 190
problematic, 295
protective sweep, 123
real, 186
rebuttal, 297
revealed, 269
rules of, 184-185
sexual assault case and, 42
state's, 189
surveillance, 167
testimonial, 186
witness character, 191
Evidence rules, relevance and, 185
Evidence seizure with home search, 112
Evidence technician
  definition of, 178
Evidence technicians, police as, 167
Evidence types, 185, 199
Evidentiary hearing, 266
*Ex Parte Crouse*, 230
*Ex Parte Sharpe*, 237
Exceptional sentence, 303-304
Exceptions to general rule, state's code and, 90-91
Excessive bail, 106, 154
Excited utterance, 187, 290
  definition of, 198
Exclusionary evidence, 266
  impeachment and, 131
Exclusionary Rule, 112-114, 130
  civil proceedings and, 131
  definition of, 133
  exceptions, 130-131
  grand juries and, 131
  private individual and, 131
Exculpatory evidence, 260
Exculpatory oath, 7
Executing a warrant, 110-116
Execution of minors, 287
Exemplars, definition of, 305
Exhibits, 260

definition of, 305
kinds of, 293
Exigency, vehicle and, 125
Exigent circumstances, 122
  children in trouble and, 122
  hot pursuit and, 122
  police risk and, 122
  property fire, 122
  public risk and, 122
  vanishing evidence and, 122
Expectation of privacy, 112, 125
  bank account records and, 125
  car paint and, 125
  spouse and, 114
  voice and, 125
Expediency and judicial notice, 187
Expert
  evidence, 189
  testimony, 280, 293
  witness, 292
  witnesses, 81-82, 260
  stipulation of, 268
  types of, 293
Express questioning, 136
Extortion, 56, 221
  child snatchers, 44
  death penalty and, 221
  definition of, 224
  purpose of, 221
  writ of habeas corpus, 221
Eyewitness identification, lineups and, 174

**F**

Fails to prepare, 269
Failure to have I.D., 107
Failure to know, 270
"Falling through the cracks," 27
False evidence, 306
False imprisonment, 42,45
  examples of, 43
False information, questioning and, 118
False pretense, 9
  definition of, 49
False promise, home repair, 50
False testimony, 7, 192, 293
Family Court, 274
Family in need of supervision (FINS), 227
*Fare v. Michael C.*, 238